A Book Of

DISCRETE MATHEMATICS

For M.C.A. (Under Management Faculty)
Semester - I
As Per Pune University's Revised Syllabus
Effective from June 2012

M. D. Bhagat
Ex-Head of Mathematics Deptt.
Tuljaram Chaturchand College,
Baramati (Dist. Pune)

NIRALI PRAKASHAN
Advancement of knowledge

DISCRETE MATHEMATICS   ISBN 978-93-83525-86-7

First Edition : **October 2013**

© : **Authors**

The text of this publication, or any part thereof, should not be reproduced or transmitted in any form or stored in any computer storage system or device for distribution including photocopy, recording, taping or information retrieval system or reproduced on any disc, tape, perforated media or other information storage device etc., without the written permission of Authors with whom the rights are reserved. Breach of this condition is liable for legal action.

Every effort has been made to avoid errors or omissions in this publication. In spite of this, errors may have crept in. Any mistake, error or discrepancy so noted and shall be brought to our notice shall be taken care of in the next edition. It is notified that neither the publisher nor the authors or seller shall be responsible for any damage or loss of action to any one, of any kind, in any manner, therefrom.

Published By :
NIRALI PRAKASHAN
Abhyudaya Pragati, 1312, Shivaji Nagar,
Off J.M. Road, PUNE – 411005
Tel - (020) 25512336/37/39, Fax - (020) 25511379
Email : niralipune@pragationline.com

Printed By :
Repro Knowledgecast Limited
Thane

DISTRIBUTION CENTRES
PUNE

Nirali Prakashan
119, Budhwar Peth, Jogeshwari Mandir Lane
Pune 411002, Maharashtra
Tel : (020) 2445 2044, 66022708, Fax : (020) 2445 1538
Email : bookorder@pragationline.com

Nirali Prakashan
S. No. 28/27, Dhayri,
Near Pari Company, Pune 411041
Tel : (022) 24690371
Email : dhayri@pragationline.com
          bookorder@pragationline.com

MUMBAI
Nirali Prakashan
385, S.V.P. Road, Rasdhara Co-op. Hsg. Society Ltd.,
Girgaum, Mumbai 400004, Maharashtra
Tel : (022) 2385 6339 / 2386 9976, Fax : (022) 2386 9976
Email : niralimumbai@pragationline.com

DISTRIBUTION BRANCHES

NAGPUR
Pratibha Book Distributors
Above Maratha Mandir, Shop No. 3, First Floor,
Rani Jhanshi Square, Sitabuldi, Nagpur 440012,
Maharashtra, Tel : (0712) 254 7129

BENGALURU
Pragati Book House
House No. 1, Sanjeevappa Lane, Avenue Road Cross,
Opp. Rice Church, Bengaluru – 560002.
Tel : (080) 64513344, 64513355,
Mob : 9880582331, 9845021552
Email:bharatsavla@yahoo.com

JALGAON
Nirali Prakashan
34, V. V. Golani Market, Navi Peth, Jalgaon 425001,
Maharashtra, Tel : (0257) 222 0395
Mob : 94234 91860

KOLHAPUR
Nirali Prakashan
New Mahadvar Road,
Kedar Plaza, 1st Floor Opp. IDBI Bank
Kolhapur 416 012, Maharashtra. Mob : 9855046155

CHENNAI
Pragati Books
9/1, Montieth Road, Behind Taas Mahal, Egmore,
Chennai 600008 Tamil Nadu, Tel : (044) 6518 3535,
Mob : 94440 01782 / 98450 21552 / 98805 82331, Email : bharatsavla@yahoo.com

RETAIL OUTLETS
PUNE

Pragati Book Centre
157, Budhwar Peth, Opp. Ratan Talkies,
Pune 411002, Maharashtra
Tel : (020) 2445 8887 / 6602 2707, Fax : (020) 2445 8887

Pragati Book Centre
Amber Chamber, 28/A, Budhwar Peth,
Appa Balwant Chowk, Pune : 411002, Maharashtra,
Tel : (020) 20240335 / 66281669
Email : pbcpune@pragationline.com

Pragati Book Centre
676/B, Budhwar Peth, Opp. Jogeshwari Mandir,
Pune 411002, Maharashtra
Tel : (020) 6601 7784 / 6602 0855

PBC Book Sellers & Stationers
152, Budhwar Peth, Pune 411002, Maharashtra
Tel : (020) 2445 2254 / 6609 2463

MUMBAI
Pragati Book Corner
Indira Niwas, 111 - A, Bhavani Shankar Road, Dadar (W), Mumbai 400028, Maharashtra
Tel : (022) 2422 3526 / 6662 5254, Email : pbcmumbai@pragationline.com

www.pragationline.com   info@pragationline.com

Preface ...

I have great pleasure in presenting this text book on **Discrete Mathematics** to the students of M.C.A. (Under Management Faculty) Semester - I. This book is written according to the new revised syllabus of University of Pune to be implemented from June 2012.

I have taken utmost care to present the matter systematically. The book contains several selected solved examples and an ample number of graded problems in the exercises.

In each unit the mathematical concepts are explained and made clear with the help of everyday life examples.

I am thankful to **Shri Dineshbhai Furia, Shri Jignesh Furia, Shri M. P. Munde**, Mrs. Anagha Kaware, Mr. Ilyas Shaikh, Mrs. Anjali Mule and the staff of Nirali Prakashan, for the great efforts that they have taken to publish the book in time.

We welcome the valuable suggestions from our colleagues' and readers for the improvement of the book.

PUNE   **AUTHOR**
OCTOBER 2013

Syllabus ...

1. Mathematical Logic

1.1 Propositional (Statements)

1.2 Logical connectives, NOT, AND, OR, $\to$, $\leftrightarrow$, $\equiv$

1.3 Compound Statements form, Truth tables, Tautology, Implications and equivalence of statements forms logical identities

1.4 Normal forms: Disjunctive normal form and simplification. Conjunctive normal form, Logical implications, Valid arguments, Methods of proof. Theory of inference of statement calculus, Predicate calculus, Quantifiers, Free and bound variables, Theory of inference of predicate calculus.

2. Relations and Functions

2.1 Relation defined as ordered n-tuple

2.2 Unary, Binary, Ternary, n-ary

2.3 Restrict to binary relations

2.4 Complement of a relation, Converse

2.5 Relation, Compositions

2.6 Matrix representation and its properties

2.7 Graphical representation of relation

2.8 Diagraphs, Properties of binary relation

2.9 Reflexive, Irreflexive, Symmetric, Assymetric, Transitive Equivalence, Equivalence classes, transitive closure - Warshall's algorithm

2.10 Functions: Definitions and only bijection

3. Permutations and Combinations

3.1 Addition principle, Multiplication principle

3.2 Bijection principle, r-permutations of n elements

3.3 r-combination of n elements, binomial coefficients

- 3.4 Circular permutations, Permutations with repetitions
- 3.5 Multinomial theorem, Combinations with repetitions
- 3.6 Distribution of objects
- 3.7 Distinct objects in distinct cells
- 3.8 Indistinguishable objects in distinct cells

4. Number of Non-negative Integer Solutions of linear equations with conditions, Binomial identities

5. Principle of Inclusion and Exclusion

Formula Derangement - Restrictions on relative positions

6. Algebraic Structures
- 6.1 Operations on sets - Unary, Binary, Ternary
- 6.2 Definitions of algebraic systems
- 6.3 (restrict to binary operations)
- 6.4 Properties - Closure, Idempotent, Associative
- 6.5 Communicative, Associative, Commutative
- 6.6 Identity, Inverse, Semi group, Monoid, Abelian group, Permutation group, Multiplicative abelian
- 6.7 Group, Cyclic group
- 6.8 Subgroups: Cosets, Right cosets, left cosets
- 6.9 Normal subgroups, [For cosets only definitions, No derivations and proofs]
- 6.10 Group codes : In group codes only properties without derivations and problems on following subtopics should be covered
- 6.11 Weight and Hamming distance, Minimum distance of code, Generation of codes using parity checks - even parity, Odd parity, Parity check matrix - Hamming code, For detection and correction of errors, Problems on encoding functions decoding functions Application of residue - arithmetic to computers group codes

Contents ...

1. **Mathematical Logic** — 1.1 – 1.60

2. **Relations and Functions** — 2.1 – 2.68

3. **Permutations and Combinations** — 3.1 – 3.38

4. **Principle of Inclusion and Exclusion** — 4.1 – 4.22

5. **Algebraic Structures** — 5.1 – 5.72

Chapter 1...

MATHEMATICAL LOGIC

1.1 Statements (Propositions)

In our everyday life we use different types of sentences for communication. Below are given some sentences :

(i) High! Hellow!

(ii) Please bring me cup of coffee.

(iii) What are you doing ?

(iv) Earth is round.

(v) $3 + 4 = 10$

(vi) All students in MCA class are graduates.

(vii) The result of 5 multiplied by 2 is less than 100.

(viii) Sun rises in the west.

In the above list the sentences in (i), (ii), (iii) are exclamatory, order and question type sentences. They do not declare any result; whereas each of the sentences from (iv) – (viii) declare firmly something; which may be True (T) or False (F). They are called declarative sentences. The result declared in (iv), (vi) and (vii) is true but that in (v) and (viii) is false.

Let us consider the following declarative sentence.

'Their are four mistaks in this sentense'

Is it true or false ?

If we say it is true, then it is false since there are only three mistakes.

If we say it is false, then the result is true.

We shall avoid this type of declarative sentences.

Definition : A declarative sentence which is either True (T) or False (F) but not both, is called a statement or proposition.

Thus the sentences (iv), (vi) and (vii) above are true statements and (v), (viii) are false statements. We denote the statements by small case letters p, q, r etc. If the statement p is true then we say that the truth value of p is T. If p is a false statement, then the truth value of p is F.

These results are denoted by writing $p \equiv T$ or $p \equiv F$ respectively.

Consider the following statements :

p : Logic is easy.

q : It is too hot today.

r : $2x + 3 = 15$.

The truth value of statement p changes from student to student. For a student X it may be that really it is easy but for another student Y it may seem to be rather difficult.

The truth value of q changes from place to place.

The statement r has truth value T only when x = 6 and for any other value of x it is false.

A statement whose truth value depends upon certain circumstances, is called a logical variable.

Thus p, q, r are logical variables.

A statement whose truth value never changes is called a logical constant.

s : There are 26 letters in English alphabet.

t : Integer 10 is not divisible by 2.

Here the statements s and t are logical constants and we have $s \equiv T$, $t \equiv F$.

1.2 Logical Connectives

We now proceed to the methods of forming new propositions (statements) from the given two or more propositions. While communicating with each other, we always come across with the words 'not', 'and', 'or', 'if – then', 'if and only if' etc. They are called 'Logical Connectives'.

A proposition which does not involve any logical connective is called a simple statement. The statements, we have seen in Article 1.1 are all simple statements.

A proposition which involves logical connective (s) is called a compound proposition or compound statement.

Thus,   p : 5 is odd and 9 is a perfect square

q : If traffic is jam, then buses are late.

r : Children like to watch 'chhota Bhim' or 3 is not prime.

are compound propositions.

While forming a compound proposition, we use different symbols for logical connectives. These symbols are called logical operators.

Definition : Let p be a proposition. Then the negation of p denoted by $\neg p$ (or $\sim p$ or $\bar{p}$) is a proposition whose truth value is opposite to the truth value of p.

Thus suppose,

p : Signal mechanism has failed.

Then $\neg p$: Signal mechanism has not failed.

We can also say.

$\neg p$: It is not the case that signal mechanism has failed.

From the definition of $\neg p$, we have the following table called truth table for $\neg p$.

p	$\neg p$
T	F
F	T

Definition : Let p and q be propositions. Then the conjunction of p and q, denoted by p ∧ q (read p and q) is the proposition whose truth value is T, when p and q both have value T and value F in all remaining cases.

We note that there are four possible combinations of the truth values of two propositions p and q. They are TT, TF, FT and FF.

As such the truth table for p ∧ q consists of 4 rows; as given below.

p	q	p ∧ q
T	T	T
T	F	F
F	T	F
F	F	F

Let p : 5 is prime
q : 4 is even
r : 7 is a perfect square.

Then we have p ≡ T, q ≡ T, r ≡ F. The compound position '5 is prime and 4 is even' has the truth value p ∧ q ≡ T ∧ T ≡ T (See table)

Also the proposition '5 is prime and 7 is a perfect square' has truth value

p ∧ r ≡ T ∧ F ≡ F (See table)

Sometimes the word 'still', 'but' can be used while writing the conjunction of two propositions. For example, let p : It is raining and q : we go for picnic.

Then p ∧ q : It is raining and we go for picnic

can be written as

'It is raining, still we go for picnic' we can also write

'It is raining but we go for picnic'

Definition : Let p and q be propositions. Then the disjunction of p and q, denoted by p ∨ q (read p or q) is the proposition whose truth value is T when at least one of p and q has value T and value F when both p and q have value F.

The truth table for p ∨ q is as below.

p	q	p ∨ q
T	T	T
T	F	T
F	T	T
F	F	F

Consider the following propositions.

p : The word LOGIC contains 2 vowels

q : The word LOGIC contains 3 consonants

r : The world LOGIC contains 2 consonants

s : The word LOGIC contains 3 vowels.

We note that $p \equiv T, q \equiv T, r \equiv F, s \equiv F$.

The compound proposition.

'The word LOGIC contain 2 vowels or it contains 2 consonants'

$\equiv p \vee r \equiv T \vee F \equiv T$ (See table)

Also the proposition 'The word LOGIC contains 2 consonants or it contains 3 vowels' is $r \vee s \equiv F \vee F \equiv F$ (See table).

Again the proposition 'The word LOGIC contains 3 consonants or it contains 2 consonants

$\equiv q \vee r \equiv T \vee F \equiv T$ (See table)

Note : The word 'or' has two meanings viz. 'inclusive or' and 'exclusive or'.

In the above discussion, we have used 'or' in inclusive sense. It has value T when at least one of p and q has value T, and value F otherwise.

For exclusive 'or' we use the symbol $p \oplus q$. It has value T when exactly one of p and q has value T, and value F otherwise.

The examples of exclusive 'or' are :

(i)   5 is prime or 5 is not prime.
(ii) Today it is raining or not raining.
(iii) New baby is either male or female.
(iv) Today postman gave the letter or he did not.

The truth table for exclusive 'or' as given below.

p	q	$p \oplus q$
T	T	F
T	F	T
F	T	T
F	F	F

Conditional Statements :

Definition : Let p and q be propositions. Then the conditional statement denoted b $p \rightarrow q$ ($p \Rightarrow q$) is a proposition whose truth value F only when p is true and q is false. It has truth value T in all other cases.

We read $p \rightarrow q$ as 'p implies q' or 'if p then q'.

p is called anticident (hypothesis) and q is called consequent (conclusion).

The truth table for $p \rightarrow q$ is as shown below.

p	q	$p \rightarrow q$
T	T	T
T	F	F
F	T	T
F	F	T

The following are equivalent meanings of p → q.

If p then q, q if p, p only if q, p is sufficient for q, q is necessary for p, whenever p, then q.

Consider two statements 'Today is holiday' and 'I go to movie'.

Then the conditional statement 'If today is holiday, then I go to movie' is symbolically written as below.

    p : Today is holiday

    q : I go to movie

∴ The symbolic form of the given statement is p → q.

From the given conditional statement p → q, we form three more conditional statements.

The converse of p → q is q → p.

The inverse of p → q is ¬p → ¬q.

Contrapositive of p → q is ¬q → ¬p.

In the above example, the

(i)   converse is 'If I go to movie, then today is holiday'.

(ii) inverse is 'If today is not holiday, then I will not go to movie'.

(iii) contrapositive is 'If I do not go to movie, then today is not holiday.

Let us now prepare a single truth value table which shows the truth values of above 4 implications; for all possible truth values of p and q.

Clearly the table consists of $2^2 = 4$ rows.

1	2	3	4	5	6	7	8
p	q	¬p	¬q	p → q	q → p	¬p → ¬q	¬q → ¬p
T	T	F	F	T	T	T	T
T	F	F	T	F	T	T	F
F	T	T	F	T	F	F	T
F	F	T	T	T	T	T	T
				implication	converse	inverse	contrapositive

Two compound propositions $P(p_1, p_2, ..., p_r)$ and $Q(p_1, p_2, ..., p_r)$ involving simple statements $p_1, p_2, ..., p_r$ are said to be logically equivalent if they have identical truth values in all possible combinations of the truth values of $p_1, p_2, ..., p_r$.

It is denoted by $P(p_1, p_2, ..., p_r) \equiv Q(p_1, p_2, ..., p_r)$.

From the above truth table, we observe the following results.

In column (5) and column (8), the two propositions p → q and ¬q → ¬p have identical truth values in all possible combinations of the truth values of p and q.

∴ p → q ≡ ¬q → ¬p

> The given implication and its contrapositive are logically equivalent.

Also from the column (6) and column (7) of the truth table, the compound propositions $q \to p$ and $\neg p \to \neg q$ have identical truth values in all possible combinations of the truth values of p and q.

$\therefore \quad q \to p \equiv \neg p \to \neg q$

The converse and the inverse of given implication are logically equivalent.

Biconditional Statements :

Definition : Let p and q be two statements. Then the biconditional statement denoted by $(p \leftrightarrow q)$ is the proposition 'p if and only if q'. It has truth value T when p and q have identical truth values and value F when p and q have opposite truth values. It is also called double implication or bi-implication.

We read $p \leftrightarrow q$ in the following ways. p implies and implied by q.

p is necessary and sufficient for q.

If p then q and conversely. The abbreviation p iff q is used for 'p if and only if q'.

Suppose p : I catch the train and q : I arrive at the station in time.

Then $p \leftrightarrow q$ in words is

'I catch the train if and only if, I arrive at the station in time'.

As an another example, let p : x is odd, q : x^2 is odd.

Then $p \leftrightarrow q$ is in words, 'x is odd iff x^2 is odd', i.e. 'The necessary and sufficient condition for x to be odd is that x^2 is odd'.

The truth table for biconditional statement is as below.

p	q	$p \leftrightarrow q$
T	T	T
T	F	F
F	T	F
F	F	T

Example 1.1 : By preparing a truth table show that $p \to q \equiv \sim p \vee q$.

Solution :

(1)	(2)	(3)	(4)	(5)
p	q	~p	$p \to q$	~p $\vee$ q
T	T	F	T	T
T	F	F	F	F
F	T	T	T	T
F	F	T	T	T

From column (4) and column (5) of the table the propositions $p \to q$ and ~p $\vee$ q have identical truth values in all possible combinations of the truth values of p and q.

$\therefore \qquad p \to q \equiv (\sim p) \vee q$

Note : The above result $p \to q \equiv (\sim p) \vee q$ is always useful in establishing the equivalence of two propositions by using the algebra of propositions.

1.3 Compound Propositions

In the preceding article, we are acquainted with four logical connectives conjunction ($\wedge$), disjunction ($\vee$), implication ($\rightarrow$) and bi-implication ($\leftrightarrow$) together with negation ($\neg$).

Let now $P(p_1, p_2, \ldots, p_r)$ be a compound proposition involving r simple statements $p_1, p_2, \ldots, p_r$ and the logical connectives together with negation. As each simple statement p_i assumes 2 values i.e. T and F, there are $2 \times 2 \times \ldots \times 2 = 2^r$ possible combinations of the truth values of $p_1, p_2, \ldots, p_r$. Thus to prepare a truth table of $P(p_1, p_2, \ldots, p_r)$, we have to construct a table having 2^r rows.

Consider a compound proposition involving 3 simple statements p, q, r. The truth table for P(p, q, r) contains $2^3 = 8$ rows. While preparing a truth table we proceed as below.

The first three columns of the table are reserved for p, q, r as shown below.

p	q	r		...		P
T	T	T				
T	T	F				
T	F	T				
T	F	F				
F	T	T				
F	T	F				
F	F	T				
F	F	F				

Now the height of each column is 8.

In the column of p, we put first 4T^s and last 4F^s. (See table).

Then in the column of q, we put first 2T^s, next 2F^s, next 2T^s and last 2F^s (See table).

In the column of r, we put T^s and F^s alternately. (See table).

After this, we fill-up the next columns successively as given in P(p, q, r).

Example 1.2 : Construct a truth table for $(q \rightarrow \neg p) \vee (\neg p \rightarrow \neg q)$.

Solution : $P(p, q) \equiv (q \rightarrow \neg p) \vee (\neg p \rightarrow \neg q)$ involves 2 simple statements.

$\therefore$ Truth table consists of $2^2 = 4$ rows. Also the expression for P(p, q) suggests that the table needs 7 columns; as shown below.

p	q	$\neg p$	$\neg q$	$q \rightarrow \neg p$	$\neg p \rightarrow \neg q$	$(q \rightarrow \neg p) \vee (\neg p \rightarrow \neg q)$
T	T	F	F	F	T	T
T	F	F	T	T	T	T
F	T	T	F	T	F	T
F	F	T	T	T	T	T

Example 1.3 : Construct a truth table for $(\neg p \leftrightarrow \neg q) \leftrightarrow (q \leftrightarrow r)$

Solution : The given expression involves three simple statements. Therefore truth table consists of $2^3 = 8$ rows.

p	q	r	¬p	¬q	¬p ↔ ¬q	q ↔ r	(¬p ↔ ¬q) ↔ (q ↔ r)
T	T	T	F	F	T	T	T
T	T	F	F	F	T	F	F
T	F	T	F	T	F	F	T
T	F	F	F	T	F	T	F
F	T	T	T	F	F	T	F
F	T	F	T	F	F	F	T
F	F	T	T	T	T	F	F
F	F	F	T	T	T	T	T

By referring to the above examples, we see that the compound proposition $(q \to \neg p) \vee (\neg p \to \neg q)$ has truth value T in all possible combinations of the truth values of p and q. Such a compound proposition is called a tautology.

Definition : A compound proposition $P(p_1, p_2, \ldots, p_r)$ is called a tautology if P has truth value T in all possible combinations of the truth values of $p_1, p_2, \ldots, p_r$.

Definition : A compound proposition $P(p_1, p_2, \ldots, p_r)$ is called a contradiction of fallacy if P has truth value F in all possible combinations of the truth values of $p_1, p_2, \ldots, p_r$.

A proposition which is neither tautology nor contradiction is called a contingency.

Thus, $(\neg p \leftrightarrow \neg q) \leftrightarrow (q \leftrightarrow r)$ is a contingency.

From the definition of logical equivalence of two propositions $P(p_1, p_2, \ldots, p_r)$ and $Q(p_1, p_2, \ldots, p_r)$ and tautology it immediately follows that

$[P \equiv Q]$ iff $[(P \leftrightarrow Q)$ is a tautology$]$.

The symbol $\Leftrightarrow$ is used for logical equivalence.

Thus $P \equiv Q$ and $P \Leftrightarrow Q$ have the same meaning.

Example 1.4 : Show that $(\neg Q \wedge (P \to Q)) \to \neg P$ is a tautology. **(P.U. 2009)**

Solution :

P	Q	¬P	¬Q	P → Q	¬Q ∧ (P → Q)	(¬Q ∧ (P → Q)) → ¬P
T	T	F	F	T	F	T
T	F	F	T	F	F	T
F	T	T	F	T	F	T
F	F	T	T	T	T	T

From the last column of the table, the proposition $(\neg Q \wedge (P \to Q)) \to \neg P$ has truth value T in all possible combinations of the truth values of P and Q. Hence it is a tautology.

Logical Identities :

In the algebra of propositions there are some logical identities (logical equivalences). We can use them in establishing the equivalence of compound propositions. The following table gives the list of logical identities.

Commutative laws	$p \vee q \equiv q \vee p$
	$p \wedge q \equiv q \wedge p$
Distributive laws	$p \vee (q \wedge r) \equiv (p \vee q) \wedge (p \vee r)$
	$p \wedge (q \vee r) \equiv (p \wedge q) \vee (p \wedge r)$
Identity laws	$p \wedge T \equiv p$
	$p \vee F \equiv p$
Negation laws	$p \wedge \sim p \equiv T$
	$p \wedge \sim p \equiv F$
Associative laws	$p \vee (q \vee r) \equiv (p \vee q) \vee r$
	$p \wedge (q \wedge r) \equiv (p \wedge q) \wedge r$
Domination laws	$p \vee T \equiv T$
	$p \wedge F \equiv F$
Double negation law	$\sim (\sim p) \equiv p$
De Morgan's laws	$\sim (p \vee q) \equiv \sim p \wedge \sim q$
	$\sim (p \wedge q) \equiv \sim p \vee \sim q$
Absorption laws	$p \wedge (p \vee q) \equiv p$
	$p \vee (p \wedge q) \equiv p$
Idempotency laws	$p \vee p \equiv p$
	$p \wedge p \equiv p$

We shall give the proof of some of these laws below. The proofs of the remaining are left as an exercise.

Proof of associative laws :

(1)	(2)	(3)	(4)	(5)	(6)	(7)
p	q	r	$q \vee r$	$p \vee (q \vee r)$	$p \vee q$	$(p \vee q) \vee r$
T	T	T	T	T	T	T
T	T	F	T	T	T	T
T	F	T	T	T	T	T
T	F	F	F	T	T	T
F	T	T	T	T	T	T
F	T	F	T	T	T	T
F	F	T	T	T	F	T
F	F	F	F	F	F	F

From column (5) and (7), we see that $p \vee (q \vee r)$ and $(p \vee q) \vee r$ have identical truth values in all the rows.

$\therefore \qquad p \vee (q \vee r) \equiv (p \vee q) \vee r$

The other associative law i.e. $p \wedge (q \wedge r) \equiv (p \wedge q) \wedge r$ can be proved as above (Try yourself)

De Morgan's laws :

(1)	(2)	(3)	(4)	(5)	(6)	(7)	(8)	(9)	(10)
p	q	~p	~q	p ∨ q	~ (p ∨ q)	~p ∧ ~q	p ∧ q	~ (p ∧ q)	~p ∨ ~q
T	T	F	F	T	F	F	T	F	F
T	F	F	T	T	F	F	F	T	T
F	T	T	F	T	F	F	F	T	T
F	F	T	T	F	T	T	F	T	T

From column (6) and (7), we see that $\sim (p \vee q)$ and $\sim p \wedge \sim q$ have identical truth values in all the rows.

$\therefore \qquad \sim (p \vee q) \equiv \sim p \wedge \sim q$

Also from column (9) and (10) the proposition $\sim (p \wedge q)$ and $\sim p \vee \sim q$ have identical truth values in all possible rows.

$\therefore \qquad \sim (p \wedge q) \equiv \sim p \vee \sim q$

Absorption laws :

(1)	(2)	(3)	(4)	(5)	(6)
p	q	p ∧ q	p ∨ (p ∧ q)	p ∨ q	p ∧ (p ∨ q)
T	T	T	T	T	T
T	F	F	T	T	T
F	T	F	F	T	F
F	F	F	F	F	F

From column (1) and (4), we see that the proposition $p \vee (p \wedge q)$ and p have identical truth values in all the rows.

$\therefore \qquad p \vee (p \wedge q) \equiv p$

Also from column (1) and (6) the proposition $p \wedge (p \vee q)$ and p have identical truth values in all the rows.

$\therefore \qquad p \wedge (p \vee q) \equiv p$

With the help of truth table complete the proof of remaining laws given in the table.

The careful look to the table of logical identities immediately tells that all the identities (except that of double negation) occur in pairs. In each identity the second part (first part) can be obtained from the first part (second part) simply by interchanging all occurrences of (i) disjunction (∨) and conjunction (∧) and (ii) T and F.

It is called 'principle of duality' in the algebra of propositions.

For example, consider first distributive law
$$p \vee (q \wedge r) \equiv (p \vee q) \wedge (p \vee r)$$
$\wedge$ by $\vee$ everywhere.

Then we get, $\quad p \wedge (q \vee r) \equiv (p \wedge q) \vee (p \wedge r)$

which is second distributive law.

Again consider the first domination law i.e. $p \vee T \equiv T$.

Now we replace $\vee$ by $\wedge$ and also T by F.

Then, we get $p \wedge F \equiv F$; which is second domination law.

We have seen that logical equivalence of two propositions can be established with the help of a truth table.

If the two propositions whose logical equivalence is to be established, involve 2 or 3 simple statements, then we need to prepare a truth table of $2^2 = 4$ or $2^3 = 8$ rows.

It is manageable.

However, in case the number of simple statements involved is 4 or more it is quite unmanageable to prepare a truth table of $2^4 = 16$ rows or $2^5 = 32$ rows.

In such cases the equivalence can be established with the help of logical identities.

Let us prove that $A \to (B \vee C) \Leftrightarrow (A \wedge \sim B) \to C$.

We have,
$$\begin{aligned}
A \to (B \vee C) &\equiv (\sim A) \vee (B \vee C) && \because p \to q \equiv \sim p \vee q \\
&\equiv ((\sim A) \vee B) \vee C && \because \text{associative law} \\
&\equiv ((\sim A) \vee (\sim \sim B)) \vee C && \because \text{double negation} \\
&\equiv [\sim (A \wedge \sim B)] \vee C && \because \text{De Morgan's law} \\
&\equiv (A \wedge \sim B) \to C && \because p \to q \equiv \sim p \vee q \quad \text{Proved.}
\end{aligned}$$

SOLVED EXAMPLES

Example 1.5 : Let
$\quad$ P : It rains
$\quad$ Q : The atmospheric humidity increases.

Write the following statements in symbolic form :

(i) Atmospheric humidity increases only if it rains.
(ii) Sufficient condition for it to rain is that atmospheric humidity increases.
(iii) Necessary condition for it to rain is that atmospheric humidity increases.
(iv) Whenever atmospheric humidity increases it rains. **(P.U. 2009)**

Solution : (i) Atmospheric humidity increases only if it rains i.e. Q only if P.

$\quad$ Symbolically it is $Q \to P$.

(ii) Sufficient condition for it to rain is that atmospheric humidity increases i.e. sufficient condition for P is Q. i.e. Q is sufficient for P.

$\quad$ Symbolically $Q \to P$.

(iii) Necessary condition for it to rain is that atmospheric humidity increases i.e. necessary condition for P is Q i.e. Q is necessary for P.

Symbolically $P \to Q$.

(iv) Whenever atmospheric humidity increases it rains.

Symbolically $Q \to P$.

Example 1.6 : Construct truth table for the following :

(i) $P \vee \neg (P \wedge Q)$ (ii) $(P \vee Q) \vee \neg R$ (iii) $\neg (P \vee \neg Q)$.   **(P.U. 2009)**

Solution : (i)

P	Q	$P \wedge Q$	$\neg (P \wedge Q)$	$P \vee \neg (P \wedge Q)$
T	T	T	F	T
T	F	F	T	T
F	T	F	T	T
F	F	F	T	T

(ii)

P	Q	R	$\neg R$	$P \vee Q$	$(P \vee Q) \vee \neg R$
T	T	T	F	T	T
T	T	F	T	T	T
T	F	T	F	T	T
T	F	F	T	T	T
F	T	T	F	T	T
F	T	F	T	T	T
F	F	T	F	F	F
F	F	F	T	F	T

(iii)

P	Q	$\neg Q$	$P \vee \neg Q$	$\neg (P \vee \neg Q)$
T	T	F	T	F
T	F	T	T	F
F	T	F	F	T
F	F	T	T	F

Example 1.7 : Determine which is a tautology or fallacy (P.U. 2010)

(i) $p \Rightarrow q \wedge q \Rightarrow p$ (ii) $(p \wedge q) \wedge (p \vee q)$

Solution : (i)

p	q	$p \Rightarrow q$	$q \Rightarrow p$	$(p \Rightarrow q) \wedge (q \Rightarrow p)$
T	T	T	T	T
T	F	F	T	F
F	T	T	F	F
F	F	T	T	T

From the truth values of $(p \Rightarrow q) \wedge (q \Rightarrow p)$ in the last column of the truth table, we conclude that the proposition $(p \Rightarrow q) \wedge (q \Rightarrow p)$ is neither a tautology nor fallacy.

(ii)

p	q	$p \wedge q$	$p \vee q$	$(p \wedge q) \wedge (p \vee q)$
T	T	T	T	T
T	F	F	T	F
F	T	F	T	F
F	F	F	F	F

From the truth values of $(p \wedge q) \wedge (p \vee q)$ in the last column of the table conclusion is that the proposition is neither a tautology nor a fallacy.

Example 1.8 : (a) Write the converse and contrapositive of the following statements :

(i) If it is raining the grass is wet.

(ii) Rain is necessary for it to be cloudy.

(b) Write the converse and inverse of the following statement. If I am not in good health, then I will go to clinic. **(P.U. 2010)**

Solution : (a) (i) Given statement is

If it is raining the grass is wet.

Let p : It is raining.

q : Grass is wet.

Then symbolically the given statement is $p \to q$.

Now $\neg p$: It is not raining

$\neg q$: Grass is not wet.

Converse is $q \to p$, i.e. If grass is wet then it is raining. Contrapositive is $\neg q \to \neg p$.

i.e. If grass is not wet, then it is not raining.

(ii) Given statement is 'Rain is necessary for it to be cloudy'.

We know that $p \to q$ means q is necessary for p.

We take   p : It is cloudy

q : It rains

∴ Symbolically given statement is p → q.

Now   ¬ p : It is not cloudy

¬ q : It does not rain

Converse is q → p, i.e. 'If it rains, then it is cloudy'. Contrapositive is ¬ q → ¬ p.

i.e. 'If it does not rain, then it is not cloudy'.

(b) Given statement is 'If I am not in good health, then I will go to clinic'.

Let   p : I am not in good health.

q : I will go to clinic.

Then symbolically given statement is p → q.

Now   ¬ p : I am in good health.

¬ q : I will not go to clinic.

Converse is q → p i.e. 'If I go to clinic, then I am not in good health'.

Inverse is ¬ p → ¬ q, i.e. 'If I am in good health, then I will not go to clinic.'

Example 1.9 : By using truth table examine whether or not the following statements are equivalent :

(i) $(P \rightarrow Q) \wedge (R \rightarrow Q) \Leftrightarrow (P \vee R) \rightarrow Q$

(ii) $P \rightarrow (Q \vee R) \rightleftharpoons (P \rightarrow Q) \vee (P \rightarrow R) \Leftrightarrow T$ **(P.U. 2012)**

Solution : (i)

(1)	(2)	(3)	(4)	(5)	(6)	(7)	(8)
P	Q	R	P → Q	R → Q	(P → Q) ∧ (R → Q)	P ∨ R	(P ∨ R) → Q
T	T	T	T	T	T	T	T
T	T	F	T	T	T	T	T
T	F	T	F	F	F	T	F
T	F	F	F	T	F	T	F
F	T	T	T	T	T	T	T
F	T	F	T	T	T	F	T
F	F	T	T	F	F	T	F
F	F	F	T	T	T	F	T

From column (6) and column (8) of the table the propositions (P → Q) ∧ (R → Q) and (P ∨ R) → Q have identical truth values in all possible combinations of the values of P, Q, R. Hence the propositions are equivalent.

(ii)

P	Q	R	Q ∨ R	P → (Q ∨ R) (A)	P → Q	P → R	(P → Q) ∨ (P → R) (B)	A ⇌ B
T	T	T	T	T	T	T	T	T
T	T	F	T	T	T	F	T	T
T	F	T	T	T	F	T	T	T
T	F	F	F	F	F	F	F	F
F	T	T	T	T	T	T	T	T
F	T	F	T	T	T	T	T	T
F	F	T	T	T	T	T	T	T
F	F	F	F	T	T	T	T	T

The last column of the table shows that P → (Q ∨ R) ⇌ (P → Q) ∨(P → R) is not a tautology.

Hence the propositions are not equivalent.

Example 1.10 : Show that the following statements are equivalent.

$$A \to (B \vee C) \Leftrightarrow (A \wedge \sim B) \to C \qquad \text{(P.U. 2010)}$$

Solution :

(1)	(2)	(3)	(4)	(5)	(6)	(7)	(8)
A	B	C	B ∨ C	A → (B ∨ C)	~ B	A ∨ ~ B	(A ∧ ~ B) → C
T	T	T	T	T	F	F	T
T	T	F	T	T	F	F	T
T	F	T	T	T	T	T	T
T	F	F	F	F	T	T	F
F	T	T	T	T	F	F	T
F	T	F	T	T	F	F	T
F	F	T	T	T	T	F	T
F	F	F	F	T	T	F	T

From column (5) and column (8) of the table the two propositions A → (B ∨ C) and (A ∧ ~ B) → C have identical truth values in all possible combinations of the truth values of A, B, C. Hence A → (B ∨ C) ⇔ (A ∧ ~ B) → C.

Example 1.11 : Two roads cross each other at the junction point where there are two restaurants diagonally opposite to each other. The owner of one restaurant displayed a board 'cheap food is not good'. The owner of the other restaurant displayed a board 'good food is not cheap'.

Are they saying the same thing ? Justify your answer.

Solution : Let
p : food is good
q : food is cheap

Then $\neg p$: food is not good
and $\neg q$: food is not cheap.

Symbolically first board says $q \to \neg p$ and second board says $p \to \neg q$.

We know that the implication and its contrapositive are logically equivalent.

The contrapositive of $p \to \neg q$ is $\neg(\neg q) \to \neg p$ i.e. $q \to \neg p$ ∵ double negation

∴ $p \to \neg q \equiv q \to \neg p$

The two boards are saying the same thing.

Example 1.12 : Establish the following equivalence by using :
(a) truth table
(b) logical identities

$$P \to (Q \vee R) \Leftrightarrow (P \to Q) \vee (P \to R)$$

Solution :

(1)	(2)	(3)	(4)	(5)	(6)	(7)	(8)
P	Q	R	Q∨R	P→(Q∨R)	P→Q	P→R	(P→Q)∨(P→R)
T	T	T	T	T	T	T	T
T	T	F	T	T	T	F	T
T	F	T	T	T	F	T	T
T	F	F	F	F	F	F	F
F	T	T	T	T	T	T	T
F	T	F	T	T	T	T	T
F	F	T	T	T	T	T	T
F	F	F	F	T	T	T	T

From column (5) and (8) of the table, the truth values of

$P \to (Q \vee R)$ and $(P \to Q) \vee (P \to R)$ are identical in all rows.

∴ $P \to (Q \vee R) \Leftrightarrow (P \to Q) \vee (P \to R)$

Use of Logical Identities :

$$P \to (Q \vee R) \equiv (\neg P) \vee (Q \vee R) \quad \because p \to q \equiv \neg p \vee q$$
$$\equiv (\neg P \vee \neg P) \vee (Q \vee R) \quad \because \text{idempotency}$$

Now by associative law and commutative law it is

$$(\neg P \vee Q) \vee (\neg P \vee R) \equiv (P \to Q) \vee (P \to R) \quad \text{Proved.}$$

Example 1.13 : Establish the logical equivalence
$$[(\sim p \vee \sim q) \Rightarrow (p \wedge q \wedge r)] \Leftrightarrow (p \wedge q)$$
by using (a) truth table
(b) logical identities.

Solution :

(1)	(2)	(3)	(4)	(5)	(6)	(7)	(8)	(9)
p	q	r	~p	~q	~p ∨ ~q	p ∧ q ∧ r	[(~p ∨ ~q) ⇒ p ∧ q ∧ r]	p ∧ q
T	T	T	F	F	F	T	T	T
T	T	F	F	F	F	F	T	T
T	F	T	F	T	T	F	F	F
T	F	F	F	T	T	F	F	F
F	T	T	T	F	T	F	F	F
F	T	F	T	F	T	F	F	F
F	F	T	T	T	T	F	F	F
F	F	F	T	T	T	F	F	F

From column (8) and (9) of the table, we see that the two propositions
   $(\sim p \vee \sim q) \Rightarrow (p \wedge q \wedge r)$ and $p \wedge q$ have identical truth values in all the rows.
∴ $(\sim p \vee \sim q) \Rightarrow (p \wedge q \wedge r) \Leftrightarrow p \wedge q$.

Use of Logical Identities :

$$(\sim p \vee \sim q) \Rightarrow (p \wedge q \wedge r) \equiv \sim (p \wedge q) \Rightarrow (p \wedge q \wedge r) \qquad \because \text{De Morgan's law}$$
$$\equiv [\sim \sim (p \wedge q)] \vee (p \wedge q \wedge r) \qquad \because a \rightarrow b \equiv \sim a \vee b$$
$$\equiv (p \wedge q) \vee ((p \wedge q) \wedge r) \qquad \because \text{double negation}$$
$$\equiv p \wedge q \text{ Proved.} \qquad \because \text{absorption law}$$

Example 1.14 : Show the following implications :

(i) $P \wedge Q \Rightarrow P \rightarrow Q$

(ii) $P \rightarrow (Q \rightarrow R) \Rightarrow (P \rightarrow Q) \rightarrow (P \rightarrow R)$ **(P.U. Oct. 2012)**

Solution : (i)

P	Q	P ∧ Q	P → Q	(P ∧ Q) → (P → Q)
T	T	T	T	T
T	F	F	F	T
F	T	F	T	T
F	F	F	T	T

In the last column the proposition $(P \wedge Q) \rightarrow (P \rightarrow Q)$ has truth value T in all possible cases.

∴ $(P \wedge Q) \rightarrow (P \rightarrow Q)$ is a tautology.
∴ $(P \wedge Q) \Rightarrow (P \rightarrow Q)$

(ii)

P	Q	R	Q→R	P→(Q→R) (A)	P→Q	P→R	(P→Q)→(P→R) (B)	A→B
T	T	T	T	T	T	T	T	T
T	T	F	F	F	T	F	F	T
T	F	T	T	T	F	T	T	T
T	F	F	T	T	F	F	T	T
F	T	T	T	T	T	T	T	T
F	T	F	F	T	T	T	T	T
F	F	T	T	T	T	T	T	T
F	F	F	T	T	T	T	T	T

In the last column the proposition $[P \rightarrow (Q \rightarrow R)] \rightarrow [(P \rightarrow Q) \rightarrow (P \rightarrow R)]$ has truth value T in all possible cases.

∴ $[P \rightarrow (Q \rightarrow R)] \rightarrow [(P \rightarrow Q) \rightarrow (P \rightarrow R)]$ is a tautology.
∴ $[P \rightarrow (Q \rightarrow R)] \Rightarrow [(P \rightarrow Q) \rightarrow (P \rightarrow R)]$.

Example 1.15 : Show that the following formula is contradiction or not :

(i) $(P \wedge \neg Q) \wedge (P \rightarrow Q)$

(ii) $P \leftrightarrow (\neg Q \wedge R)$ **[P.U. Oct. 2012]**

Solution : (i) We prepare a truth table.

P	Q	¬Q	P∧¬Q	P→Q	(P∧¬Q)∧(P→Q)
T	T	F	F	T	F
T	F	T	T	F	F
F	T	F	F	T	F
F	F	T	F	T	F

In the last column of the truth table the truth value is F in all the possible cases of the truth values of P and Q. Therefore it is a contradiction. Alternatively,

$$(P \wedge \neg Q) \wedge (P \rightarrow Q) \equiv (\neg Q \wedge P) \wedge (P \rightarrow Q) \quad \because \text{Commutative law}$$
$$\equiv \neg Q \wedge [P \wedge (P \rightarrow Q)] \quad \because \text{Associative law}$$
$$\equiv \neg Q \wedge Q \quad \because P, P \rightarrow Q \therefore Q$$
$$\equiv F$$

(ii) We prepare a truth table.

P	Q	R	¬Q	¬Q ∧ R	P ↔ (¬Q ∧ R)
T	T	T	F	F	F
T	T	F	F	F	F
T	F	T	T	T	T
T	F	F	T	F	F
F	T	T	F	F	F
F	T	F	F	F	F
F	F	T	T	T	F
F	F	F	T	F	F

In the third row of the table the truth value of given proposition is T.

Therefore it is not a contradiction.

Example 1.16 Show that ¬P is valid from ¬(P ∧ ¬Q), (¬Q ∨ R), ¬R.   **(P.U. 2012)**

Solution : Given : ¬(P ∧ ¬Q), (¬Q ∨ R), ¬R.

∴ ¬P ∨ Q, ¬Q ∨ R, ¬R   ∵ By DeMorgan's law
∴ P → Q, Q → R, ¬R
∴ ¬R, ¬R → ¬Q, ¬Q → ¬P

Now ¬R, ¬R → ¬Q ∴ ¬Q   ∵ Law of syllogism

Further ¬Q, ¬Q → ¬P ∴ ¬P   ∵ law of syllogism

Proved.

Example 1.17 : Show that ¬(p ∨ (¬p ∧ q)) and ¬p ∧ ¬q are logically equivalent by developing a series of logical equivalences.

Solution :
$\neg(p \vee (\neg p \wedge q)) \equiv \neg((p \vee \neg p) \wedge (p \vee q))$ ∵ By distributive law
$\equiv \neg(T \wedge (p \vee q))$ ∵ $p \vee \neg p \equiv T$
$\equiv \neg(p \vee q)$ ∵ $T \wedge a = a$
$\equiv \neg p \wedge \neg q$ ∵ By DeMorgan's law

Proved.

EXERCISE (1.1)

1. Let p : Logic is difficult
      q : All houses have balcony
      r : Dogs bark

   Write each of the following in symbolic form :

   (a) Either dogs bark or both logic is difficult and all houses have balcony.
   (b) If dogs do not bark, then all houses have balcony.
   (c) Logic is difficult and if some houses do not have balcony then dogs will not bark.

2. Write the following in symbolic form :
   (a) He helps you (H) only if you are rich (R).
   (b) It is necessary to be more than 18 years old (M) to get a driving licence (L).
   (c) It is sufficient to have an average I.Q. (Q) and well guided hard work (W) to score more than 90% (S).
3. If p, q are true statements and r, s are false statements, then find the truth value of :
   (a) p ∨ (q ∧ r)
   (b) (p ∧ ~r) ∧ (~q ∨ s)
   (c) (p → q) ∨ (r ↔ s).
4. Write negation of the following :
   (a) Either economy is improving or dollar is being devalued.
   (b) If the domestic production of oil increases, then we shall not import crude oil.
   (c) The leader must have both, charisma and diplomacy.
5. Prepare a truth table and write your conclusion :
   (a) (~p ∨ q) → p ∧ (q ∨ ~q)
   (b) ¬ (P ↔ Q) ↔ [P ∧ (¬Q)] ∨ [Q ∧ (¬ P)]
   (c) Write dual of P ∧ (¬ P ∨ Q) ≡ P ∧ Q
6. Identify the pairs of statements having the same meaning : Justify your answer
   (a) If party has majority, then the government will survive.
   (b) If party has no majority, then government will collapse.
   (c) If government survives, then party has majority.
   (d) If government collapses, then party has no majority.
7. Identify the pairs of statements having the same meaning :
   (a) If thieves are caught, then police department is admired.
   (b) If thieves are not caught, then police department is not admired.
   (c) If police department is admired, then thieves are caught.
   (d) If police department is not admired, then thieves are not caught.
8. Construct a truth table for the following :
   (a) ¬ (p ↔ (Q → (R ∨ P)))
   (b) ¬ (P ∧ ¬ Q)
   (c) P ∨ ¬ (Q ∧ R)
   (d) (P ∧ ¬ Q) ∨ R
   (e) ((P ∨ Q) ∧ R) → (P ∨ R)
9. By using truth table verify that the following implication is a tautology.
   [(P ∨Q) ∧ (P → R) ∧ (Q → R)] → R. **(P.U. 2010)**
10. Prepare a truth table and verify that the following implication is a tautology :
    (a) (P ∧ (P → Q)) → Q
    (b) ((P → Q) ∧ (Q → R)) → (P → R)

11. Check the equivalence of the following statements :
    (a) $(P \leftrightarrow q) \equiv ((p \to q) \wedge (q \to p))$
    (b) $(p \to q) \equiv (\sim q) \to (\sim p)$ **(P.U. 2011)**

12. By using truth table examine whether or not
    (a) $A \to (B \vee C) \Leftrightarrow (A \wedge \neg B) \to C$
    (b) $(A \to C) \wedge (B \to C) \Leftrightarrow (A \vee B) \to C$ **(P.U. 2011)**

13. Establish the following equivalence by using :
    (a) truth table.
    (b) laws of logic
    $(P \to C) \wedge (Q \to C) \Leftrightarrow (P \vee Q) \to C$

14. Write the converse and inverse of the following statement.
    'If it is cold weather, then I wear sweater'. **(P.U. 2012)**

15. Write the converse and inverse of the statement 'If I am not in good health, then I will go to clinic'. **(P.U. 2011)**

16. Write the converse, inverse and contrapositive of each of the following statements :
    (a) If I run fast, then I can win the race.
    (b) $(\sim p) \Rightarrow q$.

17. (a) If $p \to q$ is false, find the truth value of $(\sim p \vee \sim q) \to q$.
    (b) If $p \to q$ is true, find the truth value of $\sim p \vee (p \leftrightarrow q)$.

18. Write the converse and contrapositive of the following statement.
    'If the flood destroys my house or the fire destroys my house, then my insurance company will pay me'.

19. By preparing truth table, complete the proof of all logical identities.

20. Determine whether or not :
    (a) $P \Leftrightarrow (Q \leftrightarrow (P \to Q))$
    (b) $((A \to B) \to C) \Leftrightarrow (A \to (B \to C))$

ANSWERS (1.1)

1. (a) $r \vee (p \wedge q)$ (b) $(\sim r) \to q$ (c) $p \wedge [\sim q \to \sim r]$
2. (a) $H \to R$ (b) $L \to M$ (c) $Q \wedge W \to S$
3. (a) T   (b) F   (c) T
4. (a) Economy is not improving and dollar is not being devalued.
   (b) The domestic production of oil increases, still we import crude oil.
   (c) Either the leader has no charisma or he has no diplomacy.

5. (a)

p	q	~p	~q	~p ∨ q	q ∨ ~q	p ∧ (q ∨ ~q)	(~p ∨ q) → p ∧ (q ∨ ~q)
T	T	F	F	T	T	T	T
T	F	F	T	F	T	T	T
F	T	T	F	T	T	F	F
F	F	T	T	T	T	F	F

    (b) Last column is TTFT

    (c) $P \lor (\neg P \land Q) \equiv P \lor Q$

6. (a) and (d) are contrapositives of each other. ∴ a ≡ d

    (b) and (c) are contrapositives of each other. ∴ b ≡ c

7. a ≡ d, b ≡ c

14. **Converse :** If I wear sweater, then it is cold weather.

    Inverse : If it is not cold weather, then I will not wear sweater.

15. **Converse :** If I go to clinic, then I am not in good health.

    Inverse : If I am in good health, then I win not go to clinic.

16. (a) **Converse :** If I win the race, then I run fast.

    Inverse : If I do not run fast, then I cannot with the race.

    Contrapositive : If I cannot win the race, then I don't run fast.

    (b) **Converse :** $q \Rightarrow \sim p$

    Inverse : $p \Rightarrow \sim q$

    Contrapositive : $\sim q \Rightarrow p$

17. (a) F   (b) T

18. **Converse :** If my insurance company pays me then the flood destroys my house or the fire destroys my house.

    Contrapositive : If my insurance company does not pay me, then the flood does not destroy my house and the fire does not destroy my house.

20. (a) No   (b) No

1.4 Normal Forms

Consider the logical expressions $p \to q$, $p \leftrightarrow q$ and $p \oplus q$.

We have $p \to q \equiv \sim p \lor q$.

Then
$$p \leftrightarrow q \equiv (p \to q) \land (q \to p)$$
$$\equiv (\sim p \lor q) \land (\sim q \lor p)$$

Now look to the truth table given below.

(1)	(2)	(3)	(4)	(5)	(6)	(7)	(8)
p	q	~p	~q	p ⊕ q	p ∧ ~q	q ∧ ~p	(p ∧ ~q) ∨ (q ∧ ~p)
T	T	F	F	F	F	F	F
T	F	F	T	T	T	F	T
F	T	T	F	T	F	T	T
F	F	T	T	F	F	F	F

The column (5) and (8) of the table shows that p ⊕ q and (p ∧ ~q) ∨ (q ∧ ~p) have identical truth values in all the rows.

∴ p ⊕ q ≡ (p ∧ ~q) ∨ (q ∧ ~p)

We have expressed the given logical expressions by using only the connectives ∨, ∧ and ~.

In particular p → q is written as a single disjunction; p ↔ q is expressed as the conjunction of two disjunctions and p ⊕ q is expressed as the disjunction of two conjunctions.

Let now p be a logical variable and denote by $\tilde{p}$ (p tilda) either p or ~p.

Then for n variables $p_1, p_2, \ldots, p_n$ $\wedge_i \tilde{p}_i = \tilde{p}_1 \wedge \tilde{p}_2 \wedge \ldots \wedge \tilde{p}_n$ is called a minterm and

$\vee_i \tilde{p}_i = \tilde{p}_1 \vee \tilde{p}_2 \vee \ldots \vee \tilde{p}_n$ is called a maxterm.

As $\tilde{p}_i$ is either p_i or $~p_i$, we note that there are $2 \times 2 \times \ldots \times 2 = 2^n$ minterms and 2^n maxterms in n variables.

For 2 variables p and q the 4 minterms and 4 maxterms are

        minterms : p ∧ q, p ∧ ~q, ~p ∧ q, ~p ∧ ~q

        maxterms : p ∨ q, p ∨ ~q, ~p ∨ q, ~p ∨ ~q.

Also for 3 variables $2^3 = 8$ minterms and 8 maxterms are

        minterms : p ∧ q ∧ r, p ∧ q ∧ ~r, p ∧ ~q ∧ r, p ∧ ~q ∧ ~r

                    ~p ∧ q ∧ r, ~p ∧ q ∧ ~r, ~p ∧ ~q ∧ r, ~p ∧ ~q ∧ ~r

        maxterms : p ∨ q ∨ r, p ∨ q ∨ ~r, p ∨ ~q ∨ r, p ∨ ~q ∨ ~r, ~p ∨ q ∨ r,

                    ~p ∨ q ∨ ~r, ~p ∨ ~q ∨ r, ~p ∨ ~q ∨ ~r

Disjunctive Normal Form :

Let E be the given logical expression. When we write E as the disjunction of some or all minterms it is called disjunctive normal form (DNF) of E.

It is also called 'sum of products' expansion (SOP) or disjunction of conjunctions (DOC).

Thus, DNF of p ⊕ q is (p ∧ ~q) ∨ (q ∧ ~p).

We find DNF of a given logical expression E by two methods viz. use of truth table and by using the laws of algebra of propositions.

Illustration : We find DNF of $p \wedge (q \vee \sim r)$ in two ways.

Use of truth table : First we prepare a truth table of the given expression.

p	q	r	~r	q ∨ ~r	p ∧ (q ∨ ~r)
T	T	T	F	T	T
T	T	F	T	T	T
T	F	T	F	F	F
T	F	F	T	T	T
F	T	T	F	T	F
F	T	F	T	T	F
F	F	T	F	F	F
F	F	F	T	T	F

The given expression $E \equiv p \wedge (q \vee \sim r)$ has truth value T in 1st, 2nd and 4th row.

In these three rows the corresponding truth values of p, q, r are TTT, TTF and TFF respectively. This means $p \wedge (q \vee \sim r)$ is true if and only if

$(p \equiv T, q \equiv T, r \equiv T)$ or $(p \equiv T, q \equiv T, r \equiv F)$ or $(p \equiv T, q \equiv F, r \equiv F)$

∴ DNF of $p \wedge (q \vee \sim r)$ is $(p \wedge q \wedge r) \vee (p \wedge q \wedge \sim r) \vee (p \wedge \sim q \wedge \sim r)$.   **[Note this step]**

Use of Algebra of Propositions :

We have $\qquad E \equiv p \wedge (q \vee \sim r)$

$\qquad\qquad\qquad \equiv (p \wedge q) \vee (p \wedge \sim r)$ ∵ By distributive law

Now in the first bracket the variable r is missing and in the second bracket variable q is missing.

We know that $r \vee \sim r \equiv T$ and $q \vee \sim q \equiv T$.

Also, we know $a \wedge T \equiv a$

∴ $\qquad\qquad\qquad E \equiv [(p \wedge q) \wedge (r \vee \sim r)] \vee [(p \wedge \sim r) \wedge (q \vee \sim q)]$

$\qquad\qquad\qquad \equiv [(p \wedge q \wedge r) \vee (p \wedge q \wedge \sim r)] \vee [(p \wedge \sim r \wedge q) \vee (p \wedge \sim r \wedge \sim q)]$

$\qquad\qquad\qquad \equiv [p \wedge q \wedge r] \vee [(p \wedge q \wedge \sim r) \vee (p \wedge \sim r \wedge q)] \vee (p \wedge \sim r \wedge \sim q)$

$\qquad\qquad\qquad \equiv (p \wedge q \wedge r) \vee (p \wedge q \wedge \sim r) \vee (p \wedge \sim r \wedge \sim q)$

$\qquad\qquad\qquad \equiv (p \wedge q \wedge r) \vee (p \wedge q \wedge \sim r) \vee (p \wedge \sim q \wedge \sim r)$

which is as before.

The DNF containing all 2^n minterms is called complete DNF.

Conjunctive Normal Form :

Let E be the given logical expression. When we write E as the conjunction of some or all maxterms, it is called conjunctive normal form (CNF) of E.

It is also called 'product of sums' expansion (POS) or conjunction of disjunctions (COD).

Thus, CNF of $p \leftrightarrow q$ is $(\sim p \vee q) \wedge (\sim q \vee p)$.

We find CNF of a given logical expression E by two methods viz. Use of truth table and the use of laws of algebra of propositions.

Illustration : We find CNF of $[p \wedge (\sim q \vee r)] \vee (\sim r)$ in two ways.

Use of truth table :

p	q	r	~q	~r	~q ∨ r	p ∧ (~q ∨ r)	[p ∧ (~q ∨ r)] ∨ (~r)
T	T	T	F	F	T	T	T
T	T	F	F	T	F	F	T
T	F	T	T	F	T	T	T
T	F	F	T	T	T	T	T
F	T	T	F	F	T	F	F
F	T	F	F	T	F	F	T
F	F	T	T	F	T	F	F
F	F	F	T	T	T	F	T

In the last column of the table the truth value of given expression E is F in the 5th and 7th row. The corresponding values of p, q, r are $(p \equiv F, q \equiv T, r \equiv T)$ and $(p \equiv F, q \equiv F, r \equiv T)$ respectively.

∴ CNF is $(p \vee \sim q \vee \sim r) \wedge (p \vee q \vee \sim r)$. **[Note this step]**

Use of Laws of Algebra of Propositions :

$$[p \wedge (\sim q \vee r)] \vee (\sim r) \equiv (\sim r) \vee [p \wedge (\sim q \vee r)] \quad \because \text{Commutative law}$$
$$\equiv (\sim r \vee p) \wedge (\sim r \vee (\sim q \vee r)) \quad \because \text{Distributive law}$$
$$\equiv (\sim r \vee p) \wedge [(\sim r \vee r) \vee \sim q]$$
$$\quad \because \text{By commutative and associative law}$$
$$\equiv (\sim r \vee p) \wedge [T \vee \sim q] \quad \because \sim r \vee r \equiv T$$
$$\equiv (\sim r \vee p) \wedge T \quad \because T \vee \sim q \equiv T$$
$$\equiv \sim r \vee p \quad \because a \wedge T \equiv a$$

Here q is missing

$$\equiv (\sim r \vee p) \vee (q \wedge \sim q) \quad \because q \wedge \sim q \equiv F \text{ and } a \vee F \equiv a$$
$$\equiv (\sim r \vee p \vee q) \wedge (\sim r \vee p \vee \sim q) \quad \because \text{By distributive law}$$
$$\equiv (p \vee q \vee \sim r) \wedge (p \vee \sim q \vee \sim r)$$

which is as before.

The CNF containing all 2^n maxterms is called complete CNF.

SOLVED EXAMPLES

Example 1.18 : Obtain DNF of $(\sim p \wedge q) \vee (p \wedge q) \vee q$. [P.U. 2010]

Solution : $E \equiv (\sim p \wedge q) \vee (p \wedge q) \vee q$

We prepare a truth table.

p	q	~p	~p ∧ q	p ∧ q	(~p ∧ q) ∨ (p ∧ q) ∨ q
T	T	F	F	T	T
T	F	F	F	F	F
F	T	T	T	F	T
F	F	T	F	F	F

In the last column of the table the expression E has truth value T in 1st and 3rd row.

Then corresponding values for p and q are $(p \equiv T, q \equiv T)$ and $(p \equiv F, q \equiv T)$

∴ DNF is $(p \wedge q) \vee (\sim p \wedge q)$.

Note : We have,

$$E \equiv (\sim p \wedge q) \vee [(p \wedge q) \vee q]$$
$$\equiv (\sim p \wedge q) \vee q \qquad \because \text{Absorption law}$$
$$= q \qquad \because \text{Absorption law}$$

Here variable p is missing

$$q \equiv q \wedge T \equiv q \wedge (p \vee \sim p)$$
$$\equiv (q \wedge p) \vee (q \wedge \sim p)$$
$$\equiv (p \wedge q) \vee (\sim p \wedge q)$$

Example 1.19 : Obtain CNF for the following : $(P \wedge Q) \vee (\neg P \wedge Q) \vee (P \wedge \neg Q)$

Solution :

P	Q	¬P	¬Q	P ∧ Q	¬P ∧ Q	P ∧ ¬Q	[(P ∧ Q) ∨ (¬P ∧ Q) ∨ (P ∧ ¬Q)]
T	T	F	F	T	F	F	T
T	F	F	T	F	F	T	T
F	T	T	F	F	T	F	T
F	F	T	T	F	F	F	F

In the last column of truth table F appears in the 4th row.

Then corresponding values of p and q are F, F.

∴ CNF is $P \vee Q$.

Alternatively,

$$(P \wedge Q) \vee (\neg P \wedge Q) \vee (P \wedge \neg Q) \equiv [Q \wedge [P \vee \neg P] \vee (P \wedge \neg Q) \qquad \because \text{Distributive law}$$
$$\equiv (Q \wedge T) \vee (P \wedge \neg Q)$$
$$\equiv Q \vee (P \wedge \neg Q) \qquad \because Q \wedge T \equiv Q$$
$$\equiv (Q \vee P) \wedge (Q \vee \neg Q) \qquad \because \text{Distributive law}$$
$$\equiv (Q \vee P) \wedge T$$
$$\equiv Q \vee P \qquad \because a \wedge T \equiv a$$
$$\equiv P \vee Q$$

Example 1.20 : Obtain DNF of $(\neg P \to R) \wedge (Q \rightleftharpoons P)$ (P.U. 2012)

Solution :

P	Q	R	$\neg P$	$\neg P \to R$	$Q \rightleftharpoons P$	$(\neg P \to R) \wedge (Q \rightleftharpoons P)$
T	T	T	F	T	T	T
T	T	F	F	T	T	T
T	F	T	F	T	F	F
T	F	F	F	T	F	F
F	T	T	T	T	F	F
F	T	F	T	F	F	F
F	F	T	T	T	T	T
F	F	F	T	F	T	F

In the last column of the table the expression $E \equiv (\neg P \to R) \wedge (Q \rightleftharpoons P)$ has truth value T in 1st, 2nd and 7th row.

Correspondingly in these rows values of P, Q, R are T T T, T T F and F F T respectively.

$\therefore$ DNF is $(P \wedge Q \wedge R) \vee (P \wedge Q \wedge \neg R) \vee (\neg P \wedge \neg Q \wedge R)$

Example 1.21 : Write in disjunctive normal form and conjunctive normal form in three variables P, Q, R the following :

(a) $(\neg P \wedge R) \vee (P \wedge \neg R)$

(b) $\neg P \vee Q$

Solution : (a) $E \equiv (\neg P \wedge R) \vee (P \wedge \neg R)$

In both the brackets, variable Q is missing.

$$E \equiv [(\neg P \wedge R) \wedge (Q \vee \neg Q)] \vee [(P \wedge \neg R) \wedge (Q \vee \neg Q)]$$

$\therefore \quad E \equiv (\neg P \wedge R \wedge Q) \vee (\neg P \wedge R \wedge \neg Q) \vee (P \wedge \neg R \wedge Q) \vee (P \wedge \neg R \wedge \neg Q)$

$\therefore \quad$ DNF : $(\neg P \wedge Q \wedge R) \vee (\neg P \wedge \neg Q \wedge R) \vee (P \wedge Q \wedge \neg R) \vee (P \wedge \neg Q \wedge \neg R)$

Next $\quad (\neg P \wedge R) \vee (P \wedge \neg R) \equiv [(\neg P \wedge R) \vee P] \wedge [(\neg P \wedge R) \vee \neg R]$

$\qquad\qquad\qquad\qquad\qquad\qquad\qquad\qquad\qquad\qquad \because$ Distributive law

$\equiv (P \vee \neg P) \wedge (P \vee R) \wedge (\neg R \vee \neg P) \wedge (\neg R \vee R)$

$\equiv T \wedge (P \vee R) \wedge (\neg P \vee \neg R) \wedge T$

$\equiv (P \vee R) \wedge (\neg P \vee \neg R)$

$\equiv [(P \vee R) \vee (Q \wedge \neg Q)] \wedge [(\neg P \vee \neg R) \vee (Q \wedge \neg Q)]$

$\qquad\qquad\qquad\qquad\qquad\qquad\qquad\qquad\qquad\qquad \because Q \wedge \neg Q \equiv F$

$\equiv (P \vee R \vee Q) \wedge (P \vee R \vee \neg Q) \wedge (\neg P \vee \neg R \vee Q) \wedge$

$\qquad\qquad\qquad\qquad\qquad\qquad\qquad\qquad\qquad (\neg P \vee \neg R \vee \neg Q)$

$\equiv (P \vee Q \vee R) \wedge (P \vee \neg Q \vee R) \wedge (\neg P \vee Q \vee \neg R) \wedge$

$\qquad\qquad\qquad\qquad\qquad\qquad\qquad\qquad\qquad (\neg P \vee \neg Q \vee \neg R)$

This is CNF.

(b) Consider $\neg P \vee Q$.

Here variable R is missing.

$$\neg P \vee Q \equiv (\neg P \vee Q) \vee (R \wedge \neg R)$$
$$\equiv (\neg P \vee Q \vee R) \wedge (\neg P \vee Q \vee \neg R)$$

This is CNF.

Next, $\neg P \vee Q \equiv (\neg P \vee Q) \wedge (R \vee \neg R)$
$$\equiv [(\neg P \vee Q) \wedge R] \vee [(\neg P \vee Q) \wedge \neg R]$$
$$\equiv [(R \wedge \neg P) \vee (R \wedge Q)] \vee [(\neg R \wedge \neg P) \vee (\neg R \wedge Q)]$$
$$\equiv [(R \wedge \neg P) \wedge (Q \vee \neg Q)] \vee [(R \wedge Q) \wedge (P \vee \neg P)] \vee$$
$$\qquad [(\neg R \wedge \neg P) \wedge (Q \vee \neg Q)] \vee [(\neg R \wedge Q) \wedge (P \vee \neg P)]$$
$$\equiv (R \wedge \neg P \wedge Q) \vee (R \wedge \neg P \wedge \neg Q)$$
$$\quad \vee (R \wedge Q \wedge P) \vee (R \wedge Q \wedge \neg P)$$
$$\quad \vee (\neg R \wedge \neg P \wedge Q) \vee (\neg R \wedge \neg P \wedge \neg Q)$$
$$\quad \vee (\neg R \wedge Q \wedge P) \vee (\neg R \wedge Q \wedge \neg P)$$
$$\equiv (\neg P \wedge Q \wedge R) \vee (\neg P \wedge \neg Q \wedge R) \vee (P \wedge Q \wedge R)$$
$$\quad \vee (\neg P \wedge Q \wedge \neg R) \vee (\neg P \wedge \neg Q \wedge \neg R)$$
$$\quad \vee (P \wedge Q \wedge \neg R) \vee (\neg P \wedge Q \wedge \neg R)$$

This is DNF.

Example 1.22 : Obtain the PDNF for the following $(P \vee Q) \wedge (P \to R)$. **(P.U. 2012)**

Solution : $(P \vee Q) \wedge (P \to R)$
$$\equiv (P \vee Q) \wedge (\neg P \vee R)$$
$$\equiv [(P \wedge Q) \wedge \neg P] \vee [(P \vee Q) \wedge R]$$
$$\equiv (\neg P \wedge P) \vee (\neg P \wedge Q) \vee (R \wedge P) \vee (R \wedge Q)$$
$$\equiv F \vee (\neg P \wedge Q) \vee (R \wedge P) \vee (R \wedge Q)$$
$$\equiv (\neg P \wedge Q) \vee (R \wedge P) \vee (R \wedge Q)$$
$$\equiv [(\neg P \wedge Q) \wedge (R \wedge \neg R)] \vee [(R \wedge P) \wedge (Q \vee \neg Q)] \vee$$
$$\qquad [(R \wedge Q) \wedge (P \vee \neg P)]$$
$$\equiv (\neg P \wedge Q \wedge R) \vee (\neg P \wedge Q \wedge \neg R) \vee (R \wedge P \wedge Q) \vee (R \wedge P \wedge \neg Q)$$
$$\qquad \vee (R \wedge Q \wedge P) \vee (R \wedge Q \wedge \neg P)$$
$$\equiv (\neg P \wedge Q \wedge R) \vee (\neg P \wedge Q \wedge \neg R) \vee (R \wedge P \wedge Q) \vee (R \wedge P \wedge \neg Q)$$

EXERCISE (1.2)

1. Obtain DNF and CNF of $q \wedge (p \to q)$
2. Obtain CNF of $P \vee (\neg P \to (Q \vee (\neg Q \leftrightarrow R)))$. **(P.U. 2011)**
3. Obtain DNF and CNF of $\neg P \to (Q \leftrightarrow R)$ **(P.U. 2009)**

4. Show that by using the laws of algebra, the following expression is a tautology. Hence write down DNF.

   (a) $A \to (A \land (B \to A))$

   (b) $\neg P \lor (\neg P \to (Q \lor (Q \to \neg R)))$

5. Obtain CNF of $(P \to R) \land (P \rightleftharpoons Q)$

6. Obtain DNF of $(P \lor Q) \land \neg R$ by

   (a) preparing a truth table.

   (b) using the laws of algebra of propositions.

7. The table below gives the values of E_1 and E_2. Obtain DNF of E_1 and CNF of E_2.

P	Q	R	E_1	E_2
T	T	T	F	T
T	T	F	F	F
T	F	T	T	F
T	F	F	F	F
F	T	T	F	F
F	T	F	F	T
F	F	T	T	T
F	F	F	T	F

ANSWERS (1.2)

1. DNF : $(p \land q) \lor (\sim p \land q)$

   CNF : $(\sim p \lor q) \land (p \lor q)$

2. $P \lor Q \lor R$

3. DNF : $(P \land Q \land R) \lor (P \land Q \land \neg R) \lor (P \land \neg Q \land R) \lor$
   $(P \land \neg Q \land \neg R) \lor (\neg P \land Q \land R) \lor (\neg P \land \neg Q \land \neg R)$

   CNF : $(P \lor \neg Q \lor R) \land (P \lor Q \lor \neg R)$

4. Complete DNF

5. $(\neg P \lor R \lor Q) \land (\neg P \lor \neg Q \lor R) \land (\neg P \lor Q \lor \neg R) \land (P \lor \neg Q \lor R) \land (P \lor \neg Q \lor \neg R)$

6. $(P \land Q \land \neg R) \lor (P \land \neg Q \land \neg R) \lor (\neg P \land Q \land \neg R)$

7. DNF of E_1 : $(P \land \neg Q \land R) \lor (\neg P \land \neg Q \land R) \lor (\neg P \land \neg Q \land \neg R)$

   CNF of E_2 : $(\neg P \lor \neg Q \lor R) \land (\neg P \lor Q \lor \neg R) \land (\neg P \lor Q \lor R) \land$
   $(P \lor \neg Q \lor \neg R) \land (P \lor Q \lor R)$

1.5 Argument and Validity

In this section, we begin our discussion with the following examples :
Consider the following sequences of propositions.
(i) If I were a movie star, then I would be famous.
But; I am not a movie star. Therefore, I am not famous.
(ii) If it is a Lux soap then it is a good soap.
It is a Lux soap. Hence, it is a good soap.
(iii) If my brother stands first in the class, I give him a T-shirt.
Either he stood first or I was out of station. I did not give him a T-shirt.
Therefore, I was out of station.

In each of the above examples there is a sequence of propositions; which are divided into two parts. In the first part there are some hypothetical propositions. They are called 'hypothesis' or 'premises'.

In the second part there is a proposition called 'conclusion'. It is some inference drawn from the premises.

The premises together with conclusion is called an 'argument'.

In the first example, above there are two premises viz.

'If I were a movie star, then I would be famous' and 'I am not a movie star'.

The conclusion is 'I am not famous' we write this argument as below.

If I were a movie star, then I would be famous.

<u>I am not a movie star.</u>

∴ I am not famous.

We write the above argument symbolically as below.

Let p : I were a movie star

           q : I would be famous

Then $\sim p$: I am not a movie star

           $\sim q$: I am not famous.

Hence the argument is;

$$p \rightarrow q$$
<u>$\sim p$</u>

∴ $\sim q$

The same is also written as,

$$p \rightarrow q, \neg p \vdash \neg q$$

The symbol $\vdash$ is used for 'yields'.

In the second example,

Let p : It is a Lux soap

     q : It is a good soap

Then symbolically the argument is

$$p \to q$$
$$\underline{p}$$
$$\therefore \quad q$$

or $p \to q, p \vdash q$

Also in the third example,

Let   p : My brother stands first

           q : I give him a T-shirt

           r : I was out of station

Then $\neg q$: I did not give him a T-shirt. Therefore argument is

$$p \to q$$
$$p \vee r \qquad \text{or } p \to q, p \vee r, \neg q \vdash r$$
$$\underline{\neg q}$$
$$\therefore \quad r$$

Let now $P_1, P_2, \ldots, P_n \vdash C$ be an argument where each premise P_i; $1 \le i \le n$ and the conclusion C are functions of simple statements p, q, ..., r etc.

In an argument $P_1, P_2, \ldots, P_n \vdash C$ each premise P_i can have truth value either T or F.

Also the conclusion C can have value either T or F.

Definition : The argument $P_1, P_2, \ldots, P_n \vdash C$ is called **valid** argument if 'whenever all the premises are true then conclusion is also true'. Otherwise, it is called **invalid** argument.

It follows from the definition that 'if $P_1 \wedge P_2 \wedge \ldots \wedge P_n$ is true, then C is true' is the condition for argument to be valid.

Equivalently if the condition "$(P_1 \wedge P_2 \wedge \ldots \wedge P_n) \to C$ is a tautology" then the argument "$P_1, P_2, \ldots, P_n \vdash C$" is valid argument.

Illustration : Consider the argument $P \vee Q, \neg P \therefore Q$.

We prepare a truth table as below.

(1)	(2)	(3)	(4)
P	Q	P ∨ Q	¬P
T	T	T	F
T	F	T	F
F	T	T	T
F	F	F	T

From this table, we see that in the third row both the premises $P \vee Q$ and $\neg P$ are true and the conclusion Q is also true.

Therefore, given argument is valid.

In the above illustration in which the argument involved two simple statements P and Q, we need to prepare a truth table involving $2^2 = 4$ rows and test the validity.

If the argument under consideration involves more than two atomic statements it is required to prepare reasonably a large table containing $2^3 = 8$ or $2^4 = 16$ rows etc.

Consider the following argument $P \to \neg Q, \neg R \vee Q, R \vdash \neg P$

Direct Method of Proof :

We have the following truth table.

(1)	(2)	(3)	(4)	(5)	(6)	(7)	(8)
P	Q	R	¬P	¬Q	¬R	P → ¬Q	¬R ∨ Q
T	T	T	F	F	F	F	T
T	T	F	F	F	T	F	T
T	F	T	F	T	F	T	F
T	F	F	F	T	T	T	T
F	T	T	T	F	F	T	T
F	T	F	T	F	T	T	T
F	F	T	T	T	F	T	F
F	F	F	T	T	T	T	T

The premises $P \to \neg Q, \neg R \vee Q$ and R are as shown in column (7) and column (8) and column (3) respectively. The conclusion ¬P is given by column (4).

Now in the 5th row of the table all three premises are true and conclusion is true. Therefore, given argument is valid.

Indirect Method of Proof :

We can establish the validity of an argument in the above illustration, by a truth table containing 4 rows only (instead of 8 rows). For this we make use of contrapositive of given implication. We know that an implicative statement is logically equivalent to its contrapositive i.e. $(P \to Q) \equiv (\neg Q \to \neg P)$.

Now argument is valid means 'whenever all premises are true then conclusion is true'.

This is equivalent to its contrapositive which states as below.

The argument is valid means 'whenever conclusion is false, then at least one premise is false'.

By noting the above fact, we prepare a truth table in which the conclusion is false always.

In this table if we observe that in each row at least one premise is false, then we conclude that argument is valid.

Also if we observe that in some row all the premises are true, then argument is invalid.

In the above illustration, we assume that the conclusion ¬P is false i.e. P is true always. Then Q and R are free to assume any value. There are exactly 4 combinations of the values of Q and R. Thus, we prepare a table with 4 rows only.

P	Q	R	¬P	¬Q	¬R	P → ¬Q	¬R ∨ Q
T	T	T	F	F	F	F	T
T	T	F	F	F	T	F	T
T	F	T	F	T	F	T	F
T	F	F	F	T	T	T	T

This table shows that whenever conclusion ⌈P is false, at least one of the three premises viz. P → ¬Q, ¬R ∨ Q and R is false.

Hence, the argument is valid.

Rules of Inference :

Consider the proposition $((P \vee Q) \wedge \neg P) \rightarrow Q$.

We can easily verify that this implication is a tautology.

P	Q	¬P	P ∨ Q	(P ∨ Q) ∧ ¬P	((P ∨ Q) ∧ ¬P) → Q
T	T	F	T	F	T
T	F	F	T	F	T
F	T	T	T	T	T
F	F	T	F	F	T

Such tautological propositions are called as 'Theorems' or 'Rules of Inference' in propositional calculus. We can use the rules of inference to establish the validity of argument (without preparing a truth table).

Below is the list of some rules of inference which are useful for our purpose of validity of arguments. The readers are supposed to verify these rules by truth table.

Inference Rules :

Sr. No.	Rule	Name of Rule
1.	$P \vee \neg P$	Excluded middle
2.	$P \leftrightarrow \neg \neg P$	Double negation
3.	$(P \wedge Q) \rightarrow P$	Separation
4.	$P \rightarrow (P \vee Q)$	Joining
5.	$(P \wedge (P \rightarrow Q)) \rightarrow Q$	Modus ponens or law of detachment
6.	$(P \rightarrow Q) \leftrightarrow (\neg Q \rightarrow \neg P)$	Contrapositive
7.	$((\neg P \rightarrow Q) \wedge (\neg P \rightarrow \neg Q)) \rightarrow P$	Proof by contradiction

... (Contd.)

Sr. No.	Rule	Name of Rule
8.	$((P \vee Q) \wedge \neg Q) \to P$	Disjunctive syllogism
9.	$(P \vee Q) \leftrightarrow (\neg P \to Q)$	Switcheroo
10.	$((P \to Q) \wedge (Q \to R)) \to (P \to R)$	Deduction
11.	$(((P \to Q) \wedge (R \to S)) \wedge (P \vee R)) \to (Q \vee S)$	Constructive dilemma
12.	$\neg (P \vee Q) \leftrightarrow (\neg P \wedge \neg Q)$	De Morgan's law
13.	$\neg (P \wedge Q) \leftrightarrow (\neg P \vee \neg Q)$	De Morgan's law
14.	$(P \to R) \vee (Q \to R) \equiv (P \wedge Q) \to R$	
15.	$(P \to R) \wedge (Q \to R) \equiv (P \vee Q) \to R$	
16.	$(P \to Q) \equiv \neg P \vee Q$	

Illustration : Test the validity of the following argument :

If it rains, then I wear a raincoat.

If it shines, then I do not need a sweater.

Either it rains or it shines.

Moreover, I do need a sweater.

Therefore, I wear a raincoat.

Solution : Let P : It rains
Q : It shines
R : I wear a raincoat
S : I need a sweater

Then given argument in symbolic form is

$P \to R$
$Q \to \neg S$
$P \vee Q$
$\underline{S}$
$\therefore \quad R$

$Q \to \neg S \quad \therefore S \to \neg Q$ ∵ Contrapositive

$S, S \to \neg Q \quad \therefore \neg Q$ ∵ Detachment

$P \vee Q \quad \therefore Q \vee P \quad \therefore \neg Q \to P$ ∵ $a \to b \equiv \sim a \vee b$

$\neg Q, \neg Q \to P, \quad \therefore P$ ∵ Detachment

$P, P \to R \quad \therefore R$ ∵ Detachment

Hence, the argument is valid.

SOLVED EXAMPLES

Example 1.23 : By preparing truth table test the validity of the following argument :

(i) $p \vee q, \sim q \quad \therefore p$

(ii) $(\sim p \wedge q) \wedge (q \rightarrow p), p \quad \therefore p \rightarrow \sim q$

(iii) I become famous or I will be a poet. I will not be a poet.

As a result, I will become famous.

(iv) Sudhir is either clever or lucky. Sudhir is not lucky.

If Sudhir is lucky, then he will win the lottery.

Therefore, Sudhir is clever.

Solution : (i)

p	q	~q	p ∨ q
T	T	F	T
T	F	T	T
F	T	F	T
F	F	T	F

In the second row of the table both the premises ~q and p ∨ q are true and the conclusion p is also true.

∴ Argument is valid.

(ii)

(1)	(2)	(3)	(4)	(5)	(6)	(7)	(8)
p	q	~p	~q	~p ∧ q	q → p	(~p ∧ q) ∧ (q → p)	p → ~q
T	T	F	F	F	T	F	F
T	F	F	T	F	T	F	T
F	T	T	F	T	F	F	T
F	F	T	T	F	T	F	T

Column (1) and column (7) show the two premises and column (8) shows the conclusion. Both the premises are true, does not appear in any row.

Equivalently, when the conclusion is false (see first row) then at least one premise is false.

Therefore, argument is valid.

(iii) Let   p : I become famous

q : I become poet

Then argument is, $p \vee q, \sim q \quad \therefore p$

The truth table is as below.

p	q	~q	p ∨ q
T	T	F	T
T	F	T	T
F	T	F	T
F	F	T	F

In the second row of the table both the premises ~q and p ∨ q are true and the conclusion p is also true.

∴ Argument is valid.

(iv) Let
        p : Sudhir is clever
        q : Sudhir is lucky
        r : Sudhir wins lottery

The argument is, p ∨ q, ~q, q → r ∴ p

We prepare a table with $2^3 = 8$ rows.

Premises

p	q	r	~q	p ∨ q	q → r
T	T	T	F	T	T
T	T	F	F	T	F
T	F	T	T	T	T
T	F	F	T	T	T
F	T	T	F	T	T
F	T	F	F	T	F
F	F	T	T	F	T
F	F	F	T	F	T

In the third row of the table all three premises are true and conclusion is also true.

∴ Argument is valid.

Example 1.24 : By preparing a truth table determine whether the following argument is valid or not.

$$((A \to B) \land (C \to D)), (\neg B \lor \neg D) \quad \therefore (\neg A \lor \neg C)$$

Solution : The given argument involves 4 statements A, B, C and D. So we have to prepare a truth table having $2^4 = 16$ rows. However this number 16 can be reduced to 4 rows only, as below.

Assume that the conclusion ¬A ∨ ¬C is false. Then ¬(A ∧ C) is false.

∵ De Morgan's law

∴ A ∧ C is true.

This happens only when both A and C have truth value T.

Also then B and D are free to assume any value.

∴ Truth table is as below.

A	B	C	D	¬B	¬D	A → B	C → D	(A → B) ∧ (C → D)	¬B ∨ ¬D
T	T	T	T	F	F	T	T	T	F
T	T	T	F	F	T	T	F	F	T
T	F	T	T	T	F	F	T	F	T
T	F	T	F	T	T	F	F	F	T

In this table in each row at least one premise is false.

∴ Argument is valid.

Example 1.25 : Show that the conclusion C is valid under the premises for the following without constructing truth table

$P_1 : \sim(A \wedge \sim B)$, $P_2 : \sim B \vee D$, $P_3 : \sim D$ ∴ $C : \sim A$ **(P.U. 2010)**

Solution : Given argument is, $\sim(A \wedge \sim B)$, $\sim B \vee D$, $\sim D$ ∴ $\sim A$

Now $\sim(A \wedge \sim B) \equiv \sim A \vee \sim\sim B \equiv \sim A \vee B$;   De Morgan's law

$\sim B \vee D \equiv B \to D$

$\equiv \sim D \to \sim B$ ∵ Contrapositive

Then $\sim D$, $\sim D \to \sim B$

∴ $\sim B$ ∵ Law of detachment

Also, $\sim A \vee B \equiv A \to B$

$\equiv \sim B \to \sim A$ ∵ Contrapositive

$\sim B$, $\sim B \to \sim A$

∴ $\sim A$ ∵ Law of detachment

Hence, the argument is valid.

Note : This is direct method of establishing the validity.

Example 1.26 : Without constructing truth table, determine whether the conclusion C follows logically from the premises H_1, H_2, H_3 where

$H_1 : \neg P \vee Q$, $H_2 : \neg(Q \wedge \neg R)$, $H_3 : \neg R$, $C : \neg P$ **(P.U. 2012)**

Solution : $H_1 : \neg P \vee Q$

$\neg P \vee Q \equiv P \to Q$

$H_2 : \neg(Q \wedge \neg R)$

$\neg(Q \wedge \neg R) \equiv \neg Q \vee \neg\neg R \equiv \neg Q \vee R \equiv Q \to R$

Then $P \to Q$, $Q \to R$ ∴ $P \to R$ ∵ Deduction

Then $\quad P \to R, \neg R$

$\therefore \quad \neg R \to \neg P, \neg R$

$\therefore \quad \neg R, \neg R \to \neg P$

$\therefore \quad \neg P$ Law of detachment

Therefore argument is valid.

Example 1.27 : Without using truth table show that the conclusion C is valid from the premises H_1, H_2, H_3 where $H_1 : P \vee Q$, $H_2 : P \to R$, $H_3 : Q \to R$ and $C : R$ **(P.U. 2011)**

Solution : $(P \to R) \wedge (Q \to R) \equiv (P \vee Q) \to R$

Now, $(P \vee Q), ((P \vee Q) \to R)$

$\therefore \quad R$ by law of detachment

Therefore, argument is valid.

Example 1.28 : Establish the validity of the following arguments :

(i) $(A \to (B \to C)), B \quad \therefore \quad A \to C$

(ii) $(R \to P), ((P \wedge Q) \vee R), (R \to Q) \quad \therefore P \wedge Q$

Solution : (i) Premises : $(A \to (B \to C)), B$

$B, B \to C \quad \therefore \quad C$ $\because$ Detachment

Then $\quad A \to (B \to C) \equiv A \to C$; which is the conclusion.

Therefore, argument is valid.

(ii) Premises : $(R \to P), ((P \wedge Q) \vee R), (R \to Q)$

Now, $\quad\quad\quad\quad R \to P \equiv \neg P \to \neg R$

$\quad\quad\quad\quad\quad\quad R \to Q \equiv \neg Q \to \neg R$

$\therefore \quad (R \to P) \wedge (R \to Q) \equiv (\neg P \to \neg R) \wedge (\neg Q \to \neg R)$

$\quad\quad\quad\quad\quad\quad\quad\quad\quad\quad \equiv (\neg P \vee \neg Q) \to \neg R$

$\quad\quad\quad\quad\quad\quad\quad\quad\quad\quad \equiv (\neg (P \wedge Q)) \to \neg R$ $\because$ De Morgan's law

$\quad\quad\quad\quad\quad\quad\quad\quad\quad\quad \equiv (P \wedge Q) \vee (\neg R)$ ... (1)

Also, $(P \wedge Q) \vee R$; given   ... (2)

From equation (1) and (2), we get

$\quad\quad ((P \wedge Q) \vee \neg R) \wedge ((P \wedge Q) \wedge R) \equiv (P \wedge Q) \vee (\neg R \wedge R)$ $\because$ Distributive law

$\quad\quad\quad\quad\quad\quad\quad\quad\quad\quad\quad\quad\quad\quad \equiv (P \wedge Q) \vee F$

$\quad\quad\quad\quad\quad\quad\quad\quad\quad\quad\quad\quad\quad\quad \equiv P \wedge Q$ which is the conclusion.

Therefore, argument is valid.

Example 1.29 : Show the validity of the conclusion $\neg A \vee \neg D$ from the premises $A \to (B \to C)$ and $D \to (B \wedge \neg C)$.   **[P.U. 2009]**

Solution : Assume that the conclusion $\neg A \vee \neg D$ is false.

$\therefore \quad \neg (A \wedge D)$ is false

$\therefore \quad A \wedge D$ is true

$\therefore \quad A \equiv T$ and $D \equiv T$

Now first premise is $A \to (B \to C) \equiv \neg A \lor (B \to C) \equiv F \lor (B \to C)$
$\equiv B \to C \equiv \neg B \lor C$ ... (1)

Second premise is $D \to (B \land \neg C) \equiv \neg D \lor (B \land \neg C) \equiv F \lor (B \land \neg C)$
$\equiv B \land \neg C = \neg(\neg B \lor C)$ ... (2)

From equation (1) and (2) at least one of them must be false.

Thus, when conclusion is false, at least one premise is false.

Therefore argument is valid.

Example 1.30 : Determine the validity of the argument.
    If I study, then I will pass.
    If I do not go to movie, then I will study.
    I failed.
Therefore, I went to a movie.

Solution : Let   P : I study
                Q : I pass
                R : I go to movie

In symbolic form the argument is, $P \to Q, \neg R \to P, \neg Q \quad \therefore R$

Now, $P \to Q \equiv \neg Q \to \neg P$
        $\neg Q, \neg Q \to \neg P \quad \therefore \neg P$ ∵ By law of detachment
        $\neg P, \neg R \to P$
$\therefore$ $\neg P, \neg P \to R$ ∵ Contrapositive
$\therefore$ R   ∵ By law of detachment

Therefore, argument is valid.

Example 1.31 : Test the validity of the following argument :
If I study, the I will not fail in Mathematics.
If I do not play basket ball, then I will study.
But I failed in Mathematics.
Therefore, I must have played basket ball   **(P.U. 2010)**

Solution : Let   P : I study
                Q : I failed in Mathematics
                R : I played basket ball

In symbolic form the argument is;
      $P \to \neg Q, \neg R \to P, Q \quad \therefore R$

Now $P \to \neg Q \equiv Q \to \neg P$ ∵ Contrapositive
        $Q, Q \to \neg P \quad \therefore \neg P$ By law of detachment
        $\neg P, \neg R \to P$
$\therefore$ $\neg P, \neg P \to R$ ∵ Contrapositive
$\therefore$ R   ∵ Law of detachment
$\therefore$ Argument is valid.

Example 1.32 : Test the validity of the following argument :
If my plumbing plans do not meet the construction code, then I cannot build my house.
If I hire a licensed contractor, then my plumbing plans will meet the construction code.
I hire a licensed contractor. Therefore, I can build my house.

Solution : Let P : My plumbing plans meet the construction code
Q : I can build my house
R : I hire a licenced contractor.

Symbolically the argument is, $\neg P \to \neg Q$, $R \to P$, R $\therefore Q$

We make use of contrapositive. Suppose the conclusion Q is false.
The variables P and R are free. The truth table is as below.

P	Q	R	¬P	¬Q	¬P → ¬Q	R → P
T	F	T	F	T	T	T
T	F	F	F	T	T	T
F	F	T	T	T	T	F
F	F	F	T	T	T	T

The first row of truth table suggests that all three premises $\neg P \to \neg Q$, $R \to P$ and R are true but the conclusion Q is false.

Therefore, argument is invalid.

Example 1.33 : Test the validity of the following argument :
If I like Mathematics, then I will study.
Either I don't study or I pass Mathematics.
If I don't graduate, then I don't pass Mathematics.
Therefore, If I graduated, then I studied. **(P.U. 2011)**

Solution : Let   P : I like Mathematics
Q : I study
R : I pass Mathematics
S : I become graduate

Then symbolically argument is, $P \to Q$, $\neg Q \vee R$, $\neg S \to \neg R$ $\therefore S \to Q$

We use the method of contrapositive. So suppose the conclusion $S \to Q$ is false. This happens when S is true and Q is false.

The variables P and R are free.

∴   Truth table consists of 4 rows.

P	Q	R	S	¬Q	¬R	¬S	P → Q	¬Q ∨ R	¬S → ¬R
T	F	T	T	T	F	F	F	T	T
T	F	F	T	T	T	F	F	T	T
F	F	T	T	T	F	F	T	T	T
F	F	F	T	T	T	F	T	T	T

In the 3rd and 4th row all premises are true and conclusion is false.

∴   Argument is invalid.

Example 1.34 : Test the validity of the following argument :

If there was a game, then swimming was impossible.
If they started on right time, then swimming was possible.
They started on right time.
Therefore, there was no game.   **(P.U. 2010)**

Solution : Let
- P : There was a game
- Q : Swimming was possible
- R : They started on right time.

In symbolic form the argument is, $P \to \neg Q$, $R \to Q$, R $\therefore \neg P$.

We shall prove in two ways that the argument is valid.

Use of Truth Table :

Assume that the conclusion $\neg P$ is false. This means P is true. The variables Q and R are free. The truth table is as below.

P	Q	R	¬Q	P → ¬Q	R → Q
T	T	T	F	F	T
T	T	F	F	F	T
T	F	T	T	T	F
T	F	F	T	T	T

We see that when $\neg P$ is false i.e. P is true then in each row at least one of three premises i.e. $P \to \neg Q$, $R \to Q$, R is false.

∴ Argument is valid.

Use of rules of inference :

$R, R \to Q$ ∴ Q	By law of detachment
$Q, P \to \neg Q$	
∴ $Q, Q \to \neg P$	∵ Contrapositive
∴ $\neg P$	∵ Law of detachment

Therefore, argument is valid.

Example 1.35 : Test the validity of the following argument :

If Lucy has bought a fur coat, then either she has robbed a bank or her rich uncle has died.
Her rich uncle has not died.
Therefore, if Lucy has not robbed a bank, she has not bought a fur coat.

Solution : Let
- P : Lucy bought a fur coat
- Q : Lucy robbed a bank
- R : Her rich uncle died

Then symbolically the argument is, $P \to Q \vee R$, $\neg R$ $\therefore \neg Q \to \neg P$

We use the method of contrapositive. So we assume that the conclusion $\neg Q \to \neg P$ is false.

This happens when $\neg Q$ is true and $\neg P$ is false i.e. when Q is false and P is true.

The variable R is free.

∴ Truth table consists of two rows only.

P	Q	R	Q ∨ R	P → (Q ∨ R)	¬S
T	F	T	T	T	F
T	F	F	F	F	T

In this table in each row at least one of the premise is false.

Therefore, argument is valid.

Example 1.36 : Examine the validity of the following argument :

If there is life on mars, then the experts are wrong and the government is lying.

If the government is lying, then the experts are right or there is no life on mars.

The government is lying.

Therefore, there is life on mars.

Solution : Let
P : There is life on mars
Q : Experts are right
R : Government is lying

Then the given argument is symbolically, $P \to \neg Q \wedge R, R \to Q \vee \neg P, R \quad \therefore P$

We use the method of contrapositive. Assume that the conclusion P is false.

Then the truth table is as below.

P	Q	R	¬P	¬Q	¬Q ∧ R	Q ∨ ¬P	R → Q ∨ ¬P	P → ¬Q ∧ R
F	T	T	T	F	F	T	T	T
F	T	F	T	F	F	T	T	T
F	F	T	T	T	T	T	T	T
F	F	F	T	T	F	T	T	T

From column (3), (8), (9) of the three premises R, R → Q ∨ ¬P and P → ¬Q ∧ R we see that in the first and third row all the premises are true and the conclusion is false.

Therefore, argument is invalid.

Example 1.37 : Show that the following set of premises are inconsistent.

$A \to (B \to C), D \to (B \wedge \neg C),$ and $A \wedge D$

Solution : $A \to (B \to C) \equiv A \to (\neg B \vee C)$

$D \to (B \wedge \neg C) \equiv \neg (B \wedge \neg C) \to \neg D$

$\equiv \neg B \vee \neg \neg C \to \neg D$

$\equiv \neg B \vee C \to \neg D$

Now, $A \to (\neg B \vee C), (\neg B \vee C) \to \neg D$

$\therefore \quad A \to \neg D \equiv \neg A \vee \neg D$

$\equiv \neg (A \wedge D)$

This is inconsistent with $A \wedge D$.

Example 1.38 : Show that the following premises are inconsistent.

If Jack misses many classes through illness, then he fails in the examination.

If Jack fails in the examination then he is uneducated.

If Jack reads a lot of books, then he is educated.

Jack misses many classes through illness and reads a lot of books. **(P.U. 2010)**

Solution : Let
- P : Jack misses many classes through illness
- Q : Jack fails in the examination
- R : Jack is uneducated
- S : Jack reads lot of books

Then symbolically given premises are $P \to Q,\ Q \to R,\ S \to \neg R, P \wedge S$.

Now $P \to Q, Q \to R \quad \therefore P \to R$ (deduction)

and $S \to \neg R \equiv R \to \neg S$ ∵ Contrapositive

Then $P \to R,\ R \to \neg S$

$\therefore \quad P \to \neg S$ ∵ Deduction

$P \to \neg S \equiv \neg P \vee \neg S$

$\equiv \neg (P \wedge S)$ De Morgan's law

$P \wedge S$ and $\neg (P \wedge S)$ have opposite truth values.

Therefore, the given premises are inconsistent.

EXERCISE (1.3)

1. Prove by using (i) direct method and (ii) indirect method that the following argument is valid :

    $P \to \neg Q, Q \vee R, P \quad \therefore R$

2. Test the validity of the following argument :

    $R \to C,\ S \to \neg W,\ R \vee S,\ W \vdash C$

3. Test the validity of the following argument by using indirect method :

    $p \vee q,\ p \to r,\ \sim r \vdash q$

4. Give indirect proof of validity of the following argument :

    $P \vee \neg Q,\ \neg Q \to R,\ P \to S, \neg R \quad \therefore S$

5. Test the validity of :

    (i) $\sim p \wedge q,\ r \to p, \sim r \to s,\ s \to t \vdash t$

    (ii) $r \to c,\ s \to \sim w,\ r \vee s,\ w \vdash c$

6. Test the validity of the following arguments :
   (i) $p \vee \sim q, r \rightarrow \sim q, q \vdash r$
   (ii) $R \rightarrow P, G \rightarrow M, P \vee M \rightarrow S, \neg S \vdash \neg (R \vee G)$
   (iii) $P \vee Q, Q \rightarrow R, P \rightarrow M, \neg M \therefore R \wedge (P \vee Q)$

7. Show that the conclusion C follows from the premises H_1 and H_2.

   $H_1 : B \wedge C, \ H_2 : (B \rightleftharpoons C) \rightarrow (H \vee G), \ C : G \vee H$

8. Use statement calculus to derive the following argument :

   $P, P \rightarrow (Q \rightarrow (R \wedge S)) \vdash (Q \rightarrow S)$

9. Test the validity of the following argument by using method of indirect proof :
   If my brother stands first in the class, then I give him T-shirt.
   Either he stood first or I was out of station.
   I did not give him T-shirt.
   Therefore conclusion is that I was out of station.

10. Test the validity of the following argument :
    (i) Team A will win the cricket match if and only if they are playing against team B.
    I team A does not win then team C will take away the trophy.
    Team C does not get the trophy.
    Hence, team A does not play against team B.
    (ii) Wages will increase only if there is inflation.
    If there is inflation, then the cost of living will increase. Wages will increase.
    Therefore, the cost of living will increase.
    (iii) Either Hari attends the lecture or he watches the movie.
    If Hari attends the lecture, then he will have a cup of coffee.
    Hari will go to hotel, if he watches the movie.
    Therefore, either Hari will have a cup of coffee or he will go to hotel.
    (iv) If I clear my backlogs then I shall be allowed to go to the next class.
    If I am not allowed to go to the next class then I will have to leave my studies.
    However, I cleared my backlogs. Hence, I won't have to leave my studies.
    (v) If I work, I cannot study.
    Either I work or I pass in C.A.
    I passed in C.A.
    Therefore, I studied.
    (vi) If Teena marries Rahul, she will be in Pune.
    If Teena marries Ganesh, she will be in Mumbai.
    If she is either in Pune or in Mumbai, she will definitely be settled in life.
    But Teena is not settled in life.
    Therefore, she did not marry Rahul or Ganesh.

(vii) The project will complete iff Prasanna does the field work fast. Either Prasanna does the field work fast or he reads a book. Prasanna does not read a book. Hence the project will be incomplete.

11. Show that the following statements are inconsistent :

If Mugdha does not take a course in Discrete Mathematics, then she will not graduate. If Mugdha does not graduate then she is not qualified for the job appointment. If Mugdha reads this book then she is qualified for the job appointment. Mugdha does not take a course in Discrete Mathematics however she reads this book.

ANSWERS (1.3)

2. Valid
3. Valid
5. (i) Valid (ii) Valid
6. (i) Invalid (ii) Valid (iii) Invalid
9. Valid
10. (i) Invalid (ii) Valid (iii) Valid (iv) Invalid (v) Invalid (vi) Valid (vii) Invalid

1.6 Predicates

Consider the open sentence '$x + 4 = 10$'. We denote it by $P(x) : x + 4 = 10$.

We cannot determine the truth value of $P(x)$ unless we assign some particular value to x.

Thus, when $x = 1$, $P(1) : 1 + 4 = 10$ has truth value F and when $x = 6$, the truth value of $P(6)$ is T.

In the above example $P(x) : x + 4 = 10$, x is called a variable and the property P : 'plus 4 equals to 10' is called predicate.

The predicate becomes a proposition after assigning some particular value to the variable, and P is a function of x.

It can be such that there are 2 or more variables appearing in the propositions.

For example, if $Q(x, y) : x + 3y = 10$ then $Q(1, 3) = 1 + 3 \times 3 = 1 + 9 = 10$.

∴ $Q(1, 3)$ has truth value T but, $Q(3, 1) = 3 + 3 \times 1 = 3 + 3 = 6 \neq 10$

∴ $Q(3, 1)$ has value F

Also if $R(x, y, z) : x^2 + y^2 = z^2$ then $R(3, 4, 5) \equiv 3^2 + 4^2 = 5^2$ i.e. $9 + 16 = 25$ i.e. $25 = 25$.

∴ $R(3, 4, 5)$ has value T but $R(1, 2, 3) : 1^2 + 2^2 = 3^2$ i.e. $1 + 4 = 9$ i.e. $5 = 9$ which is not true.

∴ $R(1, 2, 3)$ has value F.

A proposition involving n variables $x_1, x_2, \ldots, x_n$ is called 'n place' predicate.

In the above examples,

$P(x)$ is 1 place predicate, $Q(x, y)$ is 2 place predicate and $R(x, y, z)$ is 3 place predicate.

Quantifiers :

In order to determine the truth value of P(x); for a specified value of x; the variable x is allowed to assume the values from some set. This set is called the 'universe of discourse' or 'domain of discourse'.

For example, consider $P(x) : 2x < 5$ and the universe of discourse is the set
$$S = \{1, 2, 3, 4, 5\}$$
As x varies in S, we observe that
$P(1) : (2) (1) < 5$ i.e. $2 < 5$ is T
$P(2) : (2) (2) < 5$ i.e. $4 < 5$ is T
But $P(3) : (2) (3) < 5$ i.e. $6 < 5$ is F
Similarly, P(4) and P(5) have value F.

Again let $Q(x, y) : x + y$ is odd, and the universe of discourse is $S = \{1, 2, 3, 4, 5\}$.
Then x and y can assume the values from S.
We have $Q(2, 3) : 2 + 3$ is odd i.e. 5 is odd.
It is true statement.
But $Q(1, 3) : 1 + 3$ is odd i.e. 4 is odd.
It is false statement.

In the first example above, there is at least one value of x in the set S; which satisfies the required property $2x < 5$. In fact in our example, there are 2 values of x viz. 1 and 2.

In verbal language we write this situation as below.

'There exists at least one $x \in S$ such that $2x < 5$ holds'.

We write this symbolically as below.

We use the symbol $\exists$ for 'there exists'.

Then symbolically above statement can be written as '$\exists x\ P(x)$'.

This symbol $\exists$ is called 'existential quantifier'.

Illustration : Suppose the universe of discourse is the set $S = \{1, 2, 3\}$ and for $x \in S$; $P(x) : 2x + 1$ is a perfect square.

Then $P(1) : (2) (1) + 1 = 3$ is a perfect square which is not true.

∴ P(1) is false.

In the same manner P(2) and P(3) are false statements.

In this example there is no $x \in S$ for which the property P(x) holds. Therefore the quantification $\exists x\ P(x)$ has the truth value F.

Now with the same universal set $S = \{1, 2, 3\}$
Let $Q(x) : 2x + 3$ is a perfect square.
Then Q(1) is false since $(2) (1) + 3 = 2 + 3 = 5$ which is not a perfect square.
Also Q(2) is false since $(2) (2) + 3 = 4 + 3 = 7$ which is not a perfect square.
However, when x = 3, we have $Q(3) : (2) (3) + 3 = 6 + 3 = 9$; which is a perfect square.
Therefore Q(3) is true.

Thus, there exists at least one x in the universe of discourse S such that Q(x) holds.

∴ The quantification $\exists x\, Q(x)$ has truth value T.

Note : From the algebra of propositions, we know that if $p_1, p_2, \ldots, p_n$ are n statements, then their disjunction $p_1 \vee p_2 \vee \ldots \vee p_n$ has true value T iff at least one p_i has truth value T.

It then immediately follows that,

If the universe of discourse is the finite set $S = \{x_1, x_2, \ldots, x_n\}$, then the existential quantification $\exists x\, P(x)$ has truth value T iff at least one of $P(x_1), P(x_2), \ldots, P(x_n)$ has truth value T.

Next we introduce another quantifier called universal quantifier. We consider the following example from our everyday life.

Suppose the universe of discourse is the set S of 2 staired houses; in a certain area of the city. Now for $x \in S$ [i.e. x is a 2-staired house].

Let P(x) : x has electric bulb operated by two switches.

We know that in a 2 staired house always there is a bulb in the staircase which is operated by two switches, one switch located at the ground floor and the other switch located at the first floor.

In this case, we see that the property holds for all members of the set S.

Symbolically, we write this as $\forall x\, P(x)$ [or $(x)\, P(x)$] and read as 'for every x, P(x)'.

The symbol $\forall$ is called universal quantifier.

Illustration : Suppose the universe of discourse is the set $S = \{1, 2, 3\}$.

Let $P(x) : x^3 < 30$ and $Q(x) : x^3 < 25$.

Firstly, consider the truth value of P(x).

For x = 1, P(1) : $1^3 < 30$ i.e. 1 < 30. It is true.

For x = 2, P(2) : $2^3 < 30$ i.e. 8 < 30, it is true.

Finally for x = 3, P(3) : $3^3 < 30$ i.e. 27 < 30, it is true.

Thus, P(x) is true for all $x \in S$.

Symbolically, we have $\forall x\, P(x)$ has the truth value T.

Now, consider the truth value of Q(x).

For x = 1, Q(1) : $1^3 < 25$ i.e. 1 < 25; it is true.

For x = 2, Q(2) : $2^3 < 25$ i.e. 8 < 25; it is true.

For x = 3, Q(3) : $3^3 < 25$ i.e. 27 < 25; it is false.

We see that the property Q(x) does not hold for all $x \in S$.

For some values of $x \in S$; Q(x) is true but not for all values of $x \in S$.

Symbolically, we write $\forall(x)\, Q(x)$ has truth value F.

Example 1.39 : What is the truth value of $\exists x\ (x^2 \leq x)$ if the domain consists of all real numbers ? What is the truth value of this statement if the domain consists of all integers ? Justify.

Solution : Consider $\exists x\ (x^2 \leq x)$ and x is a real number. We note that for any real number from 0 to 1, $x^2 \leq x$.

For example, $\quad x = 0,\ x^2 = 0 \qquad \therefore x^2 = x$

$$x = \frac{1}{2},\ x^2 = \frac{1}{4} \qquad \therefore x^2 < x$$

$$x = 1,\ x^2 = 1 \qquad \therefore x^2 = x$$

Given statement is true. Again $\exists x\ (x^2 \leq x)$ and x is integer

$$x = 0,\ x^2 = 0 \qquad \therefore x^2 = x$$

$$x = 1,\ x^2 = 1 \qquad \therefore x^2 = x$$

Given statement is true.

Note : From the algebra of propositions, we note that if $p_1, p_2, ..., p_n$ are n statements, then their conjunction $p_1 \wedge p_2 \wedge ... \wedge p_n$ has truth value T iff each p_i has truth value T.

It then follows that if the universe of discourse is the set $S = \{x_1, x_2, ..., x_n\}$ then the universal quantification $\forall x\ P(x)$ has truth value T iff each of $P(x_1), P(x_2), ..., P(x_n)$ has truth value T.

Example 1.40 : Suppose that the universe of discourse of the propositional function P(x) is the set $S = \{-2, -1, 0, 1, 2\}$ write each of the following propositions using disjunction, conjunction and negation.

(a) $\exists x\ P(x)$ (b) $\forall x\ P(x)$ (c) $\exists x\ \neg P(x)$ (d) $\forall x\ \neg P(x)$

Solution : We know that if the universe of discourse is the set $S = \{x_1, x_2, ..., x_n\}$ then

$$\exists x\ P(x) \equiv P(x_1) \vee P(x_2) \vee ... \vee P(x_n)$$

and $\qquad \forall x\ P(x) \equiv P(x_1) \wedge P(x_2) \wedge ... \wedge P(x_n)$

(a) $\quad \exists x\ P(x) \equiv P(-2) \vee P(-1) \vee P(0) \vee P(1) \vee P(2)$

(b) $\quad \forall x\ P(x) \equiv P(-2) \wedge P(-1) \wedge P(0) \wedge P(1) \wedge P(2)$

(c) $\quad \exists x\ \neg P(x) \equiv \neg P(-2) \vee \neg P(-1) \vee \neg P(0) \vee \neg P(1) \vee \neg P(2)$

(d) $\quad \forall x\ \neg P(x) \equiv \neg P(-2) \wedge \neg P(-1) \wedge \neg P(0) \wedge \neg P(1) \wedge \neg P(2)$

Restricted Domain :

In some instances, we need to restrict the domain to some elements in it, by avoiding the remaining ones.

Consider the following situation. The universe of discourse is the set of all those students who have passed XII science examination. Some of these students may not have offered Mathematics as one of their subjects. Such students are not eligible to apply for engineering degree course admission. So we restrict our domain to those students who have offered Mathematics as one of their subjects at the XII science examination.

Let now P(x) : x applied for admission for engineering degree course.

We write this situation symbolically as below.

$\forall x$, (x offered Mathematics) P(x).

Here the condition 'x offered Mathematics' appears immediately to the right of quantifier.

The meaning of this symbolic statement is that all those students who have offered Mathematics can apply for admission to engineering degree course.

Equivalently 'if x has offered Mathematics then he can apply for admission'.

Thus, the restriction of a universal quantification is universal quantification of a conditional statement.

$$\boxed{\forall x \text{ (condition) } (P(x)) \equiv \forall x \text{ (condition} \to P(x))}$$

In the above problem, we note that there is at least one student who has offered Mathematics and applied for the admission. Symbolically this is written as :

$\exists x$, (x offered Mathematics) (x applied for admission)

Thus, the restriction of existential quantification is equivalent to existential quantification of the conjunction of the condition and P(x).

$$\boxed{\exists x \text{ (condition) } (P(x)) \equiv \exists x \text{ (condition} \land P(x))}$$

Example 1.41 : Explain the meaning of the following; assuming that the universe of discourse is the set of real numbers.

(a) $\forall x < 0 \ (x^2 > 0)$

(b) $\forall x \neq 0 \ (x^3 \neq 0)$

(c) $\exists x > 0 \ (x^2 = 3)$

Solution : We know that,

$$\forall x \text{ (condition) } P(x) \equiv \forall x \text{ (condition} \to P(x))$$

and $\quad \exists x \text{ (condition) } P(x) \equiv \exists x \text{ (condition} \land P(x))$

(a) $\quad \forall x < 0 \ (x^2 > 0) \equiv \forall x \ (x < 0) \ (x^2 > 0)$

$\quad\quad\quad\quad\quad\quad\quad \equiv \forall x \ [(x < 0) \to x^2 > 0]$

In words 'the square of any negative number is positive'.

(b) $\quad \forall x \neq 0 \ (x^3 \neq 0) \equiv \forall x \ (x \neq 0) \ (x^3 \neq 0)$

$\quad\quad\quad\quad\quad\quad\quad \equiv \forall x \ [(x \neq 0) \to (x^3 \neq 0)]$

In words 'the cube of non-zero real number is non-zero'.

(c) $\quad \exists x > 0 \ (x^2 = 3) \equiv \exists x \ (x > 0) \ (x^2 = 3)$

$\quad\quad\quad\quad\quad\quad\quad \equiv \exists x \ [(x > 0) \land (x^2 = 3)]$

In words 'there is a positive real number whose square is 3'.

Note : We know that in the algebra of real numbers while evaluating the given arithmetic expression, we perform the arithmetic operations in a particular order 'BEDMAS'. It is called hierarchy of operations.

B : bracket evaluation, E : exponentiation, D : division, M : multiplication,

A : addition, S : subtraction.

For example, $(2 + 3 \times 4) - 4^3 + 12 \div 4 = (2 + 12) - 64 + 3 = 14 - 64 + 3 = 17 - 64 = -47$

In the algebra of propositions while evaluating logical expression the top priority goes to quantifiers $\forall$ and $\exists$.

Thus, $\forall x\ P(x) \land Q(x)$ means $(\forall x\ P(x)) \land Q(x)$.

It is different from $\forall x\ (P(x) \land Q(x))$.

Similarly, $\exists x\ P(x) \lor Q(x)$ means $(\exists x\ P(x)) \lor Q(x)$; and it is different from $\exists x\ (P(x) \lor Q(x))$.

Binding Variables :

In the logical expression, when a quantifier is used on the variable x, we say that this occurrence of the variable is bound. On the other hand the occurrence of a variable which is not bound by a quantifier nor it is assigned some particular value is described by saying that the variable is free.

In order to be able for us to determine the truth value of a propositional function it is quite necessary that all the variables appearing in it must be bound or they are assigned some particular value. This is achieved with the help of universal quantifiers, existential quantifiers and the value assignments.

In the logical expression that part to which a quantifier is applied is called 'scope' of that quantifier.

In the statement $\exists x\ (x + y = 5)$ the variable x is bound by the existential quantifier $\exists x$. The variable y is not bound by any quantifier nor that y is assigned any particular value. So y is free variable.

Also in $\forall x\ (P(x) \lor Q(x)) \land \exists x\ R(x)$ the scope of $\forall x$ is $P(x) \lor Q(x)$ and the scope of $\exists x$ is $R(x)$.

Let now P and Q be two statements involving quantifiers and predicates. We say that P is logically equivalent to Q and write $P \equiv Q$ if and only if they have the same truth value irrespective of the predicates substituted in them and irrespective of the universe of discourse.

We show that $\forall x\ (P(x) \land Q(x)) \equiv \forall x\ P(x) \land \forall x\ Q(x)$.

In words 'the universal quantifier distributes over the conjunction. **(P.U. 2010)**

Let $P(x)$ and $Q(x)$ be two given statements. Without any loss, we can assume that the universe of discourse is the same for both $P(x)$ and $Q(x)$.

We establish the equivalence by considering two parts.

In the first part, we assume that $\forall x\ (P(x) \land Q(x))$ has truth value T and show that

$\forall x\ P(x) \land \forall x\ Q(x)$ has truth value T.

In the second part, we assume that $\forall x\ P(x) \land \forall x\ Q(x)$ has truth value T and prove that $\forall x\ (P(x) \land Q(x))$ has truth value T.

First Part : $\forall x\ (P(x) \land Q(x))$ has truth value T (assumption).

Then if a is any element in the universe of discourse, we have $P(a) \land Q(a)$ is true.

$\therefore$ $P(a)$ is true and $Q(a)$ is true.

Now P(a) is true and Q(a) is true, this holds for every a in the universe of discourse.

∴ $\forall x\ P(x)$ is true and

$\forall(x)\ Q(x)$ is true.

∴ $\forall x\ P(x) \wedge \forall x\ Q(x)$ is true.

Second Part : Assume that $\forall x\ P(x) \wedge \forall x\ Q(x)$ is true.

Then, $\forall x\ P(x)$ is true and

$\forall x\ Q(x)$ is true.

∴ If a is any element in the universe of discourse, then P(a) is true and Q(a) is true.

∴ for all a, $P(a) \wedge Q(a)$ is true.

∴ $\forall x\ (P(x) \wedge Q(x))$ is true.

This completes the proof and we have $\forall x(P(x) \wedge Q(x)) \equiv (\forall x\ P(x)) \wedge (\forall x\ Q(x))$

Note : The generalization to more than two propositions is possible i.e.

$\forall x\ (P_1(x) \wedge P_2(x) \wedge \ldots \wedge P_n(x)) \equiv (\forall x\ P_1(x)) \wedge \ldots \wedge (\forall x\ P_n(x))$

Note : The universal quantifier does not distribute over disjunction. For this, suppose the universe of discourse is the set S = {3, 5, 16, 19, 25}.

Let   P(x) : x is odd

and   Q(x) : x is a perfect square

Then $P(x) \vee Q(x)$ is the statement 'x is odd or perfect square'.

We have $\forall x\ (P(x) \vee Q(x))$ is true since each member of S is odd or a perfect square.

But $\forall x\ P(x)$ is false because $16 \in S$ is not odd.

Also $\forall x\ Q(x)$ is false because $5 \in S$ and 5 is not a perfect square.

∴ $(\forall x\ P(x)) \vee (\forall x\ Q(x))$ has truth value $F \vee F \equiv F$.

Therefore $\forall x\ (P(x) \vee Q(x))$ and $\forall x\ P(x) \vee \forall x\ Q(x)$ are not logically equivalent.

Negation of Quantified Expression :

Consider the statement :

'All students in the class passed in the Discrete Mathematics course'.

Symbolically it is $\forall x\ P(x)$.

Clearly we cannot say that the negation of the above statement is 'all students in the class failed in Discrete Mathematics course'.

We note that if at least one student in the class failed in Discrete Mathematics course then we cannot say all students in the class passed.

Thus 'all students passed' and 'at least one student failed' have opposite truth values.

Now 'at least one student failed' is symbolically $\exists x\ \neg P(x)$.

∴ $\neg \forall x\ P(x) \equiv \exists x\ \neg P(x)$.

Consider now the universe of discourse S = {1, 2, 3, 4, 5}.

Let P(x) : x is a perfect square.

The statement $\exists x\ P(x)$ has truth value T since at least one member i.e. $4 \in S$ is a perfect square.

The corresponding statement whose truth value is F will be as below.

No element of S is a perfect square i.e. every element in S is a non-square quantity. Symbolically it is $\forall x \, \neg P(x)$.

Thus, $\neg \exists x \, P(x) \equiv \forall x \, \neg P(x)$

Illustration :

(a) Let $P(x)$ be the statement.

$P(x)$: For every positive integer x, $x^2 + 41x + 41$ is a prime number.

Symbolically it can be written as $\forall x \, P(x)$.

Now, negation of the above statement is

$\neg \forall x \, P(x) \equiv \exists x \, \neg P(x)$

In words 'there is at least one positive integer x for which $x^2 + 41x + 41$ is not a prime number.

(b) Let $Q(x)$ be the statement.

$Q(x)$: There is some integer x for which $4x = 20$.

Symbolically it can be written as $\exists x \, Q(x)$.

Now negation of the above statement is

$\neg \exists x \, Q(x) \equiv \forall x \, \neg Q(x)$

For every integer x, $4x \neq 20$.

SOLVED EXAMPLES

Example 1.42 : Let $P(x)$, $Q(x)$, $R(x)$ be the statements 'x is a clear explanation', 'x is satisfactory' and 'x is an acuse'.

Suppose that the universe of discourse for x is the set of all English texts. Express each of the following statements using quantifiers :

(a) All clear explanations are satisfactory.

(b) Some excuses are not clear explanations.   **(P.U. 2010)**

Solution : (a) $\forall x \, (P(x) \rightarrow Q(x))$

(b) $\exists x \, (R(x) \rightarrow \neg Q(x))$

Example 1.43 : If the universe of discourse is the set {a, b, c}, eliminate the quantifiers in the following formulae :

(a) $(x) (P(x) \rightarrow Q(x))$

(b) $(x) R(x) \vee (\exists x) S(x)$

Solution : (a) Given statement $(x) (P(x) \rightarrow Q(x))$ is $\forall x \, (P(x) \rightarrow Q(x))$

$\equiv (P(a) \rightarrow Q(a)) \wedge (P(b) \rightarrow Q(b)) \wedge (P(c) \rightarrow Q(c))$

(b) Given statement $(x) R(x) \vee (\exists x) S(x)$ is $\forall x \, R(x) \vee (\exists x) S(x)$

$\equiv [R(a) \wedge R(b) \wedge R(c)] \vee [S(a) \vee S(b) \vee S(c)]$

Example 1.44 : Indicate the variables that are free and bound and scope of the quantifiers.

(a) $(P(x) \wedge (\exists x) Q(x)) \vee ((\forall x) P(x) \rightarrow Q(x))$

(b) $(\forall x) R(x) \wedge (\forall x) S(x)$

Solution : (a) The variable x is bound by the quantifiers $\exists x$ and $\forall x$.

Scope of $\exists x$ is $Q(x)$.

Scope of $\forall x$ is $P(x)$.

(b) Given statement is $\forall x\ R(x) \wedge (\forall x) S(x)$ which is equivalent to $\forall x\ (R(x) \wedge S(x))$.

The variable x is bound by the quantifier $\forall x$.

The scope of $\forall x$ is $R(x) \wedge S(x)$.

Example 1.45 : Let $P(x, y)$ denote '$x + y = 0$'.

Find the truth values of quantifications $\exists y\ \forall x\ P(x, y)$ and $\forall x\ \exists y\ P(x, y)$; the universe of discourse being the set of all real numbers.

Solution : The quantification $\exists y\ \forall x\ P(x, y)$ says that there exists a value of y such that for any real value of x, $x + y = 0$ holds.

For a given value of y there is only one value of x viz. $x = -y$ satisfying $x + y = 0$.

Therefore, the value of the quantification $\exists y\ \forall x\ P(x, y)$ is F.

Next, consider $\forall x\ \exists y\ P(x, y)$. This quantification says that for every real value of x, we can find y such that $x + y = 0$.

We note that if x is any real number then $y = -x$ satisfies $x + y = 0$.

Therefore the value of the quantification $\forall x\ \exists y\ P(x, y)$ is T.

Example 1.46 : Write each of the following propositions using quantifiers and predicates.

(a) A man qualifies for the marathon if his best previous time is less than 3 hours and a woman qualifies for the marathon if her best previous time is less than 3.5 hours.

(b) x is father of mother of y.

Solution : (a) We write $M(x)$: x is a male person. Then $\neg M(x)$: x is a female person.

Let $T(x, y)$: A person x has best previous time less than y hours.

Let $Q(x)$: Person x is qualified for the marathon.

Then symbolic form of the given proposition is

$\forall x\ (((M(x) \wedge T(x, 3)) \vee (\neg M(x) \wedge T(x, 3.5))) \rightarrow Q(x))$

(b) Consider $P(x)$: x is person

$F(x, y)$: x is father of y.

$M(x, y)$: x is mother of y.

Then the given proposition 'x is father of mother of y' is in symbolic form

$\exists x\ \exists y\ \exists z\ F(x, z) \wedge M(z, y)$

Example 1.47 : Write the negation of the following statements :

(a) All roses in the garden are either pink or white.

(b) For some real numbers x and y, $x^2 - y^4$ is negative.

Solution : (a) Let $\quad$ P(x) : Rose is pink

$\qquad\qquad\qquad$ Q(x) : Rose is white

Then given statement in symbolic form is $\forall x\,(P(x) \vee Q(x))$.

Its negation is $\quad \neg \forall x\,(P(x) \vee Q(x)) \equiv \exists x\,\neg(P(x) \vee Q(x))$

$\qquad\qquad\qquad\qquad\qquad\qquad \equiv \exists x\,((\neg P(x)) \wedge \neg Q(x))$

i.e. there is at least one rose in the garden, which is neither pink nor white.

(b) In symbolic form the given statement is $\exists x\,\exists y\,(x^2 - y^4 < 0)$.

Its negation is $\quad \neg \exists x\,\exists y\,(x^2 - y^4 < 0) \equiv \forall x\,\neg \exists y\,(x^2 - y^4 < 0)$

$\qquad\qquad\qquad\qquad\qquad\qquad \equiv \forall x\,\forall y\,\neg(x^2 - y^4 < 0)$

$\qquad\qquad\qquad\qquad\qquad\qquad \equiv \forall x\,\forall y\,(x^2 - y^4 \geq 0)$

In words, for any two real numbers x and y, $x^2 - y^4 \geq 0$.

Example 1.48 : Write the negation of :

(a) $\exists x\,(P(x) \wedge \neg Q(x))$

(b) $\exists x\,P(x) \wedge \neg Q(x)$

(c) $\forall x\,(P(x) \wedge Q(x))$

(d) $\forall x\,(P(x) \to Q(x))$

Solution : (a) Given statement is $\exists x\,(P(x) \wedge \neg Q(x))$

$\qquad \neg \exists x\,(P(x) \wedge \neg Q(x)) \equiv \forall x\,\neg(P(x) \wedge \neg Q(x))$

$\qquad\qquad\qquad\qquad\qquad\quad \equiv \forall x\,(\neg P(x) \vee \neg\neg Q(x)) \qquad \because$ De Morgan's law

$\qquad\qquad\qquad\qquad\qquad\quad \equiv \forall x\,(\neg P(x) \vee Q(x)) \qquad\quad \because$ Double negation

(b) Given statement is $\exists x\,P(x) \wedge \neg Q(x)$

$\qquad \neg[\exists x\,P(x) \wedge \neg Q(x)] \equiv \neg \exists x\,P(x) \vee \neg\neg Q(x) \qquad \because$ De Morgan's law

$\qquad\qquad\qquad\qquad\qquad\quad \equiv \forall x\,(\neg P(x)) \vee Q(x)$

(c) Given statement is $\forall x\,(P(x) \wedge Q(x))$

$\qquad \neg \forall x\,(P(x) \wedge Q(x)) \equiv \exists x\,\neg(P(x) \wedge Q(x))$

$\qquad\qquad\qquad\qquad\qquad\quad \equiv \exists x\,(\neg P(x) \vee \neg Q(x))$

(d) Given statement is $\forall x\,(P(x) \to Q(x))$

$\qquad \neg \forall x\,(P(x) \to Q(x)) \equiv \neg \forall x\,(\neg P(x) \vee Q(x)) \qquad \because p \to q \equiv \sim p \vee q$

$\qquad\qquad\qquad\qquad\qquad\quad \equiv \exists x\,\neg(\neg P(x) \vee Q(x))$

$\qquad\qquad\qquad\qquad\qquad\quad \equiv \exists x\,(\neg\neg P(x) \wedge \neg Q(x))$

$\qquad\qquad\qquad\qquad\qquad\quad \equiv \exists x\,(P(x) \wedge \neg Q(x)) \qquad\qquad \because$ Double negation

Example 1.49 : Express the negation of the following propositions using quantifiers. Then write the negation in verbal language :

(a) There is some one in this class who does not have a good attitude.

(b) No one can keep a secret.

Solution : (a) Let the universe of discourse be the set of all students in a class and $P(x)$: x has a good attitude.

Then symbolically given statement is $\exists x\,(\neg P(x))$.

Its negation is
$$\neg \exists x\,(\neg P(x)) \equiv \forall x\,\neg(\neg P(x))$$
$$\equiv \forall x\, P(x) \qquad \because \text{By double negation}$$

In words 'All students in the class have a good attitude'.

(b) Let the universe of discourse be the set of all people and $P(x)$: x keeps a secret.

Then the given proposition in symbolic form is $\forall x\,(\neg P(x))$.

Its negation is
$$\neg \forall x\,(\neg P(x)) \equiv \exists x\,\neg(\neg P(x))$$
$$\equiv \exists x\, P(x) \qquad \because \text{By double negation}$$

In words 'there is at least one person who keeps the secret'.

This can also be described by saying that 'some persons keep secret'.

Example 1.50 : Prove that, $\exists x\,(P(x) \vee Q(x)) \equiv (\exists x\, P(x)) \vee (\exists x\, Q(x))$ i.e. the existential quantifier distributes over disjunction.

Give example to show that $\exists x\,(P(x) \wedge Q(x))$ and $\exists x\, P(x) \wedge \exists x\, Q(x)$ are not logically equivalent.

Solution : Let $P(x)$ and $Q(x)$ have the same universe of discourse. We establish the equivalence

$$\exists x\,(P(x) \vee Q(x)) \equiv (\exists x\, P(x)) \vee (\exists x\, Q(x))$$

By proving that whenever left side expression has value F, right side expression has value F. Further whenever right side expression has value F, then left side expression has value F.

First Part : Suppose $\exists x\,(P(x) \vee Q(x))$ has value F. Then for some a in the universe of discourse, we have $P(a) \vee Q(a)$ has value F.

∴ $P(a)$ has value F and $Q(a)$ has value F.

∴ $\exists x\, P(x)$ has value F and $\exists x\, Q(x)$ has value F.

∴ $\exists x\, P(x) \vee \exists x\, Q(x)$ has value F.

Second Part : Assume that $\exists x\, P(x) \vee \exists x\, Q(x)$ has value F.

Then $\exists x\, P(x)$ has value F and $\exists x\, Q(x)$ has value F.

∴ $P(a)$ is F and $Q(a)$ is F for some a in the universe of discourse.

∴ $P(a) \vee Q(a)$ is F.

∴ $P(x) \vee Q(x)$ is F for some x.

∴ $\exists x\,(P(x) \vee Q(x))$ is F.

The proof is complete and we have

$$\exists x\,(P(x) \vee Q(x)) \equiv \exists x\, P(x) \vee \exists x\, Q(x)$$

Now consider the following example $S = \{1, 2, 3, \ldots, 10\}$ is the universe of discourse.

Let $P(x)$: x is divisible by 3

and $Q(x)$: x is divisible by 4.

The elements 3, 6, 9 ∈ S are divisible by 3.

∴   ∃P(x) is true.

Also 4, 8 ∈ S are divisible by 4.

∴   ∃x Q(x) is true.

Hence (∃x P(x)) ∧ (∃x Q(x)) is T ∧ T ≡ T.

Next we note that there is no element x ∈ S which is divisible by 3 and 4 both.

∴   ∃x (P(x) ∧ Q(x)) has value F.

Thus, ∃x (P(x) ∧ Q(x)) and ∃x P(x) ∧ ∃x Q(x) do not possess identical truth values.

∴   These two propositions are not logically equivalent.

Example 1.51 : Let P(x), Q(x), R(x) be the statements 'x is a professor', x is ignorant' and 'x is vain' respectively. Express the following statements using quantifiers :

(a) No professors are ignorant.

(b) All ignorant people are vain. **(P.U. 2010)**

Solution : The universe of discourse is S = {all people}. The given problem is that of restricted domain.

(a) Given statement is 'No professors are ignorant'. This means if a person x is a professor then he/she is not ignorant.

Here 'x is a professor' is a condition and this condition implies 'x is not ignorant', we know that

$$\forall x \text{ (condition)} \wedge (x) \equiv \forall x \text{ (condition} \rightarrow A(x))$$

∴   ∀x (x is a professor → x is not ignorant)

$$\equiv \forall x \text{ (x is a professor) (x is not ignorant)}$$

$$\equiv \forall x (P(x)) (\neg Q(x))$$

(b) Given statement is 'all ignorant people are vain'.

This means 'if a person is ignorant then he/she is vain'.

Here 'a person is ignorant' is the condition and this condition implies 'a person is vain'.

We know that   ∀x (condition) (A(x)) ≡ ∀x (condition → A(x))

∴   ∀x (x is ignorant → x is vain) ≡ ∀x (x is ignorant) (x is vain)

$$\equiv \forall x (Q(x)) (R(x))$$

EXERCISE (1.4)

1. In the universe of discourse **Z** of all integers, let P(x) : x is even, Q(x) : x is a prime number and R(x, y) : x + y is even.

    (a) Write the following as a sentence in English.

    (i)   ∃x ¬ Q(x)

    (ii) ∀x P(x)

    (iii) ∀x ∃y R(x, y)

    (iv) ∃x ∀y R(x, y)

(b) Write each of the following by using quantifiers :
   (i) Every integer is an odd integer.
   (ii) The sum of any two integers is an even number.
   (iii) There are no even primes.
   (iv) Every integer is even or prime.
(c) Find the values of P(2), P(3), Q(2), Q(6) and R(3, 4).

2. In the set of all integers, determine the truth value of
   (a) $\exists x\, (x^3 < 4)$
   (b) $\forall x\, (x^2 > 0)$
   (c) $\forall x\, (x > 4x)$
   (d) $\forall x\, (x^2 \geq x)$
   (e) $\exists x\, (x < -x)$

3. Let P(x) : x is a baby
   Q(x) : x is logical
   R(x) : x is able to manage crocodile
   S(x) : x is dispised.
   The universe of discourse consists of all people. Express the following using quantifiers.
   (a) Babies are illogical.
   (b) Nobody is dispised who can manage crocodile.
   (c) Illogical persons are dispised.
   (d) Babies cannot manage crocodile.

4. The universe of discourse is the set U = {1, 2, 3, 4, 5}
   Write truth set of the following predicates :
   (a) $\exists x\, ((x^2 - 3x + 2) = 0)$
   (b) $\forall x\, x^2 \geq 9$
   (c) $\forall x\, ((x^2 - 6x + 8 = 0) \wedge (x^2 - 5x + 4 = 0))$

5. Write the truth value of :
   (a) $\forall x\, P(x)$ and (b) $\exists x\, \neg P(x)$
   where P(x) : $x^2 < 25$ and the universe of discourse is the set of non-negative integers not greater than 5.

6. Let D = {1, 2, 3, 4} be the domain of discourse. Eliminate the quantifier from each of the following :
   (a) $\forall x\, P(x)$
   (b) $\exists x\, P(x)$
   (c) $\neg \exists x\, P(x)$
   (d) $\exists x\, \neg P(x)$

7. If the universe of discourse is {a, b, c}, eliminate the quantifiers in the following :
   (a) $\forall x\, (P(x) \rightarrow Q(x))$
   (b) $\exists x\, R(x) \wedge (x)\, S(x)$

8. Over the set of integers, let

$A(x, y)$: $x + y$ is even

$B(x)$: x is a prime number

$C(x, y)$: $x + y$ is odd.

Write the following into simple English sentences :

(a) $\forall x \exists y\ A(x, y)$ (b) $\forall x \exists y\ C(x, y)$

(c) $\forall x (\forall y\ C(x, y))$ **(P.U. 2011)**

9. Rewrite the following propositions using the symbols $\exists$ and $\forall$.

  (a) All elephants have trunks.

  (b) Every clever student is successful.

  (c) Some people know all the answers.

  (d) Only judges admire judges.

  (e) All good students study hard.

  (f) There is a triangle whose sum of angles is not equal to 180°.

10. Prove that $\neg \forall x\ (P(x) \rightarrow Q(x))$ is logically equivalent to $\exists x\ (P(x) \land \neg Q(x))$.

11. Prove that the following are tautologies :

  (a) $\exists x\ (P(x) \land Q(x)) \Rightarrow \exists x\ P(x) \land \exists x\ Q(x)$

  (b) $\forall x\ (P(x) \lor Q(x)) \Rightarrow [\forall x\ P(x)] \lor [\forall x\ Q(x)]$

12. Let $Q(x, y, z) : x + y = z$. What are the truth values of :

  (a) $\forall x\ \forall y\ \exists z\ Q(x, y, z)$?   (b) $\exists z\ \forall x\ \forall y\ Q(x, y, z)$?

  Assume that $x = 1$, $y = 2$, $z = 3$.

13. Let $Q(x, y)$: x has sent e-mail message to y; and the domain D = all students in the class. Express the following in words :

  (a) $\exists x\ \exists y\ Q(x, y)$ (b) $\exists x\ \forall y\ Q(x, y)$

  (c) $\forall x\ \exists y\ Q(x, y)$ (d) $\exists y\ \forall x\ Q(x, y)$

  (e) $\forall y\ \exists x\ Q(x, y)$ (f) $\forall x\ \forall y\ Q(x, y)$

14. Write the following sentences in predicate formula :

  (i) All that glitters is not gold.

  (ii) Some birds cannot fly.

15. Translate the following sentence in symbolic form. "Some lawyers who are politicians are not congressmen".

16. Using quantifiers symbolize the following; if the universe of discourse is the set of real numbers.

  (i) For any real value of x, x^2 is atmost equal to 10.

  (ii) There is some x such that $x^2 + 3x - 2 = 0$

  (iii) For any value of x, there is some value of y such that $x \cdot y = 1$.

  (iv) There is a value of x and y such that $x^2 + y^2$ is negative.

17. Let $Q(x, y)$ be the statement "$x^2 = y - 3$". What are the truth values of the propositions $Q(1, 2)$, $Q(3, 0)$ and $Q(2, 7)$.

ANSWERS (1.4)

1. (a) (i) There is some integer x, which is not prime.
   (ii) Every integer is even integer.
   (iii) For any value of x, we can find a value of y such that x + y is even.
   (iv) There is some integer x such that for every integer y, x + y is even integer.

   (b) (i) $\forall x \neg P(x)$
   (ii) $\forall x \forall y\, R(x, y)$
   (iii) $\neg(P(x) \wedge Q(x))$ or $\neg P(x) \vee \neg Q(x)$
   (iv) $\forall x (P(x) \vee Q(x))$

   (c) P(2) : 2 is even; T
   P(3) is F, Q(2) is T, Q(6) is F, R(3, 4) is F.

2. (a) T   (b) F   (c) F   (d) T   (e) T

3. (a) $\forall x (P(x) \rightarrow \neg Q(x))$
   (b) $\forall x \neg(R(x) \wedge S(x))$
   (c) $\forall x ((\neg Q(x)) \rightarrow S(x))$ or $\forall x (Q(x) \vee S(x))$
   (d) $\forall x (P(x) \rightarrow \neg R(x))$

4. (a) {1, 2}   (b) {3, 4, 5}   (c) {4}

5. (a) T   (b) F

6. (a) $P(1) \wedge P(2) \wedge P(3) \wedge P(4)$
   (b) $P(1) \vee P(2) \vee P(3) \vee P(4)$
   (c) $(\neg P(1)) \wedge (\neg P(2)) \wedge (\neg P(3)) \wedge (\neg P(4))$
   (d) $(\neg P(1)) \vee (\neg P(2)) \vee (\neg P(3)) \vee (\neg P(4))$

7. (a) $[P(a) \rightarrow Q(a)] \wedge [P(b) \rightarrow Q(b)] \wedge [P(c) - Q(c)] [P(c) \rightarrow Q(c)]$
   i.e. $[\neg P(a) \vee Q(a)] \wedge [\neg P(b) \vee Q(b)] \wedge [\neg P(c) \vee Q(c)]$
   (b) $[R(a) \vee R(b) \vee R(c)] \wedge [S(a) \wedge S(b) \wedge S(c)]$

8. (a) If x is any given integer, we can find integer y such that the sum of x and y is even integer.
   (b) If x is any given integer, we can find integer y such that they add upto odd integer.
   (c) For all integers x and y their sum is odd integer.

9. (a) U = Set of all animals.
   P(x) : animal x is elephant
   Q(x) : animal x has trunk
   ∴ $\forall x (P(x) \rightarrow Q(x))$

   (b) U = Set of all students
   P(x) : student x is clever
   Q(x) : student x is successful
   ∴ $\forall x (P(x) \rightarrow Q(x))$

(c) U = Set of all people
   P(x) : person x knows all answers
   ∴ ∃x P(x)
(d) U = Set of all people
   P(x) : person x is a judge
   A(x, y) : x admires y.
   ∴ ∀x ∀y [P(x) ∧ P(y)) → A(x, y)] ∧ [(¬ P(x) ∧ P(y)) → ¬ A(x, y)]
(e) U = Set of all students
   P(x) : x is a good student
   Q(x) : x studies hard
   ∴ ∀x (P(x) → Q(x))
(f) U = Set of all triangles
   P(x) : In a triangle x the sum of angles is 180°
   ∴ ∃x (¬ P(x))

12. (a) T (b) F
13. (a) There are two students x and y in a class such that x has sent e-mail message to y.
    (b) There is a student x in the class, who has sent e-mail message to every student of the class.
    (c) Every student in the class has sent e-mail message to at least one student in the class.
    (d) There is some student in the class who received e-mail message from every student of the class.
    (e) Every student in the class received e-mail message from at least one student of the class.
    (f) All students in the class sent e-mail message to each other.
14. (i) P(x) : x glitters
       Q(x) : x is gold
       ∃x (P(x) ∧ ¬Q (x))
    (ii) S = {all birds}
       P(x) : x files
       ∃x (¬P(x))
15. Domain S = {all people}
    P(x) : x is a lawyer
    Q(x) : x is a politician
    R(x) : x is a congressman
    ∃x (P(x) ∧ Q(x) ∧ ¬R(x))
16. (i) ∀x ($x^2 \leq 10$), (ii) ∃x ($x^2 + 3x - 2 = 0$), (iii) ∀x ∃y (xy = 1),
    (iv) ∃x ∃y ($x^2 + y^2 < 0$)
17. F, F, T

Chapter 2...

RELATIONS AND FUNCTIONS

2.1 Cartesian Product

Consider two sets $A = \{a_1, a_2, ..., a_m\}$ and $B = \{b_1, b_2, ..., b_n\}$ containing m and n elements respectively. Then the Cartesian product of A and B denoted by $A \times B$ consists of all ordered pairs (a_i, b_j); $1 \leq i \leq m$, $1 \leq j \leq n$.

For example, if $A = \{1, 2, 3\}$ and $B = \{a, b, c, d\}$, then

$$A \times B = \{(1, a), (1, b), (1, c), (1, d), (2, a), (2, b), (2, c), (2, d),$$
$$(3, a), (3, b), (3, c), (3, d)\}$$

Also, $B \times A = \{(a, 1), (a, 2), (a, 3), (b, 1), (b, 2), (b, 3), (c, 1), (c, 2), (c, 3),$
$(d, 1), (d, 2), (d, 3)\}$

Obviously, if A has m elements and B has n elements then $A \times B$ consist of mn pairs.

The Cartesian product of the set A with itself is possible.

Thus, if $A = \{1, 2, 3\}$

then $A \times A = \{(1, 1), (1, 2), (1, 3), (2, 1), (2, 2), (2, 3), (3, 1), (3, 2), (3, 3)\}$

Obviously see that, $A \times B \neq B \times A$

For three sets A, B, C

where, $A = \{a_1, a_2, ..., a_p\}$
$B = \{b_1, b_2, ..., b_q\}$

and $C = \{c_1, c_2, ..., c_r\}$

The product $A \times B \times C$ consists of all triplets of the type (a_i, b_j, c_k) with $a_i \in A$, $b_j \in B$, $c_k \in C$.

It consists of pqr triplets, we call $A \times B \times C$ as ternary product.

Likewise the generalization to n sets $A_1, A_2, ..., A_n$ is possible. The n-ary product of n sets is

$$A_1 \times A_2 \times ... \times A_n = \{(a_1, a_2, ..., a_n); a_i \in A_i\}$$

It consists of all possible n-tuples.

Partition of a Set

Consider the set $A = \{1, 2, 3, 4, 5\}$ and its subsets $A_1 = \{1, 2\}$, $A_2 = \{3, 5\}$, $A_3 = \{4\}$.

We observe that each of A_1, A_2, A_3 is non-empty subset of A. Further these three subsets of A are pairwise disjoint i.e. $A_1 \cap A_2 = \phi$, $A_1 \cap A_3 = \phi$, $A_2 \cap A_3 = \phi$ and their union gives the set A;

$$A = A_1 \cup A_2 \cup A_3$$

(2.1)

We say that the collection P = {A_1, A_2, A_3} is a partition of the set A.

Figuratively, we have

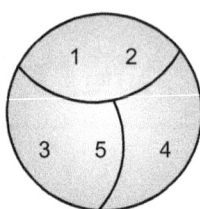

Fig. 2.1

Definition : Let A be non-empty set. Then the collection P = {A_1, A_2, ..., A_r} of subsets of A is called a partition of A if

(i) each A_i is non-empty,

(ii) A_i^s are pairwise disjoint i.e. $A_i \cap j = \phi$ for $i \neq j$, and

(iii) $\bigcup_i A_i = A$.

For the set A = {1, 2, 3, 4, 5, 6}

(a) P_1 = {{1, 3, 5}, {2, 4, 6}} is a partition.

(b) P_2 = {{1, 6}, {2, 4}, {3}, {5}} is a partition.

(c) P_3 = {{1, 2, 3, 4}, {4, 5, 6}} is not a partition since the two sets in P_1 are not disjoint.

(d) P_4 = {{1, 2, 3, 4}, {5}} is not a partition since the union of two sets in P_4 does not give original set A

EXERCISE (2.1)

1. A child has 4 shirts S_1, S_2, S_3, S_4 and 3 trousers t_1, t_2, t_3. Interpret the Cartesian product of these two sets.

2. If A, B, C are three sets, prove :

    (a) $A \times (B \cup C) = (A \times B) \cup (A \times C)$

    (b) $A \times (B \cap C) = (A \times B) \cap (A \times C)$

    Verify the results in (a) and (b) above, by taking
    A = {1, 2}, B = {a, b, c}, C = {b, d}

3. If $A \subseteq B$ and $C \subseteq D$, then prove that $A \times C \subseteq B \times D$. Is the converse true ?

4. Explain why $A \times B \times C \neq (A \times B) \times C$?

5. If A = {x; $1 \leq x \leq 2$} and B = {y; $2 \leq y \leq 3$} then show graphically $A \times B$ and $B \times A$.

6. Let A = {1, 2} and P(A) be the power set of A (i.e. the set of all subsets of A). Write $P(A) \times A$.

7. List all possible partitions of the set A = {a, b, c}.

8. A is the set of all positive integers, B is the set of all negative integers. Explain why {A, B} is not a partition of the set Z of all integers.

ANSWERS (2.1)

5.

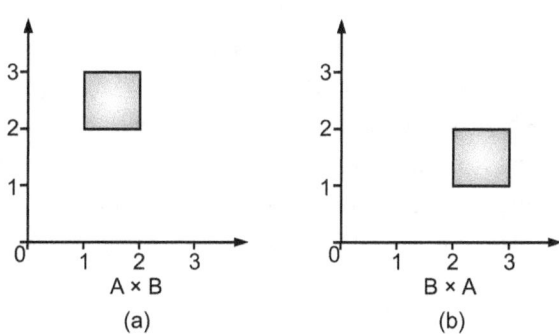

Fig. 2.2

6. $\{<\phi, 1>, <\phi, 2>, <\{1\}, 1>, <\{1\}, 2>, <\{2\}, 1>, <\{2\}, 2>, <\{1,2\}, 1>, <\{1,2\}, 2>\}$.

7. $A_1 = \{\{a\}, \{b\}, \{c\}\}$, $A_2 = \{\{a\}, \{b, c\}\}$, $A_3 = \{\{b\}, \{a, c\}\}$, $A_4 = \{\{c\}, \{a, b\}\}$, $A_5 = \{a, b, c\}$

8. $A \cup B \neq \mathbb{Z}$ because $0 \notin A \cup B$.

2.2 Relation

In our everyday life, we always come across with the word relation. For example 'is brother of' 'is sister of' 'is larger than' 'is smaller than' are some few examples. We now proceed to the precise mathematical idea of a relation.

Consider two sets

$A = \{2, 4, 5\}$ and $B = \{1, 2, 3, 4, ..., 10\}$.

Then the Cartesian product

$A \times B = \{(2, 1), (2, 2) ..., (2, 10), (4, 1), (4, 2), ..., (4, 10), (5, 1), (5, 2) ..., (5, 10)\}$

It consists of $3 \times 10 = 30$ ordered pairs.

Now we select the pairs (x, y) from $A \times B$; in which x divides y. These pairs form a subset R of $A \times B$.

$R = \{(2, 2), (2, 4), (2, 6), (2, 8), (2, 10), (4, 4), (4, 8), (5, 5), (5, 10)\}$

Definition : If A and B are two non-empty sets, then a subset R of $A \times B$ is called a binary relation from A to B.

SOLVED EXAMPLES

Example 2.1 : In the above example find the relations

$R_1 = \{(a, b); a > b\}$ $R_2 = \{(a, b); b = 2a + 1\}$.

Solution : We have $A = \{2, 4, 5\}$ and $B = \{1, 2, 3, 4, 5, 6, 7, 8, 9, 10\}$.

$$R_1 = \{(a, b); a > b\}$$
$$\therefore \quad R_1 = \{(2, 1), (4, 1), (4, 2), (4, 3), (5, 1), (5, 2), (5, 3), (5, 4)\}$$
Also,
$$R_2 = \{(a, b); b = 2a + 1\}$$
$$\therefore \quad R_2 = \{(2, 5), (4, 9)\}$$

In a relation $R \subset A \times B$; when $(a, b) \in R$, we say that $a \in A$ is related to $b \in B$ according to relation R and write aRb. It is also described by saying that 'a is R-related to b'.

If $B = A$, then a relation R from A to A itself, is called a relation on the set A.

Just like a binary relation $R \subset A \times B$; a subset $R \subset A \times B \times C$ is called a ternary relation. Also, if $A_1, A_2, A_3, \ldots, A_n$ are n sets, then a subset $R \subset A_1 \times A_2 \times \ldots \times A_n$ is called n-ary relation.

The case $n = 1$ corresponds to unary relation.

In our course, we shall deal with binary relations only. As such the word relation we shall mean a binary relation.

A relation R from set A to set B is a subset of $A \times B$. Hence the set of those elements $a \in A$; which appear as first elements in the pairs of R form a subset of A. It is called domain of R.

Likewise the set of those elements $b \in B$ which appear as the second elements in the pairs of R form a subset of B. It is called range of R.

We denote domain of R as Dom (R) and the range of R as Ran (R).

More precisely, if R is a relation from set A to set B, then
$$\text{Dom (R)} = \{a \in A; (a, b) \in R \text{ for some } b \in B\}$$
and
$$\text{Ran (R)} = \{b \in B; (a, b) \in R \text{ for some } a \in A\}$$

Example 2.2 : Let $A = \{1, 2, 3, 4, 5\}$ and $B = \{4, 5, 7, 8, 9, 10\}$.

Define a relation R from A to B as $R = \{(a, b); a + b \text{ is a perfect square}\}$

Find Dom (R) and Ran (R).

Solution : $A = \{1, 2, 3, 4, 5\}$ $B = \{4, 5, 6, 7, 8, 9, 10\}$

Then
$$R = \{(1, 8), (2, 7), (3, 6) (4, 5), (5, 4)\}$$
$$\text{Dom (R)} = \{1, 2, 3, 4, 5\}$$
$$\text{Ran (R)} = \{8, 7, 6, 5, 4\}$$

EXERCISE (2.2)

1. Let $A = \{1, 2, 3, 4, \ldots, 8\}$ and $B = \{1, -1, 2, -2, 3, -3\}$. A relation R from A to B is defined by aRb iff $a = b^2 + 1$.

   State which of the following pairs belong to R :

   (a) (5, −2) (b) (1, −1) (c) (10, 3) (d) (1, 0) (e) (2, 2) (f) (2, 1)

2. A relation R is defined on the set $\mathbf{Z}^+$ of positive integers, as below.

   aRb iff $a = b^k$, where k is some positive integer. State which of the following pairs belong to R.

(a) (1, 1) (b) (16, 2) (c) (2, 16) (d) (4, 4) (e) (3, 243) (f) (1, 6).

3. Let A = {1 2, 3, 4, 5, 6}. A relation R is defined on the set A as below.
   aRb iff a is multiple of b. Find the domain and range of R.

4. A relation R is defined on the set A = {2, 3, 5, 6, 7, 8} by (a, b) ∈ R iff a + b ≥ 12. Find the domain and range of R.

ANSWERS (2.2)

1. $(5, -2) \in R$ ∵ $5 = (-2)^2 + 1$
   $(1, -1) \notin R$ ∵ $1 \neq (-1)^2 + 1$
   $(10, 3) \notin R$ ∵ $10 \notin A$
   $(1, 0) \notin R$ ∵ $0 \notin B$
   $(2, 2) \notin R$ ∵ $2 \neq (2)^2 + 1$
   $(2, 1) \in R$ ∵ $2 = (1)^2 + 1$

2. 1 R 1   ∵ $1 = (1)^1$
   16 R 2   ∵ $16 = (2)^4$
   2 R̸ 16   ∵ $2 \neq (16)^k$ for any positive integer k
   4 R 4   ∵ $4 = (4)^1$
   3 R̸ 243   ∵ $3 \neq (243)^k$ for any positive integer k
   1 R̸ 6   ∵ $1 \neq (6)^k$ for any positive integer k

3. R = {(1, 1), (2, 1), (2, 2), (3, 1), (3, 3), (4, 1), (4, 2), (4, 4), (5, 1), (5,5), (6, 1), (6, 2), (6, 3), (6, 6)}
   Dom R = Ran (R) = A

4. R = {(5, 7), (5, 8), (6, 6), (6, 7), (6, 8), (7, 5), (7, 6), (7, 7), (7, 8), (8, 5), (8, 6), (8, 7), (8, 8)}
   Dom · R = {5, 6, 7, 8}
   Ran · R = {5, 6, 7, 8}

2.3 Combination of Relations

The relations from set A to set B or those on the set A are subsets of A × B (A × A). Hence we can find their union, intersection and get the new relations.

(i) The union of two relations R_1 and R_2 is a relation
$$R_1 \cup R_2 = \{(a, b); (a, b) \in R_1 \text{ or } (a, b) \in R_2\}$$

(ii) The intersection of two relations R_1 and R_2 is a relation
$$R_1 \cap R_2 = \{(a, b); (a, b) \in R_1 \text{ and } (a, b) \in R_2\}$$

(iii) The difference $R_1 - R_2$ of two relations is a relation
$$R_1 - R_2 = \{(a, b)\}; (a, b) \in R_1 \text{ but } (a, b) \notin R_2\}$$

(iv) The ring sum of two relations R_1 and R_2 is a relation $R_1 \oplus R_2$ which consists of the pairs in $R_1 \cup R_2$ but not in $R_1 \cap R_2$.
Thus, $R_1 \oplus R_2 = (R_1 \cup R_2) - (R_1 \cap R_2)$

(v) Let R be a relation from set A to set B, then the inverse (also called converse) relation denoted by R^{-1} is a relation from set B to set A as below.
$$R^{-1} = \{(b, a); (a, b) \in R\}.$$

(vi) Let R be a relation from set A to set B. Then the complementary relation denoted by $\overline{R}$ is
$$\overline{R} = \{(a, b); (a,b) \notin R\}$$

It is clear that $\overline{R} = A \times B - R$

Example 2.3 : Let R and S be the relations defined on the set $A = \{2, 3, 5, 9, 12\}$ as below
$$R = \{(a, b); 3 \text{ divides } a - b\}$$
$$S = \{(a, b); 2 \text{ divides } a - b\}$$

Compute the relations R and S as ordered pairs. Then find $R \cup S, R \cap S, R \oplus S, R^{-1}, \overline{S}$.

Solution : $A = \{2, 3, 5, 9, 12\}$

$R = \{(a, b); 3 \text{ divides } a - b\}$

$\therefore$ $R = \{(2, 2), (2, 5), (3, 3), (3, 9), (3, 12), (5, 2), (5, 5), (9, 3), (9, 9),$
$(9, 12), (12, 3), (12, 9), (12, 12)\}$

$S = \{(a, b); 2 \text{ divides } a - b\}$

$\therefore$ $S = \{(2, 2), (2, 12), (3, 3), (3, 5), (3, 9), (5, 3), (5, 5), (5, 9), (9, 3),$
$(9, 5), (9, 9), (12, 2), (12, 12)\}$

$R \cup S = \{(2, 2), (2, 5), (3, 3), (3, 9), (3, 12), (5, 2), (5, 5), (9, 3), (9, 9),$
$(9, 12), (12, 3), (12, 9), (12, 12), (2, 12), (3, 5), (5, 3), (5, 9),$
$(9, 5), (12, 2)\}$

$R \cap S = \{(2, 2), (3, 3), (3, 9), (5, 5), (9, 3), (9, 9), (12, 12)\}$

$R \oplus S = \{(2, 5), (3, 12), (5, 2), (9, 12), (12, 3), (12, 9), (2, 12), (3, 5),$
$(5, 3), (5, 9), (9, 5)$

$R^{-1} = \{(2, 2), (5, 2), (3, 3), (9, 3), (12, 3), (2, 5), (5, 5), (3, 9), (9, 9),$
$(12, 9), (3, 12), (9, 12), (12, 12)\}$

$\overline{S} = \{(2, 3), (2, 5), (2, 9), (3, 2), (3, 12), (5, 2), (5, 12), (9, 2),$
$(9, 12), (12, 3), (12, 5), (12, 9)\}$

Composition of Two Relations

Let R be a relation from set A to set B and S be a relation from set B to set C.

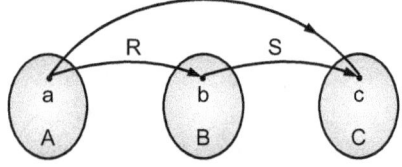

Fig. 2.3

As shown in the above figure $a \in A$, $b \in B$, $c \in C$ such that aRb and bSc i.e. $(a, b) \in R$ and $(b, c) \in S$. Ultimately then $a \in A$ is related to $c \in C$ under the relation denoted by SOR from set A to set C. It is called composition of R and S.

For example, let $A = \{1, 2, 3\}$, $B = \{b, p, d\}$ and $C = \{p, q, r\}$.

A relation R from A to B is $R = \{(1, b), (1, d), (3, p), (2, b)\}$

Also a relation S from B to C is $S = \{(p, r), (b, q), (d, r)\}$.

Then the composite relation SOR from set A to set C is SOR = $\{(1, q), (1, r), (3, r), (2, q)\}$.

We see that SOR is a relation from set A to set C such that whenever $(a, b) \in R$ and $(b, c) \in S$ then $(a, c) \in SOR$.

Example 2.4 : Let R be the relation $\{(1, 2), (1, 3), (2, 3), (2, 4), (3, 1)\}$ and S be the relatin $\{(2, 1), (3, 1), (3, 2), (4, 2)\}$. Find SOR.

Solution : $(1, 2) \in R$, $(2, 1) \in S$ ∴ $(1, 1) \in SOR$

$(1, 3) \in R$, $(3, 1) \in S$ ∴ $(1, 1) \in SOR$

$(1, 3) \in R$, $(3, 2) \in S$ ∴ $(1, 2) \in SOR$

$(2, 3) \in R$, $(3, 1) \in S$ ∴ $(2, 1) \in SOR$

$(2, 3) \in R$, $(3, 2) \in S$ ∴ $(2, 2) \in SOR$

$(2, 4) \in R$, $(4, 2) \in S$ ∴ $(2, 2) \in SOR$

∴ SOR = $\{(1, 1), (1, 2), (2, 1), (2, 2)\}$

EXERCISE (2.3)

1. Let R and S be two relations from set $A = \{1, 2, 3\}$ to set $B = \{1, 2, 3, 4\}$.

    $R = \{(1, 3), (2, 4), (3, 2), (3, 3)\}$

    $S = \{(1, 1), (2, 1), (3, 1), (3, 4), (3, 2), (3, 3), (2, 3)\}$

    Compute (a) $R \cup S$, (b) $R \cap S$, (c) $R \oplus S$ (d) $\bar{R}$.

2. Let R and S be two relations defined on the set $A = \{1, 2, 3, 4, 5\}$.

    $R = \{(1, 1), (1, 3), (1, 4), (1, 5), (2, 2), (2, 3), (3, 1), (3, 4), (4, 1), (4, 3), (5, 2), (5, 3), (5, 4), (5, 5)\}$

    $S = \{(1, 1), (1, 2), (1, 5), (2, 4), (3, 1), (3, 2), (3, 5), (4, 2), (4, 4), (4, 5), (5, 1)\}$.

    Compute ROS and SOR.

3. Let $A = \{1, 2, 3, 4, 5\}$ and R, S be two relations defined on A by

    $R = \{a, b); a^2 \leq 2b\}$

    $S = \{a, c); a^2 \leq 3c\}$

    Compute ROS and SOR.

ANSWERS (2.3)

1. (a) {(1, 3), (2, 4), (3, 2), (3, 3), (1, 1), (2, 1), (3, 1), (3, 4), (2, 3)}
   (b) {(3, 2), (3, 3)}
   (c) {(1, 3), (2, 4), (1, 1), (2, 1)}
   (d) {(1, 1), (1, 2), (1, 4), (2, 1), (2, 2), (2, 3), (3, 1), (3, 4)}
2. ROS = {(1, 1), (1, 3), (1, 4), (1, 5), (1, 2), (2, 1), (2, 3), (3, 1), (3, 3), (3, 4), (3, 5), (3, 2), (4, 2), (4, 3), (4, 1), (4, 4), (4, 5), (5, 1), (5, 3), (5, 4), (5, 5)}
   SOR = {(1, 1), (1, 2), (1, 5), (1, 4), (2, 4), (2, 1), (2, 2), (2, 5), (3, 1), (3, 2), (3, 5), (3, 4), (4, 1), (4, 2), (4, 5), (5, 4), (5, 1), (5, 2), (5, 5), (5, 4)}
3. ROS = SOR = {(1, 1), (1, 2), (1, 3), (1, 4), (1, 5)}

2.4 Representation of a Relation

We have already seen that a relation R is represented as a set of ordered pairs (a, b), where $a \in A$ and $b \in B$. We now proceed to two other representations of a relation viz. matrix representation and graphical representation. The former is useful in computer programming while the latter gives us the visual display of various properties of the relation.

Matrix Representation :

We begin the matrix representation of a relation with some introductory results about Boolean matrices. An $m \times n$ matrix A whose elements are 1 and 0 only, is called a Boolean matrix. For example, $A = \begin{bmatrix} 1 & 0 & 1 & 0 \\ 0 & 1 & 1 & 0 \\ 1 & 1 & 0 & 1 \end{bmatrix}$ and $B = \begin{bmatrix} 0 & 0 & 1 & 0 \\ 1 & 1 & 1 & 0 \\ 1 & 0 & 1 & 1 \\ 0 & 1 & 0 & 1 \end{bmatrix}$ are Boolean matrices of order 3×4 and 4×4 respectively.

Now in a two element Boolean algebra B(0, 1), we have two binary operations, one of them is called 'join' denoted by $\vee$ and the other is called 'meet' denoted by $\wedge$. Also there is one unary operation i.e. complementation and is denoted by /.

Then in Boolean algebra B(0, 1) we have

$0 \vee 0 = 0, \ 0 \vee 1 = 1, \ 1 \vee 0 = 1, \ 1 \vee 1 = 1$

and $0 \wedge 0 = 0, \ 0 \wedge 1 = 0, \ 1 \wedge 0 = 0, \ 1 \wedge 1 = 1$

Also, $0' = 1$ and $1' = 0$

For ready reference we represent the above results by composition tables as below.

$\vee$	0	1
0	0	1
1	1	1

Join operation

$\wedge$	0	1
0	0	0
1	0	1

Meet operation

a	a'
0	1
1	0

Complementation

Let now $A = [a_{ij}]$ and $B = [b_{ij}]$ be two Boolean matrices of the same order say $m \times n$. Then the join of A and B is a Boolean matrix $C = [c_{ij}]$ of order $m \times n$ such that

$c_{ij} = a_{ij} \vee b_{ij}$ for $i = 1, 2, \ldots, m$ and $j = 1, 2, \ldots, n$.

Similarly, the meet of A and B is a Boolean matrix $D = [d_{ij}]$ of order $m \times n$ such that $d_{ij} = a_{ij} \wedge b_{ij}$ for $i = 1, 2, \ldots, m$ and $j = 1, 2, \ldots, n$.

As an illustration consider

$$A = \begin{bmatrix} 1 & 1 & 0 & 1 \\ 0 & 1 & 1 & 0 \\ 0 & 0 & 1 & 1 \end{bmatrix}_{3 \times 4} \text{ and } B = \begin{bmatrix} 0 & 1 & 1 & 0 \\ 0 & 0 & 1 & 1 \\ 1 & 0 & 1 & 0 \end{bmatrix}_{3 \times 4}$$

Then

$$A \vee B = \begin{bmatrix} 1 \vee 0 & 1 \vee 1 & 0 \vee 1 & 1 \vee 0 \\ 0 \vee 0 & 1 \vee 0 & 1 \vee 1 & 0 \vee 1 \\ 0 \vee 1 & 0 \vee 0 & 1 \vee 1 & 1 \vee 0 \end{bmatrix}$$

$$= \begin{bmatrix} 1 & 1 & 1 & 1 \\ 0 & 1 & 1 & 1 \\ 1 & 0 & 1 & 1 \end{bmatrix}_{3 \times 4} \qquad \text{[See table of } \vee \text{]}$$

Also

$$A \wedge B = \begin{bmatrix} 1 \wedge 0 & 1 \wedge 1 & 0 \wedge 1 & 1 \wedge 0 \\ 0 \wedge 0 & 1 \wedge 0 & 1 \wedge 1 & 0 \wedge 1 \\ 0 \wedge 1 & 0 \wedge 0 & 1 \wedge 1 & 1 \wedge 0 \end{bmatrix}$$

$$= \begin{bmatrix} 0 & 1 & 0 & 0 \\ 0 & 0 & 1 & 0 \\ 0 & 0 & 1 & 0 \end{bmatrix} \qquad \text{[See table of } \wedge \text{]}$$

We define another binary operation on Boolean matrices, called Boolean multiplication of matrices. It is denoted by $\odot$.

The Boolean product $A \odot B$ of two matrices A and B in this order is defined only when the number of columns in the prefactor A is equal to the number of rows in the post factor B. Thus, if A is $m \times n$ Boolean matrix and B is $n \times p$ Boolean matrix, then $A \odot B$ is $m \times p$ Boolean matrix.

In order to find the $i - j^{th}$ element in $A \odot B$, our left hand finger runs on the ith row of prefactor A, at the same time right hand finger runs on the jth column of B at equal speed. In this way, we find the join of the meets to get $i - j^{th}$ element of $A \odot B$. We illustrate this by an example.

Let $A = \begin{bmatrix} 1 & 1 & 0 \\ 0 & 1 & 1 \end{bmatrix}$ and $B = \begin{bmatrix} 1 & 1 \\ 0 & 1 \\ 1 & 0 \end{bmatrix}$.

Here A is 2×3 and B is 3×2 matrix. Therefore $A \odot B$ is 2×2 matrix.

$C = A \odot B = \begin{bmatrix} C_{11} & C_{12} \\ C_{21} & C_{22} \end{bmatrix}$. To find C_{11}, we consider first row of A and first column of B.

$\therefore \qquad C_{11} = (1 \wedge 1) \vee (1 \wedge 0) \vee (0 \wedge 1) = 1 \vee 0 \vee 0 = 1$

Similarly,
$$C_{12} = (1 \wedge 1) \vee (1 \wedge 1) \vee (0 \wedge 0) = 1 \vee 1 \vee 0 = 1$$
$$C_{21} = (0 \wedge 1) \vee (1 \wedge 0) (1 \wedge 1) = 0 \vee 0 \vee 1 = 1$$
$$C_{22} = (0 \wedge 1) \vee (1 \wedge 1) \vee (1 \wedge 0) = 0 \vee 1 \vee 0 = 1$$

$\therefore \quad A \odot B = \begin{bmatrix} 1 & 1 \\ 1 & 1 \end{bmatrix}_{2 \times 2}$

For the matrices A and B given above; the product $B \odot A$ is also defined.

We have, $\quad B \odot A = \begin{bmatrix} 1 & 1 \\ 0 & 1 \\ 1 & 0 \end{bmatrix} \odot \begin{bmatrix} 1 & 1 & 0 \\ 0 & 1 & 1 \end{bmatrix}$

$\therefore \quad B \odot A = \begin{bmatrix} 1 & 1 & 1 \\ 0 & 1 & 1 \\ 1 & 1 & 0 \end{bmatrix}_{3 \times 3}$

Let now $A = \{a_1, a_2, \ldots, a_m\}$ and $B = \{b_1, b_2, \ldots, b_n\}$ be two finite sets with m and n elements respectively. Let R be the relation defined from A to B. Then a relation R is represented by $m \times n$ matrix $M_R = [m_{ij}]$ such that
$$m_{ij} = \begin{cases} 1; & \text{if } (a_i, b_j) \in R \\ 0; & \text{if } (a_i, b_j) \notin R \end{cases}$$

For example, let $A = \{1, 2, 3, 4\}$, $B = \{1, 2, 3\}$ and relation R from A to B is
$$R = \{(1, 3), (4, 1), (3, 2), (2, 2), (2, 3)\}$$

The matrix M_R associated with this relation is 4×3 matrix and $M_R = \begin{bmatrix} 0 & 0 & 1 \\ 0 & 1 & 1 \\ 0 & 1 & 0 \\ 1 & 0 & 0 \end{bmatrix}$.

Conversely, if we know $m \times n$ Boolean matrix, then we can write the relation R represented by this matrix.

For example, if $M = \begin{bmatrix} 0 & 1 & 1 & 1 \\ 1 & 1 & 0 & 0 \\ 1 & 0 & 0 & 1 \\ 0 & 1 & 1 & 0 \end{bmatrix}$.

It is 4×4 matrix. So it represents a relation from the set $A = \{a_1, a_2, a_3, a_4\}$ to the set $B = \{b_1, b_2, b_3, b_4\}$ and $R = \{(a_1, b_2), (a_1, b_3), (a_1, b_4), (a_2, b_1), (a_2, b_2), (a_3, b_1), (a_3, b_4), (a_4, b_2), (a_4, b_3)\}$.

Example 2.5 : Let $A = \{a, b, c, d, e\}$ and $M_R = \begin{bmatrix} 1 & 1 & 0 & 0 & 0 \\ 0 & 0 & 1 & 1 & 0 \\ 0 & 0 & 0 & 1 & 1 \\ 0 & 1 & 1 & 0 & 0 \\ 1 & 0 & 0 & 0 & 0 \end{bmatrix}$.

Find the relation R defined on the set A.

Solution : The entries 1 in the matrix M_R suggest the pairs in the relation R.

$\therefore \quad R = \{(a, a), (a, b), (b, c), (b, d), (c, d), (c, e), (d, b), (d, c), (e, a)\}$

Graphical Representation

Suppose $A = \{a_1, a_2, ..., a_n\}$ is a finite set of n elements. A relation R from A to A itself can be represented pictorially, called directed graph (digraph) of that relation. In a digraph of R each element of the set A is enclosed in a small circle, which is called a vertex in a digraph. Further when a_i R a_j i.e. the pair $(a_i, a_j) \in R$ we draw an arrowed edge joining the vertices corresponding to a_i and a_j, the arrow being directed from a_i towards a_j.

Consider a relation R defined on the set $A = \{1, 2, 3, 4\}$.

$R = \{(2, 2), (2, 1), (1, 2), (1, 1), (1, 4), (1, 3), (4, 3), (3, 2)\}$

The digraph of this relation looks as below.

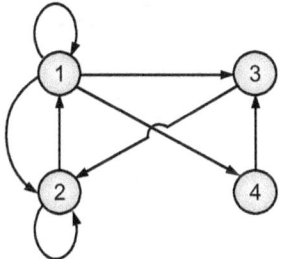

Fig. 2.4

The edges in a digraph are called directed edges or simply diedges.

A diedge whose beginning vertex coincides with the ending vertex, is said to form a loop. In the above digraph, the edges (1, 1) and (2, 2) form a loop at the vertex 1 and 2 respectively.

Consider now the edge corresponding to the pair (4, 3) in the above digraph. This edge leaves the vertex 4 and enters into the vertex 3. We describe this situation by saying that this diedge contributes one out degree at the leaving vertex 4 and one indegree at the entering vertex 3.

In the same manner each edge in a digraph contributes one outdegree at the leaving vertex and one indegree at the entering vertex.

In particular a loop in a digraph contributes one outdegree and one indegree at the same vertex.

SOLVED EXAMPLES

Example 2.6 : Let $A = \{a, b, c, d\}$ and R be the relation on A, whose matrix is

$$M_R = \begin{bmatrix} 0 & 1 & 1 & 0 \\ 1 & 1 & 1 & 0 \\ 0 & 1 & 0 & 1 \\ 1 & 0 & 1 & 0 \end{bmatrix}$$

Draw the digraph of R, verify that the sum of all indegrees and outdegrees is equal to twice the number of edges.

Solution :

$$M_R = \begin{bmatrix} 0 & 1 & 1 & 0 \\ 1 & 1 & 1 & 0 \\ 0 & 1 & 0 & 1 \\ 1 & 0 & 1 & 0 \end{bmatrix}$$

∴ R = {(a, b), (a, c), (b, a), (b, b), (b, c), (c, b), (c, d), (d, a), (d, c)}

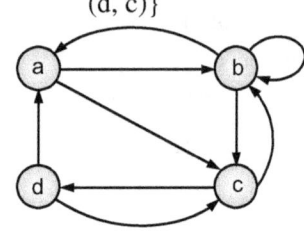

Fig. 2.5

Vertex :	a	b	c	d
Indegree :	2	3	3	1
Outdegree	2	3	2	2

Total indegree = 9

Total outdegree = 9

∴ Total degree = 9 + 9 = 18

which is twice the number of edges.

Example 2.7 : A digraph of a relation R is given as below.

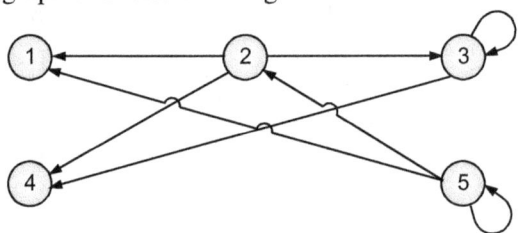

Fig. 2.6

Write the relation R as a set of pairs and write its matrix.

Solution : From the given diagraph

R = {(2, 1), (2, 3), (2, 4), (3, 3), (3, 4), (5, 2), (5, 1), (5, 5)}

$$M_R = \begin{bmatrix} 0 & 0 & 0 & 0 & 0 \\ 1 & 0 & 1 & 1 & 0 \\ 0 & 0 & 1 & 1 & 0 \\ 0 & 0 & 0 & 0 & 0 \\ 1 & 1 & 0 & 0 & 1 \end{bmatrix}$$

Let now R and S be the two relations from set A to set B, where A and B are finite sets. Then R ∪ S, R ∩ S, R ⊕ S are also relations from set A to set B.

We shall now prove that the matrix of R ∪ S is the matrix $M_R \vee M_S$.

Clearly $M_{R \cup S}$, M_R and M_S are $m \times n$ matrices. Let m_{ij}, p_{ij}, q_{ij} denote the $i-j^{th}$ element in $M_{R \cup S}$, M_R and M_S respectively. We have to prove $m_{ij} = p_{ij} \vee q_{ij}$. Suppose $m_{ij} = 1$. Then $a_i \in A$ is related to $b_j \in B$ under the relation $R \cup S$. i.e. $a_i \, R \cup S \, b_j$. This implies that $a_i \, R b_j$ or $a_i \, S b_j$ or both.

$\therefore \quad p_{ij} = 1$ or $q_{ij} = 1$ or both

$\therefore \qquad\qquad\qquad p_{ij} \vee q_{ij} = 1 \qquad\qquad [\because 1 \vee 0 = 1,\ 0 \vee 1 = 1,\ 1 \vee 1 = 1]$

$\therefore \qquad\qquad\qquad m_{ij} = p_{ij} \vee q_{ij}$

Suppose now $\qquad\qquad m_{ij} = 0$.

Then $a_i \in A$ is not related to $b_j \in B$ under the relation $R \cup S$.

$\therefore \quad (a_i, b_j) \notin R$ and $(a_i, b_j) \notin S$

$\therefore \quad p_{ij} = 0$ and $q_{ij} = 0$

$\therefore \quad p_{ij} \vee q_{ij} = 0 \vee 0 = 0$

In any case, we get

$\qquad m_{ij} = p_{ij} \vee q_{ij}$ for $i = 1, 2, ..., m$ and $j = 1, 2, ..., n$

Hence, $\qquad\qquad\qquad M_{R \cup S} = M_R \vee M_S$

On the same lines the proof of following result is straight forward

$$M_{R \cap S} = M_R \wedge M_S$$

Suppose next that the three sets A, B, C have m, n, p elements respectively. Further R is a relation from A to B and S is a relation from B to C so that the composite relation SOR is from set A to set C.

Let M_R, M_S and M_{SOR} be the Boolean matrices of R, S and SOR.

Let $i-j^{th}$ element in M_R be p_{ij}, that in M_S be q_{ij} and in M_{SOR} be m_{ij}.

Now the ordered pair (a_i, c_j) is in SOR if and only if there is an element b_k in B such that $(a_i, b_k) \in R$ and $(b_k, c_j) \in S$.

From this it immediately follows that $m_{ij} = 1$ if and only if $p_{ik} = 1$ and $q_{kj} = 1$, for some k.

Then from the definition of Boolean product, we get

$$M_{SOR} = M_R \odot M_S$$

Example 2.8 : Let $A = \{1, 2, 3, 4\}$ and R, S be two relations defined on A as below.

$R = \{(1, 1), (1, 2), (2, 3), (2, 4), (3, 4), (4, 1), (4, 2)\}$

$S = \{(2, 3), (4, 4), (3, 1), (1, 1), (1, 4), (2, 4)\}$

Verify the following results

$M_{R \cup S} = M_R \vee M_S, \quad M_{R \cap S} = M_R \wedge M_S,$

$M_{SOR} = M_R \odot M_S, \quad M_{ROS} = M_S \odot M_R.$

Solution : We have,

$R = \{(1, 1), (1, 2), (2, 3), (2, 4), (3, 4), (4, 1), (4, 2)\}$

$S = \{(2, 3), (4, 4), (3, 1), (1, 1), (1, 4), (2, 4)\}$

Then, $M_R = \begin{bmatrix} 1 & 1 & 0 & 0 \\ 0 & 0 & 1 & 1 \\ 0 & 0 & 0 & 1 \\ 1 & 1 & 0 & 0 \end{bmatrix}$, $M_S = \begin{bmatrix} 1 & 0 & 0 & 1 \\ 0 & 0 & 1 & 1 \\ 1 & 0 & 0 & 0 \\ 0 & 0 & 0 & 1 \end{bmatrix}$

Now, $R \cup S = \{(1, 1), (1, 2), (2, 3), (2, 4), (3, 4), (4, 1), (4, 2), (4, 4)$
$(3, 1), (1, 4)\}$

$R \cap S = \{(1, 1), (2, 3), (2, 4)\}$

$SOR = \{(1, 1), (1, 4), (1, 3), (2, 1), (2, 4), (3, 4), (4, 1), (4, 4),$
$(4, 3)\}$

$ROS = \{(2, 4), (4, 1), (4, 2), (3, 1), (3, 2), (1, 1), (1, 2), (2, 1), (2, 2)\}$

(i) $M_{R \cup S} = \begin{bmatrix} 1 & 1 & 0 & 1 \\ 0 & 0 & 1 & 1 \\ 1 & 0 & 0 & 1 \\ 1 & 1 & 0 & 1 \end{bmatrix}$

$M_R \vee M_S = \begin{bmatrix} 1 & 1 & 0 & 0 \\ 0 & 0 & 1 & 1 \\ 0 & 0 & 0 & 1 \\ 1 & 1 & 0 & 0 \end{bmatrix} \vee \begin{bmatrix} 1 & 0 & 0 & 1 \\ 0 & 0 & 1 & 1 \\ 1 & 0 & 0 & 0 \\ 0 & 0 & 0 & 1 \end{bmatrix}$

$= \begin{bmatrix} 1 & 1 & 0 & 1 \\ 0 & 0 & 1 & 1 \\ 1 & 0 & 0 & 1 \\ 1 & 1 & 0 & 1 \end{bmatrix}$

$\therefore \quad M_{R \cup S} = M_R \vee M_S$

(ii) $M_{R \cap S} = \begin{bmatrix} 1 & 0 & 0 & 0 \\ 0 & 0 & 1 & 1 \\ 0 & 0 & 0 & 0 \\ 0 & 0 & 0 & 0 \end{bmatrix}$

$M_R \wedge M_S = \begin{bmatrix} 1 & 1 & 0 & 0 \\ 0 & 0 & 1 & 1 \\ 0 & 0 & 0 & 1 \\ 1 & 1 & 0 & 0 \end{bmatrix} \wedge \begin{bmatrix} 1 & 0 & 0 & 1 \\ 0 & 0 & 1 & 1 \\ 1 & 0 & 0 & 0 \\ 0 & 0 & 0 & 1 \end{bmatrix}$

$= \begin{bmatrix} 1 & 0 & 0 & 0 \\ 0 & 0 & 1 & 1 \\ 0 & 0 & 0 & 0 \\ 0 & 0 & 0 & 0 \end{bmatrix}$

$\therefore \quad M_{R \cap S} = M_R \wedge M_S$

$M_{SOR} = \begin{bmatrix} 1 & 0 & 1 & 1 \\ 1 & 0 & 0 & 1 \\ 0 & 0 & 0 & 1 \\ 1 & 0 & 1 & 1 \end{bmatrix}$

$$M_R \odot M_S = \begin{bmatrix} 1 & 1 & 0 & 0 \\ 0 & 0 & 1 & 1 \\ 0 & 0 & 0 & 1 \\ 1 & 1 & 0 & 0 \end{bmatrix} \odot \begin{bmatrix} 1 & 0 & 0 & 1 \\ 0 & 0 & 1 & 1 \\ 1 & 0 & 0 & 0 \\ 0 & 0 & 0 & 1 \end{bmatrix}$$

$$\therefore \quad M_R \odot M_S = \begin{bmatrix} 1 & 0 & 1 & 1 \\ 1 & 0 & 0 & 1 \\ 0 & 0 & 0 & 1 \\ 1 & 0 & 1 & 1 \end{bmatrix}$$

$$\therefore \quad M_{SOR} = M_R \odot M_S$$

(iv) $$M_{ROS} = \begin{bmatrix} 1 & 1 & 0 & 0 \\ 1 & 1 & 0 & 1 \\ 1 & 1 & 0 & 0 \\ 1 & 1 & 0 & 0 \end{bmatrix}$$

$$M_S \odot M_R = \begin{bmatrix} 1 & 0 & 0 & 1 \\ 0 & 0 & 1 & 1 \\ 1 & 0 & 0 & 0 \\ 0 & 0 & 0 & 1 \end{bmatrix} \odot \begin{bmatrix} 1 & 1 & 0 & 0 \\ 0 & 0 & 1 & 1 \\ 0 & 0 & 0 & 1 \\ 1 & 1 & 0 & 0 \end{bmatrix}$$

$$= \begin{bmatrix} 1 & 1 & 0 & 0 \\ 1 & 1 & 0 & 1 \\ 1 & 1 & 0 & 0 \\ 1 & 1 & 0 & 0 \end{bmatrix}$$

$$\therefore \quad M_{ROS} = M_S \odot M_R$$

Finally, we consider the matrices of the inverse relation and complementary relation.

We know that if R is a relation from set A to set B, then its inverse R^{-1} is a relation from set B to set A.

The inverse relation of the relation R is denoted by R^{-1}. Thus $bR^{-1}a$ iff aRb.

Let $\quad A = \{1, 2, 3, 4\}$
and $\quad B = \{2, 5, 6, 7, 8\}$
and $\quad R = \{(1, 8), (3, 5), (3, 7), (2, 6), (2, 7), (4, 5), (4, 6), (4, 7)\}$

We have, $$M_R = \begin{bmatrix} 0 & 0 & 0 & 0 & 1 \\ 0 & 0 & 1 & 1 & 0 \\ 0 & 1 & 0 & 1 & 0 \\ 0 & 1 & 1 & 1 & 0 \end{bmatrix}$$

Now, $\quad R^{-1} = \{(8, 1), (5, 3), (7, 3), (6, 2), (7, 2), (5, 4), (6, 4), (7, 4)\}$

$$M_{R^{-1}} = \begin{bmatrix} 0 & 0 & 0 & 0 \\ 0 & 0 & 1 & 1 \\ 0 & 1 & 0 & 1 \\ 0 & 1 & 1 & 1 \\ 1 & 0 & 0 & 0 \end{bmatrix}$$

We observe that the matrix of R^{-1} is the transpose of the matrix of R

$$M_{R^{-1}} = (M_R)^T$$

In the above example the complementary relation $\bar{R}$ defined as

$(a, b) \in \bar{R}$ iff $(a, b) \notin R$ is

$\bar{R} = \{(1, 2), (1, 5), (1, 6), (1, 7), (2, 2), (2, 5), (2, 8), (3, 2), (3, 6),$
$(3, 8), (4, 2), (4, 8)\}$

Then
$$M_{\bar{R}} = \begin{bmatrix} 1 & 1 & 1 & 1 & 0 \\ 1 & 1 & 0 & 0 & 1 \\ 1 & 0 & 1 & 0 & 1 \\ 1 & 0 & 0 & 0 & 1 \end{bmatrix}$$

The matrix of $\bar{R}$ can be obtained from the matrix of R; simply by replacing all occurrences of 1 by 0 and all occurrence of 0 by 1.

Path in a Relation

Let R be a relation on the set A. Let a and b be two vertices in the digraph of R. Consider a finite sequence a, x_1, x_2, ..., x_{n-1}, b of elements of A such that a Rx_1, x_1Rx_2, ..., x_{n-1} Rb.

It is called a path of length n in R. In a path there may be repetition of a vertex.

For example : Let A = {1, 2, 3, 4, 5} and relation R on A be

$R = \{(1, 2), (1, 3), (1, 4), (2, 2), (2, 3), (4, 1), (4, 4), (4, 5)\}$

The digraph of this relation looks as below.

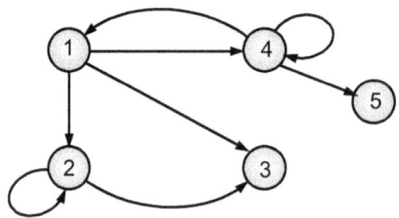

Fig. 2.7

We observe that, π_1 : 1, 4; π_2 : 2, 3; π_3 : 4, 4 are paths of length 1.

Also π_4 : 1, 4, 5; π_5 : 4, 1, 2 and π_6 : 1, 2, 2 are paths of length 2 and π_7 : 4, 1, 2, 3 is path of length 3.

A path in which ending vertex coincides with the beginning vertex is called a cycle.

We see that, 1, 4, 1 is a cycle of length 2.

In fact every loop is a cycle of length 1.

Each pair appearing in R is a path of length 1.

Now consider the matrix of R and R^2.

$$M_R = \begin{bmatrix} 0 & 1 & 1 & 1 & 0 \\ 0 & 1 & 1 & 0 & 0 \\ 0 & 0 & 0 & 0 & 0 \\ 1 & 0 & 0 & 1 & 1 \\ 0 & 0 & 0 & 0 & 0 \end{bmatrix}$$

$$M_{R^2} = M_R \odot M_R = \begin{bmatrix} 0 & 1 & 1 & 1 & 0 \\ 0 & 1 & 1 & 0 & 0 \\ 0 & 0 & 0 & 0 & 0 \\ 1 & 0 & 0 & 1 & 1 \\ 0 & 0 & 0 & 0 & 0 \end{bmatrix} \odot \begin{bmatrix} 0 & 1 & 1 & 1 & 0 \\ 0 & 1 & 1 & 0 & 0 \\ 0 & 0 & 0 & 0 & 0 \\ 1 & 0 & 0 & 1 & 1 \\ 0 & 0 & 0 & 0 & 0 \end{bmatrix}$$

$$\therefore \quad M_{R^2} = \begin{bmatrix} 1 & 1 & 1 & 1 & 1 \\ 0 & 1 & 1 & 0 & 0 \\ 0 & 0 & 0 & 0 & 0 \\ 1 & 1 & 1 & 1 & 1 \\ 0 & 0 & 0 & 0 & 0 \end{bmatrix}$$

$$R^2 = \{(1,1), (1,2), (1,3), (1,4), (1,5), (2,2), (2,3), (4,1), (4,2), (4,3), (4,4), (4,5)\}$$

The digraph of R^2 is as below.

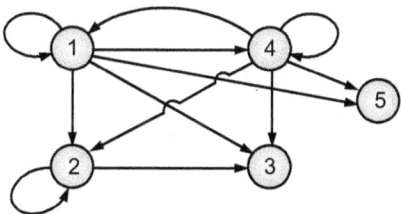

Fig. 2.8

We have the following result

$1R^2 1$; path of length 2 from 1 to 1 is 1, 4, 1

$1R^2 2$; path of length 2 from 1 to 2 is 1, 2, 2

$1R^2 3$; path of length 2 from 1 to 3 is 1, 2, 3

$1R^2 4$; path of length 2 from 1 to 4 is 1, 4, 4

$1R^2 5$; path of length 2 from 1 to 5 is 1, 4, 5

$2R^2 2$; path of length 2 from 2 to 2 is 2, 2, 2

$2R^2 3$; path of length 2 from 2 to 3 is 2, 2, 3

$4R^2 1$; path of length 2 from 4 to 1 is 4, 4, 1

$4R^2 2$; path of length 2 from 4 to 2 is 4, 1, 2

$4R^2 3$; path of length 2 from 4 to 3 is 4, 1, 3

$4R^2 4$; path of length 2 from 4 to 4 is 4, 1, 4

$4R^2 5$; path of length 2 from 4 to 5 is 4, 4, 5

Thus R^2 is a relation on A such that for a, b $\in$ A; aR^2b iff there is a path of length 2 from a to b. We accept this result without proof.

Similarly, R^3 is a relation on A such that for a, b $\in$ A; aR^3b iff there is a path of length 3 from a to b.

For any positive integer n, $aR^n b$ iff there is a path of length n from a to b.

We define the relation R^∞ on A as below.

$aR^\infty b$ iff there exists some path from a to b in R.

Hence R^∞ is called a connectivity relation. By using matrices the relation R^∞ is obtained by $M_{R^\infty} = M_R \vee M_{R^2} \vee M_{R^3} \vee \ldots\ldots$

SOLVED EXAMPLES

Example 2.9 : A relation R is defined on the set A = {a, b, c, d, e, f} by

$R = \{(a, b), (a, f), (b, c), (c, c), (c, d), (d, a), (d, c), (d, e), (f, d)\}$

(a) Draw the digraph of R.

(b) List all paths of length 1, 2, 3

(c) Find a cycle starting at vertex b.

Solution :

(a)

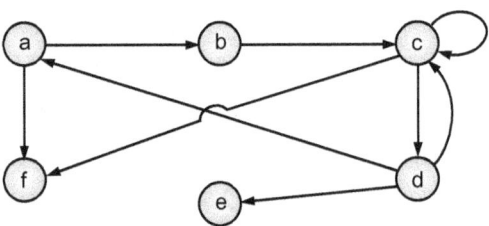

Fig. 2.9

(b) π_1 : a, b; π_2 : b, c; π_3 : c, c; π_4 : c, d; π_5 : d, c; π_6 : d, e; π_7 : f, d; π_8 : a, f are the paths of length 1.

π_9 : a, b, c; π_{10} : a, f, d; π_{11} : b, c, c; π_{12} : b, c, d; π_{13} : c, c, d; π_{14} : c, d, c; π_{15} : c, d, e; π_{16} : c, d, a; π_{17} : d, a, f; π_{18} : d, c, c; π_{19} : d, c, d are paths of length 2.

π_{20} : a, b, c, c; π_{21} : a, b, c, d; π_{22} : a, f, d, e; π_{23} : b, c, c, d; π_{24} : b, c, d, e; π_{25} : b, c, d, a; π_{26} : c, c, d, c; π_{27} : c, d, a, b; π_{28} : c, d, a, f; π_{29} : f, d, c, c; are paths of length 3.

(c) A cycle starting at vertex b is b, c, d, a, b.

Example 2.10 : A relation R on the set A = {1, 2, 3, 4} is as below.

$R = \{(1, 2), (1, 3), (3, 2), (4, 1), (4, 4)\}$

(a) Write M_R

(b) Draw the graph of R

(c) Find R^2, R^3 and R^∞.

Solution : $R = \{(1, 2), (1, 3), (3, 2), (4, 1), (4, 4)\}$

(a) $$M_R = \begin{bmatrix} 0 & 1 & 1 & 0 \\ 0 & 0 & 0 & 0 \\ 0 & 1 & 0 & 0 \\ 1 & 0 & 0 & 1 \end{bmatrix}$$

(b)

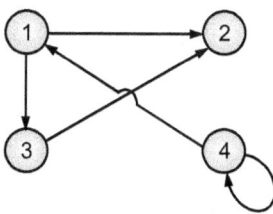

Fig. 2.10

(c) $M_{R^2} = M_R \odot M_R = \begin{bmatrix} 0 & 1 & 1 & 0 \\ 0 & 0 & 0 & 0 \\ 0 & 1 & 0 & 0 \\ 1 & 0 & 0 & 1 \end{bmatrix} \odot \begin{bmatrix} 0 & 1 & 1 & 0 \\ 0 & 0 & 0 & 0 \\ 0 & 1 & 0 & 0 \\ 1 & 0 & 0 & 1 \end{bmatrix} = \begin{bmatrix} 0 & 1 & 0 & 0 \\ 0 & 0 & 0 & 0 \\ 0 & 0 & 0 & 0 \\ 1 & 1 & 1 & 1 \end{bmatrix}$

$M_{R^3} = M_{R^2} \odot M_R = \begin{bmatrix} 0 & 1 & 0 & 0 \\ 0 & 0 & 0 & 0 \\ 0 & 0 & 0 & 0 \\ 1 & 1 & 1 & 1 \end{bmatrix} \odot \begin{bmatrix} 0 & 1 & 1 & 0 \\ 0 & 0 & 0 & 0 \\ 0 & 1 & 0 & 0 \\ 1 & 0 & 0 & 1 \end{bmatrix}$

$= \begin{bmatrix} 0 & 0 & 0 & 0 \\ 0 & 0 & 0 & 0 \\ 0 & 0 & 0 & 0 \\ 1 & 1 & 1 & 1 \end{bmatrix}$

$M_{R^4} = M_{R^3} \odot M_R = \begin{bmatrix} 0 & 0 & 0 & 0 \\ 0 & 0 & 0 & 0 \\ 0 & 0 & 0 & 0 \\ 1 & 1 & 1 & 1 \end{bmatrix} \odot \begin{bmatrix} 0 & 1 & 1 & 0 \\ 0 & 0 & 0 & 0 \\ 0 & 1 & 0 & 0 \\ 1 & 0 & 0 & 1 \end{bmatrix}$

$= \begin{bmatrix} 0 & 0 & 0 & 0 \\ 0 & 0 & 0 & 0 \\ 0 & 0 & 0 & 0 \\ 1 & 1 & 1 & 1 \end{bmatrix}$

Here, $\quad M_{R^4} = M_{R^3}$

$\therefore \quad M_{R^\infty} = M_R \vee M_{R^2} \vee M_{R^3}$

$= \begin{bmatrix} 0 & 1 & 1 & 0 \\ 0 & 0 & 0 & 0 \\ 0 & 1 & 0 & 0 \\ 1 & 0 & 0 & 1 \end{bmatrix} \vee \begin{bmatrix} 0 & 1 & 0 & 0 \\ 0 & 0 & 0 & 0 \\ 0 & 0 & 0 & 0 \\ 1 & 1 & 1 & 1 \end{bmatrix} \vee \begin{bmatrix} 0 & 0 & 0 & 0 \\ 0 & 0 & 0 & 0 \\ 0 & 0 & 0 & 0 \\ 1 & 1 & 1 & 1 \end{bmatrix}$

$= \begin{bmatrix} 0 & 1 & 1 & 0 \\ 0 & 0 & 0 & 0 \\ 0 & 1 & 0 & 0 \\ 1 & 1 & 1 & 1 \end{bmatrix}$

Example 2.11 : Let S and R be two relations defined over the set A = {1, 2, 3, ..., 29, 30}

where, $\quad R = \{<x, 2x> | x \in A\}$

and $\quad S = \{<x, 3x> | x \in A\}$

Compute (i) ROS, (ii) SOR

Solution : A = {1, 2, 3, ..., 29, 30}

$R = \{<x, 2x> | x \in A\}$
= {<1, 2>, <2, 4>, <3, 6>, <4, 8>, <5, 10>, <6, 12>, <7, 14>, <8, 16>, <9, 18>, <10, 20>, (11, 22>, <12, 24>, <13, 26>, <14, 28>, <15, 30>}

Also, $\quad S = \{<x, 3x> | x \in A\}$
= {<1, 3>, <2, 6>, <3, 9>, <4, 12>, <5, 15>, <6, 18>, <7, 21>, <8, 24<, <9, 27>, <10, 30>}

(i) To find ROS

<1, 3> ∈ S, <3, 6> ∈ R ∴ <1, 6> ∈ ROS
<2, 6> ∈ S, <6, 12> ∈ R ∴ <2, 12> ∈ ROS
<3, 9> ∈ S, <9, 18> ∈ R ∴ <3, 18> ∈ ROS
<4, 12> ∈ S, <12, 24> ∈ R ∴ <4, 24> ∈ ROS
<5, 15> ∈ S, <15, 30> ∈ S ∴ <5, 30> ∈ ROS

∴ ROS = {<1, 6>, <2, 12>, <3, 18>, <4, 24>, <5, 30>}

(ii) To find SOR

<1, 2> ∈ R, <2, 6> ∈ S ∴ <1, 6> ∈ SOR
<2, 4> ∈ R, <4, 12> ∈ S ∴ <2, 12> ∈ SOR
<3, 6> ∈ R, <6, 18> ∈ S ∴ <3, 18> ∈ SOR
<4, 8> ∈ R, <8, 24> ∈ S ∴ <4, 24> ∈ SOR
<5, 10> ∈ R, <10, 30> ∈ S ∴ <5, 30> ∈ SOR

∴ SOR = {<1, 6>, <2, 12>, <3, 18>, <4, 24>, <5, 30>}

Example 2.12 : Given the relation matrices M_R and M_S. Find M_{ROS} and M_{SOR}

$$M_R = \begin{bmatrix} 1 & 0 & 1 \\ 1 & 1 & 0 \\ 1 & 1 & 1 \end{bmatrix}, \quad M_S = \begin{bmatrix} 1 & 0 & 0 & 1 & 0 \\ 1 & 0 & 1 & 0 & 1 \\ 0 & 1 & 0 & 1 & 0 \end{bmatrix}$$

Solution : M_R is 3 × 3 matrix and M_S is 3 × 5 matrix. So we consider the set A = {1, 2, 3, 4, 5} on which the relations are defined

$$M_R = \begin{bmatrix} 1 & 0 & 1 & 0 & 0 \\ 1 & 1 & 0 & 0 & 0 \\ 1 & 1 & 1 & 0 & 0 \\ 0 & 0 & 0 & 0 & 0 \\ 0 & 0 & 0 & 0 & 0 \end{bmatrix} \quad M_S = \begin{bmatrix} 1 & 0 & 0 & 1 & 0 \\ 1 & 0 & 1 & 0 & 1 \\ 0 & 1 & 0 & 1 & 0 \\ 0 & 0 & 0 & 0 & 0 \\ 0 & 0 & 0 & 0 & 0 \end{bmatrix}$$

Now, $M_{ROS} = M_S \odot M_R = \begin{bmatrix} 1 & 0 & 0 & 1 & 0 \\ 1 & 0 & 1 & 0 & 1 \\ 0 & 1 & 0 & 1 & 0 \\ 0 & 0 & 0 & 0 & 0 \\ 0 & 0 & 0 & 0 & 0 \end{bmatrix} \odot \begin{bmatrix} 1 & 0 & 1 & 0 & 0 \\ 1 & 1 & 0 & 0 & 0 \\ 1 & 1 & 1 & 0 & 0 \\ 0 & 0 & 0 & 0 & 0 \\ 0 & 0 & 0 & 0 & 0 \end{bmatrix}$

$\therefore \quad M_{ROS} = \begin{bmatrix} 1 & 0 & 1 & 0 & 0 \\ 1 & 1 & 1 & 0 & 0 \\ 1 & 1 & 0 & 0 & 0 \\ 0 & 0 & 0 & 0 & 0 \\ 0 & 0 & 0 & 0 & 0 \end{bmatrix}$

$M_{SOR} = M_R \odot M_S = \begin{bmatrix} 1 & 0 & 1 & 0 & 0 \\ 1 & 1 & 0 & 0 & 0 \\ 1 & 1 & 1 & 0 & 0 \\ 0 & 0 & 0 & 0 & 0 \\ 0 & 0 & 0 & 0 & 0 \end{bmatrix} \odot \begin{bmatrix} 1 & 0 & 0 & 1 & 0 \\ 1 & 0 & 1 & 0 & 1 \\ 0 & 1 & 0 & 1 & 0 \\ 0 & 0 & 0 & 0 & 0 \\ 0 & 0 & 0 & 0 & 0 \end{bmatrix}$

$\therefore \quad M_{SOR} = \begin{bmatrix} 1 & 1 & 0 & 1 & 0 \\ 1 & 0 & 1 & 1 & 1 \\ 1 & 1 & 1 & 1 & 1 \\ 0 & 0 & 0 & 0 & 0 \\ 0 & 0 & 0 & 0 & 0 \end{bmatrix}$

Example 2.13 : Let A = {1, 2, 3, 4}. Let
R = {<1, 2>, <1, 3>, <1, 4>, <2, 3>, <3, 1>, <3, 3>, <4, 2>} and
S = {<1, 3>, <2, 2>, <3, 2>, <4, 2>}
Find (i) RO(SOS), (ii) IS ROS = SOR ? (iii) ROROR

Solution : $M_R = \begin{bmatrix} 0 & 1 & 1 & 1 \\ 0 & 0 & 1 & 0 \\ 1 & 0 & 1 & 0 \\ 0 & 1 & 0 & 0 \end{bmatrix}$, $M_S = \begin{bmatrix} 0 & 0 & 1 & 0 \\ 0 & 1 & 0 & 0 \\ 0 & 1 & 0 & 0 \\ 0 & 1 & 0 & 0 \end{bmatrix}$

(i) $M_{RO(SOS)} = M_{SOS} \odot M_R = (M_S \odot M_S) \odot M_R$

$= \begin{bmatrix} 0 & 0 & 1 & 0 \\ 0 & 1 & 0 & 0 \\ 0 & 1 & 0 & 0 \\ 0 & 1 & 0 & 0 \end{bmatrix} \begin{bmatrix} 0 & 0 & 1 & 0 \\ 0 & 1 & 0 & 0 \\ 0 & 1 & 0 & 0 \\ 0 & 1 & 0 & 0 \end{bmatrix} \begin{bmatrix} 0 & 1 & 1 & 1 \\ 0 & 0 & 1 & 0 \\ 1 & 0 & 1 & 0 \\ 0 & 1 & 0 & 0 \end{bmatrix}$

$= \begin{bmatrix} 0 & 1 & 0 & 0 \\ 0 & 1 & 0 & 0 \\ 0 & 1 & 0 & 0 \\ 0 & 1 & 0 & 0 \end{bmatrix} \begin{bmatrix} 0 & 1 & 1 & 1 \\ 0 & 0 & 1 & 0 \\ 1 & 0 & 1 & 0 \\ 0 & 1 & 0 & 0 \end{bmatrix} = \begin{bmatrix} 0 & 0 & 1 & 0 \\ 0 & 0 & 1 & 0 \\ 0 & 0 & 1 & 0 \\ 0 & 0 & 1 & 0 \end{bmatrix}$

$\therefore \quad$ RO(SOS) = {<1, 3>, <2, 3>, <3, 3>, <4, 3>}

(ii) $M_{ROS} = M_S \odot M_R = \begin{bmatrix} 0 & 0 & 1 & 0 \\ 0 & 1 & 0 & 0 \\ 0 & 1 & 0 & 0 \\ 0 & 1 & 0 & 0 \end{bmatrix} \begin{bmatrix} 0 & 1 & 1 & 1 \\ 0 & 0 & 1 & 0 \\ 1 & 0 & 1 & 0 \\ 0 & 1 & 0 & 0 \end{bmatrix}$

$$\therefore \quad M_{ROS} = \begin{bmatrix} 1 & 0 & 1 & 0 \\ 0 & 0 & 1 & 0 \\ 0 & 0 & 1 & 0 \\ 0 & 0 & 1 & 0 \end{bmatrix}$$

$\therefore \quad ROS = \{<1, 1>, <1, 3>, <2, 3>, <3, 3>, <4, 3>\}$

$$M_{SOR} = M_R \odot M_S = \begin{bmatrix} 0 & 1 & 1 & 1 \\ 0 & 0 & 1 & 0 \\ 1 & 0 & 1 & 0 \\ 0 & 1 & 0 & 0 \end{bmatrix} \begin{bmatrix} 0 & 0 & 1 & 0 \\ 0 & 1 & 0 & 0 \\ 0 & 1 & 0 & 0 \\ 0 & 1 & 0 & 0 \end{bmatrix}$$

$$\therefore \quad M_{SOR} = \begin{bmatrix} 0 & 1 & 0 & 0 \\ 0 & 1 & 0 & 0 \\ 0 & 1 & 1 & 0 \\ 0 & 1 & 0 & 0 \end{bmatrix}$$

$\therefore \quad SOR = \{<1, 2>, <2, 2>, <3, 2>, <3, 3>, <4, 2>\}$

$\therefore \quad ROS \neq SOR$

(iii) $M_{ROROR} = M_R \odot M_R \odot M_R$

$$= \begin{bmatrix} 0 & 1 & 1 & 1 \\ 0 & 0 & 1 & 0 \\ 1 & 0 & 1 & 0 \\ 0 & 1 & 0 & 0 \end{bmatrix} \begin{bmatrix} 0 & 1 & 1 & 1 \\ 0 & 0 & 1 & 0 \\ 1 & 0 & 1 & 0 \\ 0 & 1 & 0 & 0 \end{bmatrix} \begin{bmatrix} 0 & 1 & 1 & 1 \\ 0 & 0 & 1 & 0 \\ 1 & 0 & 1 & 0 \\ 0 & 1 & 0 & 0 \end{bmatrix}$$

$$= \begin{bmatrix} 0 & 1 & 1 & 1 \\ 0 & 0 & 1 & 0 \\ 1 & 0 & 1 & 0 \\ 0 & 1 & 0 & 0 \end{bmatrix} \begin{bmatrix} 1 & 1 & 1 & 0 \\ 1 & 0 & 1 & 0 \\ 1 & 1 & 1 & 1 \\ 0 & 0 & 1 & 0 \end{bmatrix}$$

$$= \begin{bmatrix} 1 & 1 & 1 & 1 \\ 1 & 1 & 1 & 1 \\ 1 & 1 & 1 & 1 \\ 1 & 0 & 1 & 0 \end{bmatrix}$$

$\therefore \quad ROR = \{<1, 1>, <1, 2>, <1, 3>, <1, 4>, <2, 1>, <2, 2>,$
$<2, 3>, <2, 4>, <3, 1>, <3, 2>, <3, 3>, <3, 4>,$
$<4, 1>, <4, 3>\}$

Example 2.14 : Let R and S be the following relations on B = {a, b, c, d};

$R = \{(a, a), (a, c), (c, b), (c, d), (d, b)\}$

and $S = \{(b, a), (c, c), (c, d), (d, a)\}$

Find the following composite relations : (i) SOR (ii) SOROS [P.U. 2010]

Solution : The matrices of the relations R and S are

$$R = \begin{array}{c} \\ a \\ b \\ c \\ d \end{array} \begin{array}{cccc} a & b & c & d \\ \begin{bmatrix} 1 & 0 & 1 & 0 \\ 0 & 0 & 0 & 0 \\ 0 & 1 & 0 & 1 \\ 0 & 1 & 0 & 0 \end{bmatrix} \end{array} \quad S = \begin{array}{c} \\ a \\ b \\ c \\ d \end{array} \begin{array}{cccc} a & b & c & d \\ \begin{bmatrix} 0 & 0 & 0 & 0 \\ 1 & 0 & 0 & 0 \\ 0 & 0 & 1 & 1 \\ 1 & 0 & 0 & 0 \end{bmatrix} \end{array}$$

$$M_{SOR} = M_R \odot M_S = \begin{bmatrix} 1 & 0 & 1 & 0 \\ 0 & 0 & 0 & 0 \\ 0 & 1 & 0 & 1 \\ 0 & 1 & 0 & 0 \end{bmatrix} \begin{bmatrix} 0 & 0 & 0 & 0 \\ 1 & 0 & 0 & 0 \\ 0 & 0 & 1 & 1 \\ 1 & 0 & 0 & 0 \end{bmatrix}$$

$$\therefore \quad M_{SOR} = \begin{bmatrix} 0 & 0 & 1 & 1 \\ 0 & 0 & 0 & 0 \\ 1 & 0 & 0 & 0 \\ 1 & 0 & 0 & 0 \end{bmatrix}$$

$\therefore \quad$ SOR $= \{(a, c), (a, d), (c, a), (d, a)\}$

(ii) $M_{SOROS} = M_{(SOR)OS} = M_S \odot M_{SOR}$

$$= \begin{bmatrix} 0 & 0 & 0 & 0 \\ 1 & 0 & 0 & 0 \\ 0 & 0 & 1 & 1 \\ 1 & 0 & 0 & 0 \end{bmatrix} \begin{bmatrix} 0 & 0 & 1 & 1 \\ 0 & 0 & 0 & 0 \\ 1 & 0 & 0 & 0 \\ 1 & 0 & 0 & 0 \end{bmatrix}$$

$$= \begin{bmatrix} 0 & 0 & 0 & 0 \\ 0 & 0 & 1 & 1 \\ 1 & 0 & 0 & 0 \\ 0 & 0 & 1 & 1 \end{bmatrix}$$

$\therefore \quad$ SOROS $= \{(b, c), (b, d), (c, a), (d, c), (d, d)\}$

Example 2.15 : Given A = {1, 2, 3, 4, 5} and B = {1, 3, 5}. Let R be relation from Let A $\to$ B defined by "x is less than y". Write relation R, its matrix and draw its graph.

[P.U. 2009]

Solution : A = {1, 2, 3, 4, 5}, B = {1, 3, 5} $x \in$ A is related to $y \in$ B iff $x < y$

$\therefore \quad$ R = {(1, 3), (1, 5), (2, 3), (2, 5), (3, 5), (4, 5)}

The matrix of R is
$$R = \begin{array}{c} \\ 1 \\ 2 \\ 3 \\ 4 \\ 5 \end{array} \begin{array}{c} 1 \quad 3 \quad 5 \\ \begin{bmatrix} 0 & 1 & 1 \\ 0 & 1 & 1 \\ 0 & 0 & 1 \\ 0 & 0 & 1 \\ 0 & 0 & 0 \end{bmatrix} \end{array}$$

Graphically R is represented as below.

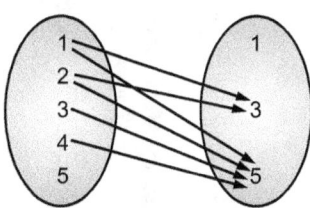

Fig. 2.11

Example 2.16 : Let R = {<1, 2>, <3, 4>, <2, 3>} and
S = {<4, 2>, <2, 5>, <3, 1>, <1, 3>}
Find SO(ROR) and (ROS)OR.

Solution : The relations and S are defined on the set A = {1, 2, 3, 4, 5}

$$M_R = \begin{bmatrix} 0 & 1 & 0 & 0 & 0 \\ 0 & 0 & 1 & 0 & 0 \\ 0 & 0 & 0 & 1 & 0 \\ 0 & 0 & 0 & 0 & 0 \\ 0 & 0 & 0 & 0 & 0 \end{bmatrix}, M_S = \begin{bmatrix} 0 & 0 & 1 & 0 & 0 \\ 0 & 0 & 0 & 0 & 1 \\ 1 & 0 & 0 & 0 & 0 \\ 0 & 1 & 0 & 0 & 0 \\ 0 & 0 & 0 & 0 & 0 \end{bmatrix}$$

$$M_{ROR} = M_R \odot M_R = \begin{bmatrix} 0 & 1 & 0 & 0 & 0 \\ 0 & 0 & 1 & 0 & 0 \\ 0 & 0 & 0 & 1 & 0 \\ 0 & 0 & 0 & 0 & 0 \\ 0 & 0 & 0 & 0 & 0 \end{bmatrix} \begin{bmatrix} 0 & 1 & 0 & 0 & 0 \\ 0 & 0 & 1 & 0 & 0 \\ 0 & 0 & 0 & 1 & 0 \\ 0 & 0 & 0 & 0 & 0 \\ 0 & 0 & 0 & 0 & 0 \end{bmatrix}$$

$$= \begin{bmatrix} 0 & 0 & 1 & 0 & 0 \\ 0 & 0 & 0 & 1 & 0 \\ 0 & 0 & 0 & 0 & 0 \\ 0 & 0 & 0 & 0 & 0 \\ 0 & 0 & 0 & 0 & 0 \end{bmatrix}$$

$$M_{ROS} = M_S \odot M_R = \begin{bmatrix} 0 & 0 & 1 & 0 & 0 \\ 0 & 0 & 0 & 0 & 1 \\ 1 & 0 & 0 & 0 & 0 \\ 0 & 1 & 0 & 0 & 0 \\ 0 & 0 & 0 & 0 & 0 \end{bmatrix} \begin{bmatrix} 0 & 1 & 0 & 0 & 0 \\ 0 & 0 & 1 & 0 & 0 \\ 0 & 0 & 0 & 1 & 0 \\ 0 & 0 & 0 & 0 & 0 \\ 0 & 0 & 0 & 0 & 0 \end{bmatrix}$$

$$= \begin{bmatrix} 0 & 0 & 0 & 1 & 0 \\ 0 & 0 & 0 & 0 & 0 \\ 0 & 1 & 0 & 0 & 0 \\ 0 & 0 & 1 & 0 & 0 \\ 0 & 0 & 0 & 0 & 0 \end{bmatrix}$$

$$M_{SO(ROR)} = M_{ROR} \odot M_S = \begin{bmatrix} 0 & 0 & 1 & 0 & 0 \\ 0 & 0 & 0 & 1 & 0 \\ 0 & 0 & 0 & 0 & 0 \\ 0 & 0 & 0 & 0 & 0 \\ 0 & 0 & 0 & 0 & 0 \end{bmatrix} \begin{bmatrix} 0 & 0 & 1 & 0 & 0 \\ 0 & 0 & 0 & 0 & 1 \\ 1 & 0 & 0 & 0 & 0 \\ 0 & 1 & 0 & 0 & 0 \\ 0 & 0 & 0 & 0 & 0 \end{bmatrix}$$

$$= \begin{bmatrix} 1 & 0 & 0 & 0 & 0 \\ 0 & 1 & 0 & 0 & 0 \\ 0 & 0 & 0 & 0 & 0 \\ 0 & 0 & 0 & 0 & 0 \\ 0 & 0 & 0 & 0 & 0 \end{bmatrix}$$

∴ SO(ROR) = {<1, 1>, <2, 2>}

$$M_{(ROS)OR} = M_R \odot M_{ROS}$$

$$= \begin{bmatrix} 0 & 1 & 0 & 0 & 0 \\ 0 & 0 & 1 & 0 & 0 \\ 0 & 0 & 0 & 1 & 0 \\ 0 & 0 & 0 & 0 & 0 \\ 0 & 0 & 0 & 0 & 0 \end{bmatrix} \begin{bmatrix} 0 & 0 & 0 & 1 & 0 \\ 0 & 0 & 0 & 0 & 0 \\ 0 & 1 & 0 & 0 & 0 \\ 0 & 0 & 1 & 0 & 0 \\ 0 & 0 & 0 & 0 & 0 \end{bmatrix}$$

$$= \begin{bmatrix} 0 & 0 & 0 & 0 & 0 \\ 0 & 1 & 0 & 0 & 0 \\ 0 & 0 & 1 & 0 & 0 \\ 0 & 0 & 0 & 0 & 0 \\ 0 & 0 & 0 & 0 & 0 \end{bmatrix}$$

∴ (ROS)OR = {<2, 2>, <3, 3>}

EXERCISE (2.4)

1. Let R and S be two relations defined on
   A = {1, 2, 3, 4) as
   R = {(1, 2), (1, 3), (2, 3), (2, 4), (3, 1)}
   S = {(2, 1), (3, 2), (4, 2), (3, 1)}
   By using matrices find the relations SOR and ROS and write them as ordered pairs.

2. Let R be the relation defined on A = {1, 2, 3, 4, 5} as below.
   R = {(2, 2), (2, 3), (2, 4), (3, 4), (3, 5), (4, 2), (4, 5), (4, 1), (5, 3), (5, 1),
   (1, 2), (1, 3), (1, 5)}
   Find R^2 = ROR and R^3 = ROROR

3. Find the relation represented by the following digraph. Also write its matrix.

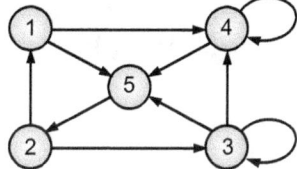

Fig. 2.12

4. Let A = {a, b, c, d, e} and R be the relation on A, whose matrix is

$$M_R = \begin{bmatrix} 1 & 1 & 0 & 0 & 0 \\ 0 & 0 & 1 & 1 & 0 \\ 0 & 0 & 0 & 1 & 1 \\ 0 & 1 & 1 & 0 & 0 \\ 1 & 0 & 0 & 0 & 0 \end{bmatrix}$$

Find R and draw its digraph.

5. A = {1, 2, 3, 4}. A relation R is defined on A as
   R = {(1, 1), (1, 2), (1, 3), (1, 4), (2, 3), (3, 2), (4, 2), (4, 3), (4, 4)}
   (a) Draw the graph of R and also write the matrix.
   (b) Compute M_{R^2}, M_{R^3}, M_{R^4} and write your conclusion; where
   $M_{R^2} = M_{RoR}$, M_{RoRoR}
   (c) Compute M_{R^∞}.

ANSWERS (2.4)

1. $M_{ROS} = \begin{bmatrix} 0 & 0 & 0 & 0 \\ 0 & 1 & 1 & 0 \\ 0 & 1 & 1 & 1 \\ 0 & 0 & 1 & 1 \end{bmatrix}$ ROS = {(2, 2), (2, 3), (3, 2), (3, 3), (3, 4), (4, 3), (4, 4)}

   $M_{SOR} = \begin{bmatrix} 1 & 1 & 0 & 0 \\ 1 & 1 & 0 & 0 \\ 0 & 0 & 0 & 0 \\ 0 & 0 & 0 & 0 \end{bmatrix}$ $\therefore$ SOR = {(1, 1), (1, 2), (2, 1), (2, 2)}

2. $M_{R^2} = \begin{bmatrix} 1 & 1 & 1 & 1 & 1 \\ 1 & 1 & 1 & 1 & 1 \\ 1 & 1 & 1 & 0 & 1 \\ 1 & 1 & 1 & 1 & 1 \\ 0 & 1 & 1 & 1 & 1 \end{bmatrix}$

   R^2 = {(1, 1), (1, 2), (1, 3), (1, 4), (1, 5), (2, 1), (2, 2), (2, 3), (2, 4), (2, 5), (3, 1), (3, 2), (3, 3), (3, 5), (4, 1), (4, 2), (4, 3), (4, 4), (4, 5), (5, 2), (5, 3), (5, 4), (5, 5)}

   $M_{R^3} = \begin{bmatrix} 1 & 1 & 1 & 1 & 1 \\ 1 & 1 & 1 & 1 & 1 \\ 1 & 1 & 1 & 1 & 1 \\ 1 & 1 & 1 & 1 & 1 \\ 1 & 1 & 1 & 1 & 1 \end{bmatrix}$ $R^3 = A \times A$

3. R = {(1, 4), (1, 5), (2, 1), (2, 3), (3, 3), (3, 4), (3, 5), (4, 5), (4, 4), (5, 2)}

   $M_R = \begin{bmatrix} 0 & 0 & 0 & 1 & 1 \\ 1 & 0 & 1 & 0 & 0 \\ 0 & 0 & 1 & 1 & 1 \\ 0 & 0 & 0 & 1 & 1 \\ 0 & 1 & 0 & 0 & 0 \end{bmatrix}$

4. R = {(a, a), (a, b), (b, c), (b, d), (c, d), (c, e), (d, b), (d, c), (e, a)}

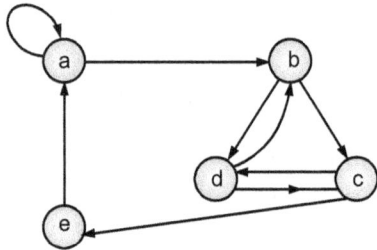

Fig. 2.13

5. (a) $M_R = \begin{bmatrix} 1 & 1 & 1 & 1 \\ 0 & 0 & 1 & 0 \\ 0 & 1 & 0 & 0 \\ 0 & 1 & 1 & 1 \end{bmatrix}$

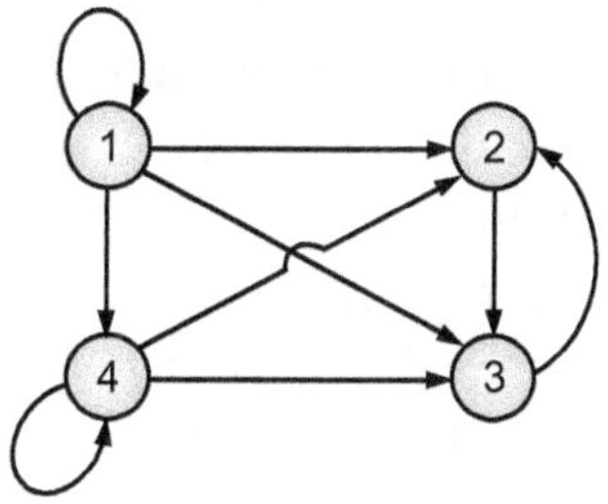

Fig. 2.14

(b) $M_{R^2} = \begin{bmatrix} 1 & 1 & 1 & 1 \\ 0 & 1 & 0 & 0 \\ 0 & 0 & 1 & 0 \\ 0 & 1 & 1 & 1 \end{bmatrix}$ $M_{R^3} = \begin{bmatrix} 1 & 1 & 1 & 1 \\ 0 & 0 & 1 & 0 \\ 0 & 1 & 0 & 0 \\ 0 & 1 & 1 & 1 \end{bmatrix}$ $M_{R^4} = \begin{bmatrix} 1 & 1 & 1 & 1 \\ 0 & 1 & 0 & 0 \\ 0 & 0 & 1 & 0 \\ 0 & 1 & 1 & 1 \end{bmatrix}$

Here $M_{R^2} = M_{R^4}$. The paths in the digraph of R, of length 4 and of length 2 are given by the same digraph.

(c) As $M_{R^4} = M_{R^2}$ we have

$$M_{R^\infty} = \begin{bmatrix} 1 & 1 & 1 & 1 \\ 0 & 0 & 1 & 0 \\ 0 & 1 & 0 & 0 \\ 0 & 1 & 1 & 1 \end{bmatrix} \vee \begin{bmatrix} 1 & 1 & 1 & 1 \\ 0 & 1 & 0 & 0 \\ 0 & 0 & 1 & 0 \\ 0 & 1 & 1 & 1 \end{bmatrix} \vee \begin{bmatrix} 1 & 1 & 1 & 1 \\ 0 & 0 & 1 & 0 \\ 0 & 1 & 0 & 0 \\ 0 & 1 & 1 & 1 \end{bmatrix}$$

$$= \begin{bmatrix} 1 & 1 & 1 & 1 \\ 0 & 1 & 1 & 0 \\ 0 & 1 & 1 & 0 \\ 0 & 1 & 1 & 1 \end{bmatrix}$$

2.5 Types of Relations

We always come across with the relations defined on the set A, instead of relations from set A to set B. We now discuss the properties satisfied (not satisfied) by the relations defined on set A.

Reflexivity : A relation R on the set A is called reflexive relation if every element of A is related to itself according to relation R i.e. aRa for every $a \in A$. Equivalently $(a, a) \in R$ for every $a \in A$.

If no element of A is related to itself according to relation R, then R is called irreflexive relation. Following are some examples of reflexive and irreflexive relations.

(a) The relation of equality in the set $\mathbb{R}$ of all real numbers is reflexive because every real number is equal to itself.

(b) The relation of divisibility in the set $\mathbb{N} = \{1, 2, 3, ...\}$ of positive integers is reflexive because every positive integer divides itself. We write this as $a \mid a$ for every $a \in \mathbb{N}$.

(c) Let n be any (but fixed) positive integer greater than 1. We define a relation R on the set $Z = \{0, \pm 1, \pm 2, \pm 3, ...\}$ of all integers as below.

For $a, b \in Z$ we have aRb iff n divides the difference $a - b$.

It is called 'congruence modulo n' relation. When aRb i.e. $n \mid (a - b)$ we denote this by $a \equiv b$ (mod. n) and read 'integer a is congruent to integer b modulo n'.

For example : $13 \equiv 5$ (mod. 4) because $13 - 5 = 8$ is divisible by 4. Also $9 \equiv -21$ (mod. 6), since $9 - (-21) = 9 + 21 = 30$ which is divisible by 6.

But $23 \not\equiv 6$ (mod. 5) because $23 - 6 = 17$ which is not divisible by 5.

If now $a \in Z$ is any member of Z, then $a - a = 0$, which is clearly divisible by n. Hence $a \equiv a$ (mod. n) for every $a \in Z$.

Therefore the congruence relation modulo n is reflexive relation.

(d) The relation R = {(a, b), (b, d), (c, c), (d, c), (d, d)} defined on the set A = {a, b, c, d} is not reflexive. The reason is that $a \in A$ and $(a, a) \notin R$. Also $b \in A$ and $(b, b) \notin R$.

(e) The relation R = {(1, 3), (2, 1), (4, 2), (2, 4)} on A = {1, 2, 3, 4} is irreflexive. For any $a \in A$, we see that $(a, a) \notin R$.

(f) Consider the relation R = {(1, 1), (2, 4), (3, 2), (4, 1)} on A = {1, 2, 3, 4}.

R is not reflexive because $(2, 2) \notin R$, $(3, 3) \notin R$, $(4, 4) \notin R$. Also R is not irreflexive due to the presence of the pair $(1, 1) \in R$.

In the matrix M_R of reflexive relation R, on the set A; each entry on the main diagonal (top left to right bottom) must be 1; while in case of irreflexive relation, each entry on the main diagonal is 0.

When we look to the digraph of reflexive relation there is a loop at each vertex and in the digraph of irreflexive relation, there is no loop at any vertex.

Symmetric Relation

A relation R defined on the set A is called symmetric if, whenever $(a, b) \in R$, $(b, a) \in R$. i.e. if aRb $\Rightarrow$ bRa.

From this it follows that if there exist two elements a and $b \in A$ such that $(a, b) \in R$ but $(b, a) \notin R$, then the relation R fails to be symmetric.

A relation R on A is called asymmetric if whenever $(a, b) \in R$ then $(b, a) \notin R$. From this it follows that if there exist $a, b \in A$ such that $(a, b) \in R$ and $(b, a) \in R$, then R is not asymmetric.

A relation R on set A is called antisymmetric if whenever $(a, b) \in R$ and $(b, a) \in R$ then $a = b$. This is equivalent to say that if $a \neq b$ in A, then either $(a, b) \notin A$ or $(b, a) \notin A$.

(a) The relation of equality in the set $\mathbb{R}$ of all real numbers is symmetric because $a = b \Rightarrow b = a$.

(b) The relation of divisibility in the set $\mathbb{N}$ of positive integers is not symmetric because $5\,|\,20$ but $20\,\nmid\,5$. However, this relation is antisymmetric because if a and b are two positive integers with $a \neq b$ then either a does not divide b or b does not divide a.

(c) The congruence relation modulo n in the set Z of all integers is symmetric relation. This is because

$$a \equiv b \pmod{n} \Rightarrow n\,|\,(a - b)$$
$$\Rightarrow a - b = nk; \ k \text{ is integer}$$
$$\Rightarrow b - a = n(-k); \ -k \text{ is integer}$$
$$\Rightarrow b \equiv a \pmod{n}$$

(d) Consider the relation 'less than' on the set Z of integers.

$aRb \Rightarrow a < b \Rightarrow b \not< a \Rightarrow b\cancel{R}a$. Therefore, it is not symmetric.

Further $a < b \Rightarrow b \not< a$. Therefore, it is asymmetric.

Also it is antisymmetric because, if $a \neq b$ then either $a \not< b$ or $b \not< a$.

(e) Consider the set $A = \{a, b, c, d\}$ and relation $R = \{(a, b), (b, b), (c, d), (d, a)\}$.

R is not symmetric because $(a, b) \in R$ but $(b, a) \notin R$.

Also R is not asymmetric because $(b, b) \in R$. However R is antisymmetric because $a \neq b \Rightarrow (a, b) \notin R$ or $(b, a) \notin R$.

Now in a symmetric relation, we have $a_i R a_j \Leftrightarrow a_j R a_i$. This means in the matrix M_R of a symmetric relation; $a_{ij} = a_{ji}$. If $a_{ij} = 1$, then $a_{ji} = 1$ and if $a_{ij} = 0$ then $a_{ji} = 0$. Therefore the matrix of a symmetric relation is symmetric matrix.

In the matrix of asymmetric relation, we have the following result. If $m_{ij} = 1$, then $m_{ji} = 0$ and on the main diagonal $m_{ii} = 0$ for every i.

The matrix M_R of antisymmetric relation has the following property. If $i \neq j$, the neither $m_{ij} = 0$ or $m_{ji} = 0$.

Example 2.17 : Let $M_R = \begin{bmatrix} 0 & 1 & 1 & 0 \\ 1 & 1 & 0 & 0 \\ 1 & 0 & 1 & 1 \\ 0 & 0 & 1 & 1 \end{bmatrix}$

Examine the relation R for reflexivity and symmetry. Is R (i) irreflexive (ii) asymmetric (iii) antisymmetric ?

Solution : $M_R = \begin{bmatrix} 0 & 1 & 1 & 0 \\ 1 & 1 & 0 & 0 \\ 1 & 0 & 1 & 1 \\ 0 & 0 & 1 & 1 \end{bmatrix}$; $A = \{1, 2, 3, 4\}$

In M_R; $m_{11} = 0$ ∴ $1\cancel{R}1$

∴ R is not reflexive.

The matrix M_R is a symmetric matrix because $m_{ij} = m_{ji}$ for $i = 1, 2, 3, 4$ and $j = 1, 2, 3, 4$.

∴ Relation R is symmetric.

R is not irreflexive because $(2, 2) \in R$.

In the matrix of asymmetric relation all diagonal elements must be 0. This condition is violated in M_R. Therefore relation R is not asymmetric.

Also the relation R is not antisymmetric, since 1 and 2 are distinct elements of A and $(1, 2) \in R$, $(2, 1) \in R$.

The digraph of a relation R possesses the following characteristics with respect to the above properties.

(i) In the reflexive relation R defined on set A, $(a, a) \in R$ for every $a \in A$.

Therefore in the digraph of R, there is a loop at each vertex.

(ii) If R is irreflexive, then there cannot be a loop at any vertex.

(iii) The equirement of a symmetric relation viz. $(a_i, a_j) \in R \Rightarrow (a_j, a_i) \in R$ suggests that whenever there is an edge from vertex a_i to vertex a_j, there is also an edge from vertex a_j to vertex a_i.

Also it may or may not have a loop at some vertex.

(iv) In the digraph of asymmetric relation, again there is no loop at any vertex. Further whenever there is an edge from vertex a_i to vertex a_j; there is no edge from vertex a_j to vertex a_i.

(v) If R is antisymmetric relation then for $i \neq j$ there cannot be simultaneously edge from a_i to a_j and an edge from a_j to a_i. Further there is no any restriction about the loop at any vertex.

Example 2.18 : A digraph of a relation R is given below. Comment about R.

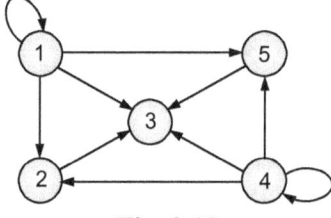

Fig. 2.15

Solution : In the given digraph, there is no loop at the vertex 2 and vertex 5.

∴   2$\cancel{R}$2, 5$\cancel{R}$5

∴   Relation R is not reflexive.

The existence of loop at the vertex 1 and 4 suggests that 1R1, 4R4.

∴   Relation R is not irreflexive.

There are no antiparallel edges in the graph.

   1R2 but 2$\cancel{R}$1

∴   Relation R is not symmetric.

Also 1R1, 4R4 suggests that R is not asymmetric.

The relation R is antisymmetric because from the diagraph, we see that for any two different vertices antiparallel edges are not there. The loop at vertex 1 and 4 is allowed.

Transitivity of a Relation

A relation R on the set A is called transitive if whenever aRb, and bRc then aRc; for a, b, c ∈ A.

Obviously then if there exist a, b, c ∈ A such that aRb and bRc but a$\not R$ c then we can say R is not transitive.

(a) The relation of equality in the set $\mathbb{R}$ of real numbers is transitive since $a = b, b = c \Rightarrow a = c$.

(b) The relation of divisibility in the set $\mathbb{N}$ of all positive integers is transitive. Suppose $a \mid b$ and $b \mid c$.

Then we have $b = ak_1$, and $c = bk_2$ where k_1, k_2 are integers.

Then $c = bk_2 = (ak_1)k_2 = a(k_1k_2) = ak_3$ ∵ $k_3 = k_1k_2$ is integer

∴ $a \mid c$.

(c) Consider now the congruence relation modulo n in the set Z of all integers.

Let $a \equiv b \pmod{n}$ and $b \equiv c \pmod{n}$ where a, b, c ∈ **Z**.

Then by the definition of congruence relation, we have

$n \mid (a - b)$ and $n \mid (b - c)$

∴ $a - b = nk_1$; k_1 is integer

and $b - c = nk_2$; k_2 is integer

Adding these two results,

$$a - b + b - c = nk_1 + nk_2$$

∴ $a - c = n(k_1 + k_2)$

∴ $a - c = nk_3$ ∵ $k_3 = k_1 + k_2$ is integer

∴ $a \equiv c \pmod{n}$

Hence the relation is transitive.

(d) Consider the relation, $R = \{(1, 3), (2, 2), (2, 4), (3, 1), (4, 2)\}$ defined on the set $A = \{1, 2, 3, 4\}$, we see that $(1, 3) \in R, (3, 1) \in R$ but $(1, 1) \notin R$.

Also $(4, 2) \in R, (2, 4) \in R$ but $(4, 4) \notin R$. Hence this relation fails to be transitive.

We note that a relation R on set A is transitive if and only if the following condition holds in M_R.

If $m_{ij} = 1$ and $m_{jk} = 1$ then $m_{ik} = 1$.

The 'if' part of this condition clearly suggests that in M_{R^2} the $i - k^{th}$ entry is 1. So, the transitivity of relation R means that if M_{R^2} has entry 1 in any position, then M_R must have entry 1 in that position.

Hence, if $M_{R^2} = M_R$, then the relation R is transitive. In other words, $M_{R^2} = M_R$ is a sufficient condition for relation R to be transitive.

This condition however is not necessary condition for R to be transitive, i.e. a relation R can be transitive even if $M_{R^2} \neq M_R$.

For example, consider the relation $R = \{(1, 2), (1, 3), (1, 4), (2, 3), (2, 4), (3, 4)\}$ on the set $A = \{1, 2, 3, 4\}$.

In this relation $(a, b) \in R$, $(b, c) \in R$ but $(a,c) \notin R$ such pairs are not there. Therefore R is transitive relation.

Now, $$M_R = \begin{bmatrix} 0 & 1 & 1 & 1 \\ 0 & 0 & 1 & 1 \\ 0 & 0 & 0 & 1 \\ 0 & 0 & 0 & 0 \end{bmatrix}$$

Then $$M_{R^2} = \begin{bmatrix} 0 & 1 & 1 & 1 \\ 0 & 0 & 1 & 1 \\ 0 & 0 & 0 & 1 \\ 0 & 0 & 0 & 0 \end{bmatrix} \odot \begin{bmatrix} 0 & 1 & 1 & 1 \\ 0 & 0 & 1 & 1 \\ 0 & 0 & 0 & 1 \\ 0 & 0 & 0 & 0 \end{bmatrix}$$

$$= \begin{bmatrix} 0 & 0 & 1 & 1 \\ 0 & 0 & 0 & 1 \\ 0 & 0 & 0 & 0 \\ 0 & 0 & 0 & 0 \end{bmatrix}$$

Thus, $M_{R^2} \neq M_R$

A necessary and sufficient condition for a relation R defined on the set A to be transitive is that $R^n \subseteq R$, for all $n \geq 1$. We accept this result without proof.

EXERCISE (2.5)

1. Give example of a relation on the set $A = \{1, 2, 3\}$ which is :
   (a) reflexive and symmetric but not transitive.
   (b) reflexive and transitive but not symmetric.
   (c) symmetric and transitive but not reflexive.
2. L is a set of straight lines in a plane. R is a relation of parallelism of lines and S is a relation of perpendicularity of lines.
   Determine whether or not R, S is (a) reflexive, (b) symmetric, (c) transitive.
3. A relation R on the set
   $A = \{a, b, c, d\}$ is defined as $R = \{(a, a), (a, c), (c, a), (a, b), (c, c), (d, d)\}$.
   Determine whether or not R is reflexive, irreflexive, symmetric, asymmetric, antisymmetric, transitive.
4. The matrix M_R of a relation R on $A = \{1, 2, 3, 4\}$ is $M_R = \begin{bmatrix} 0 & 1 & 0 & 1 \\ 1 & 0 & 1 & 1 \\ 0 & 1 & 0 & 0 \\ 1 & 1 & 0 & 0 \end{bmatrix}$

   Is R (a) symmetric, (b) transitive, (c) antisymmetric ?
5. A digraph of relation R is given below.

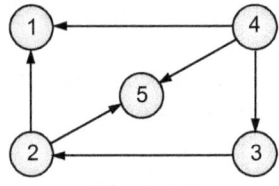

Fig. 2.16

Determine whether or not R is reflexive, symmetric, antisymmetric, transitive.

ANSWERS (2.5)

1. (a) R = {(1, 1), (2, 2), (3, 3), (1, 2), (2, 1), (2, 3), (3, 2)}
   (b) R = {(1, 1), (2, 2), (3, 3), (1, 2), (2, 3), (1, 3)}
   (c) R = {(1, 3), (3, 1), (1, 1), (3, 3)}
2. (a) R is reflexive, S is irreflexive.
   (b) R and S both are symmetric.
   (c) R is transitive but S is not transitive.
3. Not reflexive, not irrefleixve,
   Not symmetric, not asymmetric,
   Not antisymmetric, not transitive.
4. R is symmetric, not transitive, not antisymmetric.
5. Not reflexive, not symmetric, antisymmetric, not transitive.

2.6 Equivalence Relations

A relation R on a set A is called an equivalence relation if it is reflexive, symmetric and transitive.

(a) Let A be the set of all people in Maharashtra state. Let R be the relation defined on A as follows. aRb if and only if a and b belong to the same district of Maharashtra state.

Clearly then for every a ∈ A, a and a belong to the same district i.e. aRa for every a ∈ A. Therefore R is a reflexive. Secondly, if a and b belong to the same district, then b and a belong to the same district. Thus aRb implies bRa. So the relation is symmetric.

Finally, if a and b belong to the same district and also b and c belong to the same district, then a and c belong to the same district. This means aRb and bRc implies aRc. Hence it is transitive relation.

The relation R satisfies all three properties required by an equivalence relation. Hence R is an equivalence relation.

(b) The relation of equality in the set of real numbers is reflexive symmetric and transitive. So the equality relation on $\mathbb{R}$ is an equivalence relation.

(c) The relation 'congruence modulo 3' defined on the set $\mathbb{Z}$ of all integers is an equivalence relation.

(d) Consider the relation of divisibility defined on the set $\mathbb{N}$ of positive integers. It is reflexive and transitive but not symmetric. Therefore it is not equivalence relation.

(e) Let A = {1, 2, 3, 4, 5}. Consider the relation R defined on A as a set of pairs.
   R = {(1, 1), (2, 5), (1, 4), (3, 4), (1, 3), (3, 1), (3, 3), (4, 1), (4, 4), (4, 3), (5, 2), (5, 5), (2, 2)}

One can easily check that R is reflexive, symmetric and transitive, so it is an equivalence relation. Consider the equivalence relation in (e) above. We find the set of those elements of A which are related to 1 under this equivalence relation, and denote it by R(1).

$R(1) = \{x \in A; (1, x) \in R\} = \{1, 4, 3\}$

Similarly, we get

$R(2) = \{x \in A; (2, x) \in R\} = \{5, 2\}$

$R(3) = \{x \in A; (3, x) \in R\} = \{4, 1, 3\}$

$R(4) = \{x \in A; (4, x) \in R\} = \{1, 4, 3\}$

$R(5) = \{x \in A; (5, x) \in R\} = \{2, 5\}$

These sets are called equivalence classes; of respective elements. The equivalence class of an element a i.e. R(a) is also denote by [a].

In the above example, we have $R(1) = [1] = \{1, 4, 3\}$ and $R(1) = R(3) = R(4)$.

Also, $R(2) = R(5)$.

Below, we prove some elementary results. We recall that a partition $\mathbf{P} = \{A_1, A_2, \ldots A_k\}$ of a set $A = \{a_1, a_2, \ldots, a_n\}$ is a collection of non-empty and pairwise disjoint subsets of A, whose union is the set A.

The sets $A_1, A_2, \ldots, A_k$ in a partition are called blocks.

In the above example, $P = \{\{1, 4, 3\}, \{2, 5\}\}$ is a partition consisting of two blocks viz $\{1, 4, 3\}$ and $\{2, 5\}$.

We now prove that any partition of a given set defines an equivalence relation on that set.

Theorem : A partition $\mathbf{P} = \{A_1, A_2, \ldots, A_k\}$ of the set $A = \{a_1, a_2, \ldots, a_n\}$ defines an equivalence relation on A.

Proof : Let $\mathbf{P} = \{A_1, A_2, \ldots, A_k\}$ be the partition of the set $A = \{a_1, a_2, \ldots, a_n\}$.

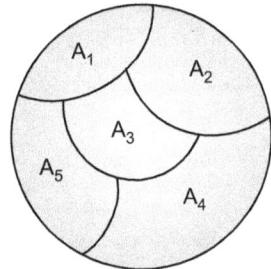

Fig. 2.17

We define a relation R on the set A as below.

$a_i R a_j$ if and only if a_i and a_j are in the same block of partition **P**.

Reflexivity : It is clear that for every i, a_i and a_i belong to the same block of **P**.

∴ $a_i R a_i$ for every i

∴   Relation R is reflexive.

Symmetry : Suppose $a_i R a_j$. Then a_i and a_j are in the same block of **P**. Therefore clearly it follows that a_j and a_i are in the same block of **P**. Therefore $a_j R a_i$.

Thus $a_iRa_j \Rightarrow a_jRa_i$.

∴   Relation R is symmetric.

Transitivity : Suppose a_iRa_j and a_jRa_k.

Then a_i and a_j are in the same block of **P**.

Also a_j and a_k are in the same block of **P**.

Therefore, a_i and a_k must be in the same block of **P** in which a_j lies.

∴ a_iRa_k

Thus $a_iRa_j, a_jRa_k \Rightarrow a_iRa_k$

∴   Relation R is transitive.

The relation R being reflexive, symmetric and transitive, it is an equivalence relation on the set A, determined by the partition **P** of A.

We now proceed to the converse problem. Does every equivalence relation on the set A generates some partition of A ?

The answer to this question is YES. To prove it we need the following result.

Theorem : Let R be an equivalence relation on set A. If a and b are two elements of A, then aRb if and only if $R(a) = R(b)$.

Proof : R is an equivalence relation on set A. So R is reflexive, symmetric and transitive.

Let a, b be two elements in A.

First Part : Suppose $R(a) = R(b)$.

Now, $b \in R(b)$; by reflexivity

∴ $b \in R(a)$; ∵ $R(a) = R(b)$

∴   aRb.

Second Part : Suppose aRb.

Now to prove that $R(a) = R(b)$, we need to prove that

$R(a) \subseteq R(b)$ and $R(b) \subseteq R(a)$.

Let x be any member of $R(a)$. Then we have aRx.

Now aRb and aRx.

$\Rightarrow$ bRa and aRx; ∵ by symmetry of R

$\Rightarrow$ bRx;   ∵ by transitivity of R

$\Rightarrow$ $x \in R(b)$

Thus $x \in R(a) \Rightarrow x \in R(b)$

Therefore $R(a) \subseteq R(b)$.

Again let y be any member of $R(b)$ i.e. $y \in R(b)$.

Then we have bRy.

Now aRb and bRy.

$\Rightarrow$ aRy   ∵ by transitivity of R

$\Rightarrow$ $y \in R(a)$.

We have $y \in R(b) \Rightarrow y \in R(a)$

$\therefore \quad R(b) \subseteq R(a)$

Finally $R(a) \subseteq R(b)$ and $R(b) \subseteq R(a)$

Therefore $R(a) = R(b)$.

Now we are prepared to prove the following theorem.

Theorem : Let R be an equivalence relaion on the set A. Let **P** denote the collection of all disjoint equivalence classes $R(a)$; $a \in A$. Then **P** is a partition of A.

Proof : R is an equivalence relation on set A and **P** is a collection of all disjoint equivalence classes $R(a)$; $a \in A$.

To prove that **P** is a partition of A, we need to prove following two results.

(a) Every element of A is in some $R(a)$.

But by reflexivity of R it is clear that $a \in R(a)$.

(b) When $R(a) \neq R(b)$, then $R(a) \cap R(b) = \phi$.

To prove this result, we make use of contrapositive.

Assume that $R(a) \cap R(b) \neq \phi$.

Then $c \in R(a) \cap R(b)$ for some $c \in A$.

$\therefore \quad c \in R(a)$ and $c \in R(b)$

$\therefore \quad$ aRc and bRc; by symmetry

$\therefore \quad$ aRc and cRb; by symmetry

$\therefore \quad$ aRb; by transitivity

$\therefore \quad R(a) = R(b)$

Thus, (b) part is proved.

Then **P** is a partition of A.

The collection of the sets in **P** above is also called the quotient set of A by R and it is denoted by A/R. Thus **P** = A/R.

SOLVED EXAMPLES

Example 2.19 : If $\{1, 3, 5\}$, $\{2, 4\}$ is a partition of the set $A = \{1, 2, 3, 4, 5\}$, determine the corresponding equivalence relation. **[P.U. 2010]**

Solution : $A = \{1, 2, 3, 4, 5\}$ and $\mathbf{P} = \{\{1, 3, 5\}, \{2, 4\}\}$ is a partition of A.

The blocks in the partition **P** are $\{1, 3, 5\}$ and $\{2, 4\}$.

Define a relation R on A as below. For $a, b \in A$; aRb if and only if a and b belong to the same block. Then we know that R is an equivalence relation.

$\therefore \quad R = \{<1, 1>, <1, 3>, <1, 5>, <3, 1>, <3, 3>, <3, 5>, <5, 1>, <5, 3>, <5, 5>, <2, 2>,$
$\qquad <2, 4>, <4, 2>, <4, 4>\}$

Example 2.20 : Let $A = \{1, 2, 3, 4, 5, 6, 7\}$. Define a relation R on A by aRb iff 3 divides $(a - b)$. Show that R is an equivalence relation. Also, determine the partition generated by R.

(P.U. 2010)

Solution : $A = \{1, 2, 3, 4, 5, 6, 7\}$, aRb iff 3 divides $(a - b)$.

∴ The relation R contains the following pairs
  $R = \{(1, 1), (1, 4), (1, 7), (2, 2), (2, 5), (3,3), (3, 6), (4, 1), (4, 4), (4, 7), (5, 2), (5, 5),$
  $(6, 3), (6, 6), (7, 1), (7, 4), (7, 7)\}$

We see that $(a, a) \in R$ for every $a \in A$.

∴ Relation is reflexive.

If $(a, b) \in R$, then 3 divides.

∴ 3 divides $b - a$. Therefore bRa i.e. $(b, a) \in R$.

∴ Relation is symmetric.

If $(a, b) \in R$ and $(b, c) \in R$, then 3 divides $(a - b)$ and 3 divides $(b - c)$.

∴ 3 divides $[(a - b) + (b - c)]$ i.e. 3 divides $a - c$. Therefore aRc i.e. $(a, c) \in R$.

∴ Relation is transitive.

Hence R is an equivalence relation.

The equivalences of various elements are as below.

  $R(1) = R(4) = R(7) = \{1, 4, 7\}$
  $R(2) = R(5) = \{2, 5\}$
  $R(3) = R(6) = \{3, 6\}$

∴ Partition generated by R is $\{\{1, 4, 7\}, \{2, 5\}, \{3, 6\}\}$.

Example 2.21 : Let $A = \{1, 2, 3, 4, 5, 6\}$.
Let $R = \{(a, b) \mid a \equiv b \pmod{2}\}$. Is R an equivalence relation ? **(P.U. 2010)**

Solution : $A = \{1, 2, 3, 4, 5, 6\}$ for $a, b \in A$; $R = \{(a, b) \mid a \equiv b \pmod{2}\}$.

Reflexivity : Let a be any element of A. Then clearly $a - a = 0$ is divisible by 2.

∴ $a \equiv a \pmod{2}$ for every $a \in A$.

∴ Relation is reflexive.

Symmetry : Suppose $a, b \in A$ such that $a \equiv b \pmod{2}$

Then by definition of congruence relation, 2 divides $a - b$.

Clearly then 2 divides $b - a$

∴ $b \equiv a \pmod{2}$

Thus $a \equiv b \pmod{2} \Rightarrow b \equiv a \pmod{2}$

∴ Relation is symmetric.

Transitivity : Suppose $a, b, c \in A$ such that $a \equiv b \pmod{2}$ and $b \equiv c \pmod{2}$

Then 2 divides $a - b$ and 2 divides $b - c$.

∴ 2 divides $[(a - b) + (b - c)]$

∴ 2 divides $(a - c)$

∴ $a \equiv c \pmod{2}$

∴ Relation is transitive. Hence R is an equivalence relation.

Example 2.22 : Let $A = \{1, 2, 3\}$. Determine whether the relations R and S whose matrices M_R and M_S are given below, are equivalence relations or not.

(i) $M_R = \begin{bmatrix} 1 & 0 & 0 \\ 0 & 1 & 1 \\ 0 & 1 & 1 \end{bmatrix}$, (ii) $M_S = \begin{bmatrix} 1 & 0 & 1 \\ 0 & 1 & 0 \\ 1 & 0 & 0 \end{bmatrix}$

Solution : (i) $M_R = \begin{bmatrix} 1 & 0 & 0 \\ 0 & 1 & 1 \\ 0 & 1 & 1 \end{bmatrix}$ Here all the diagonal elements are 1.

∴ 1R1, 2R2, 3R3

∴ R is reflexive.

The matrix M_R is symmetric $a_{ij} = a_{ji}$ for every i and j.

∴ Relation R is symmetric.

Now. $M_{R^2} = \begin{bmatrix} 1 & 0 & 0 \\ 0 & 1 & 1 \\ 0 & 1 & 1 \end{bmatrix} \odot \begin{bmatrix} 1 & 0 & 0 \\ 0 & 1 & 1 \\ 0 & 1 & 1 \end{bmatrix} = \begin{bmatrix} 1 & 0 & 0 \\ 0 & 1 & 1 \\ 0 & 1 & 1 \end{bmatrix}$

$M_{R^2} = M_R$ ∴ Relation R is transitive.

Therefore R is an equivalence relation.

(ii) $M_S = \begin{bmatrix} 1 & 0 & 1 \\ 0 & 1 & 0 \\ 1 & 0 & 0 \end{bmatrix}$ Here 3, 3 entry is 0. Therefore, relation S is not reflexive.

M_S is a symmetric matrix.

∴ Relation is a symmetric matrix.

Now 3, 1 entry is 1 and 1, 3 entry is 1.

∴ 3S1 and 1S3 but 3$\cancel{S}$3

∴ S is fails to be transitive.

∴ S is symmetric but not reflexive, not transitive.

∴ S is not an equivalence relation

Example 2.23 : A relation

$R = \{<1, 1>, <1, 2>, <1, 4>, <2, 1>, <2, 2>, <3, 2>, <3, 3>, <4, 4>\}$ is defined over the set $A = \{1, 2, 3, 4\}$. Is R and equivalence relation ?

Solution : $A = \{1, 2, 3, 4\}$

$R = \{<1, 1>, <1, 2>, <1, 4>, <2, 1>, <2, 2>, <3, 2>, <3, 3>, <4, 4>\}$

We see that each element of A is related with itself according to relation R.

$<1, 1> \in R, <2, 2> \in R, <3, 3> \in R, <4, 4> \in R$.

Therefore R is reflexive.

Now $<1, 4> \in R$ but $<4, 1> \notin R$

Also $<3, 2> \in R$ but $<2, 3> \notin R$

Therefore relation R is not symmetric.

Again $<2, 1> \in R$ and $<1, 4> \in R$ but $<2, 4> \notin R$

Also, $<3, 2> \in R$ and $<2, 1> \in R$ but $<3, 1> \notin R$.

Therefore R is not transitive. Thus R is reflexive, not symmetric, not transitive.

Therefore R is not an equivalence relation.

Example 2.24 : If A = {a, e, i, o, u} and **P** = {{a, i}, {e, o}, {u}} is a partition of A, find the equivalence relation determined by **P**.

Solution : The set A = {a, e, i, o, u} and partition **P** = {{a, i}, {e, o}, {u}}.

We know that R is an equivalence relation determine by the partition **P** when each element of the same block is related to each element, including itself of that block.

∴ R = {(a, a), (a, i), (i, a), (i, i), (e, e), (e, o), (o, e), (o, o), (u, u)}

This is required equivalence relation.

Example 2.25 : Let X = {a, b, c, d, e} and C = {{a, b}, {c}, {d, e}}. Show that partition 'C' defines an equivalence relation on X.

Solution : X = {a, b, c, d, e} and C = {{a, b}, {c}, {d, e}} is a partition of X. The blocks in the partition C are {a, b}, {c} and {d, e}.

Consider the relation R on X such that two elements of X are related iff they belong to the same block. Then we have,

R = {(a, a), (a, b), (b, a), (b, b), (c, c), (d, d), (d, e), (e, d), (e, e)}

This relation R is an equivalence relation on set X, determined by partition C.

Example 2.26 : Let S = {1, 2, 3, 4} and A = S × S. Define a relation R on A = S × S as follows.

(a, b) R (c, d) if and only if a + b = c + d.

(a) Show that R is an equivalence relation.

(b) Compute A/R.

Solution : Two pairs (a, b) and (c, d) are R-related if and only if a + b = c + d.

(a) Reflexivity : Let (a, b) be any pair belonging to A = S × S.

We have a + b = a + b.

∴ (a, b) R (a, b)

∴ Relation R is reflexive.

Symmetry : Let (a, b) and (c, d) be two pairs in A such that (a, b) R (c, d).

Then a + b = c + d; by definition of R.

∴ c + d = a + b

∴ (c, d) R (a, b)

∴ Relation R is symmetric.

Transitivity : Let (a, b), (c, d), (e, f) be three pairs in A such that (a, b) R (c, d) and (c, d) R (e, f).

Then $a + b = c + d$ and $c + d = e + f$; by definition of R

∴ $a + b = e + f$

∴ $(a, b)\ R\ (e, f)$

∴   Relation R is transitive. The relation R being reflexive, symmetric and transitive it is an equivalence relation on $A = S \times S$.

(b) Now $A = S \times S$ consist of $4 \times 4 = 16$ pairs; $(1, 1)\ (1, 2), \ldots, (4, 3), (4, 4)$.

Consider the first pair $(1, 1)$, we have $1 + 1 = 2$.

Then for any pair $(a, b) \in A$, we have $a + b = 2$ only when $a = 1$, and $b = 1$.

∴   Equivalence class of $(1, 1)$ consists of $(1, 1)$ itself.

$$R((1, 1)) = \{(1, 1)\}$$

Consider the next pair $(1, 2)$ in A. We have $1 + 2 = 3$, then for any pair $(a, b) \in A$, $a + b = 3$ only when $a = 1, b = 2$ and $a = 2, b = 1$.

∴   Equivalence class of $(1, 2)$ consists of two pairs.

$$R((1, 2)) = \{(1, 2), (2, 1)\} = R((2, 1))$$

After continuing in this way we get,

$$R((1, 3)) = \{(1, 3), (2, 2), (3, 1)\}$$
$$R((1, 4)) = \{(1, 4), (2, 3), (3, 2), (4, 1)\}$$
$$= R((2, 3)) = R((3, 2)) = R((4, 1))$$
$$R((2, 4)) = \{(2, 4), (4, 2), (3, 3)\}$$
$$= R((4, 2)) = R((3, 3))$$
$$R((3, 4)) = \{(3, 4), (4, 3)\} = R((4, 3))$$
$$R((4, 4)) = \{(4, 4)\}$$

∴ $A/R = \{A_1 = \{(1, 1)\}, A_2 = \{(1, 2), (2, 1)\}$
$A_3 = \{(1, 3), (2, 2), (3, 1)\}$
$A_4 = \{(1, 4), (2, 3), (3, 2), (4, 1)\}$
$A_5 = \{(2, 4), (4, 2), (3, 3)\}\ A_6 = \{(3, 4), (4, 3)\}$
$A_7 = \{(4, 4)\}\ \}$

Example 2.27 : Let R be a transitive and reflexive relation on A. Let T be a relation on A such that (a, b) is in T if and only if both (a, b) and (b, a) are in R. Show that T is an equivalence relation on A.

Solution : Given : R is transitive and reflexive.

Also given; $(a, b) \in T$ if and only if (a, b) and (b, a) are in R.

Reflexivity of T : Let a be any element of A. Then by reflexivity of R, we have

$(a, a) \in R$ and $(a, a) \in R$.

∴ $(a, a) \in T$; by definition of T.

∴   Relation T is reflexive.

Symmetry of T : Let a and b be two elements of A such that $(a, b) \in T$.

$(a, b) \in T$ $\therefore (a, b) \in R$ and $(b, a) \in R$
$\therefore (b, a) \in R$ and $(a, b) \in R$
$\therefore (b, a) \in T$ by definition of T.

Thus, $(a, b) \in T \Rightarrow (b, a) \in T$

$\therefore$ Relation T is symmetric.

Transitivity of T : Let a, b, c be elements of A such that $(a, b) \in T$ and $(b, c) \in T$.
Then $(a, b) \in R, (b, a) \in R, (b, c) \in R, (c, b) \in R$ by definition of T.
Now by transitivity of R, we have $(a, b) \in R, (b, c) \in R \Rightarrow (a, c) \in R$.
Also $(c, b) \in R, (b, a) \in R \Rightarrow (c, a) \in R$.
Finally, $(a, c) \in R, (c, a) \in R \Rightarrow (a, c) \in T$;   by definition of T.
Thus, $(a, b) \in T, (b, c) \in T \Rightarrow (a, c) \in T$.
Hence the relation T is transitive.

We proved that relation T is reflexive, symmetric and transitive. Therefore it is an equivalence relation.

Example 2.28 : If R and S are equivalence relations on a set A, prove that $R \cap S$ is an equivalence relation on A.   **(P.U. 2011)**

Solution : Given that R and S are equivalence relations on set A.

$\therefore$ R and S both are reflexive, symmetric and transitive.

Now consider the relation $R \cap S$.

Reflexivity : We have for any $a \in A$ that $(a, a) \in R$ and $(a, a) \in S$ by reflexivity of R and S.

$\therefore$ $(a, a) \in R \cap S$ for every $a \in A$.

$\therefore$ $R \cap S$ is reflexive.

Symmetry : Suppose $a \, R \cap S \, b$. Then $(a,b) \in R \cap S$.

$\therefore$ $(a, b) \in R$ and $(a, b) \in S$

$\therefore$ $(b, a) \in R$ and $(b, a) \in S$; by symmetry of R and S

$\therefore$ $(b, a) \in R \cap S$

$\therefore$ $b \, R \cap S \, a$

Hence $R \cap S$ is symmetric.

Transitivity : Suppose $a \, R \cap S \, b$ and $b \, R \cap S \, c$. Then $(a, b) \in R \cap S$ and $(b, c) \in R \cap S$

$\therefore$ $(a, b) \in R, (a, b) \in S, (b, c) \in R, (b, c) \in S$.

Now $(a, b) \in R, (b, c) \in R$. $\therefore (a, c) \in R$ by transitivity of R.

Also $(a, b) \in S, (b, c) \in S \Rightarrow (a, c) \in S$ by transitivity of S.

Therefore $(a, c) \in R \cap S$.

$\therefore$ $a \, R \cap S \, c$

$\therefore$ Relation $R \cap S$ is transitive. Thus finally, $R \cap S$ being reflexive, symmetric and transitive, it is an equivalence relation.

EXERCISE (2.6)

1. By stating the required result, determine the equivalence relation on the set A, by the partition **P**.

    (a) A = {2, 4, 6, 8, 9, 10}

    P = {{2, 8, 9}, {6, 10}, {4}}

    (b) A = {p, q, r, s, t}

    P = {{p}, {q}, {r, s, t}}

    (c) A = {3, 4, 5, 6, 7, 8, 9}

    P = {{3, 7}, {4, 8}, {5, 9}, {6}}

2. A relation R is defined on the set A = {1, 3, 5, 6, 7, 9} as below. aRb if and only if a − b is divisible by 4. Determine the relation R. Show that it is an equivalence relation. Determine the partition of A generated by R. Draw the digraph of R.

3. Let A = {1, 2, 3, 4, 5, 6, 7} and R = {<x, y> | x − y is divisible by 3}, show that R is an equivalence relation. Draw the graph of R.   **[P.U. 2009]**

4. R and S are two relations on A = {1, 2, 3} whose matrices are given below.

    $$M_R = \begin{bmatrix} 1 & 1 & 0 \\ 1 & 1 & 0 \\ 0 & 0 & 1 \end{bmatrix}, \quad M_S = \begin{bmatrix} 1 & 0 & 1 \\ 0 & 1 & 0 \\ 1 & 0 & 1 \end{bmatrix}$$

    (a) Show that R and S both are equivalence relations.

    (b) Write R ∩ S as a set of ordered pairs. Is R ∩ S an equivalence relation ?

    (c) Write R ∪ S as a set of ordered pairs. Is R ∪ S an equivalence relation ?

5. A relation R is defined on the A = {1, 2, 3, 4} by the matrix $M_R = \begin{bmatrix} 1 & 0 & 0 & 0 \\ 0 & 1 & 1 & 1 \\ 0 & 1 & 1 & 1 \\ 0 & 1 & 1 & 1 \end{bmatrix}$.

    Show that R is an equivalence relation. Compute A/R.

6. Let S = {1, 2, 3, 4} and A = S × S. A relation R is defined on A = S × S as follows.

    (a, b) R (c, d) if and only if ad = bc.

    (a) Show that R is an equivalence relation.

    (b) Compute A/R.

ANSWERS (2.6)

1. (a) R = {(2, 2), (2, 8), (2, 9), (8, 2), (8, 8), (8, 9), (9, 2), (9, 8), (9, 9), (6, 6), (6, 10), (10, 6), (10, 10), (4, 4)}

    (b) R = {(p, p), (q, q), (r, r), (r, s), (r, t), (s, r), (s, s), (s, t), (t, r), (t, s), (t, t)}

    (c) R = {(3, 3), (3, 7), (7, 3), (7, 7), (4, 4), (4, 8), (8, 4), (8, 8), (5, 5), (5, 9), (9, 5), (9, 9), (6, 6)}

2. R = {(1, 1), (1, 5), (1, 9), (3, 3), (3, 7), (5, 1), (5, 5), (5, 9), (6, 6), (7, 3), (7, 7), (9, 1), (9, 5), (9, 9)}
P = {{1, 5, 9}, {3, 7}, {6}}

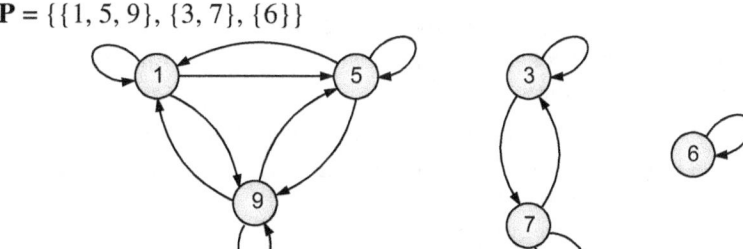

Fig. 2.18

3. R = {(1, 1), (1, 4), (1, 7), (4, 1),(4, 4), (4, 7), (7, 1), (7, 4), (7, 7), (2, 2), (2, 5), (5, 2), (5, 5), (3, 3), (3, 6), (6, 3), (6, 6)}

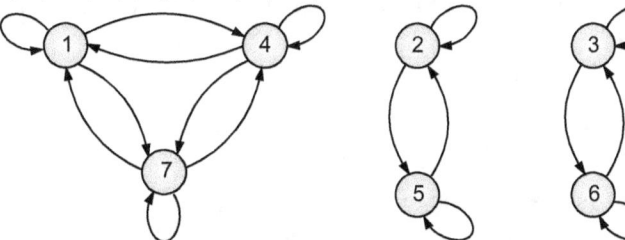

Fig. 2.19

4. (b) R ∩ S = {(1, 1), (2, 2), (3, 3)} It is an equivalence relation.
   (c) R ∪ S = {(1, 1), (2, 2), (3, 3), (1, 2), (2, 1), (1, 3), (3, 1)}
   It is not equivalence relation (3, 1) ∈ R ∪ S, (1, 2) ∈ R ∪ S but (3, 2) ∉ R ∪ S.

5. A/R = {A_1 = {(1, 1)},
   A_2 = {(2, 2), (2, 3), (2, 4), (3, 2), (3, 3), (3, 4), (4, 2), (4, 3), (4, 4)}

6. A/R = {A_1 = {(1, 1)},
   A_2 = {(1, 2), (2, 4)}
   A_3 = {(1, 3)}
   A_4 = {(1, 4)}
   A_5 = {(2, 1), (4, 2)}
   A_6 = {(2, 2), (3, 3), (4, 4)}
   A_7 = {(2, 3)}
   A_8 = {(3, 1)}
   A_9 = {(3, 2)}
   A_{10} = {(3, 4)}
   A_{11} = {(4, 1)}
   A_{12} = {(4, 3)}}

2.7 Closure of a Relation

Consider a relation R on the set $A = \{a_1, a_2, ..., a_n\}$. If for some or few values of i, $1 \leq i \leq n$ it happens that the pair $(a_i, a_i) \notin R$, then the relation R fails to be reflexive. Now we extend the relation R by adding such missing pairs so that the new relation is reflexive. It is called reflexive closure of the relation.

Likewise if a pair $(a_i, a_j) \in R$ but $(a_j, a_i) \notin R$, then R fails to be symmetric. If R is extended by adding such minimum pairs, then the resulting relation becomes symmetric.

For example let,
$$A = \{1, 2, 3, 4, 5\}$$
and
$$R = \{(1, 2), (5, 4), (3, 3), (5, 5), (4, 5), (5, 1), (3, 2)\}$$

This relation is not reflexive because $(1, 1) \notin R$, $(2, 2) \notin R$, $(4, 4) \notin R$. We add these missing pairs to R and get the relation.

$R_1 = \{(1, 2), (5, 4), (3, 3), (5, 5), (4, 5), (5, 1), (3, 2), (1, 1), (2, 2), (4, 4)\}$ which is reflexive closure of R.

Again $(1, 2) \in R$ but $(2, 1) \notin R$
$(5, 1) \in R$ but $(1, 5) \notin R$
$(3, 2) \in R$ but $(2, 3) \notin R$

We add these missing pairs to the relation R and get,

$R_2 = \{(1, 2), (5, 4), (3, 3), (5, 5), (4, 5), (5, 1), (3, 2), (2, 1), (1, 5), (2, 3)\}$

which is symmetric closure of R.

It may be noted that it is not sometimes possible to find the reflexive closure or symmetric closure of a given relation R.

We now proceed to transitive closure of a relation. We recall that the transitivity needs whenever $(a_i, a_j) \in R$ and $(a_j, a_k) \in R$, then $(a_i, a_k) \in R$.

In the relation R discussed above, we note that $(4, 5) \in R$, $(5, 4) \in R$ but $(4, 4) \notin R$.

Again $(4, 5) \in R$, $(5, 1) \in R$ but $(4, 1) \notin R$.

$(5, 1) \in R$, $(1, 2) \in R$ but $(5, 2) \notin R$.

After adding the three missing terms to R, it is extended to

$R_3 = \{(1, 2), (5, 4), (3, 3), (5, 5), (4, 5), (5, 1), (3, 2), (4, 4), (4, 1), (5, 2)\}$.

R_3 is now a transitive relation. Here only three new terms are required to convert the relation R into a transitive one.

R_3 is transitive closure of R.

To find the transitive closure of a given relation, we use Warshall's algorithm.

In this algorithm, we start with the matrix W_0 of given relation R. We then go on improving this matrix step by step; $W_0 \to W_1 \to W_2 \to W_{k-1} \to W_k \to ..... \to W_n$, where n denotes the number of elements in the set A on which the relation R is defined. For the improvement from W_{k-1} to W_k the following procedure is adopted. Suppose entries of W_{k-1} are denoted by s_{ij} and that of W_k be t_{ij}.

All the entries 1 in W_{k-1} will appear as 1 in W_k i.e. if $s_{ij} = 1$ then $t_{ij} = 1$.

In addition some entries 0 in W_{k-1} will be converted to 1 in W_k. For this we use the fact that if $s_{ik} = 1$ and $s_{kj} = 1$ then $t_{ij} = 1$; which is the requirement of transitivity. In this process the matrix W_n is the matrix of transitive closure of the relation R.

SOLVED EXAMPLES

Example 2.29 : Let A = {1, 2, 3} and R = {<1, 1>, <1, 2>, <1, 3>, <2, 3>, <3, 1>, <3, 2>}.

Find the transitive closure by using Warshall's algorithm. **(P.U. 2011)**

Solution : A = {1, 2, 3}

R = {(1, 1), (1, 2), (1, 3), (2, 3), (3, 1), (3, 2)}.

The matrix of given relation is

$$W_0 = \begin{bmatrix} 1 & 1 & 1 \\ 0 & 0 & 1 \\ 1 & 1 & 0 \end{bmatrix}$$

Step 1 : To find W_1 ∴ k = 1

All entries 1 in W_0 appear as they are, in W_1.

In addition $s_{31} = 1$ and $s_{13} = 1$ ∴ $t_{33} = 1$

∴ $$W_1 = \begin{bmatrix} 1 & 1 & 1 \\ 0 & 0 & 1 \\ 1 & 1 & 1 \end{bmatrix}$$

Step 2 : To find W_2 ∴ k = 2

$s_{32} = 1$ and $s_{23} = 1$ implies $t_{33} = 1$

$s_{12} = 1$ and $s_{23} = 1$ implies $t_{13} = 1$

∴ $$W_2 = \begin{bmatrix} 1 & 1 & 1 \\ 0 & 0 & 1 \\ 1 & 1 & 1 \end{bmatrix}$$

Step 3 : To find W_3 ∴ k = 3

$s_{13} = 1$ and $s_{31} = 1$ implies $t_{11} = 1$

$s_{22} = 1$ and $s_{31} = 1$ implies $t_{21} = 1$

$s_{23} = 1$ and $s_{32} = 1$ implies $t_{22} = 1$

$s_{23} = 1$ and $s_{33} = 1$ implies $t_{23} = 1$

∴ $$W_3 = \begin{bmatrix} 1 & 1 & 1 \\ 1 & 1 & 1 \\ 1 & 1 & 1 \end{bmatrix}$$

∴ Transitive closure is

R* = {(1, 1), (1, 2), (1, 3), (2, 1), (2, 2), (2, 3), (3, 1), (3, 2), (3, 3)}

Example 2.30 : Use Warshall's algorithm, to find the transitive closure of the relation R = {(1, 2), (2, 3), (3, 4), (2, 1)} on A = {1, 2, 3, 4}. **(P.U. 2009)**

Solution : A = {1, 2, 3, 4} and R = {(1, 2), (2, 3), (3, 4), (2, 1)}.

The matrix of the given relation is

$$W_0 = \begin{bmatrix} 0 & 1 & 0 & 0 \\ 1 & 0 & 1 & 0 \\ 0 & 0 & 0 & 1 \\ 0 & 0 & 0 & 0 \end{bmatrix}$$

Step 1 : To find W_1 ∴ k = 1

$s_{21} = 1$ and $s_{12} = 1$ ∴ $t_{22} = 1$

∴ $$W_1 = \begin{bmatrix} 0 & 1 & 0 & 0 \\ 1 & 1 & 1 & 0 \\ 0 & 0 & 0 & 1 \\ 0 & 0 & 0 & 0 \end{bmatrix}$$

Step 2 : To find W_2 ∴ k = 2

$s_{12} = 1$ and $s_{21} = 1$ ∴ $t_{11} = 1$

$s_{12} = 1$ and $s_{22} = 1$ ∴ $t_{12} = 1$

$s_{12} = 1$ and $s_{23} = 1$ ∴ $t_{13} = 1$

∴ $$W_2 = \begin{bmatrix} 1 & 1 & 1 & 0 \\ 1 & 1 & 1 & 0 \\ 0 & 0 & 0 & 1 \\ 0 & 0 & 0 & 0 \end{bmatrix}$$

Step 3 : To find W_3 ∴ k = 3

$s_{13} = 1$ and $s_{34} = 1$ ∴ $t_{14} = 1$

Also $s_{23} = 1$ and $s_{34} = 1$ ∴ $t_{24} = 1$

∴ $$W_3 = \begin{bmatrix} 1 & 1 & 1 & 1 \\ 1 & 1 & 1 & 1 \\ 0 & 0 & 0 & 1 \\ 0 & 0 & 0 & 0 \end{bmatrix}$$

Step 4 : To find W_4 ∴ k = 4

Since fourth row has all zeros, there is no further improvement in W_3 ∴ $W_4 = W_3$

∴ $$W_4 = \begin{bmatrix} 1 & 1 & 1 & 1 \\ 1 & 1 & 1 & 1 \\ 0 & 0 & 0 & 1 \\ 0 & 0 & 0 & 0 \end{bmatrix}$$

∴ The transitive closure of a given relation is

R* = {(1, 1), (1, 2), (1, 3), (1, 4), (2, 1), (2, 2), (2, 3), (2, 4), (3, 4)}

Example 2.31 : Obtain the transitive closure of the following relational matrix using Warshall's algorithm.

$$M_R = \begin{bmatrix} 1 & 0 & 0 & 1 \\ 1 & 1 & 0 & 0 \\ 0 & 0 & 1 & 0 \\ 0 & 0 & 0 & 1 \end{bmatrix}$$

(P.U. 2011)

Solution : The matrix of the given relation is

$$W_0 = \begin{bmatrix} 1 & 0 & 0 & 1 \\ 1 & 1 & 0 & 0 \\ 0 & 0 & 1 & 0 \\ 0 & 0 & 0 & 1 \end{bmatrix}$$

Step 1 : To find W_1 $\therefore$ $k = 1$

$s_{11} = 1$ and $s_{11} = 1$ $\therefore$ $t_{11} = 1$
$s_{11} = 1$ and $s_{14} = 1$ $\therefore$ $t_{14} = 1$
$s_{21} = 1$ and $s_{11} = 1$ $\therefore$ $t_{21} = 1$
$s_{21} = 1$ and $s_{14} = 1$ $\therefore$ $t_{24} = 1$

$\therefore$ $W_1 = \begin{bmatrix} 1 & 0 & 0 & 1 \\ 1 & 1 & 0 & 1 \\ 0 & 0 & 1 & 0 \\ 0 & 0 & 0 & 1 \end{bmatrix}$

Step 2 : To find W_2 $\therefore$ $k = 2$

$s_{22} = 1$ and $s_{21} = 1$ $\therefore$ $t_{21} = 1$
$s_{22} = 1$ and $s_{22} = 1$ $\therefore$ $t_{22} = 1$

$\therefore$ $W_2 = \begin{bmatrix} 1 & 0 & 0 & 1 \\ 1 & 1 & 0 & 1 \\ 0 & 0 & 1 & 0 \\ 0 & 0 & 0 & 1 \end{bmatrix}$

Step 3 : To find W_3 $\therefore$ $k = 3$

$s_{33} = 1$ and $s_{33} = 1$ $\therefore$ $t_{33} = 1$

$\therefore$ $W_3 = \begin{bmatrix} 1 & 0 & 0 & 1 \\ 1 & 1 & 0 & 1 \\ 0 & 0 & 1 & 0 \\ 0 & 0 & 0 & 1 \end{bmatrix}$

Step 4 : To find W_4 $\therefore$ $k = 4$

$s_{14} = 1$ and $s_{44} = 1$ $\therefore$ $t_{14} = 1$
$s_{24} = 1$ and $s_{44} = 1$ $\therefore$ $t_{24} = 1$
$s_{44} = 1$ and $s_{44} = 1$ $\therefore$ $t_{44} = 1$

$\therefore$ $W_4 = \begin{bmatrix} 1 & 0 & 0 & 1 \\ 1 & 1 & 0 & 1 \\ 0 & 0 & 1 & 0 \\ 0 & 0 & 0 & 1 \end{bmatrix}$

Relation R = {(1, 1), (1, 4), (2, 1), (2, 2), (3, 3), (4, 4)}. Its transitive closure is
R* = {(1, 1), (1, 4), (2, 1), (2, 2), (2, 4), (3, 3), (4, 4)}

Example 2.32 : Use Warshall's algorithm to find the transitive closure of the relation.

R = {(1, 2), (1, 3), (1, 4), (2, 3), (2, 4), (3, 4)} on A = {1, 2, 3, 4}.

Solution : The matrix of the relation is

$$W_0 = \begin{bmatrix} 0 & 1 & 1 & 1 \\ 0 & 0 & 1 & 1 \\ 0 & 0 & 0 & 1 \\ 0 & 0 & 0 & 0 \end{bmatrix}$$

Step 1 : To find W_1 ∴ k = 1

In the first column, there are all zeros.

∴ $$W_1 = W_0 = \begin{bmatrix} 0 & 1 & 1 & 1 \\ 0 & 0 & 1 & 1 \\ 0 & 0 & 0 & 1 \\ 0 & 0 & 0 & 0 \end{bmatrix}$$

Step 2 : To find W_2 ∴ k = 2

$s_{12} = 1$ and $s_{23} = 1$ ∴ $t_{13} = 1$

$s_{12} = 1$ and $s_{24} = 1$ ∴ $t_{14} = 1$

∴ $$W_2 = \begin{bmatrix} 0 & 1 & 1 & 1 \\ 0 & 0 & 1 & 1 \\ 0 & 0 & 0 & 1 \\ 0 & 0 & 0 & 0 \end{bmatrix}$$

Step 3 : To find W_3 ∴ k = 3

$s_{13} = 1$ and $s_{34} = 1$ ∴ $t_{14} = 1$

$s_{23} = 1$ and $s_{34} = 1$ ∴ $t_{24} = 1$

∴ $$W_3 = \begin{bmatrix} 0 & 1 & 1 & 1 \\ 0 & 0 & 1 & 1 \\ 0 & 0 & 0 & 1 \\ 0 & 0 & 0 & 0 \end{bmatrix}$$

Step 4 : To find W_4 ∴ k = 4

Since fourth row contains all zeros, there is no further improvement in W_3.

∴ $$W_4 = \begin{bmatrix} 0 & 1 & 1 & 1 \\ 0 & 0 & 1 & 1 \\ 0 & 0 & 0 & 1 \\ 0 & 0 & 0 & 0 \end{bmatrix}$$

∴ Transitive closure of relation R is

R* = {(1, 2), (1, 3), (1, 4), (2, 3), (2, 4), (3, 4)}

Here R* = R

Example 2.33 : By using Warshall's algorithm find the transitive closure of the relation
R = {(1, 1), (1, 4), (2, 2), (2, 3), (3, 2), (3, 3), (4, 1), (4, 4)} defined on the set
A = {1, 2, 3, 4}.

Solution : The matrix of the relation is

$$W_0 = \begin{bmatrix} 1 & 0 & 0 & 1 \\ 0 & 1 & 1 & 0 \\ 0 & 1 & 1 & 0 \\ 1 & 0 & 0 & 1 \end{bmatrix}$$

Step 1 : To find W_1 ∴ k = 1

$s_{11} = 1$ and $s_{11} = 1$ ∴ $t_{11} = 1$
$s_{11} = 1$ and $s_{14} = 1$ ∴ $t_{14} = 1$
$s_{41} = 1$ and $s_{11} = 1$ ∴ $t_{41} = 1$
$s_{41} = 1$ and $s_{14} = 1$ ∴ $t_{44} = 1$

∴ $$W_1 = \begin{bmatrix} 1 & 0 & 0 & 1 \\ 0 & 1 & 1 & 0 \\ 0 & 1 & 1 & 0 \\ 1 & 0 & 0 & 1 \end{bmatrix}$$

Step 2 : To find W_2 ∴ k = 2

$s_{22} = 1$ and $s_{22} = 1$ ∴ $t_{22} = 1$
$s_{22} = 1$ and $s_{23} = 1$ ∴ $t_{23} = 1$
$s_{32} = 1$ and $s_{22} = 1$ ∴ $t_{32} = 1$
$s_{32} = 1$ and $s_{23} = 1$ ∴ $t_{33} = 1$

∴ $$W_2 = \begin{bmatrix} 1 & 0 & 0 & 1 \\ 0 & 1 & 1 & 0 \\ 0 & 1 & 1 & 0 \\ 1 & 0 & 0 & 1 \end{bmatrix}$$

Step 3 : To find W_3 ∴ k = 3

$s_{23} = 1$ and $s_{32} = 1$ ∴ $t_{22} = 1$
$s_{23} = 1$ and $s_{33} = 1$ ∴ $t_{23} = 1$
$s_{33} = 1$ and $s_{32} = 1$ ∴ $t_{32} = 1$
$s_{33} = 1$ and $s_{33} = 1$ ∴ $t_{33} = 1$

∴ $$W_3 = \begin{bmatrix} 1 & 0 & 0 & 1 \\ 0 & 1 & 1 & 0 \\ 0 & 1 & 1 & 0 \\ 1 & 0 & 0 & 1 \end{bmatrix}$$

Step 4 : To find W_4 ∴ k = 4

$s_{14} = 1$ and $s_{41} = 1$ ∴ $t_{11} = 1$
$s_{14} = 1$ and $s_{44} = 1$ ∴ $t_{14} = 1$
$s_{44} = 1$ and $s_{41} = 1$ ∴ $t_{41} = 1$
$s_{44} = 1$ and $s_{44} = 1$ ∴ $t_{44} = 1$

$$W_4 = \begin{bmatrix} 1 & 0 & 0 & 1 \\ 0 & 1 & 1 & 0 \\ 0 & 1 & 1 & 0 \\ 1 & 0 & 0 & 1 \end{bmatrix}$$

Transitive closure of R is

R* = R = {(1, 1), (1, 4), (2, 2), (2, 3), (3, 2), (3, 3), (4, 1), (4, 4)}

EXERCISE (2.7)

1. By using Warshall's algorithm find the transitive closure of the relation :
   (a) R = {(1, 2), (2, 3), (3, 4)} defined on A = {(1, 2, 3, 4}.
   (b) R = {(1, 3), (1, 1), (3, 1), (1, 2), (3, 3), (4, 4)} defined on A = {1, 2, 3, 4}
   (c) R = {(1, 1), (1, 2), (2, 2), (3, 3), (4, 2), (4, 4)} defined on A = {1, 2, 3, 4}
   (d) R = {(1, 3), (2, 1), (2, 3), (3, 1)} defined on A = {1, 2, 3}.

2. By using Warshall's algorithm find the transitive closure of the relation represented by the matrix
$$\begin{bmatrix} 0 & 0 & 0 & 1 \\ 0 & 0 & 0 & 0 \\ 0 & 1 & 0 & 0 \\ 0 & 0 & 1 & 0 \end{bmatrix}$$

ANSWERS (2.7)

1. (a) R* = {(1, 2), (2, 3), (3, 4), (1, 3), (2, 4), (1, 4)}
   (b) R* = {(1, 3), (1, 1), (3, 1), (1, 2), (3, 3), (4, 4), (3, 2)}
   (c) R* = R
   (d) R* = {(1, 3), (2, 1), (2, 3), (3, 1), (1, 1), (3, 3)}
2. R* = {(1, 2), (1, 3), (1, 4), (3, 2), (4, 2), (4, 3)}

2.8 Compatibility Relation

A relation defined on the set A, which is reflexive and symmetric is called a compatibility relation.

It is then clear that every equivalence relation is compatibility relation.

Consider the relation R defined on A = {a, b, c, d, e}.

R = {(a, a), (a, b), (a, c), (b, a), (b, b), (b, c), (c, a), (c, b), (c, c), (d, d), (d, e), (e, d), (e, e)}

The matrix of this relation is

$$M_R = \begin{bmatrix} 1 & 1 & 1 & 0 & 0 \\ 1 & 1 & 1 & 0 & 0 \\ 1 & 1 & 1 & 0 & 0 \\ 0 & 0 & 0 & 1 & 1 \\ 0 & 0 & 0 & 1 & 1 \end{bmatrix}$$

All the diagonal elements are 1. Therefore xRx for every $x \in A$. Hence R is reflexive. Further the matrix M_R is a symmetric matrix, $a_{ij} = a_{ji}$ for every i and j. Therefore R is a symmetric relation. Hence R is a compatibility relation.

The above relation fails to be transitive since aRc and cRd but a$\not R$d.

Hence it is not an equivalence relation.

Consider again the set A = {All students in a class} and a relation R be defined on A as below, $(a, b) \in R$ iff a is a friend of b.

It is clear that this relation is reflexive and symmetric. However, if a friend of b and b is a friend of c, it does not necessarily imply that a is a friend of c.

Thus, $(a, b) \in R$, $(b, c) \in R \not\Rightarrow (a, c) \in R$.

Therefore R is not a transitive relation. Finally we conclude that in this example, R is a compatibility relation but not an equivalence relation.

Let now A be the given set. Then a collection $\{A_1, A_2, ..., A_k\}$ of subsets of A is called covering of A if $\bigcup_{i=1}^{k} A_i = A$.

For example if A = {1, 2, 3, 4, 5, 6}, then A_1 = {1, 2, 4, 5}, A_2 = {1, 3, 4}

A_3 = {2, 3, 4, 6} form the covering of A.

A maximal compatibility block of the set A is a subset B of A such that :

(i)   each element of B, is R-related with each element of B, and

(ii) no element of A − B is R-related with every element of B.

As an illustration consider the relation R = {(1, 1), (2, 2), (3, 3), (4, 4), (5, 5), (6, 6), (1, 2), (2, 1), (2, 3), (3, 2), (2, 4), (4, 2), (3, 5), (5, 3), (3, 6), (6, 3), (4, 5), (5, 4), (4, 6), (6, 4), (5, 6), (6, 5)} defined on the set A = {1, 2, 3, 4, 5, 6}.

Consider the set B = {3, 5, 6}. Each element of B is related with each element of B. Now consider $4 \in A - B$. We observe that $4 \in A - B$ is related with $5 \in B$ and $6 \in B$ but 4 is not related $3 \in B$. Similar result holds for $1 \in A - B$ and $2 \in A - B$.

Hence B = {3, 5, 6} is maximal compatibility block. The other maximal compatibility blocks are = C = {1, 2} and D = {4, 5, 6}.

In order to find the maximal compatibility blocks in a given relation, the digraph of a relation in its simplified form is useful.

In the simplified form of a digraph of a relation, we enclose each element in a small circle without any arrow. (reflexivity).

Also whenever aRb and bRa by symmetry, the circles corresponding to the elements a and b, are joined by a single line segment without any arrow.

In this digraph, two elements joined by a line segment give a maximal compatibility block, provided those two elements together with line segment is not a part of a triangle. Likewise three elements together with three line segments forming a triangle give a maximal compatibility block, provided they do not form a part of a complete rectangle. Also the four elements together with four sides and two diagonals, forming a complete rectangle give a maximal compatibility block, provided they do not form a part of complete pentagon.

It may be noted that just like an equivalence relation defined on a set corresponds to the partition of the set, the compatibility relation defined on a set corresponds to the covering of that set.

SOLVED EXAMPLES

Example 2.34 : A relation R is defined on A = {1, 2, 3, 4, 5} as below.

R = {(1, 1), (2, 2), (3, 3), (4, 4), (5, 5), (1, 2), (2, 1), (1, 3), (3, 1), (1, 4), (4, 1), (2, 3), (3, 2), (2, 4), (4, 2), (4, 5), (5, 4)}

(i) Write the matrix of R.

(ii) Draw simplified digraph of R.

(iii) Write all maximal compatibility blocks of R.

Solution : (i) $M_R = \begin{bmatrix} 1 & 1 & 1 & 1 & 0 \\ 1 & 1 & 1 & 1 & 0 \\ 1 & 1 & 1 & 0 & 0 \\ 1 & 1 & 0 & 1 & 1 \\ 0 & 0 & 0 & 1 & 1 \end{bmatrix}$

Another notation

2	1			
3	1	1		
4	1	1	0	
5	0	0	0	1
	1	2	3	4

The simplified digraph of R is as below.

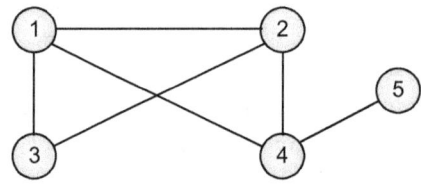

Fig. 2.20

(iii) From the digraph, we observe that the maximal compatibility blocks are

B = {1, 2, 3}, C = {1, 2, 4}, D = {4, 5}.

Example 2.35 : The compatibility relation on a set {1, 2, 3, 4, 5} is given by the following matrix

2	1			
3	0	1		
4	1	1	0	
5	0	1	1	1
	1	2	3	4

Draw the graph and find all the maximal compatibility blocks of the relation. **(P.U. 2010)**

Solution : The digraph of the given relation is as below.

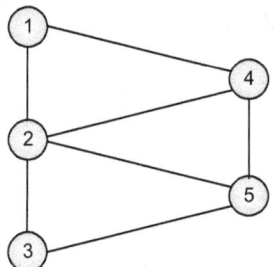

Fig. 2.21

The maximal compatibility blocks are B = {1, 2, 4}, C = {2, 4, 5}, D = {2, 3, 5}

Example 2.36 : The compatibility relation on a set $(x_1, x_2, ..., x_6)$ is given by the matrix.

$$
\begin{array}{c|ccccc}
x_2 & 1 & & & & \\
x_3 & 1 & 0 & & & \\
x_4 & 1 & 1 & 0 & & \\
x_5 & 0 & 1 & 0 & 0 & \\
x_6 & 0 & 0 & 1 & 0 & 1 \\
\hline
 & x_1 & x_2 & x_3 & x_4 & x_5
\end{array}
$$

Draw the graph and find all the maximal compatibility blocks of the relation. **[P.U. 2010]**

Solution : The graph of the relation is as below.

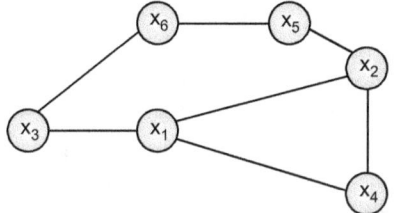

Fig. 2.22

The maximal compatibility blocks are :

$B_1 = \{x_1, x_2, x_4\}$, $B_2 = \{x_1, x_3\}$, $B_3 = \{x_3, x_6\}$, $B_4 = \{x_5, x_6\}$ $B_5 = \{x_2, x_5\}$

Example 2.37 : A relation R on the set A = {1, 2, 3, 4, 5, 6, 7} is defined by the matrix below.

$$
\begin{array}{c|cccccc}
2 & 0 & & & & & \\
3 & 1 & 0 & & & & \\
4 & 1 & 1 & 0 & & & \\
5 & 0 & 1 & 0 & 1 & & \\
6 & 1 & 0 & 1 & 1 & 0 & \\
7 & 0 & 1 & 0 & 1 & 1 & 0 \\
\hline
 & 1 & 2 & 3 & 4 & 5 & 6
\end{array}
$$

Draw the simplified digraph and find all maximal compatibility blocks of R.

Solution :

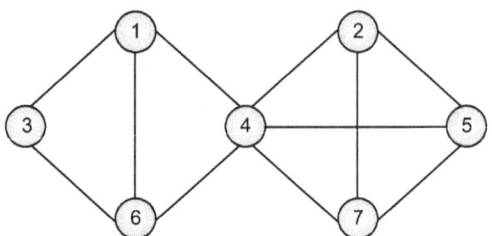

Fig. 2.23

From the graph the maximal compatibility blocks are
$B_1 = \{1, 3, 6\}$, $B_2 = \{1, 4, 6\}$, $B_3 = \{2, 4, 5, 7\}$

EXERCISE (2.8)

1. A relation R is defined on the set A by the following matrix. Draw the graph of R and find all the maximal compatibility blocks of R.

(i)
$$\begin{array}{c|ccccc} 2 & 1 & & & & \\ 3 & 0 & 1 & & & \\ 4 & 1 & 0 & 1 & & \\ 5 & 0 & 0 & 1 & 1 & \\ 6 & 0 & 0 & 0 & 0 & 1 \\ \hline & 1 & 2 & 3 & 4 & 5 \end{array}$$

(ii)
$$\begin{array}{c|ccccc} 2 & 1 & & & & \\ 3 & 0 & 1 & & & \\ 4 & 0 & 1 & 1 & & \\ 5 & 0 & 0 & 1 & 1 & \\ 6 & 0 & 0 & 1 & 1 & 1 \\ \hline & 1 & 2 & 3 & 4 & 5 \end{array}$$

(iii)
$$\begin{array}{c|cccc} 2 & 1 & & & \\ 3 & 1 & 1 & & \\ 4 & 0 & 1 & 1 & \\ 5 & 0 & 0 & 1 & 1 \\ \hline & 1 & 2 & 3 & 4 \end{array}$$

(iv)
$$\begin{array}{c|ccccc} 2 & 1 & & & & \\ 3 & 1 & 1 & & & \\ 4 & 1 & 1 & 1 & & \\ 5 & 1 & 1 & 1 & 1 & \\ 6 & 1 & 0 & 0 & 0 & 1 \\ \hline & 1 & 2 & 3 & 4 & 5 \end{array}$$

ANSWERS (2.8)

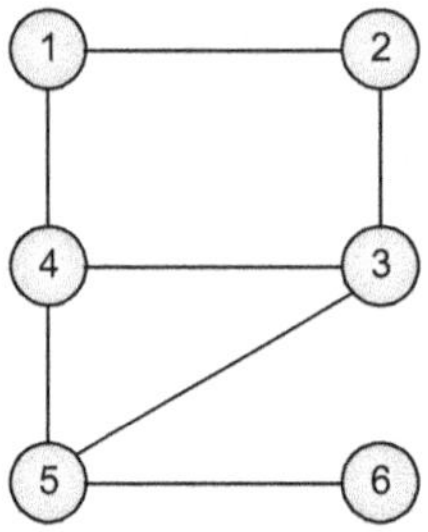

1. (i) $B_1 = \{5, 6\}$, $B_2 = \{3, 4, 5\}$, $B_3 = \{1, 2\}$, $B_4 = \{1, 4\}$, $B_5 = \{2, 3\}$

Fig. 2.24

(ii)

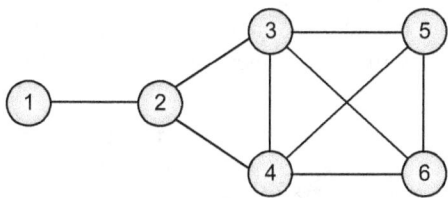

Fig. 2.25

$B_1 = \{1, 2\}$, $B_2 = \{2, 3, 4\}$, $B_3 = \{3, 4, 5, 6\}$

(iii)

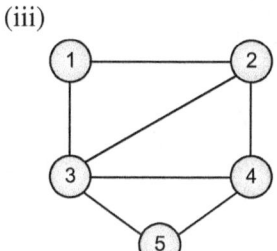

Fig. 2.26

$B_1 = \{1, 2, 3\}$, $B_2 = \{2, 3, 4\}$, $B_3 = \{3, 4, 5\}$

(iv)

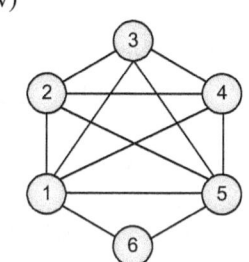

Fig. 2.27

$B_1 = \{1, 5, 6\}$, $B_2 = \{1, 2, 3, 4, 5\}$

2.9 Functions

A function is a special type of relation. Let A and B be two non-empty sets and D is some nonempty subset of A; $\phi \neq D \subseteq A$. Then a relation R from A to B which associates exactly one element of B for each element of D is called a function with its domain D and codomain B. The following diagram will clear this.

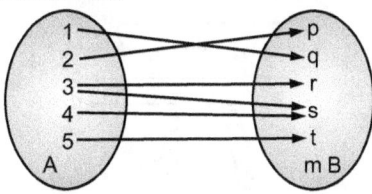

Fig. 2.28

We denote the function by f, g, h etc.

In the above diagram the elements 1, 2, 4, 5 ∈ A are associated with unique element of set B; but 3 ∈ A is associated with two elements viz. q and s in B. The above relation is not a function from A to B.

On the other hand consider a relation represented by the diagram below.

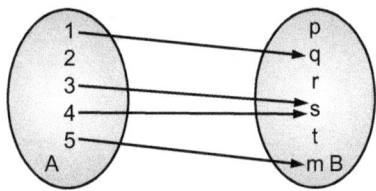

Fig. 2.29

According to this relation the elements 1, 3, 4, 5 ∈ A are related to unique element of B and 2 ∈ A is not related to any element of B. This relation represents a function denoted by say f. The domain of function f is D = {1, 3, 4, 5}. The element 2 ∈ A does not belong to domain of f; 2 ∉ domain f.

Codomain of function f is set B. We also say that under the function (mapping) f;

image of 1 is q and write f(1) = q

image of 3 is s and write f(3) = s

Similarly, f(4) = s, f(5) = m.

The set of all image points is called range of the function. In the above example, the range of the function f is Range f = {q, s, m} which is a subset of the codomain.

Example : let A = {p, q, r} and B = {x, y, z}. Consider the relations.

R = {(p, y), (r, y)} and S = {(p, x), (p, y), (q, z), (r, y)}

The relation R is a function whose domain is D = {p, r} and range is {y}. The relation S however is not a function because p ∈ A is related to two different elements x and y in B.

Let now f be a function from set A to set B; i.e. f : A → B such that the range of f consists of a single element of B i.e. every element of A maps onto the same point of B, then f is called a constant function. In the above example, the function represented by relation R is a constant function, and Range f = {y}.

Let now f be a function from set A to A itself; f : A → A such that every element of A maps onto itself i.e. f(x) = x for every x ∈ A. Such a function is called identity function denoted by $I_A(x)$.

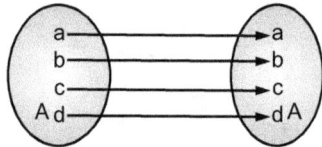

Fig. 2.30

This diagram represents identity function.

Composition of Functions :

Suppose A, B, C are three sets of f : A → B and g : B → C are functions, so that for a ∈ A, f(a) = b ∈ B and for b ∈ B, g(b) = c ∈ C. This is shown in the following diagram.

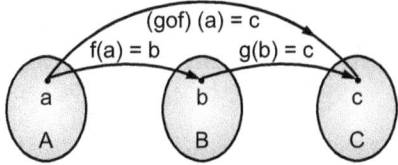

Fig. 2.31

It then follows that every element a ∈ A is related to unique element c ∈ C according to a function called composite function of g and f; which is denoted by gof.

Thus, (gof) (a) = g(f(a)) = g(b) = c.

Example : Let f : ℝ → ℝ and g : ℝ → ℝ be defined by f(x) = 2x + 1 and g(x) = x^2.

Then   (gof) (2) = g(f(2)) = g(2(2) + 1) = g(5) = 5^2 = 25

Also   (fog) (2) = f(g(2)) = f(2^2) = f(4) = (2) (4) + 1 = 9

Note that (gof) (2) ≠ (fog) (2).

We can find formulae for composite functions as below.

In the above example, we have

    (gof) (x) = g(f(x)) = g(2x + 1) = $(2x + 1)^2$ = $4x^2 + 4x + 1$

and   (fog) (x) = f(g(x)) = f(x^2) = $2x^2 + 1$

Special Types of Functions :

From the discussion above, we note the following results about a function f(x) defined from set A to set B.

Let   f : A → B

Then (i) different elements of A have different images in B.

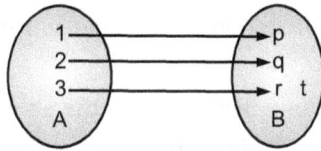

Fig. 2.32

(ii) there is at least one pair of elements x_1, x_2 ∈ A having the same image in B; if |B| < |A|.

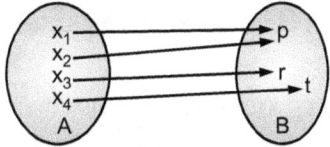

Fig. 2.33

(iii) the range of the function is equal to set B i.e. codomain. This means every element of B is image of some element of A under the function f.

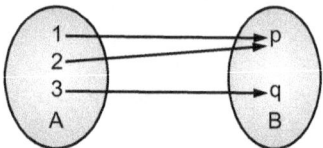

Fig. 2.34

(iv) The range of the function is a proper subset of set B i.e. there is at least one element of B which is not image of any element of A; if $|A| < |B|$.

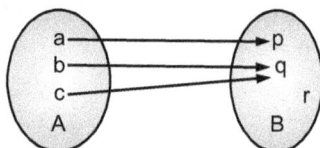

Fig. 2.35

Definition : A function $f : A \to B$ is called one-one function (mapping) or injective mapping if every pair of different elements in the domain A have different images in the codomain B i.e. $x_1 \neq x_2$ in A $\Rightarrow f(x_1) \neq f(x_2)$ in B.

Definition : A function $f : A \to B$ is called onto mapping (surjective mapping) if every element $b \in B$ is image of some element $a \in A$ i.e. Range $f = B$.

In the diagram (i) above the function is one-one but not onto; since $t \in B$ is not image of any element of A. It is into function.

In the diagram (ii) the function is onto; Range $f = B$; but f is not one-one because

$x_1 \neq x_2$ in A while $f(x_1) = f(x_2) = p$.

In the diagram(iii) again the function is onto but not one-one and in the diagram (iv) function is one-one but not onto.

Now our main aim is to examine that which of the above diagrams allow us to define a function. $g : B \to A$ i.e. in the reverse direction ?

Clearly the diagrams in (i) and (iv) cannot define a function $g : B \to A$ since in diagram (i) $t \in B$ has not image in A and in diagram (iv) $r \in B$ has no image in A.

Also diagrams in (ii) and (iii) cannot define a function in the reverse direction; since in (ii) $p \in B$ is related to two distinct elements x_1 and $x_2 \in A$ and in (iii) $p \in B$ is related to two distinct elements $1, 2 \in A$.

Now consider two sets, $A = \{x_1, x_2, x_3, x_4\}$ and $B = \{y_1, y_2, y_3, y_4\}$.

Let R be the relation from A to B and $R = \{(x_1, y_1), (x_2, y_2), (x_3, y_4), (x_4, y_3)\}$.

This relation is diagrammatically represented as below.

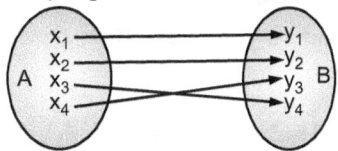

Fig. 2.36

This relation R defines a mapping $f : A \to B$; which is one-one (injective) and onto (surjective).

Definition : A mapping $f : A \to B$ is called a bijective mapping if it is injective and surjective.

The mapping $f : A \to B$ in the above diagram is clearly a bijective mapping and in this case it is quite possible for us to define a mapping $g : B \to A$ in the reverse direction; as below.

$$g(y_1) = x_1, \ g(y_2) = x_2, \ g(y_3) = x_4, \ g(y_4) = x_3$$

We say that the mapping g is the inverse mapping of f and f is said to be invertible.

Also then we write $g = f^{-1}$.

The following theorem gives the necessary and sufficient condition for the existence of inverse function.

Theorem : Let f be a function from set A to set B. Then the inverse function $f^{-1} : B \to A$ exists if and only if f is one-one and onto.

Proof : Suppose $f : A \to B$ is one-one and onto function. Then our claim is that for every $b \in B$, we can assign unique element $a \in A$. Let $b \in B$.

Since f is onto B, there exists $a \in A$ such that $f(a) = b$. Also it is impossible that $a_1 \neq a_2$ in A but $f(a_1) = f(a_2) = b$; since f is one-one.

Thus, for each $b \in B$ there corresponds unique $a \in A$; and it defines inverse function from B to A.

Conversely suppose $f^{-1} : B \to A$ exists. To prove that f is one-one.

Suppose $f : A \to B$ is not one-one. Then $f(a_1) = f(a_2) = b$.

∴ b is related to two elements in A; which is contradiction.

Also to prove that f is onto. Suppose f is not onto. Then there exists $b \in B$ which is not related to any $a \in A$; which is a contradiction to the fact $f^{-1}; B \to A$ is defined.

Permutation Functions :

Let $A = \{x_1, x_2, ..., x_n\}$ be a finite set of n elements. Then a one-one onto mapping f from A to A itself is called a permutation on the set A.

For the above set A suppose $f(x_1) = y_1, f(x_2) = y_2, ..., f(x_n) = y_n$ where each y_i is some x_j then we write the above permutation f by using the notation as below.

$$f = \begin{pmatrix} x_1 & x_2 & x_3 & ... & x_n \\ y_1 & y_2 & y_3 & ... & y_n \end{pmatrix}$$

In this notation the elements of set A are written in the first row and the respective images are written in the second row. Clearly then the second row gives some another arrangement of elements in the first row.

Again for simplicity, we write the set A as A = {1, 2, ..., n}.

There are n! = 1 × 2 × 3 × ... × n different permutations (arrangements) of n distinct objects in a row. Hence there are n! one-one onto functions from the set A to A itself; when A = {1, 2, 3, ..., n}.

For example, if A = {1, 2, 3} then there are 3! = 1 × 2 × 3 = 6 permutations on the set A.

The Greek letters $\alpha, \beta, \gamma, ..., \mu, \sigma, \rho$ etc. are used generally to denoted the permutations.

Thus, for A = {1, 2, 3} the 6 permutations are

$$i = \begin{pmatrix} 1 & 2 & 3 \\ 1 & 2 & 3 \end{pmatrix}, \quad \alpha = \begin{pmatrix} 1 & 2 & 3 \\ 1 & 3 & 2 \end{pmatrix}, \quad \beta = \begin{pmatrix} 1 & 2 & 3 \\ 2 & 1 & 3 \end{pmatrix}$$

$$\mu = \begin{pmatrix} 1 & 2 & 3 \\ 2 & 3 & 1 \end{pmatrix}, \quad \sigma = \begin{pmatrix} 1 & 2 & 3 \\ 3 & 1 & 2 \end{pmatrix}, \quad \rho = \begin{pmatrix} 1 & 2 & 3 \\ 3 & 2 & 1 \end{pmatrix}$$

We again make it clear that the meaning of permutation $\alpha = \begin{pmatrix} 1 & 2 & 3 \\ 1 & 3 & 2 \end{pmatrix}$ is that there is one-one onto function say f : A → A such that f(1) = 1, f(2) = 3 and f(3) = 2.

Also if g is one-one onto mapping corresponding to permutation β, then we have g(1) = 2, g(2) = 1, g(3) = 3. Now consider two composite mappings viz. gof and fog.

$$(gof)(x) = g(f(x))$$

∴   (gof) (1) = g(f(1)) = g(1) = 2

          (gof) (2) = g(f(2)) = g(3) = 3

          (gof) (3) = g(f(3)) = g(2) = 1

This composite mapping is represented by the permutation μ above; and we write $\beta\alpha = \mu$.

i.e. $\begin{pmatrix} 1 & 2 & 3 \\ 2 & 1 & 3 \end{pmatrix} \begin{pmatrix} 1 & 2 & 3 \\ 1 & 3 & 2 \end{pmatrix} = \begin{pmatrix} 1 & 2 & 3 \\ 2 & 3 & 1 \end{pmatrix}$.

Again (fog) (x) = f(g(x))

∴   (fog) (1) = f(g(1)) = f(2) = 3

          (fog) (2) = f(g(2)) = f(1) = 1

          (fog) (3) = f(g(3)) = f(3) = 2

This composite mapping is represented by the permutation σ above; and we write $\alpha\beta = \sigma$.

i.e. $\begin{pmatrix} 1 & 2 & 3 \\ 1 & 3 & 2 \end{pmatrix} \begin{pmatrix} 1 & 2 & 3 \\ 2 & 1 & 3 \end{pmatrix} = \begin{pmatrix} 1 & 2 & 3 \\ 3 & 1 & 2 \end{pmatrix}$.

This composition of mappings is called multiplication of permutation; which is performed from right to left. The word multiplication is used for composition. The multiplication $\begin{pmatrix} 1 & 2 & 3 \\ 1 & 3 & 2 \end{pmatrix} \begin{pmatrix} 1 & 2 & 3 \\ 2 & 1 & 3 \end{pmatrix}$ is performed as below.

$1 \to 2 \to 3 \qquad \therefore 1 \to 3$

$2 \to 1 \to 1 \qquad \therefore 2 \to 1$

$3 \to 3 \to 2 \qquad \therefore 3 \to 2$

$\therefore \begin{pmatrix} 1 & 2 & 3 \\ 1 & 3 & 2 \end{pmatrix} \begin{pmatrix} 1 & 2 & 3 \\ 2 & 1 & 3 \end{pmatrix} = \begin{pmatrix} 1 & 2 & 3 \\ 3 & 1 & 2 \end{pmatrix}$

We ask the students to perform the multiplications of permutations on 3 symbols 1, 2, 3 and verify the following table :

·	i	α	β	μ	σ	ρ
i	i	α	β	μ	σ	ρ
α	α	i	σ	ρ	β	μ
β	β	μ	i	α	ρ	σ
μ	μ	β	ρ	σ	i	α
σ	σ	ρ	α	i	μ	β
ρ	ρ	σ	μ	β	α	i

Since the permutation is one-one onto mapping from a finite set A to A itself, its inverse exists.

Consider the permutation, $r = \begin{pmatrix} 1 & 2 & 3 & 4 & 5 \\ 4 & 3 & 1 & 2 & 5 \end{pmatrix}$

If f is the function corresponding to this permutation, then we have f(1) = 4, f(2) = 3, f(3) = 1, f(4) = 2 and f(5) = 5.

The inverse mapping is given as $f^{-1}(4) = 1$, $f^{-1}(3) = 2$, $f^{-1}(1) = 3$, $f^{-1}(2) = 4$, $f^{-1}(5) = 5$.

The resulting permutation is $\begin{pmatrix} 4 & 3 & 1 & 2 & 5 \\ 1 & 2 & 3 & 4 & 5 \end{pmatrix}$.

Now we write the elements of the first row in natural order.

$\therefore \qquad r^{-1} = \begin{pmatrix} 1 & 2 & 3 & 4 & 5 \\ 3 & 4 & 2 & 1 & 5 \end{pmatrix}$

Thus to find the inverse permutation of a given permutation, we first interchange the rows and then write the elements in the new first row in natural order and their images below them.

SOLVED EXAMPLES

Example 2.38 : Consider the permutations $\alpha = \begin{pmatrix} 1 & 2 & 3 & 4 \\ 3 & 1 & 4 & 2 \end{pmatrix}$ and $\beta = \begin{pmatrix} 1 & 2 & 3 & 4 \\ 4 & 3 & 1 & 2 \end{pmatrix}$ on 4 symbols Find : (i) α^{-1} (ii) $\beta\alpha$ (iii) $(\alpha\beta^{-2})^{-1}$.

Solution : $\alpha = \begin{pmatrix} 1 & 2 & 3 & 4 \\ 3 & 1 & 4 & 2 \end{pmatrix}$, $\beta = \begin{pmatrix} 1 & 2 & 3 & 4 \\ 4 & 3 & 1 & 2 \end{pmatrix}$

(i) $\alpha = \begin{pmatrix} 1 & 2 & 3 & 4 \\ 3 & 1 & 4 & 2 \end{pmatrix}$

$\therefore \quad \alpha^{-1} = \begin{pmatrix} 3 & 1 & 4 & 2 \\ 1 & 2 & 3 & 4 \end{pmatrix}$

$\therefore \quad \alpha^{-1} = \begin{pmatrix} 1 & 2 & 3 & 4 \\ 2 & 4 & 1 & 3 \end{pmatrix}$

(ii) $\beta\alpha = \begin{pmatrix} 1 & 2 & 3 & 4 \\ 4 & 3 & 1 & 2 \end{pmatrix} \begin{pmatrix} 1 & 2 & 3 & 4 \\ 3 & 1 & 4 & 2 \end{pmatrix} = \begin{pmatrix} 1 & 2 & 3 & 4 \\ 1 & 4 & 2 & 3 \end{pmatrix}$

(iii) $\alpha\beta^2 = \alpha\beta\beta$

$= \begin{pmatrix} 1 & 2 & 3 & 4 \\ 3 & 1 & 4 & 2 \end{pmatrix} \begin{pmatrix} 1 & 2 & 3 & 4 \\ 4 & 3 & 1 & 2 \end{pmatrix} \begin{pmatrix} 1 & 2 & 3 & 4 \\ 4 & 3 & 1 & 2 \end{pmatrix}$

$\therefore \quad \alpha\beta^2 = \begin{pmatrix} 1 & 2 & 3 & 4 \\ 1 & 3 & 2 & 4 \end{pmatrix}$

Then $(\alpha\beta^2)^{-1} = \begin{pmatrix} 1 & 3 & 2 & 4 \\ 1 & 2 & 3 & 4 \end{pmatrix} = \begin{pmatrix} 1 & 2 & 3 & 4 \\ 1 & 3 & 2 & 4 \end{pmatrix}$

Now consider a permutation on 8 symbols.

$$\sigma = \begin{pmatrix} 1 & 2 & 3 & 4 & 5 & 6 & 7 & 8 \\ 1 & 7 & 8 & 4 & 3 & 2 & 5 & 6 \end{pmatrix}$$

In this permutation the elements 1 and 4 map onto themselves. As regards the remaining elements, we observe that

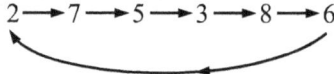

As shown, the elements 2, 7, 5, 3, 8 map onto the next element and 6 maps onto 2 thus completing the cycle. Thus σ is a cyclic permutation. It is called a cycle and denoted by

$$\sigma = (2\ 7\ 5\ 3\ 8\ 6)$$

Note again that according to this notation each element is mapped onto the next element and the last element is mapped onto the first element, where cycle starts.

The elements which do not appear in the cycle, are unchanged. they map onto themselves.

Thus in σ; $1 \to 1$ and $4 \to 4$.

It is clear that every cycle is a permutation but not conversely. For example, suppose

$$\mu = \begin{pmatrix} 1 & 2 & 3 & 4 & 5 & 6 & 7 \\ 3 & 5 & 7 & 4 & 2 & 1 & 6 \end{pmatrix}$$

which is a permutation on 7 symbols, we start with first element 1.

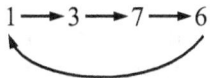

This completes the first cycle, viz. (1 3 7 6).

The next element which does not appear in the above cycle is 2 and we get $2 \longrightarrow 5$.

It gives a cycle (2 5).

The next element which does not appear in the above two cycles is 4 which maps onto itself.

We have then $\quad \mu = (2\ 5)(1\ 3\ 7\ 6)$

We observe that the permutation μ is not a cycle. However it is a product of disjoint cycles.

The disjoint cycles commute for their multiplication (verify this yourself).

The number of elements appearing in a cycle is called length of that cycle. Thus the cycles (2 5) and (1 3 7 6) are of lengths 2 and 4 respectively.

A cycle of length 2 is called a transposition. Thus in the above example (2 5) is a transposition but (1 3 7 6) is not.

Consider again the cycle (1 3 7 6) above; which is not a transposition. We have

$$(1\ 3\ 7\ 6) = \begin{pmatrix} 1 & 2 & 3 & 4 & 5 & 6 & 7 \\ 3 & 2 & 7 & 4 & 5 & 1 & 6 \end{pmatrix} \qquad \ldots (i)$$

Consider now the transpositions (1 3), (1 7) and (1 6).

We find their product (1 6) (1 7) (1 3) [see the order].

$$(1\ 6)(1\ 7)(1\ 3) = \begin{pmatrix} 1 & 2 & 3 & 4 & 5 & 6 & 7 \\ 6 & 2 & 3 & 4 & 5 & 1 & 7 \end{pmatrix} \begin{pmatrix} 1 & 2 & 3 & 4 & 5 & 6 & 7 \\ 7 & 2 & 3 & 4 & 5 & 6 & 1 \end{pmatrix} \begin{pmatrix} 1 & 2 & 3 & 4 & 5 & 6 & 7 \\ 3 & 2 & 1 & 4 & 5 & 6 & 7 \end{pmatrix}$$

$$= \begin{pmatrix} 1 & 2 & 3 & 4 & 5 & 6 & 7 \\ 3 & 2 & 7 & 4 & 5 & 1 & 6 \end{pmatrix}$$

$$= (1\ 3\ 7\ 6) \qquad \ldots (ii)$$

We have expressed the cycle as a product of transportations.

In fact $\quad$ (a b c) = (a c) (a b)

(a b c d) = (a d) (a c) (a b)

(a b c d e) = (a e) (a d) (a c) (a b)

After combining the two results :

(i) Every permutation can be written as a product of disjoint cycles and

(ii) Every cycle can be expressed as a product of transpositions, we get the following result.

"Every permutation can be expressed as a product of transpositions".

SOLVED EXAMPLES

Example 2.39 : Express the permutation $\sigma = \begin{pmatrix} 1 & 2 & 3 & 4 & 5 & 6 & 7 & 8 & 9 \\ 6 & 1 & 7 & 2 & 9 & 4 & 3 & 5 & 8 \end{pmatrix}$ on 9 symbols as a product of disjoint cycles and then as a product of transpositions. Is the number of transpositions even or odd ?

Solution : $\sigma = \begin{pmatrix} 1 & 2 & 3 & 4 & 5 & 6 & 7 & 8 & 9 \\ 6 & 1 & 7 & 2 & 9 & 4 & 3 & 5 & 8 \end{pmatrix} = (5\ 9\ 8)\ (3\ 7)\ (1\ 6\ 4\ 2)$

$\therefore \quad \sigma = (5\ 8)\ (5\ 9)\ (3\ 7)\ (1\ 2)\ (1\ 4)\ (1\ 6)$

The number of transpositions is 6 i.e. even. A permutation is called an even or odd permutation according as it is written as a product of even or odd number of transpositions.

It is interesting to look to the above problem from diagrammatic point of view.

A one-one onto function of corresponding to permutation σ is shown below.

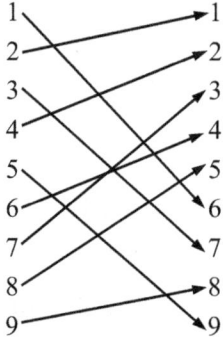

Fig. 2.37

Observe that the number of intersections of lines in this diagram is 4 which is even number. Therefore the permutation σ is even.

Example 2.40 : Let A = {1, 2, 3, 4} and B = {a, b, c, d}. Determine if the following functions are one-one, onto or both.

(i) f = {<1, a>, <2, a>, <3, b>, <4, d>}

(ii) g = {<1, c>, <2, b>, <3, a>, <4, a>}

(iii) h = {<1, a>, <2, b>, <3, a>, <4, c>}

Solution : (i) f = {<1, a>, <2, a>, <3, b>, <4, d>}

Here f(1) = f(2) = a.

∴ f is not one-one.

Range f = {a, b, d} is a proper subset of codomain B; c ∉ Range f.

∴ f is not onto.

(ii) g = {<1, c>, <2, b>, <3, a>, <4, a>}

f(3) = f(4) = a

∴ f is not one-one

Also d ∈ B is not image of any element of A.

∴ g is not onto

(iii) h = {<1, a>, <2, b>, <3, a>, <4, c>}

h(1) = h(3) = a

∴ h is not one-one.

Also d ∈ B has not preimage in A

∴ h is not onto.

Example 2.41 : Let $f : \mathbb{R} \to \mathbb{R}$ be a function given by $f(x) = 3 - x^3$. Show that f is invertible and find the formula for f^{-1}.

Solution : $f : \mathbb{R} \to \mathbb{R}$ is $f(x) = 3 - x^3$.

Then equation $\quad f(x_1) = f(x_2)$

$\Rightarrow \quad 3 - x_1^3 = 3 - x_2^3$

$\Rightarrow \quad x_1^3 = x_2^3$

$\Rightarrow \quad x_1 = x_2$

∴ f is one-one.

Let y be any element in the codomain $\mathbb{R}$.

$f(x) = y \Rightarrow 3 - x^3 = y \Rightarrow x^3 = 3 - y \Rightarrow x = \sqrt[3]{3-y}$

This shows that for any $y \in \mathbb{R}$ there exits preimage $x = \sqrt[3]{3-y}$ in $\mathbb{R}$.

∴ f is onto.

As f is one-one and onto, f is invertible.

Now $y = f(x) \Rightarrow x = f^{-1}(y)$

∴ $\quad \sqrt[3]{3-y} = f^{-1}(y)$

∴ $\quad f^{-1}(y) = \sqrt[3]{3-y}$

∴ $\quad f^{-1}(x) = \sqrt[3]{3-x}$; This gives the formula for f^{-1}.

Example 2.42 : Let $f : A \to B$ such that $f(x) = x - 1$ and $g : B \to C$ such that $g(y) = y^2$.
Find : (i) (fog) (2), (ii) (gof) (y), (iii) (fof) (y) **(P.U. 2011)**

Solution : $f(x) = x - 1$, $g(y) = y^2$; Given :

(i)   (fog) (2) = f(g(2)) = f(2^2) = f(4) = 4 - 1 = 3
(ii)   (gof) (y) = g(f(y)) = g(y - 1) = $(y - 1)^2$
(iii)   (fof) (y) = f(f(y)) = f(y - 1) = (y - 1) - 1 = y - 2

Example 2.43 : Let $f : A \to B$ be a function and $A = \{1, 2, 3, 4\}$, $B = \{a, e, i, o\}$ and $f = \{(1, a), (2, i), (3, e), (4, 0)\}$. Is f^{-1} a function ?

Solution : A $A = \{1, 2, 3, 4\}$, $B = \{a, e, i, o\}$
$$f = \{(1, a), (2, i), (3, e), (4, 0)\}$$

We note that under the function $f : A \to B$; distinct elements of domain A have distinct images in codomain.

Therefore f is one-one.

Also every element of codomain B is image of some element of domain A i.e. f(1) = a, f(2) = i, f(3) = e and f(4) = 0. Therefore, mapping f is onto.

Since f is one-one and onto, f^{-1} exists and $f^{-1} = \{(a, 1), (i, 2), (e, 3), (0, 4)\}$

Example 2.44 : Let $A = \{1, 2, 3, 4, 5, 6\}$.
Let $f = (6, 3, 1, 4)$ and $g = (5, 2, 4)$ be permutations of A.
Determine (i) fog, (ii) $f^{-1} o g^{-1}$. **[P.U. 2010]**

Solution : The permutations f and g are cycles.

$$f = (6\ 3\ 1\ 4) = \begin{pmatrix} 1 & 2 & 3 & 4 & 5 & 6 \\ 4 & 2 & 1 & 6 & 5 & 3 \end{pmatrix}$$

$$g = (5\ 2\ 4) = \begin{pmatrix} 1 & 2 & 3 & 4 & 5 & 6 \\ 1 & 4 & 3 & 5 & 2 & 6 \end{pmatrix}$$

(i) $\quad fog = \begin{pmatrix} 1 & 2 & 3 & 4 & 5 & 6 \\ 4 & 2 & 1 & 6 & 5 & 3 \end{pmatrix} \begin{pmatrix} 1 & 2 & 3 & 4 & 5 & 6 \\ 1 & 4 & 3 & 5 & 2 & 6 \end{pmatrix}$

$\therefore \quad fog = \begin{pmatrix} 1 & 2 & 3 & 4 & 5 & 6 \\ 4 & 6 & 1 & 5 & 2 & 3 \end{pmatrix}$

$= (1\ 4\ 5\ 2\ 6\ 3)$

(ii) $\quad f^{-1} = \begin{pmatrix} 4 & 2 & 1 & 6 & 5 & 3 \\ 1 & 2 & 3 & 4 & 5 & 6 \end{pmatrix} = \begin{pmatrix} 1 & 2 & 3 & 4 & 5 & 6 \\ 3 & 2 & 6 & 1 & 5 & 4 \end{pmatrix}$

$g^{-1} = \begin{pmatrix} 1 & 4 & 3 & 5 & 2 & 6 \\ 1 & 2 & 3 & 4 & 5 & 6 \end{pmatrix} = \begin{pmatrix} 1 & 2 & 3 & 4 & 5 & 6 \\ 1 & 5 & 3 & 2 & 4 & 6 \end{pmatrix}$

$\therefore \quad f^{-1} o g^{-1} = \begin{pmatrix} 1 & 2 & 3 & 4 & 5 & 6 \\ 3 & 2 & 6 & 1 & 5 & 4 \end{pmatrix} \begin{pmatrix} 1 & 2 & 3 & 4 & 5 & 6 \\ 1 & 5 & 3 & 2 & 4 & 6 \end{pmatrix}$

$\therefore \quad f^{-1} o g^{-1} = \begin{pmatrix} 1 & 2 & 3 & 4 & 5 & 6 \\ 3 & 2 & 6 & 1 & 5 & 4 \end{pmatrix}$

$= (1\ 3\ 6\ 4\ 2\ 5)$

EXERCISE (2.9)

1. The set $A = \{x; x \text{ is real and } x \geq 0\}$ A function $f : \mathbb{R} \to A$ is given as $f(x) = x^2$. Determine whether or not (a) f is one-one, (b) f is onto, (c) f^{-1} exists.

2. Let f be a function from set A to set B. Show that f^{-1} exists and find f^{-1} :

   (a) $A = B = \mathbb{R}$; $f(x) = \dfrac{3x - 1}{2}$

   (b) $A = B = \{1, 2, 3, 4, 5\}$
   $f = \{(1, 2), (2, 3), (3, 1), (4, 5), (5, 4)\}$

3. f and g are two functions defined on the set $\mathbb{R}$ of all real numbers as below.
   $f(x) = x + 2$, $g(x) = x^2 + 1$. Compute :
   (a) (fog) (–3), (b) (gof) (x), (c) (fof) (5), (d) (gof) (–3), (e) (fogof) (x).

4. Determine whether each of the following is a bijective mapping from $\mathbb{R}$ to $\mathbb{R}$.

   (a) $f(x) = 4x + 3$, (b) $f(x) = x^2 + 4$, (c) $f(x) = x^3$, (d) $f(x) = \dfrac{x^2 + 2}{x^2 + 1}$

   Justify your answer.

5. Let $A = \{1, 2, 3, 4, 5, 6\}$. Compute :
   (a) (4 2 3 6) (5 1 4), (b) (5 1 4) (4 2 3 6)
   Are they equal ?

6. Let $A = \{1, 2, 3, 4, 5, 6\}$ and $\alpha = \begin{pmatrix} 1 & 2 & 3 & 4 & 5 & 6 \\ 1 & 3 & 2 & 5 & 4 & 6 \end{pmatrix}$, $\beta = \begin{pmatrix} 1 & 2 & 3 & 4 & 5 & 6 \\ 2 & 3 & 1 & 5 & 6 & 4 \end{pmatrix}$

   $\gamma = \begin{pmatrix} 1 & 2 & 3 & 4 & 5 & 6 \\ 6 & 4 & 2 & 5 & 1 & 3 \end{pmatrix}$. Compute :

   (a) α^{-1}, (b) $\gamma\alpha$, (c) $\alpha\gamma\beta^{-1}$, (d) $\alpha^{-1}\beta^{-1}$, (e) $\gamma(\beta\alpha)^{-1}$.

7. Let $A = \{1, 2, 3, 4, 5, 6, 7, 8\}$. Express the following permutations on A as product of disjoint cycles and then product of transpositions. State whether the permutation is even or odd.

   (a) $\begin{pmatrix} 1 & 2 & 3 & 4 & 5 & 6 & 7 & 8 \\ 2 & 3 & 1 & 4 & 6 & 7 & 8 & 5 \end{pmatrix}$ (b) $\begin{pmatrix} 1 & 2 & 3 & 4 & 5 & 6 & 7 & 8 \\ 4 & 2 & 3 & 5 & 8 & 1 & 6 & 7 \end{pmatrix}$

   (c) (4 2 6) (8 4 5 2) (d) (6 2 8) (8 6 4) (1 5 3)

8. Consider the permutation $\sigma = \begin{pmatrix} 1 & 2 & 3 & 4 & 5 & 6 \\ 4 & 3 & 5 & 1 & 2 & 6 \end{pmatrix}$ on 6 symbols.

   (a) Write σ as a product of disjoint cycles.
   (b) Compute α^{-1}
   (c) Compute α^2
   (d) Find the smallest positive integer n such that α^n is identity permutation.

9. (a) Let $A = \{x, y, z, t\}$ and $B = \{1, 2, 3\}$ A relation R on A is
   $R = \{(x, 1), (y, 2), (z, 1), (t, 2)\}$
   Is R a function ? If yes then what is the range ?

(b) Let f be a function from {1, 2, 3, 4} to {p, q, r, s} defined as
f = {4, p), (2, q), (1, r), (3, s)}
State whether or not f is a bijective mapping.

(c) Which of the following functions from **Z** to **Z** are one-one ?
$f(x) = x + 1$, $g(x) = x^2 + 1$, $h(x) = x^3$, $r(x) = x^4 + x$.

(d) Show that if f(x) and g(x) are both one-one (onto) then fog is also one-one (onto); where g is a function from A to B and f is a function from B to C.

ANSWERS (2.9)

1. (a) f is not one-one, (b) if is onto, (c) f^{-1} does not exist.

2. (a) $f^{-1}(x) = \dfrac{2x+1}{3}$, (b) f^{-1} {(1, 3), (2, 1), (3, 2), (4, 5), (5, 4)}

3. (a) 12, (b) $x^2 + 4x + 5$, (c) 9, (d) 2, (e) $x^2 + 4x + 7$

4. (a) Yes, (b) No, (c) Yes, (d) No

5. (a) $\begin{pmatrix} 1 & 2 & 3 & 4 & 5 & 6 \\ 2 & 3 & 6 & 5 & 1 & 4 \end{pmatrix}$, (b) $\begin{pmatrix} 1 & 2 & 3 & 4 & 5 & 6 \\ 4 & 3 & 6 & 2 & 1 & 5 \end{pmatrix}$

6. (a) $\begin{pmatrix} 1 & 2 & 3 & 4 & 5 & 6 \\ 1 & 3 & 2 & 5 & 4 & 6 \end{pmatrix}$ (b) $\begin{pmatrix} 1 & 2 & 3 & 4 & 5 & 6 \\ 6 & 2 & 4 & 1 & 5 & 3 \end{pmatrix}$ (c) $\begin{pmatrix} 1 & 2 & 3 & 4 & 5 & 6 \\ 3 & 6 & 5 & 2 & 4 & 1 \end{pmatrix}$

   (d) $\begin{pmatrix} 1 & 2 & 3 & 4 & 5 & 6 \\ 2 & 1 & 3 & 6 & 5 & 4 \end{pmatrix}$ (e) $\begin{pmatrix} 1 & 2 & 3 & 4 & 5 & 6 \\ 4 & 6 & 2 & 3 & 1 & 5 \end{pmatrix}$

7. (a) odd, (b) odd, (c) odd, (d) even

8. (a) (2 3 5) (1 4), (b) $\begin{pmatrix} 1 & 2 & 3 & 4 & 5 & 6 \\ 4 & 5 & 2 & 1 & 3 & 6 \end{pmatrix}$, (c) $\begin{pmatrix} 1 & 2 & 3 & 4 & 5 & 6 \\ 1 & 5 & 2 & 4 & 3 & 6 \end{pmatrix}$

   (d) n = 6 = L.C.M. of the lengths of disjoint cycles.

9. (a) Yes, {1, 2}
   (b) f is bijective
   (c) f(x) and h(x) are one-one functions.

Chapter 3...

PERMUTATIONS AND COMBINATIONS

3.1 Two Basic Rules

In out everyday life we always come across with the problems of counting the object, together with their selections, arrangements and distribution. We discuss in this unit the above problems. There is no too much theory part involved while discussing these problems. However keen observation to the problem and step-by-step logical thinking for its solution is quite necessary.

Factorial notation: In this unit we need a factorial notation.

If n is a positive integer then the product $n(n-1)(n-2) \ldots 3 \times 2 \times 1$ is called factorial of n. It is denoted by n! (Read 'factorial n').

Thus, $5! = 5 \times 4 \times 3 \times 2 \times 1 = 120$

$3! = 3 \times 2 \times 1 = 6$

$2! = 2 \times 1 = 2$

$1! = 1$; also $0! = 1$

Two basic Rules:

There are two basic rules for the purpose of counting the objects. They are 'Rule of addition' and 'Rule of multiplication'. We explain them by an example.

Rule of addition:

Suppose in a certain area of the city there are two residential buildings under construction. In the first building there are 8 flats available for booking while 10 flats are available in the second building.

Now if Mr. X is interested in booking a flat, then how many choices he has ?

Clearly Mr. X has $8 + 10 = 18$ choices for booking a flat.

Note that in this problem we added the two numbers 8 and 10 to find the total number of choices. This is the rule of addition for counting.

Here all 8 flats in the first building are different.

Also all 10 flats in the second building are different.

Further no flat is common to the two buildings.

We can easily extend the above discussion to any (finite) number of buildings under construction.

Thus the rule of addition is as follows:

If a set A_1 contains r_1 different objects, set A_2 contains r_2 different objects, ... , set A_n contains r_n different objects and the sets $A_1, A_2, ... , A_n$ are pairwise disjoint then the number of ways to select an object from the above collection is $r_1 + r_2 + ... + r_n$.

Here we can select an object from set A_1 or from set $A_2, ... ,$ or from set A_n.

Rule of multiplication:

Suppose a child has 3 pants and 4 shirts. The process of wearing a dress consists of two stages viz. wearing a shirt and wearing a pant.

If S_1, S_2, S_3, S_4 denote four shirts and P_1, P_2, P_3 denote 3 pants then that child can have his dress in $4 \times 3 = 12$ different ways as:

$S_1P_1, S_1P_2, S_1P_3, S_2P_1, S_2P_2, S_2P_3, S_3P_1, S_3P_2, S_3P_3, S_4P_1, S_4P_2, S_4P_3$

This is the rule of multiplication for the purpose of counting.

Thus the rule of multiplication is as follows:

Suppose a certain procedure consists of n successive stages resulting in r_1 outcomes in the first stage, r_2 outcomes in the second stage, ... , r_n outcomes in the nth stage. If the composite outcomes are all distinct, then the procedure has total $r_1 r_2, ... r_n$ different composite outcomes.

SOLVED EXAMPLES

Example 3.1 : In a circus family, there are 10 animals and 10 cages. The four cages are too small to occupy five animals. Find in how many ways the animals can be put into the cages; one each.

Solution: From the data there are 5 small animals and 5 big animals say a_1, a_2, a_3, a_4, a_5, A_1, A_2, A_3, A_4, A_5. Also there are 4 small cages and 6 big cages say $c_1, c_2, c_3, c_4, C_1, C_2, C_3, C_4, C_5, C_6$.

We note that as compared to small animals, there is a restriction on big animals. So first we take care of big animals.

Then A_1 has 6 choices, A_2 has 5 choices, A_3 has 4 choices, A_4 has 3 choices, A_5 has 2 choices.

Also then a_1 has 5 choices, a_2 has 4 choices, a_3 has 3 choices, a_4 has 2 choices, a_5 has 1 choice.

By the rule of multiplication the total number of ways of putting 10 animals into 10 cages is $6 \times 5 \times 4 \times 3 \times 2 \times 5 \times 4 \times 3 \times 2 \times 1 = 86400$.

Example 3.2 : The letters are of the word SKUMAR are arranged in a line with possible repetition of letters. In how many arrangements the pattern RAMU does not appear?

Solution: An arrangement of six letters looks as below:

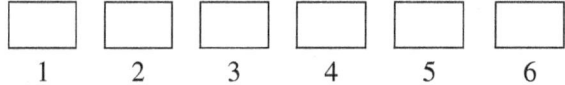

Since repetition is allowed, each box can be filled in 6 ways.

By the rule of multiplication the six boxes can be filled in $6 \times 6 \times 6 \times 6 \times 6 \times 6 = 46656$ ways.

Now we find the number of cases in which the pattern RAMU appears. This pattern appears when the letters R, A, M, U occupy the boxes labelled 1, 2, 3, 4 or 2, 3, 4, 5 or 3, 4, 5, 6. In each of these 3 cases the remaining 2 boxes can be filled in $6 \times 6 = 36$ ways.

Therefore the pattern RAMU appears in $3 \times 36 = 108$ arrangements.

Then the total number of arrangements in which the pattern RAMU does not appear is $46656 - 108 = 46548$.

Example 3.3 : A multiple choice examination consists of 10 questions. Each question has 4 alternative answers out of which exactly one is correct. In how many ways a student can answer his paper if he (i) gives answers to all questions (ii) leaves some questions blank?

Solution:
(i) A student answers all questions. To answers each question he has 4 alternatives.

   Therefore by the rule of multiplication total number of ways of answering all questions is $4 \times 4 \times \ldots \times 4 = 4^{10}$.

(ii) If some questions are answered and the remaining are left blank in this case each of the 10 questions have 5 alternatives. Therefore, the total number of ways of answering the paper is $5 \times 5 \times \ldots \times 5 = 5^{10}$.

Example 3.4 : A box contains 10 blue balls, 8 green balls and 9 red balls which are identical in all respects except the colour. Find the number of ways in which one or more balls can be drawn from the box.

Solution: The drawing of a green ball happens in $8 + 1 = 9$ ways i.e. 0, 1, 2, 3, ... , 8.

The drawing of red ball happens in $9 + 1 = 10$ ways i.e. 0, 1, 2, ... , 9.

The drawing of a blue ball happens in $10 + 1 = 11$ ways i.e. 0, 1, 2, ... , 10.

In our selection of balls suppose the selection includes some or none of each colour. Then by the rule of multiplication the total number of selections is $9 \times 10 \times 11 = 990$.

This includes the case none of each colour i.e. blue 0, green 0 balls and Red 0 balls.

Our requirement of selection is that there must be atleast one ball in the selection.

Hence the required number of selections is $990 - 1 = 989$.

Example 3.5 : How many ways are there to pick 2 successive cards from 52 playing cards such that:

(i) the first card is an Ace and the second card is not a king ?
(ii) the first card is a diamond and the second card is not a king ?

Solution:
(i) There are 4 Aces. Therefore, in the first stage an Ace can be drawn in 4 ways.

   Now there are 51 cards in the deck, which include 4 kings.

   In the second stage we don't want king.

   Thus, there are $51 - 4 = 47$ choices in the second stage.

   By the rule of multiplication total number of choices is $4 \times 47 = 188$.

(ii) In this first stage of the given procedure we may or may not draw a diamond king.

We split-up the problem into two disjoint cases.

First case: In the first stage we draw a diamond card which is not a diamond king. This can be done in 12 ways.

Now there are 51 cards in the deck which include 4 kings.

We are not interested in the king card. Therefore second stage can be performed in $51 - 4 = 47$ ways.

Thus in this case the whole procedure, by the rule of multiplication can be performed in $12 \times 47 = 564$ ways.

Second case: In this first stage we draw a diamond king. This happens only one way.

Now there are 51 cards in the deck which include 3 kings. Therefore, second stage of the procedure can be performed in $51 - 3 = 48$ ways.

By the rule of multiplication the whole procedure can be performed in $1 \times 48 = 48$ ways.

Finally the two cases discussed above are disjoint.

Therefore, by the rule of addition the total number of ways of performing the given procedure is $564 + 48 = 612$.

Example 3.6 : A string of length 3 is to be formed by using the letters A, B, C, D, E, F.

In how many ways the string can be formed if

(i) repetition of letter is not allowed.

(ii) repetition of letter is allowed.

(iii) the string contains the letter A and repetition of any letter is not allowed.

(iv) the string contains the letter A and repetition of letters is allowed.

Solution: A string of length 3 looks like

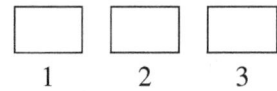

(i) The procedure consists of 3 stages of filling the three boxes. The first box can be filled in 6 ways. Then since repetition is not allowed, the second box can be filled in 5 ways and then the third box can be filled in 4 ways. By the rule of multiplication the total number of ways is $6 \times 5 \times 4 = 120$.

(ii) The first box can be filled in 6 ways and then the second box can be filled in 6 ways. Also then the third box can be filled in 6 ways. By the rule of multiplication the total number of ways of filling the three boxes is $6 \times 6 \times 6 = 216$.

(iii) Repetition of letters is not allowed and the string contains letters A. Letter A has three choices available i.e. box 1 or box 2 or box 3. In each of these three cases the remaining two boxes have 5 choices and 4 choices respectively. Thus in each case the two boxes can be filled in $5 \times 4 = 20$ ways. Now by the rule of addition the three boxes are filled in $20 + 20 + 20 = 60$ ways.

(iv) We have to proceed as below. We consider three cases.
First case: Letter A appears first time in the box 1, as below

| A | | |

Now since repetition of letters is allowed the box 2 has 6 choices and box 3 has 6 choices. The two boxes can be filled in $6 \times 6 = 36$ ways.

Second case : Letter A appears first time in the box 2, as below

| | A | |

Now box 1 has only 5 choices but box 3 has 6 choices. Therefore, the two boxes can be filled in $5 \times 6 = 30$ ways.

Third case: Letter A appears first time in box 3 as below

| | | A |

Now box 1 has 5 choices and box 2 has also 5 choices.

Therefore, the two boxes can be filled in $5 \times 5 = 25$ days.

The above three cases are disjoint. So by the rule of addition now, the three boxes can be filled in $36 + 30 + 25 = 91$ ways.

Example 3.7 : A box contains 10 pairs of shoes. Find the number of ways in which 8 shoes are selected without forming any complete pair.   **(P.U. October 2012)**

Solution : From the given condition, when a shoe is selected then its pair is to be eliminated at the time of next selection.

1st shoe can be selected in 20 ways.

2nd shoe can be selected in $20 - 2 = 18$ ways.

3rd shoe can be selected in $18 - 2 = 16$ ways continuing in this way.

8th shoe can be selected in 6 ways.

By the rule of multiplication 8 shoes can be selected in

$20 \times 18 \times 16 \times 14 \times 12 \times 10 \times 8 \times 6$ ways.

i.e. $2^8 \times [10 \times 9 \times 8 \times 7 \times 6 \times 5 \times 4 \times 3]$ ways.

i.e. $2^7 (10!)$ ways.

Example 3.8 : 10 couples are attending a party. They have to be seated in a straight line such that :

(i) Males and females alternatively.

(ii) Husband and wife sit together.

Find the number of seating arrangements in each case.   **(P.U. October 2012)**

Solution : There are 20 chairs numbered 1, 2, ..., 20 in a line.

| 1 | 2 | ..... | 19 | 20 |

(i) 10 male occupy odd numbered 10 chairs in 10! ways and 10 female occupy even numbered 10 chairs in 10! ways. OR

10 male occupy even numbered 10 chairs in 10! ways and 10 female occupy odd numbered 10 chairs in 10! ways.

The total number of possible arrangements is

$(10!) \times (10!) + (10!) \times (10!) = 2 \times (10!)^2$

(ii) First two chairs reserved for one couple.

Next two chairs reserved for second couple.

In this way last two chairs reserved for 10th couple.

In this arrangement 10 couples occupy their places in 10! ways.

Further husband and wife and change their places in 2 ways.

Total number of arrangements is $2 \times (10!)$.

EXERCISE (3.1)

1. A six faced die is thrown 4 times. How many four digit sequences will be formed?
2. There are 11 colleges giving admission to a particular course. In how many ways 4 students can take the admission to a course if (i) all students take admission to different colleges? (ii) two or more students can take admission to the same college?
3. How many bytes (8-bit strings) are there?
4. In an athletic meet 5 are taking part in high jump event, 7 are participating in discus throw, 8 are participating in hundred meters race and 6 are participating in two hundred meters race. In how many ways the first prize in the four events can be given?
5. The letters of the word SQUARE are arranged in a line. Find the total number of arrangements in which the vowels appear in the alphabetic order.
6. A variable name in a programming language must be either a letter or a letter followed by a decimal digit. How many different variables names will be there in the language?
7. A True/False test of 5 questions is given to a student. Find the number of ways in which he/she can answer the test if he/she (i) attempts all questions (ii) leaves some question blank.
8. Find the number of non-empty collections of :
   (i) $4 A^s$ and $5 B^s$
   (ii) $5 A^s$, $6 B^s$ and $4 C^s$
9. There are 5 roads from city A to city B and 4 roads from city B to city C. A journey form A to C is possible via B only. In how many ways you can
   (i) travel from A to C?
   (ii) travel from A to C and return to A?
   (iii) travel from A to C and return to A without travelling along any road which you have already used?
10. Three digit numbers without repetition are formed by using the digits 2, 3, 4, 5, 7, 9.
    (i) How many numbers are formed?
    (ii) How many of them are less than 400?
    (iii) How many of them are even?
    (iv) How many are multiple of 5?
    (v) How many are multiple of 4?

11. A store carries eight styles of pants. For each style, there are 10 different possible waist size, six pant lengths and four colour choices. How many different types of pants could the store have?

12. Give 4 bands, 7 floats and 3 equestrian units:
    (i) They go for parade down the street with the order bands followed by floats followed by equestrian units. How many parades are possible?
    (ii) Suppose they parade with each type still sticking together, but with no requirement about which type goes first, second or third. How many parades are possible?
    (iii) Suppose they forget it and just parade randomly. How many parades are possible?

ANSWERS (3.1)

1. 1296
2. (i) 7920, (ii) 14641
3. 256
4. 1680
5. 120
6. 286
7. (i) 32, (ii) 243
8. (i) 29, (ii) 209
9. (i) 20, (ii) 400, (iii) 240
10. (i) 120, (ii) 40, (iii) 40, (iv) 20, (v) 20
11. 1920
12. (i) 4! 7! 3! (ii) 3! 4! 7! 3! (iii) 14!

3.2 Permutations and Combinations

An arrangement or ordering of given n distinct objects is called a permutation. For example, if we consider 3 distinct objects say a, b and c then their permutations are

a, b, c ;   a, c, b ;   b, a, c ;   b, c, a ;   c, a, b ;   c, b, a

The permutations of 3 objects are 6 in number.

An r-permutation of n distinct objects is an arrangement of r objects out of given n objects. Thus 2-permutations of 3 objects a, b, c are

a, b;   b, a;   a, c;   c, a;   b, c;   c, b.

Also 2-permutations of 4 objects a, b, c, d are

a, b;   b, a;   a, c;   c, a;   a, d;   d, a;   b, c;   c, b;   b, d;   d, b;   c, d;   d, c.

We see that 2-permutations of 3 objects are 6 in number and 2-permutations of 4 objects are 12 in number.

The number of r-permutations of n distinct objects is denoted by $P(n, r)$ or ^nP_r.

Thus, $P(3, 2) = {}^3P_2 = 6$; $P(4, 2), {}^4P_2 = 6$.

We shall now obtain a formula for ^nP_n and ^nP_r where $r \leq n$.

To find ^nP_n i.e. the number of permutations of n objects in a row we consider n boxes arranged in a line.

$$\boxed{}\ \boxed{}\ \boxed{}\ \text{---------}\ \boxed{}$$
$$\ \ 1\ \ \ \ \ 2\ \ \ \ \ 3\ \ \ \ \ \ \ \ \ \ \ \ \ \ \ \ \ n$$

The first box can be filled in n ways. Then the second box can be filled in $(n - 1)$ ways.

The third box can be filled in $(n - 2)$ ways continuing in this way the last i.e. n^{th} box can be filled in only one way.

Therefore, by the rule of multiplication for counting, the procedure of filling all the n boxes can be completed in $n(n - 1)(n - 2) \ldots \times 4 \times 3 \times 2 \times 1$ ways, i.e. n! ways.

Our problem is solved and we have $^nP_n = n!$.

Next to find ^nP_r i.e. the number of permutations of n distinct objects taken r at a time we consider r boxes arranged in a row.

$$\boxed{}\ \boxed{}\ \boxed{}\ \text{---------}\ \boxed{}$$
$$\ \ 1\ \ \ \ \ 2\ \ \ \ \ 3\ \ \ \ \ \ \ \ \ \ \ \ \ \ \ \ \ r$$

The first box can be filled in n ways. Then the second box can be filled in $(n - 1)$ ways. Then the third box can be filled in $(n - 2)$ ways.

After continuing in this way the last box i.e. r^{th} box can be filled in $n - (r - 1) = n - r + 1$ ways.

Therefore by the rule of multiplication for counting, the total number of ways of filling the r boxes is $n(n - 1)(n - 2)(n - 3) \ldots (n - r + 1)$.

We can write this as

$$[n(n-1)(n-2)(n-3)\ldots(n-r+1)]\left[\frac{(n-r)(n-r-1)\ldots 3\times 2\times 1}{(n-r)(n-r-1)\ldots 3\times 2\times 1}\right]$$

$$= \frac{n(n-1)(n-2)\ldots\times 3\times 2\times 1}{(n-r)(n-r-1)\ldots\times 3\times 2\times 1}$$

$$= \frac{n!}{(n-r)!}$$

Hence $\quad {}^nP_r = \dfrac{n!}{(n-r)!}$

$$\boxed{{}^nP_n = n!,\ \text{distinct objects}} \quad \boxed{{}^nP_r = \dfrac{n!}{(n-r)!},\ \text{distinct objects}}$$

Clearly we have $^6P_6 = 6! = 720$ and

$$^7P_4 = \frac{7!}{(7-4)!} = \frac{7!}{3!} = \frac{7\times 6\times 5\times 4\times (3!)}{3!}$$

$$= 7 \times 6 \times 5 \times 4 = 840$$

Example 3.9 : A family consisting of 4 adults, 2 children and old man appears for dinner in a row. The two children demand for end chairs and old man does not want a child on either side of him. Find in how many ways the 7 members can occupy their chairs.

Solution : Consider 7 chairs arranged in a row

$$\square \ \square \ \square \ \square \ \square \ \square \ \square$$
$$1 \quad 2 \quad 3 \quad 4 \quad 5 \quad 6 \quad 7$$

We split-up the procedure of occupying the chairs by 7 members into 3 stages.

Firstly, two children will occupy two end chairs (box 1 and box 2) in 2! = 2 ways.

Secondly, old man does not want a child on either side of him.

This means old man cannot sit on second and sixth chairs.

Thus old man can occupy his seat on chair 3 or 4 or 5.

Thus second stage is performed in 3 ways.

Now 4 adults can occupy remaining 4 chairs in 4! = 24 ways.

Therefore, by the rule of multiplication the total number of arrangements is

$$(2) \times (3) \times (24) = 144$$

We now define r-combination. An r-combination of n distinct objects consists of an unordered selection of r objects out of n objects. It is only a subset of r objects out of n objects.

The r-combination is denoted by C(n, r) or ^nC_r or $\binom{n}{r}$.

Consider the set of three distinct elements a, b, c.

It has three 2-element subsets which are {a, b}, {a, c} and {b, c}.

Hence the number of 2-combinations of 3 distinct objects is 3 i.e. $\binom{3}{2} = 3$.

Again if we consider the set of 4 distinct objects a, b, c, d. It has 6 different subsets of 2 elements each. They are {a, b}, {a, c}, {a, d}, {b, c}, {b, d} and {c, d}.

Therefore, $\binom{4}{2} = 6$.

Verify yourself that $\binom{4}{3} = 4$.

The formula for the number of combinations (selections) of r object out of n distinct objects is obtained by using the formula $^nP_r = \dfrac{n!}{(n-r)!}$.

The problem of finding ^nP_r i.e. the number of arrangements of n (distinct) objects taken r at a time is equivalent to first select r objects from the collection of n objects [This is done in ^nC_r ways] and then find the number of these arrangements among themselves [These are r! in number]

∴ $\qquad ^nP_r = (^nC_r)(r!) \qquad$ ∵ by the rule of multiplication

$$\therefore \quad {}^nC_r = \frac{{}^nP_r}{r!}$$

$$\therefore \quad {}^nC_r = \frac{n!}{(n-r)!\, r!}$$

$$\boxed{{}^nC_r = \binom{n}{r} = \frac{n!}{r!\,(n-r)!}\,;\ \text{distinct objects}}$$

Thus we have,
$$\binom{7}{3} = \frac{7!}{3!\,(7-3)!} = \frac{7!}{3!\,4!}$$
$$= \frac{7 \times 6 \times 5 \times 4!}{6 \times 4!} = 35$$

We also have
$$\binom{n}{n-r} = \frac{n!}{(n-r)!\,[n-(n-r)]!} = \frac{n!}{(n-r)!\,r!} = \binom{n}{r}$$

This is obvious since in finding $\binom{n}{r}$ we are selecting r objects out of n objects which is equivalent to say that we are rejecting n − r objects out of given n objects.

$$\boxed{\binom{n}{r} = \binom{n}{n-r},\ \binom{n}{0} = 1,\ \binom{n}{n} = 1}$$

We advise the students to remember

$$\binom{n}{0} = 1,\ \binom{n}{1} = n,\ \binom{n}{2} = \frac{n(n-1)}{2},\ \binom{n}{3} = \frac{n(n-1)(n-2)}{6}.$$

Permutations of Identical Objects :

Consider 4 letters in the word KAKA. The number of permutations (arrangements) of these 4 letters is not 4! = 24 as given by the formula ${}^nP_n = n!$.

The reason is that the interchange of two K^s (or two A^s) does not give us different arrangement.

To find the number of different permutations in this case, we proceed as below.

First we reserve two boxes out of the four boxes for the letter K.

☐ ☐ ☐ ☐
1   2   3   4

It can be done in 6 ways i.e. box 1 and 2, or box 1 and 3, or box 1 and 4, or box 2 and 3, or box 2 and 4, or box 3 and 4.

In each of these 6 cases the remaining two boxes are used for two A^s; which are filled uniquely.

Thus, there are six different permutations of the letters of KAKA. These are listed below.

KKAA, KAKA, KAAK, AKKA, AKAK, AAKK. On this ground we prove the result below.

If there are r_1 identical objects of type 1, r_2 identical objects of type 2, ..., r_k identical objets of type k, and $r_1 + r_2 + ... + r_k = n$ then the number of different arrangements of these n object is

$$\frac{n!}{r_1! \, r_2! \, ... \, r_k!}.$$

Proof : Consider n boxes arranged in a row for given n objects.

$$\square \quad \square \quad \square \quad ... \quad \square$$
$$1 \quad\quad 2 \quad\quad 3 \quad\quad\quad\quad n$$

In first stage, we reserve r_1 boxes for the objects of type 1 and put r_1 objects into them. The selection of these r_1 boxes out of n boxes is done in $\binom{n}{r_1} = \frac{n!}{r_1! \, (n - r_1)!}$ ways.

In the second stage, now there are $n - r_1$ boxes empty.

Out of $n - r_1$ boxes, we select r_2 boxes for objects of type 2 and put these r_2 identical objects into r_2 boxes.

Here the r_2 boxes can be selected out of $n - r_1$ boxes in $\binom{n - r_1}{r_2}$ ways i.e. $\frac{(n - r_1)!}{r_2! \, (n - r_1 - r_2)!}$ ways.

Continue this process.

The last r_k boxes are filled by remaining r_k objects.

Now by the rule of multiplication the total number of ways of filling all the boxes is

$$\frac{n!}{r_1!(n - r_1)!} \times \frac{(n - r_1)!}{r_2!(n - r_1 - r_2)!} \times \, ... \, \times 1 = \frac{n!}{r_1! \, r_2! \, r_3! \, ... \, r_k!}$$

Example 3.10 : Find the number of permutations of the letters of 'INTERPRETATION'.

Solution : The word INTERPRETATION has 14 letters.

I : 2
N : 2
T : 3
E : 2
R : 2
P : 1
A : 1
O : 1
Total 14

The number of permutations is

$$\frac{14!}{(2!) \, (2!) \, (3!) \, (2!) \, (2!) \, (1!) \, (1!) \, (1!)}$$

$$= \frac{14!}{(2) \, (2) \, (6) \, (2) \, (2)} = \frac{14!}{96} \text{ [we can stop here]}$$

$$= 180180 \times 5040$$

$$= 908107200$$

Combinations of Identical Objects :

First, we explain the problem with an example.

Suppose three friends A, B, C go to the restaurant where four types of dishes D_1, D_2, D_3, D_4 are available. now the question is in how many ways they can place the order of three dishes to the waiter ?

The answer to this question is 20. These 20 types of orders are enumerated as below.

D_1 : 3 2 2 2 1 1 1 1 1 1 0 0 0 0 0 0 0 0 0 0

D_2 : 0 1 0 0 2 0 0 1 1 0 3 2 2 1 1 1 0 0 0 0

D_3 : 0 0 1 0 0 2 0 1 0 1 0 1 0 2 1 0 1 2 3 0

D_4 : 0 0 0 1 0 0 2 0 1 1 0 0 1 0 1 2 2 1 0 3

Suppose the order of 3 dishes is $D_1 = 1$, $D_3 = 2$.

The waiter will write on his paper 1//2/ and handover this paper to the supply room.

Now each worker in the restaurant knows the meaning of this order.

The four items are separated by three slashes.

Thus in our example it looks as $D_1 / D_2 / D_3 / D_4$.

Similarly, if the order consists of 3 dishes of D_4 then it is written as / / / 3.

Now we are in a position to obtain the formula for the number of selections (unordered samples) of size s from the collection of t different types of identical objects.

Suppose a collection of objects consists of r_1 identical objects of type 1, r_2 identical objects of type 2, ..., r_t identical objects of type t; then the total number of ways of selecting s objects ($s \leq r_i$ for every i) is $\binom{s+t-1}{s}$.

Proof : We have a collection of t types of objects containing $r_1, r_2, ..., r_t$ objects respectively and $s \leq r_i$ for each i. We separate the t types (called compartments) by t − 1 slashes between them as shown below.

$$\text{type 1 / type 2 / type 3 / ... / type t.}$$

Thus there is a collection of t types and t − 1 slashes now.

Suppose our selection of s objects includes i objects of type j. Then corresponding to this situation, we put i stars (*) in the compartment j. The picture looks as below.

$$\text{type 1 / ** / type 3 / ... / *** / ... / type t}$$

This arrangement consists of t − 1 slashes and s stars in a row.

Conversely the sequence of s stars and t − 1 slashes gives selection of size s out of s + t − 1 objects.

Thus, there is a one - one correspondence between two sets :

Set I : the set of selections of size s and

Set II : the set of different sequences of s stars and t − 1 slashes.

Now the number of different sequences of t − 1 slashes and s starts is exactly equal to the number of ways in which t − 1 slashes can choose their positions out of available s + t − 1 positions. This number is $\binom{s+t-1}{t-1}$.

We know that, $\binom{n}{r} = \binom{n}{n-r}$

$\therefore \binom{s+t-1}{t-1} = \binom{s+t-1}{s+t-1-(t-1)}$

$\quad = \binom{s+t-1}{s}$

If there are t types of identical objects, then s objects can be selected in $\binom{s+t-1}{s}$ ways.

SOLVED EXAMPLES

Example 3.11 : Find the number of arrangements of letters in the word 'MADAM'. Find in how many arrangements the two M^s are separated.

Solution : There are 5 letters in the word 'MADAM'.

$\quad$ M : 2
$\quad$ A : 2
$\quad$ D : 1
$\quad$ Total 5

The number of different arrangements is $\dfrac{5!}{2!\,2!\,1!} = 30$. ... (1)

Now, we first find the number of arrangements in which two M^s remain together as a single block. The number of arrangements of

$\quad$ MM, A, A, D is $\dfrac{4!}{1!\,2!\,1!} = 12$ ... (2)

From equation (1) and (2) the number of arrangements of letters of MADAM such that two M^s are separated is $30 - 12 = 18$.

Alternatively consider the following arrangement

$\quad\quad * A * D * A *$

Out of 4 places of *, we choose two places for two M^s in $\binom{4}{2} = 6$ ways; so that two M^s will remain separated. Then each time A, D, A can be arranged in $\dfrac{3!}{2!\,1!} = 3$ ways.

$\therefore$ Total number of arrangements in which two M^s are separated is $6 \times 3 = 18$.

Example 3.12 : Find the number of arrangements of the letters in the word SEEDLESS. In how many cases all three E^s are separated ?

Solution : The word SEEDLESS contains 8 letters

$\quad$ S : 3
$\quad$ E : 3
$\quad$ D : 1
$\quad$ L : 1
$\quad$ **Total 8**

The total number of arrangements is $\frac{8!}{3!\,3!\,1!\,1!} = 1120$.

Now consider the arrangement of S, D, L, S, S and 6 stars as below.

$$* S * D * L * S * S *$$

We select 3 star places for 3E^s so that all 3E^s will remain separated. This is done in $\binom{6}{3} = 20$ ways; and every time the 5 letters SDLSS can be arranged in $\frac{5!}{3!\,1!\,1!} = 20$ ways.

By the rule of multiplication such arrangements are $20 \times 20 = 400$.

Example 3.13 : A committee of k students is to be formed out of 7 students from junior class and 4 students from senior class; (where k > 0).

In each of the following, find in how many ways the committee can be formed.

(i) The committee contains 5 students out of which 3 are from junior class and 2 from senior class.

(ii) The committee includes equal number of students from junior class and senior class.

(iii) The committee consists of 4 students including at least two from junior class.

(iv) The committee consists of 4 students and one of them must be a topper from senior class.

(v) The committee consists of 4 students out of which 2 are from junior class, 2 are from senior class but the topper from senior class and the topper from junior class cannot both be in the committee.

Solution :

(i) 3 students out of 7 (junior class) can be selected in $\binom{7}{3} = \frac{7 \times 6 \times 5}{6} = 35$ ways and 2 students out of 4 (senior class) can be selected in $\binom{4}{2} = \frac{4 \times 3}{2} = 6$ ways.

By the rule of multiplication the total number of ways the committee can be formed is $35 \times 6 = 210$.

(ii) From the given condition the committee consist of

1 student from junior class and 1 student from senior class.

OR

2 from junior class and 2 from senior class

OR

3 from junior class and 3 from senior class

OR

4 from junior class and 4 from senior class.

By using the rule of multiplication and the rule of addition the total number is

$$\binom{7}{1}\binom{4}{1} + \binom{7}{2}\binom{4}{2} + \binom{7}{3}\binom{4}{3} + \binom{7}{4}\binom{4}{4}$$

$$= (7)(4) + (21)(6) + (35)(4) + (35)(1)$$
$$= 28 + 126 + 140 + 35$$
$$= 329$$

(iii) From the given condition the committee can be formed as below.

2 from 7 (junior class) and 2 out of 4 (senior class)

OR

3 out of 7 (junior class) and 1 out of 4 (senior class)

OR

4 out of 7 (junior class) and 0 out of 4 (senior class).

By the rule of multiplication and rule of addition the total number of ways of forming a committee is

$$\binom{7}{2}\binom{4}{2} + \binom{7}{3}\binom{4}{1} + \binom{7}{4}\binom{4}{0} = (21)(6) + (35)(4) + (35)(1)$$
$$= 126 + 140 + 35 = 301$$

(iv) A committee of 4 students includes a topper from senior class. There is no any other restriction.

Hence, we have to select 3 more students out of 7 + 3 = 10 students [7 from junior class and 3 from senior class because topper is already included in the committee]

Required answer is $\binom{10}{3} = \dfrac{10 \times 9 \times 8}{6} = 120$

(v) The committee consists of 4 students with the condition that the topper of junior class and the topper of senior class both cannot be included in the committee at a time. We split the problem into 3 cases.

First Case : The topper from junior class is included in the committee.

In this case, we have to select one more student from junior class out of remaining 6 students and 2 students out of 3 (senior class).

This happens in $\binom{6}{1} \times \binom{3}{2} = 6 \times 3 = 18$ ways.

Second Case : The topper from senior class is included in the committee.

In this case, we have to select 2 students out 6 (junior class) and one more student from senior class out of remaining 3 students.

This happens in $\binom{6}{2} \times \binom{3}{1} = 15 \times 3 = 45$ ways.

Third Case : Neither the topper from junior class nor the topper from senior class is included in the committee.

In this case, we have to select 2 students out of 6 remaining students (junior class) and 2 students out of remaining 3 remaining students (senior class).

This happens in $\binom{6}{2}\binom{3}{2} = 15 \times 3 = 45$ ways.

Now by the rule of addition the total number of ways of forming a committee is

$$18 + 45 + 45 = 108$$

Example 3.14 : There is a collection of 60 red balls, 50 blue balls and 25 green balls. The balls are identical in all respects except the colour.

(i) In how many was 10 balls can be selected ?

(ii) In how many ways 12 balls can be selected if the selection includes at 6 green balls?

(iii) In how many ways 8 balls can be selected if the selection includes at least one ball of each colour ?

Solution : (i) Number of types, t = 3

Size of selection, s = 10

The number of selections is $\binom{s+t-1}{s} = \binom{10+3-1}{10} = \binom{12}{10} = 66$.

(ii) First, we select 6 green balls. Then we have to select 6 more balls.

Here Number of types = t = 3

Size of selection s = 6

The number of selections is

$$\binom{s+t-1}{s} = \binom{6+3-1}{6} = \binom{8}{6} = 28.$$

(iii) First, we select one ball of each colour.

Then we have to select 5 more balls.

The number of types t = 3

Size of selection s = 5

The number of selections is

$$\binom{s+t-1}{s} = \binom{5+3-1}{5} = \binom{7}{5} = 21$$

Note : Suppose t is the number of types and s is the size of selection.

Consider the condition that the selection of size s includes at least one item of each type.

After selecting one item of each type, we have selected t items. Therefore, we have to select s − t more items.

∴ New size of selection is s − t.

The required number of selections under the given condition is then

$$\binom{size + types - 1}{size} = \binom{(s-t)+t-1}{s-t} = \binom{s-1}{s-t}$$

$$= \binom{s-1}{(s-1)-(s-t)} \qquad \because \binom{n}{r} = \binom{n}{n-r}$$

$$= \binom{s-1}{t-1}$$

By using this formula in example (iii) above, we get

$$\binom{8-1}{3-1} = \binom{7}{2} = 21; \text{ which is as before}$$

Example 3.15 : A child has a repertoire of 4 peano pieces P_1, P_2, P_3, P_4. Her parents expect her to practice 10 pieces each day.

(i) How many possible practice sessions are there ?

(ii) How many possible sessions are there if she must play each piece at least once ?

(iii) How many possible sessions are there if she must play P_3 exactly once ?

Solution : (i)   Number of types t = 4

Size of selection s = 10

Number of sessions is

$$\binom{s+t-1}{s} = \binom{10+4-1}{10} = \binom{13}{10} = 286$$

(ii) Here t = 4, s = 10.

If each piece is played at lest once then the number of sessions is

$$\binom{s-1}{t-1} = \binom{10-1}{4-1} = \binom{9}{3} = 84$$

(iii) Suppose P_3 is played exactly once. Then remaining 9 sessions are to be played by using P_1, P_2 and P_4.

∴   Number of sessions is

$$\binom{s+t-1}{s} = \binom{9+3-1}{9} = \binom{11}{9} = 55.$$

Example 3.16 : Find the number of solutions of the equation $x + y + z + w = 18$ where x, y, z, w are non-negative integers. How many solutions are there satisfying $x \geq 1$ and $z \geq 3$?

Solution : This problem is equivalent to the following.

There are 4 boxes X, Y, Z, W.

These boxes are full of identical red balls, white balls, yellow balls and green balls.

We have to select 18 balls.

Therefore number of types t = 4, size of selection s = 18.

Then the number of ways of selecting 18 balls is

$$\binom{s+t-1}{s} = \binom{18+4-1}{18} = \binom{21}{18} = 1330.$$

In the second part, we first select 1 red ball from the box X and 3 yellow balls from the box Z.

Then we have to select 14 more balls from the 4 boxes.

Then number of types   t = 4

Size of selection   s = 14.

Required number of ways of selection is

$$\binom{s+t-1}{s} = \binom{14+4-1}{14} = \binom{17}{14} = 680.$$

EXERCISE (3.2)

1. How many arrangements of A, B, ..., Z contain the string 'TRIANGLE' ?
2. Find the number of arrangements of A, B, C, D, E, F such that B is always immediately to the left of A.

   In how many arrangements B is any where to the left of A ?
3. In a meeting of 5 members A, B, C, D, E each of them speaks :
   (i) In how many cases A speaks before B ?
   (ii) In how many cases A speaks immediately before B ?
4. (i) How many 10 letter words with $4A^s$ and $6B^s$ can be formed ?
   (ii) How many 12 letter words with $3A^s$, $4B^s$ and $5C^s$ can be formed ?
5. If the vowels remain together find the number or permutations of letters in the word:
   (i) FIELD   (ii) FORTRAN
   (iii) PERFORMED   (iv) ENGAGEMENT
6. An urn contains 8 red and 7 blue balls. The balls are identical in all respects except the colour. Five balls are drawn from the urn.

   In how many cases the draw includes :
   (i) 2 red and 3 blue balls ?
   (ii) at least 2 red balls ?
   (iii) 3 red and 2 blue balls ?
7. In how many ways 5 persons can be chosen out of a group of 10 persons ?

   In how many cases the selection includes the tallest and the shortest person ?
8. How many was are there to select 3 unordered elements from a set of 5 elements assuming that the repetition is allowed ?
9. By using the letters in EVERGREEN how many strings of length ≥ 7 can be formed ?
10. In how many ways can we choose 8 notes from the collection of 100 ten rupee notes and 80 five rupee notes ?
11. From 6 different novels and 3 different dictionaries, 4 novels and 1 dictionary are to be selected and arranged in a row on a shelf so that the dictionary is always in the middle. Find the number of such arrangements.
12. Find the number of permutations of letters in the word INFORMATION.

    In how many cases the two I^s remain separated ?

13. In how many ways can one choose 3 out of 7 fiction books and 2 out of 6 non-fiction books ?

14. Five fair coins are tossed and the results noted.
    (i) How many different sequences of H and T are formed ?
    (ii) How many of them contain exactly one H ?
    (iii) How many of them contain exactly three H ?

15. Five people are to be chosen from a group of twenty for a trip.
    (i) In how many ways can this be done ?
    (ii) In how many ways selection can be done if two persons A and B refuse to travel together ?
    (iii) In how many ways selection can be done if two persons A and B refuse to travel without each other ?

16. In a class of 100 students, 40 are boys.
    (i) In how many ways a committee of 10 students can be formed ?
    (ii) In how many ways a committee of 10 students with equal number of boys and girls can be formed ?
    (iii) How many committees of 10 students are there which include 6 boys and 4 girls or 4 boys and 6 girls ?

17. Given 10 men $M_1, M_2, ..., M_{10}$. In how many ways can they :
    (i) line up ?
    (ii) line up if M_2, M_6, M_9 are together ?
    (iii) line up if M_2, M_6, M_9 are not together, even not any two of them ?

18. Given 3 men, 7 women and 8 children. Find the number of committees of size 5 that can be formed containing
    (i) no men
    (ii) M_3 and no other men
    (iii) M_3 and exactly 2 women
    (iv) M_3, W_1, W_7
    (v) Exactly one man

19. A child has 3 mangoes, 2 papayas and 2 kiwi fruits. If he eats one piece of fruit each day and only the type of fruit matters in how many different ways can the fruits be consumed ?

20. A box contains 3 red distinct balls. Another box contains 9 blue distinct balls.
    Two balls are transferred from each box to the other box simultaneously. In how many ways this can be done ?

21. A coin is tossed 20 times.
    (i) How many possible sequences of H and T are there ?
    (ii) How many possible sequences with exactly 13 heads and 7 tails ?
    (iii) How many possible sequences with exactly 5 heads in the first 10 tosses ?

22. Find the number of solutions of the equation $x_1 + x_2 + x_3 = 11$; in non-negative integers. How many of they satisfy $x_1 \geq 1, x_2 \geq 1, x_3 \geq 1$? How many satisfy $x_1 \geq 1, x_2 \geq 2, x_3 \geq 3$?

23. Find the number of solutions of the equation $x_1 + x_2 + x_3 + x_4 + x_5 = 21$ in non-negative integers satisfying
    (i) $x_1 \geq 1$
    (ii) $x_i \geq 2$ for every i
    (iii) $0 \leq x_1 \leq 10$

24. In how many ways can the letters of the word VISITING be arranged in a row such that there are no consecutive I^s ?

25. A dealer offers 5 models of cars M_1, M_2, M_3, M_4, M_5.
    A big concern is interested in purchasing 6 cars for their top level officers.
    (i) In how many ways can 6 cars be purchased ?
    (ii) In how many ways 6 cars of exactly two models are purchased ?

26. Find the number of ways to choose :
    (i) 3 out of 7 days with repetition.
    (ii) 7 out of 3 days with repetition.

27. A donut store offers 15 different kinds of donuts. In how many ways can we buy 7 ?

28. Find the number of way in which a committee of 5 members can be formed out of 10 persons so as to exclude the youngest when oldest is included.

29. A committee of 4 members is to be formed out of 6 men and 4 women.
    If the committee has to include at least 2 women and a particular women is always included in the committee, find in how many ways committee can be formed.

ANSWERS (3.2)

1. 19!
2. 120, 360
3. (i) 60, (ii) 24
4. (i) 210 (ii) 27720
5. (i) 48 (ii) 720 (iii) 7560 (iv) 5040
6. (i) 980 (ii) 1176 (iii) 2702
7. 252, 56
8. 35
9. 19635
10. 9
11. 1080
12. $\dfrac{11!}{8}, \dfrac{11!}{8} - \dfrac{10!}{4}$
13. 525

14. (i) 32   (ii) 5   (iii) 10
15. (i) 15504   (ii) 14688   (iii) 9384
16. (i) $\binom{100}{10}$

    (ii) $\binom{40}{5} \times \binom{60}{5}$

    (iii) $\binom{40}{6}\binom{60}{4} + \binom{40}{4}\binom{60}{6}$
17. (i) 10!   (ii) 8! 3!   (iii) 10! – 8! 3!
18. (i) 3003   (ii) 1365   (iii) 945   (iv) 105   (v) 4095
19. 210
20. 108
21. (i) 1048576   (ii) 77520   (iii) 258048
22. 78, 45, 21
23. (i) 10626   (ii) 1365   (iii) 11649
24. 2400
25. (i) 210   (ii) 70
26. (i) 84   (ii) 36
27. 116280
28. 196
29. 64

3.3 Circular Permutations

When we arrange n distinct objects in a row there is beginning and end. We can label the elements as first, second, third and so on. But, when the objects are arranged around a circle there is no such beginning or end.

For example, if 4 ladies appear around a circle for Garba Dance, we cannot distinguish among them that a particular lady is first, second, third or fourth.

Suppose the 4 ladies appear in the order a, b, c, d.

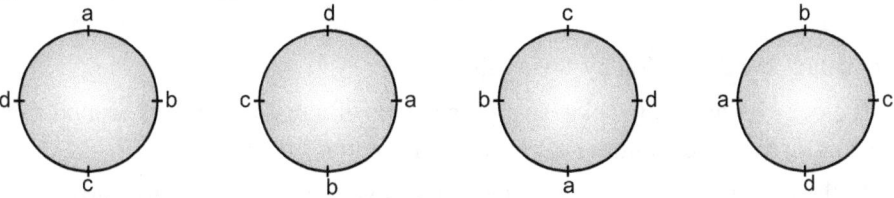

Fig. 3.1

From observer's point of view it is clear that these four arrangements are not distinct.

To find the number of permutations of n distinct objects around a circle we have to proceed as below.

We fix a place for any one of n objects on the circumference of a circle. Then the remaining n – 1 objects will occupy n – 1 places in (n – 1)! ways.

Thus, there are (n – 1)! circular permutations of n distinct objects.

Consider now 3 boys Ramesh (R), Yogesh (Y) and Girish (G). They will stand around the circle in (3 – 1)! = 2! = 2 ways as below.

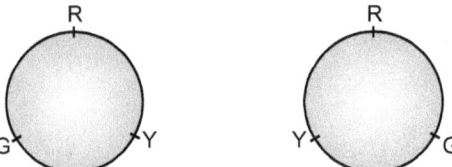

Fig. 3.2

In the first figure the order RYG is in clockwise sense whereas in second figure the order RYG is in anticlockwise sense. We take these two arrangements as distinct circular permutations.

Now consider three flowers Red (R), Yellow (Y) and Green (G). As before, we make a garland using them.

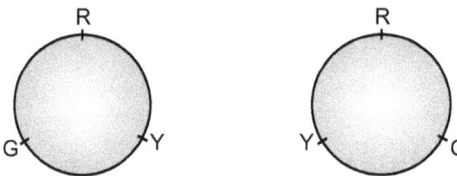

Fig. 3.3

Apparently it seems that these two garlands are different. But it is not the case.

When the garland in the first figure is rotated through 180° in a vertical plane, we get second garland.

Thus, in this case the clockwise arrangement and anticlockwise arrangement give the same garland.

We conclude the discussion by saying that

(i) If clockwise and anticlockwise arrangements of n distinct objects around a circle are considered as distinct, then number of circular permutations is (n – 1)!

(ii) If there is no distinction between clockwise and anticlockwise arrangements of objects around a circle then the number of circular permutations is $\frac{1}{2}[(n-1)!]$

SOLVED EXAMPLES

Example 3.17 : Find the number of ways in which six persons can occupy the seats around a circular table :

(i) without any restriction.

(ii) two particular persons are never together.

Solution :

(i) Without any restriction the number of circular permutations is $(6 - 1)! = 5! = 120$.

(ii) Suppose, two persons A and B out of A, B, C, D, E, F are together. This happens in 2 ways i.e. AB, BA, and every time remaining 4 persons can change their seats in $4! = 24$ ways.

So the total number of ways in which A and B are together is $2 \times 24 = 48$.

Therefore the number of ways in which A and B are not together is $120 - 48 = 72$.

Example 3.18 : Find in how many ways 8 different flowers can be strung to form a garland so that 4 particular flowers are never separated.

Solution : We consider 4 particular flowers as a single element. Then $8 - 4 + 1 = 5$ different objects are arranged around a circle.

This happens in $(5 - 1)! = 4! = 24$ ways.

Also 4 flowers which are different, can change their places in $4! = 24$ ways every time.

Therefore, by the rule of multiplication, the total number of garlands is $24 \times 24 = 576$.

Example 3.19 : Seven men and seven women sit round a circular table in such a way that there is a man on either side of every woman. How many arrangements will be there ?

Solution : Seven women take their seats around a table in 6! ways.

Then seven men occupy their seven seats in 7! ways.

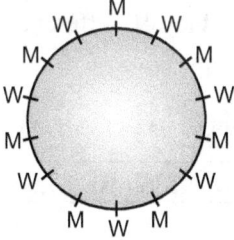

Fig. 3.4

Total number of arrangements by the rule of multiplication is

$$6! \times 7! = 720 \times 5040$$
$$= 3628800$$

Example 3.20 : Six men and 5 women sit around a circular dining table in such a way that no two women are together. How many arrangements will be there ?

Solution :

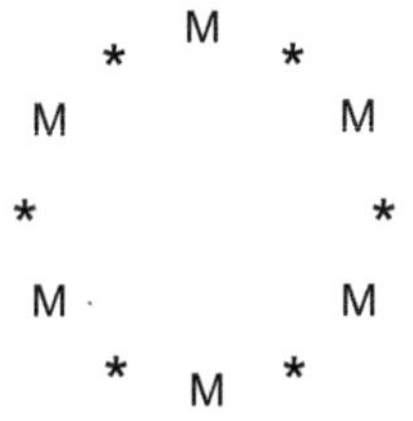

```
        M
     *     *
   M         M
   *         *
   M         M
     *  M  *
```
Fig. 3.5

As shown in the Fig. 3.5 men can occupy their seats around a circular table in $(6 - 1)! = 5! = 120$ ways.

Then 5 women have 6 choices for their seats.

This happens in $^6P_5 = \frac{6!}{1!}$ ways i.e. $6! = 720$ ways.

By the rule of multiplication the total number of arrangements under the given condition is $120 \times 720 = 86400$.

EXERCISE (3.3)

1. In how many ways five boys and five girls can sit around a circular table so that boys and girls sit alternately ?
2. The eleven members of a selection committee sit around a circular table so that the chairman and the secretary are always together. How many such arrangements are there ?
3. A 15 member committee includes one director, one assistant director and one expert. They seat around a circular table in such a way that assistant director is on one side and the expert is on the other side of the director.
   How many arrangements will be there ?
4. There are six different red roses and 4 different white roses. A garland is to be made out of them in such a way that any two of the white roses will not be together. In how many ways a garland can be made ?
5. Find the number of ways in which 10 differently coloured beads can be :
   (i) arranged in a line ?
   (ii) arranged around a circle ?
   (iii) arranged around a circle so as to form a garland ?

ANSWERS (3.3)

1. 2880
2. (2) (9!)
3. (2) (12!)
4. 21600
5. $10!, 9!, \frac{9!}{2}$

3.4 Binomial Theorem

An expression of the type $x + y$ where x and y can be constants or variables is called Binomial Expression. If n is a positive integer and by actual multiplication, we find $(x + y)^2$, $(x + y)^3$ etc., we get an expression as a sum of the terms of the type $x^k y^j$.

For example, $(x + y)^2 = x^2 + 2xy + y^2$, $(x + y)^3 = x^3 + 3x^2y + 3xy^2 + y^3$.

The coefficients of various terms of the type $x^k y^j$ are called Binomial Coefficients.

In above two expansions the Binomial Coefficients are 1, 2, 1 and 1, 3, 3, 1 respectively, we note in the first set

$$1 = \binom{2}{0}, \ 2 = \binom{2}{1}, \ 1 = \binom{2}{2}$$

and in the second set

$$1 = \binom{3}{0}, \ 3 = \binom{3}{1}, \ 3 = \binom{3}{2}, \ 1 = \binom{3}{3}$$

Therefore

$$(x + y)^2 = \binom{2}{0} x^2 + \binom{2}{1} xy + \binom{2}{2} y^2$$

and

$$(x + y)^3 = \binom{3}{0} x^3 + \binom{3}{1} x^2y + \binom{3}{2} xy^2 + \binom{3}{3} y^3 .$$

Let us now consider $(x + y)^n = (x + y) (x + y) \ldots (x + y)$; which is a product of $x + y$ with itself n times; n being a positive integer.

While performing the multiplication on right side, we shall be choosing x from i brackets and y from remaining $j = n - i$ brackets giving us x x y x y ... y.

How many such terms will be there ? Clearly these are the permutations of i identical objects i.e. x and j identical objects i.e. y.

They are

$$\frac{n!}{i! \ j!} = \frac{n!}{i! \ (n - i)!} = \binom{n}{i} \text{ in number}$$

After collecting them together, we get $\binom{n}{i} x^i y^{n-i}$; $0 \leq i \leq n$.

$$\therefore \ (x + y)^n = \binom{n}{0} x^0 y^n + \binom{n}{1} x^1 y^{n-1} + \binom{n}{2} x^2 y^{n-2} + \ldots + \binom{n}{r} x^r y^{n-r} + \ldots + \binom{n}{n} x^n y^0.$$

This is called 'Binomial Theorem'

$$\boxed{\text{Binomial Theorem} : (x + y)^n = \sum_{r=0}^{n} x^r y^{n-r}}$$

Example 3.21 : (i) Find the expansion of $(x + y)^5$.
(ii) Find the coefficient of $x^3 y^4$ in $(3x + 4y)^7$.
(iii) Find the expansion of $(2x - 3y)^6$.

Solution : (i)

$$(x + y)^5 = \binom{5}{0} x^{5-0} y^0 + \binom{5}{1} x^{5-1} y^1 + \binom{5}{2} x^{5-2} y^2$$

$$+ \binom{5}{3} x^{5-3} y^3 + \binom{5}{4} x^{5-4} y^4 + \binom{5}{5} x^{5-5} y^5$$

$$= x^5 + 5x^4y + 10x^3 y^2 + 10x^2y^3 + 5xy^4 + y^5$$

(ii) In the expansion $(3x + 4y)^7$ the term containing x^3y^4 is

$$\binom{7}{3}(3x)^3(4y)^{7-3} = \binom{7}{3} \times 3^3 \times x^3 \times 4^4 \times y^4 = 35 \times 27 \times x^3 \times 256 \times y^4$$
$$= 241920\, x^3y^4$$

Required coefficient is 241920.

(iii) $(2x - 3y)^6 = [2x + (-3y)]^6$

$$= \binom{6}{0}(2x)^6(-3y)^0 + \binom{6}{1}(2x)^{6-1}(-3y)^1 + \binom{6}{2}(2x)^{6-2}(-3y)^2$$
$$+ \binom{6}{3}(2x)^{6-3}(-3y)^3 + \binom{6}{4}(2x)^{6-4}(-3y)^4$$
$$+ \binom{6}{5}(2x)^{6-5}(-3y)^5 + \binom{6}{6}(2x)^{6-6}(-3y)^6$$
$$= (2x)^6 + 6(2x)^5(-3y) + 15(2x)^4(-3y)^2 + 20(2x)^3(-3y)^3$$
$$+ 15(2x)^2(-3y)^4 + 6(2x)(-3y)^5 + 1 \times (-3y)^6$$
$$= 64x^6 - 576\, x^5y + 2160\, x^4y^2 - 4320\, x^3y^3$$
$$+ 4860\, x^2y^4 - 2916\, xy^5 + 729\, y^6$$

Some Deductions from Binomial Theorem :

(1) $$\sum_{k=0}^{n}\binom{n}{k} = \binom{n}{0} + \binom{n}{1} + \binom{n}{2} + \ldots + \binom{n}{n} = 2^n$$

$$(x + y)^n = \binom{n}{0}x^n + \binom{n}{1}x^{n-1}y + \binom{n}{2}x^{n-2}y^2 + \ldots + \binom{n}{n}y^n$$

Put $x = 1$, $y = 1$

$\therefore \quad (1 + 1)^n = \binom{n}{0} + \binom{n}{1} + \binom{n}{2} + \ldots + \binom{n}{n}$

$\therefore \quad \binom{n}{0} + \binom{n}{1} + \binom{n}{2} + \ldots + \binom{n}{n} = 2^n$

For a given positive integer n, the sum of the Binomial coefficients is 2^n.

(2) Put $x = 1$, $y = -1$ in binomial theorem

$$(x + y)^n = \binom{n}{0}x^n + \binom{n}{1}x^{n-1}y + \binom{n}{2}x^{n-2}y^2 + \ldots + \binom{n}{n}y^n$$

$\therefore \quad (1 - 1)^n = \binom{n}{0}(1)^n + \binom{n}{1}(1)^{n-1}(-1) + \binom{n}{2}(1)^{n-2}(-1)^2$
$$+ \ldots + \binom{n}{n-1}(1)(-1)^{n-1} + \binom{n}{n}(-1)^n$$

$\therefore \quad 0 = \binom{n}{0} - \binom{n}{1} + \binom{n}{2} - \binom{n}{3} + \ldots + \binom{n}{n}(-1)^n$

From this we get

$$\binom{n}{0} + \binom{n}{2} + \binom{n}{4} + \ldots = \binom{n}{1} + \binom{n}{3} + \binom{n}{5} + \ldots$$

(3) $$\sum_{k=0}^{n} 2^r \cdot \binom{n}{r} = 3^n$$

We have, $(x+y)^n = \binom{n}{0} x^n + \binom{n}{1} x^{n-1} y + \binom{n}{2} x^{n-2} y^2 + \ldots + \binom{n}{n} y^n$

Put $x = 1$, $y = 2$

$\therefore \quad (1+2)^n = \binom{n}{0} + \binom{n}{1}(2) + \binom{n}{2}(2)^2 + \binom{n}{3}(2)^3 + \ldots + \binom{n}{n} \cdot (2)^n$

$\therefore \quad \binom{n}{0} 2^0 + \binom{n}{1} 2^1 + \binom{n}{2} 2^2 + \ldots + \binom{n}{n} \cdot 2^n = 3^n$

$\therefore \quad \sum_{k=0}^{n} 2^r \cdot \binom{n}{r} = 3^n$

(4) Let m, n, r be non-negative integers and $r \leq m$, $r \leq n$.

Then, $$\binom{m+n}{r} = \sum_{k=0}^{n} \binom{m}{k} \binom{n}{r-k}$$

For this consider a set containing m + n elements. We can choose r elements out of these m + n elements in $\binom{m+n}{r}$ ways. ... (1)

This gives us left side of the identity.

Now, we split up the given set into two sets A and B containing m elements and n elements respectively.

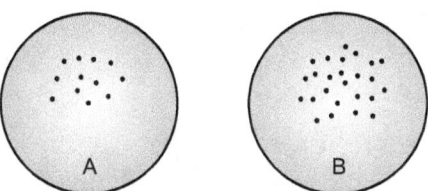

Fig. 3.6

We can choose r elements from set A and set B as follows :

r elements from A and 0 from B

OR

r – 1 elements from A and 1 from B

OR

r – 2 elements from A and 2 from B

OR

0 elements from A and r from B

Therefore, from the rule of multiplication and rule of addition for counting, the total number of ways of choosing r elements from A and B is

$$\binom{m}{r}\binom{n}{0} + \binom{m}{r-1}\binom{n}{1} + \binom{m}{r-2}\binom{n}{2} + \ldots + \binom{m}{0}\binom{n}{r} \qquad \ldots (2)$$

From equation (1) and (2)

$$\binom{m+n}{r} = \sum_{k=0}^{n} \binom{m}{r-k}\binom{n}{k}$$

This is called Vander Monde's identity.

(5) $\qquad \binom{n}{r}\binom{r}{k} = \binom{n}{k}\binom{n-k}{r-k}$

Suppose Mr. X is a chairman of a big industrial concern and there are say n other share holders.

The chairman selects r share holders on the director board and then out of them k directors are selected in the purchase committee.

This he can do in $\binom{n}{r}\binom{r}{k}$ ways. $\qquad \ldots (1)$

The same thing Mr. X can do in another way as follows.

First he selects k out of n share holders, as members of the purchase committee. These k members are then considered as directors.

Then r − k more directors are to be selected out of n − k share holders.

This happens in $\binom{n}{k}\binom{n-k}{r-k}$ ways. $\qquad \ldots (2)$

From equations (1) and (2), we have,

$$\binom{n}{r}\binom{r}{k} = \binom{n}{k}\binom{n-k}{r-k}$$

Multinomial Theorem :

An expression of the type $x_1 + x_2 + x_3 + \ldots + x_k$ is called 'Multinomial'.

Now consider the expansion of $(x_1 + x_2 + \ldots + x_k)^n$; where n is a positive integer.

We write $(x_1 + x_2 + \ldots + x_k)^n$ as a product of n factors

$(x_1 + x_2 + \ldots + x_k) \ldots (x_1 + x_2 + \ldots + x_k)$

In this product, the general term is of the type

$x_1^{n_1} x_2^{n_2} x_3^{n_3} \ldots x_k^{n_k}$; where $n_1 + n_2 + \ldots + n_k = n$.

Here two questions arise viz. What is the coefficient of the general term $x_1^{n_1} x_2^{n_2} \ldots x_k^{n_k}$? and how many terms are there in the expansion ?

The answer to the first question is as follows.

Note that $x_1^{n_1} x_2^{n_2} \cdots x_k^{n_k}$ is a permutation of k types of objects $x_1, x_2, \ldots, x_k$ such that

x_1 is repeated n_1 times
x_2 is repeated n_2 times
- - - - - - - - - - - - - - - - - -
x_k is repeated n_k times

and $n_1 + n_2 + \ldots + n_k = n$.

The number of such permutations is $\dfrac{n!}{n_1! \, n_2! \, \ldots \, n_k!}$

These terms are called multinomial coefficients.

$\dfrac{n!}{n_1! \, n_2! \, \ldots \, n_k!}$ is also written as $\binom{n}{n_1, n_2, \ldots, n_k}$.

For answer to the second question, we note that we are selecting unordered samples of size n from k types of elements with repetition allowed.

There are $\binom{n+k-1}{n}$ such samples.

The two results above, together constitute a multinomial theorem.

> In the expansion $(x_1 + x_2 + \ldots + x_k)^n$ coefficient of general term is $\dfrac{n!}{n_1! \, n_2! \, \ldots \, n_k!}$ and the number of terms is $\binom{n+k-1}{n}$

Example 3.22 : Find the coefficient of x^2yz^2 in the expansion $(x + y + z)^5$. How many terms are there in the expansion ?

Solution : The coefficient of x^2yz^2 is

$$\dfrac{5!}{2! \, 1! \, 2!} = \dfrac{120}{4} = 30$$

The number of terms is

$$\binom{n+k-1}{n} = \binom{5+3-1}{5} = \binom{7}{5} = 21$$

Example 3.23 : In the expansion of $(x_1 - x_2 + 2x_3 - 2x_4)^8$

(i) Find the coefficient of $x_1^2 x_2^3 x_3 x_4^2$.

(ii) Find the number of terms.

Solution : Given expansion $[x_1 + (-x_2) + 2x_3 + (-2x_4)]^8$

(i) Coefficient of $x_1^2 (-x_2)^3 (2x_3) (-2x_4)^2$ is $\dfrac{8!}{2! \, 3! \, 1! \, 2!} = 1680$

∴ Coefficient of $(x_1^2)(-x_2^3)(2x_3)(4x_4^2)$ is 1680

∴ Coefficient of $-8(x_1^2 x_2^3 x_3 x_4^2)$ is 1680

∴ Coefficient of $x_1^2 x_2^3 x_3 x_4^2$ is $-8 \times 1680 = -13440$. [Note this]

(ii) The number of terms is

$$\binom{8+4-1}{8} = \binom{11}{8} = \dfrac{11 \times 10 \times 9}{6} = 165.$$

Example 3.24 : State the multinomial theorem. Find the coefficient of $x^3 \, y \, z^8$ in the expansion of $(2x - 2y + 3z^2)^8$. **(P.U. October 2012)**

Solution : Multinomial Theorem : In the expansion of $(x_1 + x_2 + \ldots + x_k)^n$

(i) The number of terms is $\binom{n + k - 1}{n}$

(ii) The coefficient of $x_1^{n_1} \cdot x_2^{n_2} \ldots x_k^{n_k}$,

where $n_1 + n_2 + \ldots + n_k = n$ is $\dfrac{n!}{n_1! \, n_2! \ldots n_k!}$.

In the expansion $(2x - 2y + 3z^2)^8$ the coefficient of $(2x)^3 \, (-2y)^1 \, (3z^2)^4$ is

$$\frac{8!}{3! \, 1! \, 4!} = 280$$

Then that term is $280 \, (2x)^3 \, (-2y)^1 \, (3z^2)^4$ i.e. $[280 \times 8 \times (-2) \times 81] \, x^3 \, y \, z^8$.
i.e. $-362880 \, x^3 \, y \, z^8$.
Therefore coefficient of $x^3 \, y \, z^8$ is -362880.

EXERCISE (3.4)

1. Give combinatorial proof of the following identities :

    (i) $\binom{2n}{3} = 2 \binom{n}{3} + n^2 (n - 1)$

    (ii) $\binom{3n}{2} = 3 \binom{n}{2} + 3n^2$

    (iii) $\binom{n}{0} + \binom{n + 1}{1} + \binom{n + 2}{2} + \ldots + \binom{n + r}{r} = \binom{n + r + 1}{r}$

    (iv) $\sum_{k = 1}^{n} k \binom{n}{k} = n \times 2^{n-1}$

2. Prove that the number of dissimilar terms in $(a + b + c)^n$ is $\dfrac{(n + 1)(n + 2)}{2}$.

3. Find the coefficient of $x_2^3 \, x_3 \, x_4^4$ in the expansion $(x_1 + x_2 + x_3 + x_4)^8$.

4. How many terms are there in the expansion $(x_1 + x_2 + x_3)^7$? What is the coefficient of $x_1^4 \, x_2 \, x_3^2$?

5. Show that the coefficient of x^7 in the expansion $(1 + 3x - 2x^3)^7$ is 62640.

6. Find the coefficient of $x^2 \, y z^3$ in the expansion $(x - 2y - 3z)^6$.

7. How many dissimilar terms are there in the expansion $(5 - 2x + 4x^3)^4$?

ANSWERS (3.4)

3. 280
4. 36, 105
6. 3240
7. 12

3.5 Distribution of Objects

In many counting problems the distribution of objects into the boxes helps us in solving the problems.

The objects which are to be distributed can be of two types : distinguishable and indistinguishable. Distinguishable objects are all different from each other. We can distinguish or label them by different names.

For example :

(i) 4 children.

(ii) 6 books on Discrete Mathematics published by 6 publishers.

(iii) 52 playing cards.

(iv) red ball, green, ball, blue ball.

Indistinguishable objects are those which cannot be differentiated from among themselves. Each one of them is equally preferable.

(i) 10 copies of the same book.

(ii) 5 balls having the same colour, same size, same weight and the same smoothness.

These are indistinguishable objects.

As the above boxes or compartments into which we shall put the objects, can be distinguishable or indistinguishable.

Depending upon whether the objects are distinguishable or indistinguishable and similarly the boxes are distinguishable or indistinguishable there are four types of distribution problems.

They are :

Objects	Boxes
Distinguishable	Distinguishable
Indistinguishable	Distinguishable
Distinguishable	Indistinguishable
Indistinguishable	Indistinguishable

In our curriculum, we shall discuss first two types of distribution problems. No closed formulae are available to solve the third and fourth types of problems.

Distinguishable Objects and Distinguishable Boxes :

We explain the method by two examples :

(1) Suppose there are 8 different toys which we denote by $t_1, t_2, ..., t_8$ and 3 children c_1, c_2, c_3. Here 8 toys are distinguishable objects and 3 children are distinguishable boxes. Now, our problem is in how many ways the toys can be distributed among the children without any constraint and parcelity ? We proceed as below.

The first toy t_1 can be given to any one of the three children.

Thus, there are 3 ways of doing this action.

Then the second toy can also be given to any one of three children. Continuing in this way the 8th toy can be given to any one of three children.

By the rule of multiplication the 8 toys can be distributed among 3 children in
$$3 \times 3 \times \ldots \times 3 = 3^8 = 6561 \text{ ways.}$$

> The number of ways of distributing r distinguishable objects into n distinguishable boxes is n^r.

(2) Consider a pack of 52 playing cards. There are say 4 players and each player is given 7 cards. After distributing $4 \times 7 = 28$ cards to the players there remain $52 - 28 = 24$ cards in the deck. In this example, the 52 cards are 52 distinct objects.

Each player can be considered as a box. Thus, there are 4 different boxes. Also there is one more box i.e. the deck of remaining 24 cards.

We now find in how many ways this distribution can be made.

The first player chooses 7 cards out of 52 cards in $\binom{52}{7} = \dfrac{52!}{7!\,45!}$ ways.

Now there are 45 cards available for next distribution.

Second player chooses his 7 cards out of 45 cards in $\binom{45}{7} = \dfrac{45!}{7!\,38!}$ ways.

Now, there are 38 cards available for next distribution.

Third player chooses his 7 cards out of 38 cards in $\binom{38}{7} = \dfrac{38!}{7!\,31!}$ ways.

Now, there are 31 cards available for further distribution.

Fourth player chooses his 7 cards in $\binom{31}{7} = \dfrac{31!}{7!\,24!}$ ways.

Now, remaining 24 cards go to the deck (fifth box) in only one way.

By the rule of multiplication the total number of ways in which the whole process of distribution of cards takes place is
$$\left(\dfrac{52!}{7!\,45!}\right)\left(\dfrac{45!}{7!\,38!}\right)\left(\dfrac{38!}{7!\,31!}\right)\left(\dfrac{31!}{7!\,24!}\right)(1) = \dfrac{52!}{7!\,7!\,7!\,7!\,24!}$$

> Let there be n distinguishable objects and k distinguishable boxes. Suppose the objects are distributed into the boxes such that
>
> n_1 objects go to box 1,
>
> n_2 objects go to box 2,
>
> n_k objects go to box k
>
> and $n_1 + n_2 + \ldots + n_k = n$.
>
> Then the total number of distributions is $\dfrac{n!}{n_1!\,n_2!\,\ldots\,n_k!}$

Example 3.25 : How many ways are there to distribute 12 distinguishable objects into 6 distinguishable boxes so that two objects are placed in each box ?

Solution : The objects and boxes are distinguishable. The total number of distributions is
$$\dfrac{n!}{n_1!\,n_2!\,\ldots\,n_k!} = \dfrac{12!}{2!\,2!\,2!\,2!\,2!\,2!}$$
$$= \dfrac{12!}{2^6} = \dfrac{12!}{64} = 7484400$$

Indistinguishable Objects and Distinguishable Boxes :

The problem of counting the number of distributions of n indistinguishable objects into k distinguishable boxes is identical with the problem of counting the number of n–combinations for a set with k elements; when repetition of elements is allowed.

If n indistinguishable objects are distributed among k distinguishable boxes, the number of ways in which this can be done is $\binom{n+k-1}{n}$.

SOLVED EXAMPLES

Example 3.26 : Find the number of ways that 15 balls can be tossed into 8 distinguishable boxes under the following conditions.

(i) The balls are indistinguishable.
(ii) The balls are all of different colours.

Solution : (i) The balls are indistinguishable and the boxes are distinguishable.
Number of balls is 15. Number of boxes is 8.

∴ Number of ways of distribution is

$$\eta\binom{s+t-1}{s} = \binom{15+8-1}{15} = \binom{22}{15} = \frac{22!}{15!\,7!} = 170544.$$

(ii) The 15 different balls can be tossed into 8 different boxes in 8^{15} ways.

Example 3.27 : How many ways are there to distribute :
(i) Six objects into 5 boxes ?
(ii) Five objects into 6 boxes ?

Assume that the objects and boxes are labelled (distinguishable).

Solution : The objects and the boxes are distinguishable :
(i) Six objects can be distributed into 5 boxes in $5^6 = 15625$ ways.
(ii) Five objects can be distributed into 6 boxes in $6^5 = 7776$ ways.

Example 3.28 : In how many ways 5 balls of different colours can be distributed among 3 persons so that each person gets at least one ball ?

Solution : 5 balls are different and also 3 persons are different. If each person gets at least one ball, it happens in 2 different ways; as below.

One person gets 3 balls and the remaining two persons get 1 ball each or two persons get 2 ball each and one person gets 1 ball.

First Case : Suppose person A gets 3 balls. He can choose 3 balls out of 5 balls in $\binom{5}{3} = 10$ ways.

Then second person B can choose 1 ball out of remaining 2 balls in $\binom{2}{1} = 2$ ways.

Then third person C has only one choice.
By the rule of multiplication above three activities happen in $10 \times 2 \times 1 = 20$ ways.
Further by interchanging the role of A, B, C it takes place in 3 ways.
So the distribution 3, 1, 1 takes place in $20 \times 3 = 60$ ways.

Second Case : Suppose A gets 2 balls out of 5 balls. He can choose 2 balls in $\binom{5}{2} = 10$ ways.

Now, 3 balls are remaining. Second person B chooses again 2 balls out of 3 balls, in $\binom{3}{2} = 3$ ways.

Then third person C has only one choice.

By the rule of multiplication the distribution A : 2, B : 2, C : 1 takes place in $10 \times 3 \times 1 = 30$ ways.

Also we can change the role of A, B, C in 3 ways.

Therefore, the distribution 2, 2, 1 takes place in $30 \times 3 = 90$ ways.

From the above two cases, the total number of ways of distribution is $60 + 90 = 150$.

Example 3.29 : In how many ways :

(i) 10 different MATHEMATICS books be distributed among three students ?

(ii) 20 passengers $P_1, P_2, \ldots, P_{20}$ can be accommodated in a hotel in 4 rooms R_1, R_2, R_3, R_4 whose capacities of accommodation are 5, 5, 6, 4 respectively ?

Solution : (i) The first book can be given to any of three students.

Then second book can be given to any of three students.

We continue this upto 10th book. By the rule of multiplication total number of ways of distribution is

$$\underbrace{3 \times 3 \times 3 \times \ldots \times 3}_{10 \text{ factors}} = 3^{10} = 59049$$

(ii) Here distinguishable objects (i.e. passengers) are distributed into distinguishable boxes (i.e. rooms). Total number of distributions is $\dfrac{20!}{5!\ 5!\ 6!\ 4!}$.

Example 3.30 : How many ways are there to deal hands of seven cards to each of five players from a standard deck of 52 cards ?

Solution : The cards are distinguishable and players are distinguishable.

The number of ways of distributing 7 card hands is

$$\dfrac{52!}{7!\ 7!\ 7!\ 7!\ 7!\ 17!} = \dfrac{52!}{(7!)^5 \cdot 17!} \qquad (\because 17 \text{ cards are in the deck})$$

Example 3.31 : Find the number of ways that nine identical balls can be tossed into five distinguishable boxes under the following conditions :

(i) At least one box is to be left empty.

(ii) The third box gets an even number of balls [0 is even number].

Solution : (i) Balls are identical (indistinguishable) and boxes are different i.e. distinguishable.

At least one box is to be left empty.

For this, we assume that no box is empty i..e each box gets at least one ball.

Now $s = 9, t = 5$

The number of ways of tossing the balls such that each box gets at least one ball is

$$\binom{s-1}{t-1} = \binom{9-1}{5-1} = \binom{8}{4} = 70$$

Also total number of ways of tossing the balls without any restriction is

$$\binom{s+t-1}{s} = \binom{9+5-1}{9} = \binom{13}{9} = 715$$

By subtraction the number of ways of tossing the balls such that at least one box is empty is $715 - 70 = 645$.

(ii) The condition is that the third box gets an even number of balls i.e. 0 or 2 or 4 or 6 or 8.

First Case : Third box gets 0 number of balls.

∴ $s = 9$, $t = 5 - 1 = 4$.

∴ Number of ways is $\binom{s+t-1}{s} = \binom{9+4-1}{9} = \binom{12}{9} = 220$

Second Case : Third box get 2 balls.

Then $s = 9 - 2 = 7$, $t = 5 - 1 = 4$

∴ Number of ways is $\binom{s+t-1}{s} = \binom{7+4-1}{7} = \binom{10}{7} = 120$

Third Case : Third box gets 4 balls.

Then $s = 9 - 4 = 5$, $t = 5 - 1 = 4$

∴ Number of ways is $\binom{s+t-1}{s} = \binom{5+4-1}{5} = \binom{8}{5} = 56$

Fourth Case : Third box gets 6 balls.

Then $s = 9 - 6 = 3$, $t = 5 - 1 = 4$

The number of ways is $\binom{s+t-1}{s} = \binom{3+4-1}{3} = \binom{6}{3} = 20$

Fifth Case : The third box gets 8 balls.

Then $s = 9 - 8 = 1$, $t = 5 - 1 = 4$

The number of ways is $\binom{s+t-1}{s} = \binom{1+4-1}{1} = \binom{4}{1} = 4$

Adding the results in five cases the required number of ways of distribution is

$220 + 120 + 56 + 20 + 4 = 420$.

Example 3.32 : An executive has ₹ 10,000 in ₹ 1000 notes to distribute as bonuses among 5 of his assistants. Find how many ways are there to distribute under the following conditions :

(i) There is no restriction.
(ii) Each assistant must get at least ₹ 1000.
(iii) Each assistant must get at least ₹ 1000 and one assistant A_1 must get at least ₹ 3000.

Solution : Given problem is that of distribution of indistinguishable objects among distinguishable boxes.

There are $\dfrac{10,000}{1000} = 10$ notes of ₹ 1000 each. These are indistinguishable objects.

The 5 assistants are 5 distinguishable boxes.

∴ We have s = 10, t = 5.

(i) If there is no any restriction then the number of ways of distribution is

$$\binom{s+t-1}{5} = \binom{10+5-1}{10}$$
$$= \binom{14}{10} = \frac{14!}{10!\, 4!} = \frac{14 \times 13 \times 12 \times 11}{24} = 1001$$

(ii) Each assistant must get at least ₹ 1000 i.e. each must get at least one note of ₹ 1000. The number of ways of distribution is then

$$\binom{s-1}{t-1} = \binom{10-1}{5-1} = \binom{9}{4} = \frac{9!}{4!\, 5!}$$
$$= \frac{9 \times 8 \times 7 \times 6}{24} = 126.$$

(iii) The assistant A_1 must get ₹ 3000 i.e. he must get at least 3 notes of ₹ 1000. Also each of the remaining 4 assistant must get at least 1 note.

Now, 10 − (3 + 4) = 3 notes are remaining.

∴ s = 3, t = 5.

The number of ways of distribution is

$$\binom{s+t-1}{s} = \binom{3+5-1}{3} = \binom{7}{3} = \frac{7!}{3!\, 4!}$$
$$= \frac{5 \times 6 \times 7}{6} = 35$$

Example 3.33 : How many ways are there to distribute 18 chocolate doughnuts, 12 cinnamon doughnuts, and 14 powdered doughnuts among four school principals if each principal demands at least 2 doughnuts of each kind ?

Solution : The given problem is that of distribution of indistinguishable objects into distinguishable boxes.

The four principals correspond to 4 distinguishable boxes.

First, we meet the demand of each principal by assigning 2 doughnuts of each kind to each principal.

Then (18 − 8) + (12 − 8) + (14 − 8) = 10 + 4 + 6 = 20 doughnuts remain to be distributed.

s = 20, t = 4

Number of ways of distribution is

$$\binom{s+t-1}{s} = \binom{20+4-1}{20} = \binom{23}{20}$$
$$= 1771$$

Example 3.34 : Find the number of ways in which 8 temporary employees can be put into 5 different offices when :

(i) there is no any constraint ?

(ii) each office has at least one temporary employee ?

Solution : Eight temporary employees are indistinguishable; temporary is common property.

Five offices are distinguishable. So indistinguishable objects are put into distinguishable boxes.

(i) $s = 8$, $t = 5$.

Number of distributions without any constraints is

$$\binom{s+t-1}{s} = \binom{8+5-1}{8}$$
$$= \binom{12}{8} = \frac{12!}{8!\,4!} = \frac{9 \times 10 \times 11 \times 12}{24} = 495$$

(ii) If each office has at least one temporary employee, then the number of ways of distribution is

$$\binom{s-1}{t-1} = \binom{8-1}{5-1} = \binom{7}{4} = \frac{7!}{4!\,3!}$$
$$= \frac{5 \times 6 \times 7}{6} = 35$$

Example 3.35 : In how many ways 4 identical chocolates and 6 different fruits be distributed among 5 children ?

Solution : Distribution of Chocolates : Chocolates are given to be identical.

Therefore 4 identical objects are distributed among 5 different children.

$s = 4$, $t = 5$

Number of distributions is $\binom{s+t-1}{s} = \binom{4+5-1}{4} = \binom{8}{4} = 70$

Distribution of Fruits : Fruits are different. Any fruit can be given to any one of 5 children.

This distribution is possible in $5 \times 5 \times 5 \times 5 \times 5 \times 5 = 5^6 = 15625$ ways.

Finally, by the rule of multiplication the chocolates and fruits can be distributed in $70 \times 15625 = 1093750$ ways.

EXERCISE (3.5)

1. Find the number of ways that 15 balls can be tossed into 8 distinguishable boxes under the following conditions :
   (i) The balls are indistinguishable.
   (ii) The balls are all of different colours.

2. A restaurant serves 10 different varieties of soups. Find the number of ways, we can place 6 orders under the following conditions :
   (i) All six soups are different.
   (ii) Exactly four soups are cream of mushroom.
   (iii) At least four soups are cream of mushroom.

3. The 8 different books on Mathematics are to be distributed among three students A, B, C such that one of them gets 4 books and the remaining two get 2 books each.
   In how many ways the distribution can be made ?

4. A concert promoter has 500 unreserved grandstand seats to distribute free among alumni, students, faculty and public.
   How many possibilities are there for distributing the seats ?
5. In how many ways can three examinations be scheduled within a five day period so that no two examinations are scheduled on the same day ?
6. How many ways are there to distribute 40 identical jelly beans among four children :
   (i) Without restriction ?
   (ii) With each child getting 10 beans ?
   (iii) With each child getting at least 1 bean ?
7. There is a collection of five pens, six notebooks, six books and four compass boxes. The items of each of the four types are all identical.
   In how many ways the items can be distributed among three classes :
   (i) Without any restriction ?
   (ii) With each class getting at least one book ?
8. How many ways are there to distribute 18 different story books among 6 children ?
   (i) Without any constraint ?
   (ii) Four of them get 2 story books each and 2 of them get 5 story books each ?
   (iii) Each child gets 3 story books ?
9. In how many ways :
   (i) 8 passengers can be accommodated in 3 rooms whose capacities are 4, 2, 2 respectively ?
   (ii) 8 persons can be divided into 3 teams containing 4, 2, 2 members ?
10. In how many ways 10 identical balls can be tossed into 12 boxes if :
    (i) Each box can hold only one ball ?
    (ii) Each box can hold 10 balls ?
11. In how many ways 6 identical red balls and 5 identical blue balls can be distributed among 3 children such that each child gets at least one of each kind ?

ANSWERS (3.5)

1. (i) $\binom{22}{15}$ (ii) 8^{15}
2. (i) 210   (ii) 45   (iii) 55
3. 1260
4. 126253
5. 60
6. (i) 12341   (ii) 1   (iii) 9139
7. (i) 253   (ii) 190
8. (i) 6^{18} (ii) $\dfrac{18!}{(2!)^4 (5!)^2}$ (iii) $\dfrac{18!}{(3!)^6}$
9. (i) 420   (ii) 210
10. (i) 66   (ii) 352716
11. 60

Chapter 4...

PRINCIPLE OF INCLUSION - EXCLUSION

4.1 Introduction

In some counting problems the principle of inclusion - exclusion helps us in counting the objects. While applying the principle, we need only elementary results from the algebra of sets.

If A is a finite set under consideration, we shall write $|A|$ for the number of elements in A. For example, if $A = \{1, 2, 3, ..., 10\}$, then $|A| = 10$.

In some counting problems it is required to count the number of elements in the subsets of a set; possessing or not possessing the specified properties. The diagrams from set theory called Venn diagrams are very much useful in such cases to describe the situation pictorially.

In the following discussion throughout $\cup$ stands for the universal set, which contains all the sets under consideration. Also, we assume that $\cup$ contains in all N elements, so that

$$|\cup| = N$$

Let us consider the first and the simplest case of the problem in which counting process takes care of only one property. For example, suppose there are 60 students in a class out of which 45 have offered Mathematics as a major subject. In this example, the universal set consists of 60 elements and the set M consists of 45 elements i.e. the students who have offered Mathematics as a major subject.

Now we have $\quad |\cup| = N = 60$ and
$\quad\quad\quad\quad\quad\quad |M| = 45$

The following Venn diagram will make it clear.

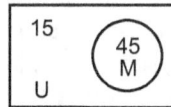

Fig. 4.1

From the diagram, one easily concludes that there are $60 - 45 = 15$ students in the class who did not offer Mathematics as a major subject.

Hence, $\quad\quad\quad |M'| = |\cup - M| = 15$

Suppose, next a problem involves two specified properties say property P_1 and property P_2.

We now consider two sets as below :

$$A = \{x \in \cup;\ x \text{ satisfies property } P_1\}$$
and
$$B = \{y \in \cup;\ y \text{ satisfies property } P_2\}$$

It is now possible that elements of $\cup$ will satisfy both the properties P_1 and P_2. Also there may be some elements in $\cup$ such that they satisfy neither property P_1 nor property P_2.

In the Venn diagram below the two circles corresponding to two sets A and B described above are shown as intersecting circles.

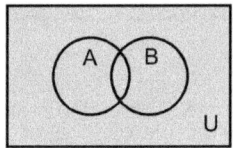

Fig. 4.2

To count the number of elements satisfying either or both the properties P_1 and P_2, we shall add $|A|$ and $|B|$.

But; in this counting the elements appearing in $A \cap B$ are counted twice. [Common region of two circles]

Therefore, we need to subtract the number $|A \cap B|$ once; giving us

$$|A \cup B| = |A| + |B| - |A \cap B|$$

This is principle of inclusion-exclusion for two sets.

From this we can find the number of elements in $\cup$ that do not satisfy any one of the properties

$$\begin{aligned}|A' \cap B'| &= |(A \cup B)'| \qquad \because \text{By De Morgan's law}\\ &= N - |A \cup B|\\ &= N - [|A| + |B| - |A \cap B|]\end{aligned}$$
$$\therefore \quad |A' \cap B'| = N - |A| - |B| + |A \cap B|$$

Illustration 1 : Among 50 students in a class, 26 secured first class in the first examination, 21 secured first class in the second examination and 17 students did not secure first class in either examination. Find how many students in the class secured first class in both examinations.

Solution : Let A = {Students who secured first class in the first examination}
and B = {Students who secured first class in the second examination}
Then $|A| = 26$, $|B| = 21$, $|A' \cap B'| = 17$; and $N = 50$; Given
Now $(A \cup B)' = A' \cap B'$ $\qquad \because$ By De Morgan's law
$\therefore \quad |(A \cup B)'| = |A' \cap B'| = 17$
$\therefore \quad N - |A \cup B| = 17$
$\therefore \quad |A \cup B| = N - 17 = 50 - 17 = 33$
$\therefore \quad |A| + |B| - |A \cap B| = 33;$ $\qquad$ By principle of inclusion - exclusion
$\therefore \quad |A \cap B| = |A| + |B| - 33$
$\qquad \qquad \qquad = 26 + 21 - 33$
$\qquad \qquad \qquad = 14$

Thus, 14 students secured first class in both examinations.

Now, we consider the problem involving 3 properties say P_1, P_2 and P_3.

Let $A = \{$Elements satisfying property $P_1\}$

$B = \{$Elements satisfying property $P_2\}$

$C = \{$Elements satisfying property $P_3\}$

$|A \cup B \cup C| = |(A \cup B) \cup C| = |A \cup B| + |C| - |(A \cup B) \cap C|$

By previous case

$|A \cup B \cup C| = [|A| + |B| - |A \cap B|] + |C| - |(A \cap C) \cup (B \cap C)|$

∵ Distributive law

∴ $|A \cup B \cup C| = [|A| + |B| - |A \cap B|] + |C| -$
$[|A \cap C| + |B \cap C| - |A \cap C \cap B \cap C|]$

∴ $|A \cup B \cup C| = |A| + |B| - |A \cap B| + |C| - |A \cap C| - |B \cap C|$
$+ |A \cap B \cap C|$

∴ $|A \cup B \cup C| = |A| + |B| + |C| - |A \cap B| - |A \cap C| - |B \cap C|$
$+ |A \cap B \cap C|$

This is principle of inclusion - exclusion for three sets.

The proof of the principle of inclusion - exclusion for n sets $A_1, A_2, \ldots, A_n$ can be given. It requires principle of induction. We omit the proof and state the result only.

If $A_1, A_2, \ldots, A_n$ are n sets, then

$|A_1 \cup A_2 \cup \ldots \cup A_n| = [|A_1| + |A_2| + \ldots + |A_n|]$
$- [|A_1 \cap A_2| + \ldots + |A_{n-1} \cap A_n|]$
$+ (-1)^{n+1} |A_1 \cap A_2 \cap \ldots \cap A_n|$

Illustration 2 : Among 100 students, 32 study Mathematics, 20 study Physics, 45 study Biology, 15 study Mathematics and Biology, 7 study Mathematics and Physics, 10 study Physics and Biology and 30 do not study any of the three subjects.

(a) Find the number of students studying all three subjects.

(b) Find the number of students studying exactly one of the three subjects.

Solution : Let M, P and B be the sets of students studying Mathematics, Physics and Biology respectively.

Then $N = 100$, $|M| = 32$, $|P| = 20$, $|B| = 45$, $|M \cap B| = 15$, $|M \cap P| = 7$,
$|P \cap B| = 10$, $|M' \cap P' \cap B'| = 30$; Given

(a) $|M' \cap P' \cap B'| = 30$ ∴ $|(M \cup P \cup B)'| = 30$

∴ $N - |M \cup P \cup B| = 30$

∴ $100 - |M \cup P \cup B| = 30$

∴ $|M \cup P \cup B| = 100 - 30 = 70$

Now by the principle of inclusion - exclusion

$|M \cup P \cup B| = |M| + |P| + |B| - |M \cap P| - |M \cap B| - |P \cap B|$
$+ |M \cap P \cap B|$

$\therefore$ $\quad 70 = 32 + 20 + 45 - 7 - 15 - 10 + |M \cap P \cap B|$
$\therefore$ $\quad |M \cap P \cap B| = 70 - 32 - 20 - 45 + 7 + 15 + 10$
$\therefore$ $\quad |M \cap P \cap B| = 5$

There are 5 students studying all three subjects.

(b)

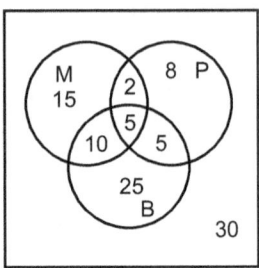

Fig. 4.3

From the diagram the number of students studying exactly one of the three subjects is
$$15 + 8 + 25 = 48$$

4.2 Derangements

We begin our discussion with a simple example below.

Suppose there are 3 locks L_1, L_2, L_3 and corresponding 3 keys K_1, K_2, K_3. A small child inserts the keys into locks at random. Now two questions arise. Firstly, in how many ways keys can be inserted into locks ? and secondly, in how many of the above cases all the keys go wrong ?

The answer to the first question is 6. As we have seen previously, the key K_1 has 3 choices, then second key has 2 choices and the third key has 1 choice. So by the rule of multiplication for counting the total number of ways of inserting 3 keys into 3 locks is
$$3 \times 2 \times 1 = 6$$

To answer the second question, we refer to the following table.

	Locks		
	L_1	L_2	L_3
Keys	K_1	K_2	K_3
	K_1	K_3	K_2
	K_2	K_1	K_3
	K_2	K_3	K_1
	K_3	K_1	K_2
	K_3	K_2	K_1

From the table, we observe that in the 1st, 2nd, 3rd and 6th row at least one key goes to the correct lock; while in the 4th and 5th row all the keys go wrong.

We know that there are 3! = 6 permutations i.e. arrangements of 3 different objects in a line. Out of these 6 arrangements there are 2 arrangements in which none of the n elements is appearing in its natural position; as shown below.

1	2	3	Natural position
1	3	2	
2	1	3	
2	3	1	
3	1	2	
3	2	1	

An arrangement in which no element appears in its natural position is called 'derangement'.

Thus the number of arrangements of 3 objects is 6; out of which 2 are derangements.

Let us consider the above situation in terms of a function. There are 6 one-one onto functions from the set A = {1, 2, 3} to itself.

$f_1(1) = 1$, $f_1(2) = 2$, $f_1(3) = 3$

$f_2(1) = 1$, $f_2(2) = 3$, $f_2(3) = 2$

$f_3(1) = 2$, $f_3(2) = 1$, $f_3(3) = 3$

$f_4(1) = 2$, $f_4(2) = 3$, $f_4(3) = 1$

$f_5(1) = 3$, $f_5(2) = 1$, $f_5(3) = 2$

$f_6(1) = 3$, $f_6(2) = 2$, $f_6(3) = 1$

In case of two functions $f_4(x)$ and $f_5(x)$, we have $f_4(x) \neq x$ for any $x \in A$ and $f_5(x) \neq x$, for any $x \in A$.

Now by using the principle of inclusion - exclusion, we shall obtain an explicit formula for D_n; the number of derangements of n distinct objects.

We start with the set $A = \{1, 2, 3, ..., n\}$.

For i, $1 \leq i \leq n$, we denote by A_i the set of those one-one onto functions f from A to A, under which $f(i) = i$

i.e. $A_i = \{f : A \to A; \ f \text{ is bijective and } f(i) = i\}$

The number of functions belonging to A_i is found as below.

The integer i can take n values and each time the remaining n − 1 elements of A can be permuted in (n − 1)! ways. So by the rule of multiplication there are n × (n − 1)! = n! functions belonging to A_i

$\therefore \quad \sum |A_i| = n!$

Next consider two integers i and j such that $1 \leq i \leq n$, $1 \leq j \leq n$.

These two integers i and j can be selected from 1, 2, ..., n in $\binom{n}{2}$ ways and every time remaining n – 2 elements can be permuted in (n – 2)! ways.

$$\therefore \quad \sum |A_i \cap A_j| = \binom{n}{2} \times (n-2)! = \frac{n!}{2!}$$

We continue in this way and get

$$\sum |A_i \cap A_j \cap A_k| = \binom{n}{3} \times (n-3)! = \frac{n!}{3!}$$

$$|A_1 \cap A_2 \cap ... \cap A_n| = \binom{n}{n}(n-n)!$$

Now by the principle of inclusion - exclusion

$$|A_1 \cup A_2 \cup ... \cup A_n| = \sum |A_i| - \sum |A_i \cap A_j| + \sum |A_i \cap A_j \cap A_k|$$
$$... + (-1)^{n-1} |A_1 \cap A_2 \cap ... \cap A_n|$$

$$\therefore \quad |A_1 \cup A_2 \cup ... \cup A_n| = n! - \frac{n!}{2!} + \frac{n!}{3!} - \frac{n!}{4!} + ... + (-1)^{n-1} \frac{n!}{n!}$$

This is the number of functions from A to A such that in each of these function, we have $f(x) = x$ for at least one $x \in A$.

Our requirement for derangement is that $f(x) \neq x$ for any $x \in A$.

Thus, we want $|A_1' \cap A_2' \cap ... \cap A_n'| = D_n$

$$\therefore \quad D_n = n! - \left[n! - \frac{n!}{2!} + \frac{n!}{3!} - \frac{n!}{4!} + ... + (-1)^{n-1} \frac{n!}{n!} \right]$$

$$\therefore \quad D_n = n! \left[1 - \frac{1}{1!} + \frac{1}{2!} - \frac{1}{3!} + \frac{1}{4!} ... \frac{(-1)^{n-1}}{n!} \right]$$

This gives the number of derangements of n objects.

For $n = 1$, $D_1 = 1! \left[1 - \frac{1}{1!} \right] = 0$

It is obvious that, when there is only one lock and its key, that key cannot go wrong.

$$\therefore \quad D_1 = 0$$

For $n = 2$, $D_2 = 2! \left[1 - \frac{1}{1!} + \frac{1}{2!} \right] = 1$

When there are 2 locks and corresponding 2 keys, then keys can be inserted into locks in 2 ways as below.

L_1	L_2
K_1	K_2
K_2	K_1

In the 2nd row of this table, we see that both the keys go wrong and $D_2 = 1$.

Similarly, $D_4 = 4! \left[1 - \frac{1}{1!} + \frac{1}{2!} - \frac{1}{3!} + \frac{1}{4!} \right] = 9$

Verify this by considering 4 locks and 4 keys.

4.3 Number of Onto Functions

We can use the principle of inclusion - exclusion to find the number of onto functions from set X to set Y.

Let X and Y be two sets having n and m elements and m respectively. For convenience we take $X = \{1, 2, 3, ..., n\}$ and $Y = \{1, 2, 3, ..., m\}$.

Let f be a function from X to Y.

Firstly, we note that for each of n elements in X there are m choices in Y for its image. So by the rule of multiplication (not rule of addition : note this) there are in all $m \times m \times ... \times m = m^n$ functions from X to Y.

Our problem is now to find how many of these m^n functions are onto functions.

As an illustration consider

$$X = \{a, b, c\} \quad \text{and} \quad Y = \{x, y\}$$

Here $\quad |X| = 3 \quad \text{and} \quad |Y| = 2$

There are $2^3 = 8$ functions from X to Y; which are represented below.

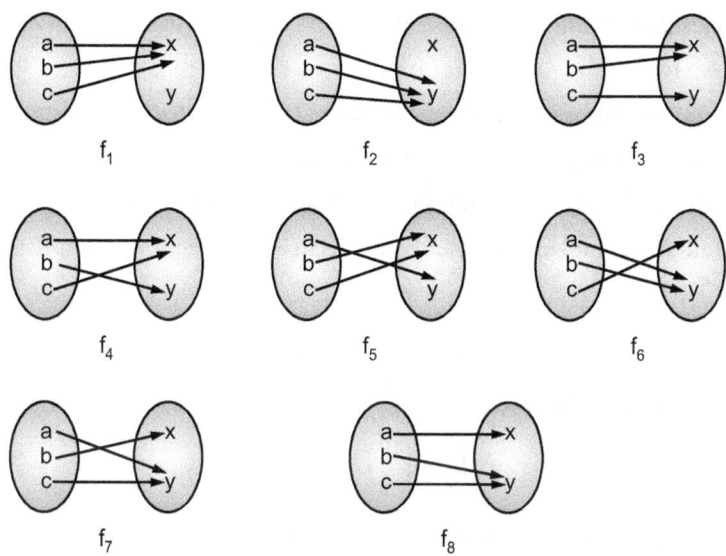

Fig. 4.4

We observe that out of 8 functions from X to Y, there are 6 functions which are onto Y. They are f_3, f_4, f_5, f_6, f_7 and f_8.

Before we obtain a formula for the number of onto functions, let us consider some particular cases.

Case - 1 : If $m > n$ then there cannot be onto function from X to Y, since there will be at least one element in Y which will not be in the range of the function.

So the number of onto functions is 0.

Case - 2 : Suppose m = n. In this case the onto function from X to Y is also one-one function and it is a permutation. We know that there are n! permutations on a set of n elements.

Hence in this case there are n! onto functions.

Case - 3 : Suppose m = 1, the codomain Y is a singleton set. Any function from X to Y is mapped onto that single element.

Hence there is only one onto function.

Case - 4 : Suppose m = 2. Total number of functions is 2^n. Out of these 2^n functions there are exactly 2 functions which are into.

In one function all elements of X map onto first element of Y and in the other all elements of X map onto the second element of Y. All remaining functions are onto. They are $2^n - 2$ in number.

We now derive a formula for the number of onto functions from X to Y; $|X| = n$, $|Y| = m$. For brevity, we use the notation "onto (n, m)" for the number of onto functions from a set of n elements to the set of m elements.

Thus, we have to find the formula for onto (n, m) when $m \leq n$.

We find the number of function which are not onto and subtract that number from 2^n.

Suppose one element say $i \in Y$ is not included in the range of a function; $1 \leq i \leq m$.

Let A_i denotes the set of those functions f such that $f(x) \neq i$, for any x in the domain.

Now i takes m values and every time there are $(m-1)^n$ functions from X to Y.

$$\therefore \quad \sum |A_i| = m(m-1)^n$$

To find $\sum |A_i \cap A_j|$, we see that the pair i, j can be selected in $\binom{m}{2}$ ways and every time there are $(m-2)^n$ functions from X to Y.

$$\therefore \quad \sum |A_i \cap A_j| = \binom{m}{2}(m-2)^n$$

Similarly, $\quad \sum |A_i \cap A_j \cap A_k| = \binom{m}{3}(m-3)^n$

and finally $|A_1 \cap A_2 \cap ... \cap A_m| = \binom{m}{m}(m-m)^n$

By inclusion - exclusion principle, we have the number of into functions from X to Y is

$$|A_1 \cup A_2 \cup ... \cup A_m| = \sum |A_i| - \sum |A_i \cap A_j| + \sum |A_i \cap A_j \cap A_k| -$$
$$... + (-1)^{m-1} |A_1 \cap A_2 \cap ... \cap A_m|$$

$$|A_1 \cup A_2 \cup ... \cup A_m| = m(m-1)^n - \binom{m}{2}(m-2)^n + \binom{m}{3}(m-3)^n$$
$$... + (-1)^{m-1}(m-m)^n$$

This give the number of into functions.

∴ $\quad \text{Onto}(n, m) = m^n - |A_1 \cup A_2 \cup \ldots \cup A_m|$

∴ $\quad \text{Onto}(n, m) = m^n - \binom{m}{1}(m-1)^n + \binom{m}{2}(m-2)^n - \binom{m}{3}(m-3)^n$
$$\ldots + (-1)^{m-1}(m-m)^n$$

Illustration 3 : Find the number of functions from $X = \{a, b, c, d, e\}$ to $Y = \{p, q, r\}$. How many of them are onto ?

Solution :
$X = \{a, b, c, d, e\}, \quad |X| = 5$
$Y = \{p, q, r\}, \quad |Y| = 3$
$f : X \to Y$

Total number of functions is $3^5 = 243$. The number of onto functions is

$$\text{Onto}(5, 3) = m^n - \binom{m}{1}(m-1)^n + \binom{m}{2}(m-2)^n \ldots$$

∴
$$\text{Onto}(5, 3) = 3^5 - \binom{3}{1}(3-1)^5 + \binom{3}{2}(3-2)^5$$
$$= 243 - (3)(2^5) + (3)(1^5)$$
$$= 243 - (3)(32) + (3)(1)$$
$$= 243 - 96 + 3$$
$$= 150$$

SOLVED EXAMPLES

Example 4.1 : How many integers between 1 to 200 are divisible by 7 or 11 ?

Solution :
$A = \{\text{Integers divisible by 7}\}$
$B = \{\text{Integers divisible by 11}\}$

The number of integers between 1 to 200 which are divisible by 7 is given by the greatest integer function.

$$\left\lfloor \frac{200}{7} \right\rfloor = \lfloor 28.57 \rfloor = 28$$

∴ $\quad |A| = 28$

Note : $\lfloor x \rfloor$ = greatest integer not greater than x.

Simiarly $\quad \left\lfloor \dfrac{200}{11} \right\rfloor = \lfloor 18.18 \rfloor = 18$

∴ $\quad |B| = 18.$

G.C.D. of 7 and 11 is 1.

∴ Integers divisible by 7 and 11 both are exactly those which are divisible by $7 \times 11 = 77$.

$$\left\lfloor \frac{200}{77} \right\rfloor = \lfloor 2.59 \rfloor = 2 \quad \therefore |A \cap B| = 2$$

By the principle of inclusion - exclusion
$$|A \cup B| = |A| + |B| - |A \cap B|$$
$$= 28 + 18 - 2$$
$$= 44$$

Example 4.2 : How many positive integers less than or equal to 1000 are divisible either by 3 or 5 or 11 ?

Solution : A = {Integers divisible by 3}
$$|A| = \left\lfloor \frac{1000}{3} \right\rfloor = \lfloor 333.33 \rfloor = 333$$

B = {Integers divisible by 5}
$$|B| = \left\lfloor \frac{1000}{5} \right\rfloor = \lfloor 200 \rfloor = 200$$

C = {Integers divisible by 11}
$$|C| = \left\lfloor \frac{1000}{11} \right\rfloor = \lfloor 90.9 \rfloor = 90$$

G.C.D. of 3 and 5 is 1.

∴ Integers divisible by 3 and 5 both are those which are divisible by 3 × 5 = 15.

∴ $$|A \cap B| = \left\lfloor \frac{1000}{15} \right\rfloor = \lfloor 66.66 \rfloor = 66$$

G.C.D. of 3 and 11 is 1.

∴ Integers divisible by 3 and 11 both are those which are divisible by 3 × 11 = 33

∴ $$|A \cap C| = \left\lfloor \frac{1000}{33} \right\rfloor = \lfloor 30.3 \rfloor = 30$$

G.C.D. of 5 and 11 is 1.

∴ Integers divisile by 5 and 11 are those which are divisible by 5 × 11 = 55

∴ $$|B \cap C| = \left\lfloor \frac{1000}{55} \right\rfloor = \lfloor 18.1 \rfloor = 18$$

Also $$|A \cap B \cap C| = \left\lfloor \frac{1000}{165} \right\rfloor = \lfloor 6.06 \rfloor = 6$$

Now $$|A \cup B \cup C| = |A| + |B| + |C| - |A \cap B| - |A \cap C| - |B \cap C| + |A \cap B \cap C|$$
$$= 333 + 200 + 90 - 66 - 30 - 18 + 6$$
$$= 515$$

Example 4.3 : The students in a hostel were asked whether they had a TV set or a computer in their rooms. The result showed that 650 students had a TV set, 150 students did not have a TV set, 175 students had a computer and 50 students had neither a TV set nor a computer. Find the number of students who :

(a) live in the hostel

(b) have both a TV set and a computer

(c) have only a computer.

Solution : $T = \{$Students having a TV set$\}$

$C = \{$Students having a computer$\}$

Then $|T| = 650, |T'| = 150, |C| = 175,$

$|T' \cap C'| = 50;$ Given

(a) Number of students in the hostel $= |T| + |T'| = 650 + 150 = 800$

(b) $|T' \cap C'| = 50$

∴ $|(T \cup C)'| = 50$

∴ $N - |T \cup C| = 50$

∴ $800 - |T \cup C| = 50$

∴ $|T \cup C| = 800 - 50 = 750$

Now by the principle of inclusion - exclusion

$|T \cup C| = |T| + |C| - |T \cap C|$

∴ $750 = 650 + 175 - |T \cap C|$

∴ $|T \cap C| = 650 + 175 - 750$

∴ $|T \cap C| = 75$

∴ There are 75 students having both a TV set and a computer.

(c) Now consider the following diagram.

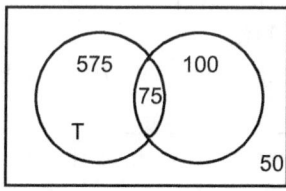

Fig. 4.5

From the diagram there are 100 students having only a computer i.e.

$|C| - |T \cap C| = 175 - 75$

$= 100$

Example 4.4 : There are 100 students in a class out of which 60 are boys; 30 students are from rural area and 10 are boys from rural area. Find how many girl students from urban area are there in the class.

Solution : Let $A = \{\text{boys}\}$
$B = \{\text{Students from rural area}\}$

Now, $N = 100$, $|A| = 60$, $|B| = 30$, $|A \cap B| = 10$; Given

Then by the inclusion - exclusion principle,
$$|A \cup B| = |A| + |B| - |A \cap B|$$
$\therefore \quad |A \cup B| = 60 + 30 - 10 = 80$

The set $A' \cap B'$ denotes the girl students from urban area.
$$|A' \cap B'| = |(A \cup B)'| = N - |A \cup B|$$
$\therefore \quad |A' \cap B'| = 100 - 80 = 20$

$\therefore$ There are 20 girl students from urban area.

Example 4.5 : At the university 60% of the students play tennis, 50% of them play bridge, 70% jog, 30% play tennis and jog, 20% play tennis and bridge, and 40% play bridge and jog. Some one claimed that 20% of the students jog and play bridge and tennis, would you believe this claim ? Justify your answer.

Solution :
$A = \{\text{Students playing tennis}\}$
$B = \{\text{Students playing bridge}\}$
$C = \{\text{Students who jog}\}$

Take $N = 100$, Then $|A| = 60$, $|B| = 50$, $|C| = 70$,
$|A \cap C| = 30$, $|A \cap B| = 20$, $|B \cap C| = 40$

Assume that the claim is true.

Then $|A \cap B \cap C| = 20$

Now by the principle of inclusion - exclusion
$$|A \cup B \cup C| = |A| + |B| + |C| - |A \cap B| - |A \cap C| - |B \cap C| + |A \cap B \cap C|$$
$\therefore \quad |A \cup B \cup C| = 60 + 50 + 70 - 20 - 30 - 40 + 20$
$\therefore \quad |A \cup B \cup C| = 110$

This contradicts to the fact that there are only 100 students at the university.

$\therefore$ Claim is not accepted.

Example 4.6 : Find the number of ways in which 8 passengers can be put in 3 rooms such that no room is vacant. Assume that there is no restriction on the accommodation capacity in any of the rooms.

Solution : The total number of ways of accommodating 8 passengers in 3 rooms is
$$3^8 = 6561$$

We shall first find the number of ways of accommodation when at least one rooms is vacant.

Let A_i denote the event that i^{th} room is vacant. In this case, 8 passengers are accommodated in 2 rooms in $2^8 = 256$ ways.

∴ $|A_1| = 256$, $|A_2| = 256$, $|A_3| = 256$

If 2 rooms are vacant, then 8 passengers are accommodated in one room in only one way.

∴ $|A_1 \cap A_2| = 1$; $|A_1 \cap A_3| = 1$, $|A_2 \cap A_3| = 1$.

It is impossible that all the three rooms are vacant.

∴ $|A_1 \cap A_2 \cap A_3| = 0$

Now by the principle of inclusion-exclusion

$|A_1 \cup A_2 \cup A_3| = |A_1| + |A_2| + |A_3| - |A_1 \cap A_2| - |A_1 \cap A_3|$
$\qquad\qquad\qquad\qquad - |A_2 \cap A_3| + |A_1 \cap A_2 \cap A_3|$

∴ $|A_1 \cup A_2 \cup A_3| = 256 + 256 + 256 - 1 - 1 - 1 + 0$

∴ $|A_1 \cup A_2 \cup A_3| = 765$

If no room is vacant, then the required number of accommodations is $6561 - 765 = 5796$.

Alternative Solution :

8 passengers are put in 3 rooms and no room remains vacant. This is equivalent to finding the number of onto functions from 8 elements set to 3 element set onto

$$(8, 3) = m^n - \binom{m}{1}(m-1)^n + \binom{m}{2}(m-2)^n \dots$$
$$= 3^8 - \binom{3}{1}(3-1)^8 + \binom{3}{2}(3-2)^8$$
$$= 6561 - (3)(2)^8 + (3)(1)^8$$
$$= 6561 - 768 + 3$$
$$= 6561 - 765$$
$$= 5796$$

Example 4.7 : How many integers out of the list 1, 2, 3, ..., 1000 are perfect squares or perfect cubes ?

Solution : The list of perfect squares is the set

$A = \{1, 4, 9, 16, 25, 36, 49, 64, 81, 100, 121, 144, 169, 196, 225, 256, 289, 324, 361, 400, 441, 484, 529, 576, 625, 676, 729, 784, 841, 900, 961\}$

∴ $|A| = 31$

The list of perfect cubes is the set

$B = \{1, 8, 27, 64, 125, 216, 343, 512, 729, 1000\}$

$|B| = 10$

Now $A \cap B = \{1, 64, 729\}$

∴ $|A \cap B| = 3$

Then by the principle of inclusion - exclusion;

$|A \cup B| = |A| + |B| - |A \cap B|$

∴ $|A \cup B| = 31 + 10 - 3$

∴ $|A \cup B| = 38$

∴ There 38 integers out of the list 1, 2, ..., 1000 which are either perfect square or perfect cube.

Example 4.8 : Thirty cars were assembled in a factory. The options available were a radio, an air conditioner and white wall tyres. It is known that 15 of the cars have radios, 8 have air conditioners and 6 have white wall tyres. Moreover, 3 of them have all three options. Then at least how many cars do not have any options at all ?

Solution : Let, A = {Cars having radio}
B = {Cars having air conditioner} and
C = {Cars having white wall tyres}

Now, $N = 30$, $|A| = 15$, $|B| = 8$, $|C| = 6$, $|A \cap B \cap C| = 3$; Given

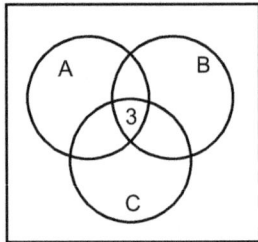

Fig. 4.6

By the principle of inclusion - exclusion

$$|A \cup B \cup C| = |A| + |B| + |C| - |A \cap B| - |A \cap C| - |B \cap C| + |A \cap B \cap C|$$

∴ $|A' \cap B' \cap C'| = N - |A \cup B \cup C|$

∴ $|A' \cap B' \cap C'| = 30 - [15 + 8 + 6 - |A \cap B| - |A \cap C| - |B \cap C| + |A \cap B \cap C|]$

∴ $|A' \cap B' \cap C'| = 30 - [29 - |A \cap B| - |A \cap C| - |B \cap C| + 3]$

∴ $|A' \cap B' \cap C'| = |A \cap B| + |A \cap C| + |B \cap C| - 2$ ... (1)

Now $|A \cap B| \geq 3$
$|A \cap C| \geq 3$ ... (2)
$|B \cap C| \geq 3$ See diagram

Use equations (2) in (1).

∴ $|A' \cap B' \cap C'| \geq 3 + 3 + 3 - 2$

∴ $|A' \cap B' \cap C'| \geq 7$

Hence at least 7 cars do not have any of the three options.

Example 4.9 : In how many ways 5 different programs can be assigned to 4 programmers, by assuming that each programmer is assigned at least one program ?

Solution : A = {P_1, P_2, P_3, P_4, P_5} is a set of programs, and
B = {a, b, c, d} is a set of 4 programmers

We have to find the number of onto functions from A to B.

$$\text{Onto } (n, m) = m^n - \binom{m}{1}(m-1)^n + \binom{m}{2}(m-2)^n \ldots$$

$$\therefore \quad \text{Onto}(5,4) = 4^5 - \binom{4}{1}(4-1)^5 + \binom{4}{2}(4-2)^5 - \binom{4}{3}(4-3)^5 + \binom{4}{4}(4-4)^5$$
$$= 4^5 - (4)(3^5) + (6)(2^5) - (4)(1^5)$$
$$= 1024 - (4)(243) + (6)(32) - (4)(1)$$
$$= 1024 - 972 + 192 - 4$$
$$= 1216 - 976$$
$$= 240$$

$\therefore$ Programs can be assigned in 240 ways.

Example 4.10 : There are 325 colleges in a certain state that have at least one of the three facilities viz. Hostel facility, credit shop and career guidance facility. 225 colleges have hostel facility, 90 colleges have credit shop facility and 60 have career guidance facility. Further 20 colleges have all three facilities.

Find how many colleges have exactly two of three facilities.

Solution : Let $\quad A = \{\text{Colleges having hostel facility}\}$
$\quad\quad\quad\quad\quad\quad B = \{\text{Colleges having credit shop facility}\}$
$\quad\quad\quad\quad\quad\quad C = \{\text{Colleges having career guidance facility}\}$

Since each college has at least one of the facilities,
$$N = |A \cup B \cup C| = 325$$
Also $|A| = 225$, $|B| = 90$, $|C| = 60$ and $|A \cap B \cap C| = 20$

By the principle of inclusion - exclusion
$$|A \cup B \cup C| = |A| + |B| + |C| - |A \cap B| - |A \cap C| - |B \cap C| + |A \cap B \cap C|$$

$\therefore \quad 325 = 225 + 90 + 60 - |A \cap B| - |A \cap C| - |B \cap C| + 20$
$\therefore \quad |A \cap B| + |A \cap C| + |B \cap C| = 225 + 90 + 60 + 20 - 325$
$\therefore \quad |A \cap B| + |A \cap C| + |B \cap C| = 70$

This sum includes $|A \cap B \cap C| = 20$, three times.

$\therefore$ The number of colleges having exactly two facilities is
$$|A \cap B| + |A \cap C| + |B \cap C| - 3 \cdot |A \cap B \cap C| = 70 - (3)(20) = 15$$

$\therefore$ There are 15 colleges having exactly two facilities.

Example 4.11 : A survey of 500 TV watchers revealed the following data. 285 watch foot ball, 195 watch hockey, 115 watch basket ball, 45 watch foot ball and basket ball, 70 watch foot ball and hockey, 50 watch hockey and basket ball 50 do not watch any of the three games.

(a) How many people in the survey watch all three games ?
(b) How many people watch exactly one game ?

Solution : $\quad\quad A = \{\text{People watching foot ball}\}$
$\quad\quad\quad\quad\quad\quad B = \{\text{People watching hockey}\}$
$\quad\quad\quad\quad\quad\quad C = \{\text{People watching basket ball}\}$

Then $N = 500$, $|A| = 285$, $|B| = 195$, $|C| = 115$, $|A \cap C| = 45$, $|A \cap B| = 70$, $|B \cap C| = 50$, $|A' \cap B' \cap C'| = 50$; Given

(a) Now $|A' \cap B' \cap C'| = 50$

$\therefore \quad |(A \cup B \cup C)'| = 50$

$\therefore \quad N - |A \cup B \cup C| = 50$

$\therefore \quad |A \cup B \cup C| = N - 50 = 500 - 50 = 450$

By the principle of inclusion - exclusion, we have

$$|A \cup B \cup C| = |A| + |B| + |C| - |A \cap B| - |A \cap C| - |B \cap C| + |A \cap B \cap C|$$

$\therefore \quad 450 = 285 + 195 + 115 - 70 - 45 - 50 + |A \cap B \cap C|$

$\therefore \quad |A \cap B \cap C| = 450 - 285 - 195 - 115 + 70 + 45 + 50$

$\therefore \quad |A \cap B \cap C| = 20$

$\therefore$ 20 people watch all three games.

(b)

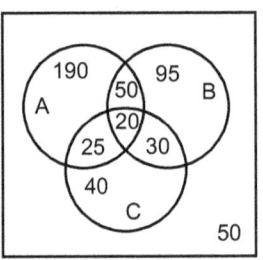

Fig. 4.7

People watching foot ball only = 190

People watching hockey only = 95

People watching basket ball only = 40

Example 4.12 : Out of 100 cups of coffee, 25 are too hot, 35 are too cold, 45 are too bitter, 15 are too hot and too bitter, and 5 are too cold and too bitter.

How many are just right ?

Solution : Let $\quad A = \{\text{too hot cups}\}$

$B = \{\text{too cold cups}\}$ and

$C = \{\text{too bitter cups}\}$

Then $N = 100$, $|A| = 25$, $|B| = 35$, $|C| = 45$, $|A \cap C| = 15$, $|B \cap C| = 5$.

Obviously $|A \cap B| = 0$ and also $|A \cap B \cap C| = 0$; since it cannot be too hot and too cold simultaneously.

By the principle of inclusion - exclusion

$$|A \cup B \cup C| = |A| + |B| + |C| - |A \cap B| - |A \cap C| - |B \cap C| + |A \cap B \cap C|$$

$|A \cup B \cup C| = 25 + 35 + 45 - 0 - 15 - 5 + 0$

$\therefore \quad |A \cup B \cup C| = 85$

Then $\quad |A' \cap B' \cap C'| = N - |A \cup B \cup C|$

$\therefore \quad |A' \cap B' \cap C'| = 100 - 85 = 15$

Hence 15 cups are just right.

Example 4.13 : Compute D_5.

Solution :
$$D_n = n! \left[1 - \frac{1}{1!} + \frac{1}{2!} - \frac{1}{3!} + \ldots + (-1)^n \frac{1}{n!} \right]$$

$$D_5 = 5! \left[1 - \frac{1}{1!} + \frac{1}{2!} - \frac{1}{3!} + \frac{1}{4!} - \frac{1}{5!} \right]$$

$$= 5! \left[1 - 1 + \frac{1}{2} - \frac{1}{6} + \frac{1}{24} - \frac{1}{120} \right]$$

$$= 120 \left[\frac{1}{2} - \frac{1}{6} + \frac{1}{24} - \frac{1}{120} \right]$$

$$= 60 - 20 + 5 - 1$$

$$= 44$$

Example 4.14 : Compute the number of functions from A = {a, b, c, d} to B = {0, 1}. How many of them are onto ?

Solution : $|A| = 4$, $|B| = 2$

There are $2^4 = 16$ functions.

The number of onto functions s $2^n - 2 = 2^4 - 2 = 16 - 2 = 14$

Example 4.15 : Consider the statement.

There are 36 onto functions from set X to set Y"

What conclusion you can draw from this statement ?

Solution : $f : X \to Y$

The number of onto functions is 36.

We shall find $|X|$ and $|Y|$.

If $|Y| = 1$, there is only one onto function from any set X to Y.

If $|Y| = 2$ and $|X| = n$ then there are $2^n - 2$ onto functions from X to Y.

Now, $2^n - 2 \neq 36$ for any value of n.

Suppose $|Y| = m = 3$ and $|X| = n = 3$.

In this case the number of onto functions is $3! = 6 \neq 36$.

Suppose m = 3 and n = 4, then the number of onto functions from X to Y is

$$m^n - \binom{m}{1}(m-1)^n + \binom{m}{2}(m-2)^n \ldots = (3)^4 - \binom{3}{1}(3-1)^4 + \binom{3}{2}(3-2)^4$$

$$= 81 - (3)(2)^4 + (3)(1)^4$$

$$= 81 - 48 + 3$$

$$= 36$$

Thus, we conclude that $|X| = 4$ and $|Y| = 3$.

Example 4.16 : At a gathering, there are 200 smokers, 300 hot beverage takers, 250 cold beverage takers. Also, 110 are smokers as well as cold beverage takers, 130 smokers and hot beverage takers and 140 who can take hot and cold beverages. There are 100 persons who are used to all the three habits. Find the number of persons at the gathering. **(P.U. Oct. 20012)**

Solution : Let A, B, C be three sets

$$A = \{\text{smokers}\}$$
$$B = \{\text{cold beverage takers}\}$$
$$C = \{\text{hot beverage takers}\}$$

Then $|A| = 200$, $|B| = 250$, $|C| = 300$, $|A \cap B| = 110$, $|A \cap C| = 130$, $|B \cap C| = 140$, $|A \cap B \cap C| = 100$.

We have to find $|A \cup B \cup C|$.

By the principle of inclusion-exclusion for three sets, we have

$$|A \cup B \cup C| = [|A| + |B| + |C|] - [|A \cap B| + |A \cap C| + |B \cap C|] + |A \cap B \cap C|$$
$$= [200 + 250 + 300] - [110 + 130 + 140] + 100$$
$$= 750 - 380 + 100$$
$$= 470$$

∴ The number of persons in the gathering is 470.

Example 4.17 : How many solutions are there to the equation $x_1 + x_2 + x_3 = 17$; where x_1, x_2 and x_3 are non-negative integers with :

(i) $x_1 > 1$, $x_2 > 2$, $x_3 > 3$?, (ii) $x_1 < 6$ and $x_3 > 5$?, (iii) $x_1 < 4$, $x_2 < 3$ and $x_3 > 5$?

Solution : (i) $x_1 + x_2 + x_3 = 17$
$$x_1 > 1,\ x_2 > 2,\ x_3 > 3$$
∴ $x_1 \geq 2,\ x_2 \geq 3,\ x_3 \geq 4$

First, we distribute 2 objects to box X_1, 3 objects to box X_2 and 4 objects to box X_3. Then $17 - (2 + 3 + 4) = 8$ objects remain to be distributed.

Now equation becomes
$$x_1 + x_2 + x_3 = 8$$
with $x_1 \geq 0,\ x_2 \geq 0,\ x_3 \geq 0$.

The number of ways in which this can be done is $\binom{8 + 3 - 1}{8} = \binom{10}{8} = \frac{10!}{8!\ 2!} = 45$.

(ii) $x_1 + x_2 + x_3 = 17$;
$$x_1 < 6,\ x_3 > 5$$

The condition $x_3 > 5 \Rightarrow x_3 \geq 6$.

First, we distribute 6 objects to the box X_3. Then $17 - 6 = 11$ objects remain to be distributed.

Now the equation is
$$x_1 + x_2 + x_3 = 11$$
$$x_1 < 6$$

All solutions of $x_1 + x_2 + x_3 = 11$ with $x_1 \geq 0,\ x_2 \geq 0,\ x_3 \geq 0$ are
$$\binom{11 + 3 - 1}{11} = \binom{13}{11} = 78$$

From this we subtract those solutions which satisfy the condition $x_1 < 6$.

Now suppose $x_1 \geq 6$, (which is opposite of $x_1 < 6$)
After assigning 6 objects into box X_1 there remain $11 - 6 = 5$ objects to be distributed.
The number of such solutions is
$$\binom{5+3-1}{5} = \binom{7}{5} = 21$$
The required number of solutions is $78 - 21 = 57$.

(iii) $x_1 + x_2 + x_3 = 17$
$x_1 < 4, \ x_2 < 3, \ x_3 > 5.$
Here $x_3 > 5$ means $x_3 \geq 6$
After distributing 6 objects to box X_3, we have
$$x_1 + x_2 + x_3 = 11$$
$$x_1 < 4, \ x_2 < 3, \ x_3 \geq 0$$
Now if $x_1 \geq 0, \ x_2 \geq 0, \ x_3 \geq 0$ then number of solutions is
$$\binom{11+3-1}{11} = \binom{13}{11} = 78 \qquad \ldots (i)$$
Next consider two conditions.
    Condition A : $x_1 < 4$
    Condition B : $x_2 < 3$
Failure of condition A i.e. A' means $x_1 \geq 4$.
Failure of condition B i.e. B' means $x_2 \geq 3$.
By using the principle of inclusion and exclusion, we now find the number of solutions such that at least one of the conditions A and B fails i.e. we find
$$|A' \cup B'| = |A'| + |B'| - |A' \cap B'|$$
To find $|A'|$ we have $x_1 \geq 4$.
After distributing 4 objects to the first box; $11 - 4 = 7$ objects remain to be distributed.
This number is $\quad |A'| = \binom{7+3-1}{7} = \binom{9}{7} = 36$
To find $|B'|$ we have $x_2 \geq 3$.
After distributing 3 objects to the second box; $11 - 3 = 8$ objects remain to be distributed.
This number is $\quad |B'| = \binom{8+3-1}{8} = \binom{10}{8} = 45$
To find $|A' \cap B'|$, we have $x_1 \geq 4$ and $x_2 \geq 3$.
After distributing 4 objects to the first box and 3 objects to the second box; $11 - (4+3) = 4$ objects remain to be distributed.

This number is $|A' \cap B'| = \binom{4+3-1}{4} = \binom{6}{4} = 15$
Then $\qquad |A' \cup B'| = |A'| + |B'| - |A' \cap B'|$
$$= 36 + 45 - 15$$
$$= 66$$
The number of solutions in which at least one of the two conditions A and B fails is 66.
The total number of solutions is 78.
Therefore, the number of solutions in which both the conditions A : $x_1 < 4$ and B : $x_2 < 3$ hold is $78 - 66 = 12$.

Example 4.18 : Find the number of integer solutions for $x_1 + x_2 + x_3 = 21$ such that $2 \leq x_1 \leq 4$, $5 \leq x_2 \leq 9$, and $x_3 > 0$. **(P.U. Oct. 2012)**

Solution : $x_1 + x_2 + x_3 = 21$
$$2 \leq x_1 \leq 4,\ 5 \leq x_2 \leq 9,\ x_3 > 0.$$

The condition is $x_3 > 0 \Rightarrow x_3 \geq 1$.

We distribute 2 objects to box X_1, 5 objects to box X_2 and 1 object to box X_3. In this way $2 + 5 + 1 = 8$ objects are distributed.

There remain $21 - 8 = 13$ objects to be distributed.

Now problem reduces to
$$x_1 + x_2 + x_3 = 13$$
$$0 \leq x_1 \leq 43,\ x_2 \leq 9,\ x_3 \geq 0$$

The total number of solutions in non-negative integers is
$$\binom{13+3-1}{13} = \binom{15}{13} = 105.$$

Now consider two condition $x_1 \leq 4$ and $x_2 \leq 9$.

By using principle of inclusion-exclusion, we find the number of solutions such that at least one of these two conditions fails.

Condition   A : $x_1 \leq 4$
$\therefore$ A' : $x_1 \geq 5$

After distributing 5 objects to box X_1 there remain $13 - 5 = 8$ objects to be distributed.

Then the number of solutions for the equation $x_1 + x_2 + x_3 = 8$ is
$$\binom{8+3-1}{8} = \binom{10}{8} = 45$$
$\therefore$ $|A'| = 45$

Condition   B : $x_2 \leq 9$
$\therefore$ B' : $x_2 \geq 10$

After distributing 10 objects to box X_2 there remain $13 - 10 = 3$ objects to be distributed.

Then the number of solutions for the equation $x_1 + x_2 + x_3 = 3$ is
$$\binom{3+3-1}{3} = \binom{5}{3} = 10$$
$\therefore$ $|B'| = 10$

Conditions A and B $\Rightarrow$ A' : $x_1 \geq 5$ and B' : $x_2 \geq 10$
$\therefore$ $|A'| + |B'| = 5 + 10 = 15$

but there are only 13 objects to be distributed.
$\therefore$ $|A' \cap B'| = 0$

By the principle of inclusion-exclusion
$$|A' \cup B'| = |A'| + |B'| - |A' \cap B'|$$
$\therefore$ $|A' \cup B'| = 45 + 10 - 0$
$\therefore$ $|A' \cup B'| = 55$

We conclude that one of total 105 solutions the 55 solutions are such that at least one of the two condition A and B fails.

Therefore, there are $105 - 55 = 50$ solutions in which both the conditions A and B are satisfied.

Answer is 50.

EXERCISE (4.1)

1. Find the number of :
   (a) Integers from 1 to 300 which are divisible by 7 or 11.
   (b) Integers from 1 to 200 inclusive, which are not divisible by any of 2, 5 or 7.
   (c) Positive integers less than 1000 which are divisible by 2 or 5 or 7.
   (d) Integers from 1 to 999 inclusive, which are divisible by 3 but not by 4.
   (e) Integers from 1 to 1000, inclusive not divisible by any one of 5 and 7.
   (f) Positive integers not exceeding 900 which are either odd or a perfect square.

2. How many integers from 100 to 999 either begin or end with 3 ?

3. How many integers from 1 to 200 inclusive, are divisible by 3 or 5 or 7 ? How many are divisible by 3 or 5 but not divisible by 7 ?

4. Suppose that 100 out of 120 Mathematics students at a college take at least one of the languages French, German, Russian. Also suppose 65 study French, 20 study French and German, 45 study German, 25 study French and Russian, 42 study Russian, 15 study German and Russian. Find the number of students who study :
   (a) all three languages.
   (b) exactly one language.
   (c) exactly two languages.

5. The college catering service must decide if the mix of food that is supplied for receptions is appropriate. Out of 100 people surveyed, 37 eat fruits, 33 eat vegetables, 9 take cheese and fruits, 12 take cheese and vegetables, 10 eat fruits and vegetables. Also 12 eat only cheese and 3 report they eat all three offerings.
   How many people surveyed eat cheese ? How many do not eat any of the offerings ?

6. A company want to hire 25 programmers to handle systems programming jobs and 40 programmers for applications programming. Out of the hired programmers 10 are expected to perform jobs of both the types. How many programmers should the company hire ?

7. A survey of households reveals that 96% have at least one TV set, 98% have telephone service and 95% have telephone service and at least one TV set. Find what percentage of households have neither telephone service nor a TV set.

8. A survey was conducted among 1000 people. Of these 595 are Democrats, 595 wear glasses and 550 like ice-cream, 395 of them are Democrats who wear glasses, 350 of them are Democrats who like ice-cream, and 400 of them wear glasses and like ice-cream; 250 of them are Democrats who wear glasses and like ice-cream.
   How many of them who are not Democrats, do not wear glasses and do not like ice-cream ?
   How many of them are Democrats who do not wear glasses and do not like ice-cream ?

9. Of 1000 applicants for a mountain climbing trip in the Himalayas, 450 get altitude sickness, 622 are not in good enough shape and 30 have allergies. An applicant qualifies if and only if this applicant does not get altitude sickness, is in good shape, and does not have allergies.

There are 111 applicants who get altitude sickness and are not in good shape, 14 who get altitude sickness and have allergies, 18 who are not in good enough shape and have allergies, and 9 who get altitude sickness, are not in good enough shape and have allergies.

Find how many applicants qualify for mountain climbing trip ?

10. A survey has been taken on methods of commuter travel. Each respondent was asked to check BUS, TRAIN, or AUTOMOBILE as a major method of travelling to work. More than one answer was permitted. The results reported were as follows :
BUS : 30, TRAIN : 35, AUTOMOBILE : 100, BUS and TRAIN : 15,
BUA and AUTOMOBILE : 15, TRAIN and AUTOMOBILE : 20 and all three methods : 5.

Find how many people completed the survey form.

11. Seventy five children visited an amusement park where there are three types of rides available : Merry-go-round, roller coaster and Ferries wheel. It is know that 20 of them have taken all three rides and 55 of them have taken at least two of the three rides. Each ride costs ₹ 5 and the total collection of amusement park in a particular day was ₹ 700.

Determine how many children did not take any of the rides.

12. Compute D_6 and D_7.
13. Compute the number of functions from the set of 6 elements to the set of 5 elements. How many of them are onto ?
14. Compute the number of functions from the set of 7 elements to the set of 4 elements. How many of them are onto ?
15. List all functions from the set A = {a, b, c} to the set B = {1, 2}. Verify that there are 6 onto functions.

ANSWERS (4.1)

1. (a) 66, (b) 69, (c) 656, (d) 250, (3) 686, (f) 465
2. 180
3. 108, 80
4. (a) 8, (b) 56, (c) 36
5. 30, 28
6. 55
7. 1%
8. 155, 100
9. 32
10. 120
11. 10
12. 265, 1854
13. 15625, 1800
14. 16384, 8400

Chapter 5...

ALGEBRAIC STRUCTURES

5.1 Operations on Sets

In the present chapter, we study algebraic system viz. a Group. We shall study subgroups, normal subgroups and isomorphic mapping and homomorphic mapping. All these mathematical tools are then used in the theory of coding and decoding of messages in various areas.

We begin with the non-empty set A = {1, 2, 3}. Let now some definite rule is given to combine any two elements (not necessarily distinct) of the set A; which will produce an element which may or may not be in the set A. For $x \in A$ and $y \in A$, let us find $x^y = x \uparrow y$. Since x can take 3 values and y also can take 3 values; in all $3 \times 3 = 9$ elements will be produced according to the above rule.

These 9 elements are :

$1 \uparrow 1 = 1^1 = 1$, $1 \uparrow 2 = 1^2 = 1$, $1 \uparrow 3 = 1^3 = 1$,
$2 \uparrow 1 = 2^1 = 2$, $2 \uparrow 2 = 2^2 = 4$, $2 \uparrow 3 = 2^3 = 8$,
$3 \uparrow 1 = 3^1 = 3$, $3 \uparrow 2 = 3^2 = 9$, $3 \uparrow 3 = 3^3 = 27$.

We can write the above conveniently as below in the table called composition table.

$\uparrow$	1	2	3
1	1	1	1
2	2	4	8
3	3	9	27

We see that out of 9 elements produced, 5 of them are in A but remaining 4 are outside A.

The elements of the set A are not necessarily numbers. They can be some other symbols also.

Consider the set A = {m, c, *l*, h}. Now to combine any two elements of A we define rule denoted by * as below. When two members of the set A come together according to rule * the result is that element who appears first in alphabetic order.

For example, m * h = h, c * *l* = c

The composition table is now as below.

*	m	c	*l*	h
m	m	c	*l*	h
c	c	c	c	c
l	*l*	c	*l*	h
h	h	c	h	h

(5.1)

In this example all $4 \times 4 = 16$ outcomes are elements of the set A itself.

Any such rule as discussed in the above two examples is called a 'binary operation' on the set A. More precisely, a function

$f : A \times A \to B$ is a binary operation on the set A.

We use the symbols $*, \oplus, \Box, \Delta$ etc. for a binary operation. Further when a, b ∈ A come together according to operation say * we write their product as a * b.

Just like binary operation, we can also have unary operation, ternary operation and in general n-ary operation defined on the set A.

In the algebra of sets, the operations of union and intersection of sets are binary operations and the 'complementation' of a set is unary operation. Similarly in the algebra of propositions the disjunction ($\vee$) and the conjunction ($\wedge$) are binary operations and the negation ($\sim$) is unary operation.

In the present chapter, we are concerned with binary operations only.

A non-empty set A together with some binary operation (operations) is called an algebraic system.

For example, the set $\mathbb{R}$ of all reals together addition and multiplication i.e. ($\mathbb{R}$, +, x) is an algebraic system. Similarly the set Q^+ of all positive rational numbers together with multiplication i.e. (Q^+, x) is also an algebraic system.

5.2 Properties of Binary Operation

Closure Property :

Let * be a binary operation on the set A. If a * b ∈ A for every a ∈ A, and b ∈ A then the set A is said to be closed under the operation *.

As we have seen in Article 5.1, in the first composition table $2 \uparrow 1 \in A$, $1 \uparrow 3 \in A$ but $3 \uparrow 2 \notin A$. Therefore the set A = {1, 2, 3} is not closed under the operation $\uparrow$.

However, in the second composition table x * y ∈ A for all x, y ∈ A. Therefore, the set A = {m, c, l, h} is closed under the operation *.

(i) Consider the binary operation addition defined on the set $\mathbb{N}$ of positive integers. We know that the sum of any two positive integers is positive. Thus, $x + y \in \mathbb{N}$ for all $x, y \in \mathbb{N}$ and $\mathbb{N}$ is closed under the operation of addition.

The set $\mathbb{N}$ is not closed under the operation of subtraction; since $5 \in \mathbb{N}$, $8 \in \mathbb{N}$ but $5 - 8 \notin \mathbb{N}$.

(ii) The set **Z** of all integers is closed under the operation of addition. Also **Z** is closed under the operation of subtraction. The reason is that if x and y are any two integers i.e. members of **Z** then $x + y \in \mathbf{Z}$ and also $x - y \in \mathbf{Z}$.

(iii) **Q** is a set of all rational numbers and for any a, b ∈ **Q** define $a * b = \frac{ab}{3}$. Clearly $\frac{ab}{3}$ is a rational number whenever a and b are rational numbers.

Therefore **Q** is closed under *.

Associative Law :

A binary operation * defined on the set A is associative if $a * (b * c) = (a * b) * c$ for every $a, b, c \in A$.

(i) The operations of addition and multiplication defined on the set $\mathbb{R}$ are associative since
$$a + (b + c) = (a + b) + c, \text{ for all } a, b, c \in \mathbb{R}$$

Also,
$$a \cdot (b \cdot c) = (a \cdot b) \cdot c, \text{ for all } a, b, c \in \mathbb{R}$$

(ii) The operation of subtraction in $\mathbb{R}$ is not associative; since
$$5 - (3 - 2) = 5 - 1 = 4$$
and
$$(5 - 3) - 2 = 2 - 2 = 0$$

(iii) Let a, b, c be any three real numbers. Define the binary operation * by
$$a * b = a + b + ab.$$

Then
$$a * (b * c) = a * (b + c + bc)$$
$$= a + (b + c + bc) + a(b + c + bc)$$
$$= a + b + c + bc + ab + ac + abc$$

Also
$$(a * b) * c = (a + b + ab) * c$$
$$= (a + b + ab) + c + (a + b + ab)(c)$$
$$= a + b + ab + c + ac + bc + abc$$

We have, $a * (b * c) = (a * b) * c$ for all $a, b, c \in \mathbb{R}$.

Therefore operation * is associative.

(iv) The operation defined by $x * y = x^y$ where $x, y \in \mathbb{N}$ fails to be associative since, by taking $x = 2, y = 3, z = 2$ in $\mathbb{N}$, we have $2 * (3 * 2) = 2 * (3^2) = 2 * 9 = 2^9 = 512$ and $(2 * 3) * 2 = (2^3) * 2 = 8 * 2 = 8^2 = 64$.

Thus, $2 * (3 * 2) \neq (2 * 3) * 2$.

Identity Element :

Let * be a binary operation defined on the set A.

If there exists an element denoted by e (e may or may not be in A) such that $a * e = a$ and $e * a = a$ for every $a \in A$, then e is called identity element w.r.t. operation *.

It is to be noted that only $a * e = a$ ($e * a = a$) for all $a \in A$ is not sufficient to say that e is identity w.r.t. operation *.

(i) Consider the operation of addition defined on the set $\mathbb{R}$ of all real numbers.

For any $x \in \mathbb{R}$; $x + 0 = x$ and $0 + x = x$. Thus 0 identity element w.r.t. operation of addition. Also $0 \in \mathbb{R}$.

If the set is $\mathbb{N} = \{1, 2, 3, ...\}$ again 0 is identity w.r.t. addition $x + 0 = x$ and $0 + x = x$ for all $x \in \mathbb{N}$ but $0 \notin \mathbb{N}$.

The operation of subtraction has no identity element $x - 0 = x$ for every $x \in \mathbb{R}$ but $0 - x \neq x$.

(ii) The positive integer 1 is identity w.r.t. operation of multiplication because $x \cdot 1 = x$ and $1 \cdot x = x$ for every $x \in \mathbb{R}$. Also $1 \in \mathbb{R}$.

Again $x \cdot 1 = x$, $1 \cdot x = x$ for every $x \in \mathbb{N}$ and also $1 \in \mathbb{N}$.

(iii) Consider the operation $*$ defined on $\mathbb{N}$ by $x * y = x^y$.

We have $x * 1 = x^1 = x$ for every $x \in \mathbb{N}$ but $1 * x = 1^x = 1 \neq x$.

This operation does not possess identity element.

(iv) Let $*$ be the operation defined on the set $\mathbb{Z}$ of all integers by $a * b = a + b - 5$.

We shall find identity w.r.t. $*$, let a be any element of $\mathbb{Z}$. Consider e such that $a * e = a$.

$\therefore \qquad a + e - 5 = a$

$\therefore \qquad e = 5$

This e also statisfies.

$e * a = 5 * a = 5 + a - 5 = a$ for every $a \in \mathbb{Z}$.

Therefore $5 \in \mathbb{Z}$ is identity w.r.t. $*$.

An element e satisfying $a * e = a$ for every a in the given set, is called right identity.

An element e is satisfying $e * a = a$ for every a in the given set is called left identity.

If e is right identity and also left identity then it is identity.

With respect to the operation of subtraction in $\mathbb{R}$, we see that $a - 0 = a$ for every $a \in \mathbb{R}$ but $0 - a \neq a$.

Therefore 0 is right identity but not identity w.r.t. operation of subtraction.

Consider the set $\mathbb{N}$ of positive integers and let $x * y = y$ for $x, y \in \mathbb{N}$.

Then we have $1 * x = x$ for all $x \in \mathbb{N}$ but $x * 1 \neq x$.

Therefore 1 is left identity but not identity w.r.t. $*$.

Let a, b, c be three boys of different heights and $S = \{a, b, c\}$. Define the operation on S by $x * y =$ taller between x and y.

Then shortest of a, b, c will act as right identity as well as left identity. Hence the shortest of a, b, c is identity element.

Inverse of an Element :

Let $*$ be a binary operation on the set A. We can talk about inverse of an element only when the operation $*$ possesses an identity element say e.

Suppose $a \in A$. If there exists element b (b may or may not be in A) such that $a * b = e$ and also $b * a = e$ then b is called inverse of a w.r.t. binary operation $*$. It is denoted by a^{-1}

$\therefore \qquad b = a^{-1}$

(i) In $\mathbb{R}$, w.r.t. addition the inverse of x is $-x$ and w.r.t. multiplication inverse of x is $\frac{1}{x}$, provided $x \neq 0$.

(ii) Consider the set $\mathbb{Z}$ of integers and the binary operation $a * b = a + b - 5$; $a, b \in \mathbb{Z}$. We have seen that identity w.r.t. $*$ is $e = 5$.

Let not x be any element of $\mathbb{Z}$.

If y is inverse of x w.r.t. $*$ then we must have $x * y = e = 5$ and $y * x = e = 5$.

We find y, $\quad x * y = 5 \Rightarrow x + y - 5 = 5$
$$\Rightarrow y = 10 - x$$

This y also satisfies $y * x = 5$ as
$$y * x = (10 - x) * x = (10 - x) + x - 5$$
$$= 10 - 5$$
$$= 5 = e$$

Thus $10 - x$ is inverse of x w.r.t. operation *.

Inverse of 2 is $10 - 2 = 8$.

Inverse of -3 is $10 - (-3) = 10 + 3 = 13$.

(iii) In the set Q^+ of positive rational numbers define the operation $a * b = \dfrac{ab}{3}$.

Now $e = 3 \in Q^+$ such that $a * 3 = \dfrac{a * 3}{3} = a$ and $3 * a = \dfrac{3a}{3} = a$.

Therefore, identity element is 3. Then for any $a \in Q^+$.
$$a * b = e \Rightarrow \dfrac{ab}{3} = 3 \Rightarrow b = \dfrac{9}{a}$$

Also then $b * a = \left(\dfrac{9}{a}\right) * a = \dfrac{\left(\dfrac{9}{a}\right)(a)}{3} = 3$; identity.

Thus $b = \dfrac{9}{a}$ is inverse of $a \in Q^+$ under *.

Inverse of 10 is $\dfrac{9}{10}$.

Inverse of 15 is $\dfrac{9}{15} = \dfrac{3}{5}$.

Commutative Law :

A binary operation * defined on the set A is called commutative if $a * b = b * a$ holds for all $a, b \in A$.

(i) The usual operations of addition and multiplication are commutative. $a + b = b + a$ and $a \cdot b = b \cdot a$ for all $a, b \in \mathbb{R}$.

(ii) The operation of subtraction is not commutative since $a - b \neq b - a$.

(iii) If $a * b = a + b - ab$ in $\mathbb{R}$ then
$$b * a = b + a - ba$$
$\therefore \qquad\qquad\qquad a * b = b * a$ for all $a, b \in \mathbb{R}$.

It is a commutative operation.

The operation $a \square b = 2a + 3b$ in $\mathbb{R}$ is not commutative since
$$5 \square 3 = (2)(5) + (3)(3) = 10 + 9 = 19$$
and
$$3 \square 5 = (2)(3) + (3)(5) = 6 + 15 = 21$$
so
$$5 \square 3 \neq 3 \square 5$$

Example 5.1 : A binary operation * defined on the set A = {a, b, c, d} has the composition table as below :

*	a	b	c	d
a	a	b	c	d
b	b	a	d	c
c	c	d	a	b
d	d	c	b	a

(i) Is A closed under * ?

(ii) Is * commutative ?

(iii) Verify that * obeys associative law.

(iv) What is identity element ?

(v) Find the inverse of each element, if it exists.

Solution : (i) In the composition table all 4 × 4 = 16 entries are from the set A itself i.e. x * y ∈ A for all x, y ∈ A. Therefore set A is closed under *.

(ii) In the composition table the entries symmetrically situated with respect to main diagonal are equal.

This means x * y = y * x for all x, y ∈ A.

Therefore * is a commutative binary operation.

(iii) Take b, c, d ∈ A

$$b * (c * d) = b * b = a$$
$$(b * c) * d = d * d = a$$

Thus, $b * (c * d) = (b * c) * d$

Associative law is verified.

(iv) In the row of element a and in the column of a, we see that elements of A appear in the order a, b, c, d.

i.e. x * a = x and a * x = x for all x ∈ A.

∴ a ∈ A is identity element.

(v) From the composition table

$$a * a = a = \text{identity} \qquad \therefore a^{-1} = a$$
$$b * b = a = \text{identity} \qquad \therefore b^{-1} = b$$
$$c * c = a = \text{identity} \qquad \therefore c^{-1} = c$$
$$d * d = a = \text{identity} \qquad \therefore d^{-1} = d$$

Here every element of A is its own inverse.

Idempotent Property :

A binary operation * on the set A is said to have an idempotent property if a * a = a for every a ∈ A.

(i) In Q, $a * b = \frac{a+b}{2}$ is idempotent because for any a ∈ Q; $a * a = \frac{a+a}{2} = \frac{2a}{2} = a$ holds.

(ii) In the set ($\mathbb{Z}^+$ of all positive integers the operation * defined by a * b = GCD of a and b, is idempotent since for any positive integer a we have a * a = GCD of a and a = a.

(iii) In $\mathbb{R}$ the operation of addition is not idempotent since a * a = a + a = 2a ≠ a.

Number of binary operations on a set :

We find the number of binary operations on a set of n elements. Also we find how many of them are commutative.

Let A be the set of n elements $a_1, a_2, ..., a_n$. The composition table for a binary operation * defined on A consist of n × n = n^2 compartments.

*	a_1	a_2	...	a_n
a_1				
a_2				
⋮				
a_n				

Each of these n^2 compartments can assume any one of n values $a_1, a_2, ..., a_n$; so that the set A is closed under the binary operation *.

By the rule of multiplication for counting, the n^2 compartments can be filled in

$$\underbrace{n \times n \times n \times ... \times n}_{n^2 \text{ factors}} = n^{(n^2)} \text{ ways.}$$

Hence, there are $n^{(n^2)}$ binary operations on the set of n elements.

To find the number of commutative binary operations, we note that the entries below the main diagonal are governed by the entries above the main diagonal, i.e. the entries below the main diagonal are not independent because $a_i * a_j = a_j * a_i$.

The n entries on the main diagonal and $\frac{n^2 - n}{2}$ entries above the main diagonal i.e. total.

$$n + \left(\frac{n^2 - n}{2}\right) = \frac{n^2 + n}{2} = \frac{n(n+1)}{2}$$

entries are independent and each of them assumes any one of $a_1, a_2, ..., a_n$ values.

Hence the number of commutative binary operations is $n^{\left[\frac{n(n+1)}{2}\right]}$.

On the set of 3 elements the number of binary operations is $n^{(n^2)} = 3^{(3^2)} = 3^9 = 19683$ and out of them the number of commutative operations is

$$n^{\left[\frac{n(n+1)}{2}\right]} = 3^{\left[\frac{3 \times 4}{2}\right]} = 3^6 = 729$$

Also on the set of 2 elements the number of binary operations is $n^{(n^2)} = 2^{(2^2)} = 2^4 = 16$ and out of them the number of commutative operations is

$$n^{\left[\frac{n(n+1)}{2}\right]} = 2^{\left[\frac{2 \times 3}{2}\right]} = 2^3 = 8.$$

5.3 Group

We are now in a position to define an algebraic system called a 'Group'.

Definition :

A non-empty set A together with a binary operation * defined on it is said to be a semigroup if :

(i) the set A is closed under operation * i.e. a * b ∈ A for all a, b ∈ A.

(ii) the operation * is associative i.e. a * (b * c) = (a * b) * c for all a, b, c ∈ A.

Definition :

A non-empty set A together with a binary operation * is called a monoid if :

(i) the set A is closed under the operation * i.e. a * b ∈ A for all a, b ∈ A.

(ii) the operation * is associative i.e. a * (b * c) = (a * b) * c for all a, b, c ∈ A.

(iii) identity element w.r.t. * exists and it belongs to set A.

Definition :

A non-empty set G together with a binary operation * is called a group if the following axioms hold:

(i) the set G is closed under the binary operation * i.e. a * b ∈ G for all a, b ∈ G.

(ii) the operation * is associative i.e. a * (b * c) = (a * b) * c for all a, b, c ∈ G.

(iii) identity element e w.r.t. operation * exists and e ∈ G and e * x = x * e = x for all x ∈ G.

(iv) each element a ∈ G possesses inverse b w.r.t. * in G i.e. b ∈ G such that a * b = b * a = e; where e is the identity element.

We denote the group by (G, *).

Definition :

A group (G, *) is called abelian group (commutative group) if the operation * obeys.

Commutative law i.e. a * b = b * a for all a, b ∈ G.

If the operation * in a group (G, *) is not commutative then G is called non-abelian group.

Briefly, we have the following picture of above algebraic structures.

Property	SEMIGROUP	MONOID	GROUP	ABELIAN GROUP
Closure property	✓	✓	✓	✓
Associative law	✓	✓	✓	✓
Existence of identity		✓	✓	✓
Existence of inverse			✓	✓
Commutative law				✓

Illustration 1 : Consider the set of all positive even integers.

$$E = \{2, 4, 6, 8, 10, \ldots\}$$

Let us define a binary operation of usual addition on the set E.

Clearly the sum of any two positive even integers is again positive even integer.

$$x \in E, \ y \in E \Rightarrow x + y \in E.$$

Therefore E is closed under operation of addition.

The usual operation of addition obeys associative law.

$$x, y, z \in E \Rightarrow x + (y + z) = (x + y) + z.$$

Hence the system $(E, +)$ is a semigroup.

However, $(E, +)$ is not a monoid. The reason is that additive identity usual 0 is not in E.

Now consider the set $E_1 = E \cup \{0\} = \{0, 2, 4, 6, 8, \ldots\}$.

The system $(E_1, +)$ is now a monoid. But it fails to be a group.

$2 \in E_1$ bit its additive inverse $-2 \notin E_1$.

Next consider the set $E_2 = \{\ldots, -4, -2, 0, 2, 4, 6, 8, \ldots\}$ of all even integers.

The set E_2 together with the operation of addition satisfies all requirements of a group structure.

Hence $(E_2, +)$ is a group. In fact it is abelian group since the operation of usual addition is commutative.

A group $(G, *)$ is called finite or infinite according as the number of elements in G is finite or infinite.

The number of elements in a finite group $(G, *)$ is called order of that group.

If $(G, *)$ contains n elements then we write $O(G) = n$.

Illustration 2 : Consider the set S_3 of $3! = 6$ permutations on three symbols 1, 2, 3. The six permutations are

$$i = \begin{pmatrix} 1 & 2 & 3 \\ 1 & 2 & 3 \end{pmatrix}, \alpha = \begin{pmatrix} 1 & 2 & 3 \\ 2 & 3 & 1 \end{pmatrix}, \beta = \begin{pmatrix} 1 & 2 & 3 \\ 3 & 1 & 2 \end{pmatrix}$$

$$\rho = \begin{pmatrix} 1 & 2 & 3 \\ 1 & 3 & 2 \end{pmatrix}, \mu = \begin{pmatrix} 1 & 2 & 3 \\ 3 & 2 & 1 \end{pmatrix}, \nu = \begin{pmatrix} 1 & 2 & 3 \\ 2 & 1 & 3 \end{pmatrix}$$

We have already seen in the chapter, 'Relations and Functions' that the permutations on the set $S = \{1, 2, 3\}$ are exactly the one-one onto mappings from the set S to itself and the multiplication of permutations is composition of mappings.

For example,

$$\mu\nu = \begin{pmatrix} 1 & 2 & 3 \\ 3 & 2 & 1 \end{pmatrix} \begin{pmatrix} 1 & 2 & 3 \\ 2 & 1 & 3 \end{pmatrix} = \begin{pmatrix} 1 & 2 & 3 \\ 3 & 1 & 2 \end{pmatrix} = \beta$$

Also,

$$\nu\mu = \begin{pmatrix} 1 & 2 & 3 \\ 2 & 1 & 3 \end{pmatrix} \begin{pmatrix} 1 & 2 & 3 \\ 3 & 2 & 1 \end{pmatrix} = \begin{pmatrix} 1 & 2 & 3 \\ 2 & 3 & 1 \end{pmatrix} = \alpha$$

We ask the students to perform these multiplications and complete the following composition table.

·	i	α	β	ρ	μ	ν
i	i	α	β	ρ	μ	ν
α	α	β	i	μ	ν	ρ
β	β	i	α	ν	ρ	μ
ρ	ρ	ν	μ	i	β	α
μ	μ	ρ	ν	α	i	β
ν	ν	μ	ρ	β	α	i

Closure Property :

From the table, we see that the multiplication of any two permutations in S_3 is again a permutation in S_3. Therefore S_3 is closed under permutation multiplication.

Associative Law :

The composition of functions is associative. This means multiplication of permutations is associative. For example,

$$\mu \cdot (\nu\beta) = \mu\rho = \alpha$$

Also $(\mu\nu)\beta = \beta\beta = \alpha$

Thus, $\mu(\nu\beta) = (\mu\nu)\beta$

Identity Element :

From the table the permutation i is identity permutation and $i \in S_3$.

Inverse of an Element :

Again from the table, $\alpha\beta = i$ and $\beta\alpha = i$ where i is identity.

Therefore, $\alpha^{-1} = \beta \in S_3$, $\beta^{-1} = \alpha \in S_3$

Similarly, $i^{-1} = i \in S_3$, $\rho^{-1} = \rho \in S_3$, $\mu^{-1} = \mu \in S_3$ and $\nu^{-1} = \nu \in S_3$.

All 4 group axioms hold. Hence $(S_3, \cdot)$ is a group. This group is non-abelian as $\mu\nu = \beta$ but $\nu\mu = \alpha$.

Further it is a finite group of order 6.

The following theorem gives some elementary properties of a group structure.

Theorem 1 : In a group $(G, *)$:

(i) identity element is unique.

(ii) inverse of an element of G is unique.

(iii) $(a * b)^{-1} = b^{-1} * a^{-1}$

(iv) cancellation laws hold; $a * x = a * y \Rightarrow x = y$ and $x * b = y * b \Rightarrow x = y$.

(v) the equation $a * x = b$ has unique solution in G.

Proof : Let $(G, *)$ be a group :

(i) If possible suppose there are two identity elements e_1 and e_2 in G.

e_1 is identity and e_2 is element of G.

$\therefore \qquad e_1 * e_2 = e_2 \qquad \ldots (1)$

Also e_2 is identity and e_1 is element of G.

$\therefore \qquad e_1 * e_2 = e_1 \qquad \ldots (2)$

From equations (1) and (2), we get $e_1 = e_2$. Hence identity is unique

(ii) Suppose if possible an element $a \in G$ has two inverses say b and c.

Then
$\qquad a * b = e \qquad \ldots (1)$
$\qquad b * a = e \qquad \ldots (2)$
$\qquad a * c = e \qquad \ldots (3)$
$\qquad c * a = e \qquad \ldots (4)$

Our claim is $b = c$.

Now
$\quad b = b * e \qquad \because e \text{ is identity}$
$\quad\quad = b * (a * c) \qquad \because \text{ by (3)}$
$\quad\quad = (b * a) * c \qquad \because \text{ by associative law}$
$\quad\quad = e * c \qquad \because \text{ by (2)}$
$\quad\quad = c \qquad \because e \text{ is identity}$

Thus, $\quad b = c$

Hence $a \in G$ has unique inverse.

(iii) Let a, b be any two elements of G having their inverses a^{-1} and b^{-1} respectively.

By closure property $a * b \in G$ and it has inverse $(a * b)^{-1}$.

Now consider $(a * b) * (b^{-1} * a^{-1})$

$(a * b) * (b^{-1} * a^{-1}) = [(a * b) * b^{-1}] * a^{-1} \qquad \because \text{ by associative law}$
$\qquad\qquad\qquad\qquad = [a * (b * b^{-1})] * a^{-1} \qquad \because \text{ by associative law}$
$\qquad\qquad\qquad\qquad = (a * e) * a^{-1} \qquad \because b * b^{-1} = e$
$\qquad\qquad\qquad\qquad = a * a^{-1} \qquad \because a * e = a$
$\qquad\qquad\qquad\qquad = e \qquad \because a * a^{-1} = e$

$\ldots (1)$

Again $(b^{-1} * a^{-1}) * (a * b) = b^{-1} * [a^{-1} * (a * b)]$ ∵ by associative law
$$= b^{-1} * [(a^{-1} * a) * b]$$ ∵ by associative law
$$= b^{-1} * [e * b]$$ ∵ $a^{-1} * a = e$
$$= b^{-1} * b$$ ∵ $e * b = b$
$$= e$$ ∵ $b^{-1} * b = e$
... (2)

From (1) and (2), we conclude that $b^{-1} * a^{-1}$ is inverse of $a * b$ in G.

∴ $b^{-1} * a^{-1} = (a * b)^{-1}$

∴ $(a * b)^{-1} = b^{-1} * a^{-1}$ Proved.

(iv) **Left cancellation law.**

$$a * x = a * y$$

Premultiply by a^{-1} on both sides.

∴ $a^{-1} * (a * x) = a^{-1} * (a * y)$

∴ $(a^{-1} * a) * x = (a^{-1} * a) * y$ ∵ by associative law

∴ $e * x = e * y$ ∵ $a^{-1} * a = e$

∴ $x = y$ ∵ e is identity

Right cancellation law.

$$x * a = y * a$$

Post multiply by a^{-1} on both sides.

∴ $(x * a) * a^{-1} = (y * a) * a^{-1}$

∴ $x * (a * a^{-1}) = y * (a * a^{-1})$ ∵ by associative law

∴ $x * e = y * e$ ∵ $a * a^{-1} = e$

∴ $x = y$ ∵ e is identity

(v) Consider the equation $a * x = b$ where $a, b \in G$.

Then premultiplication by a^{-1} on both sides of the equation gives

$$a^{-1} * (a * x) = a^{-1} * b$$

∴ $(a^{-1} * a) * x = a^{-1} * b$ ∵ by associative law

∴ $e * x = a^{-1} * b$ ∵ $a^{-1} * a = e$

∴ $x = a^{-1} * b$ ∵ $e * x = x$

Thus, $x = a^{-1} * b$ is a solution of the given equation.

Now we know that the inverse of an element is unique.

∴ $a^{-1} * b$ is unique.   Proved.

Note : The result proved in (iii) above can be generalized to more than 2 elements.

Thus $(a * b * c)^{-1} = c^{-1} * b^{-1} * a^{-1}$

$(a * b * c * d) = d^{-1} * c^{-1} * b^{-1} * a^{-1}$

This is called reversal law for inverse of the product in a group.

Integral powers of elements in a group :

Let $(G, *)$ be a group and $a \in G$.

We write $a * a$ as a^2, $a * a * a$ as a^3.

In general if n is a positive integer and $n > 1$ then

$$\underbrace{a * a * \ldots * a}_{n \text{ factors}} = a^n$$

Similarly $\underbrace{a^{-1} * a^{-1} * \ldots a^{-1}}_{n \text{ factors}} = a^{-n}$

and $a^0 = e$; which is identity element in G.

With this notation the following laws of indices hold.

$$a^m * a^n = a^{m+n}$$
$$a^m * a^{-n} = a^{m-n}$$
$$(a^m)^n = a^{mn}$$
$$a^0 = e$$

Hence forth we shall write $a * b$ as simply ab. But remember that it is not usual multiplication.

In a group $(G, *)$ with identity e, an element $a \in G$ is said to be or order r if r is a positive integer such that $a^r = e$ but $a^m \neq e$ when $m < r$.

In the group $G = \{1, 2, 3, 4\}$ under multiplication modulo 5, we see that $e = 1$ is of order 1, $2^1 = 2$, $2^2 = 4$, $2^3 = 3$, $2^4 = 1 =$ identity.

∴ Order of 2 is 4. $3^1 = 3$, $3^2 = 4$, $3^3 = 2$, $3^4 = 1 =$ identity

∴ Order of 3 is 4. $4^1 = 4$, $4^2 = 1 =$ identity

∴ Order of 4 is 2.

In the additive group of integers every element other than identity 0 is of order infinity.

SOLVED EXAMPLES

Example 5.2 : Show that $x * y = x^y$ is a binary operation on the set of positive integers.

Determine whether :

(i) $*$ is commutative ?

(ii) $*$ is associative ?

Solution : $\mathbb{N} = \{1, 2, 3, 4, \ldots\}$

For $x, y \in \mathbb{N}$, $x * y = x^y$; Given.

If x and y are any two positive integers, then x^y is also a positive integer. Thus, $x \in \mathbb{N}$, $y \in \mathbb{N} \Rightarrow x * y \in \mathbb{N}$.

∴ The set $\mathbb{N}$ is closed under the operation $*$.

∴ $*$ is a binary operation on $\mathbb{N}$.

(i) The operation * defined by $x * y = x^y$ is not commutative.
   If $x = 2$, $y = 3$ then $x * y = 2 * 3 = 2^3 = 8$ and $y * x = 3 * 2 = 3^2 = 9$.
   Thus, $x * y \neq y * x$.

(ii) The operation * is not associative.
   If $x = 2, y = 3, z = 2$ in $\mathbb{N}$ then $x * (y * z) = 2 * (3 * 2) = 2 * (3^2) = 2 * 9 = 2^9 = 512$
   and $(x * y) * z = (2 * 3) * 2 = (2^3) * 2 = 8 * 2 = 8^2 = 64$
   Thus, $x * (y * z) \neq (x * y) * z$

Example 5.3 : How many distinct binary operations are there on the set $\{0, 1\}$? Give their composition tables, which of them are commutative ?

Solution : Consider the composition table

*	0	1
0		
1		

We have to fill up 4 places.

In order that the set $\{0, 1\}$ is closed under the binary operation * there are 2 choices for each compartment.

Hence the number of binary operations is $2^4 = 16$.

They are listed below.

*	0	1
0	0	0
1	0	0

Table 1   All four 0s total 1

*	0	1
0	0	0
1	0	1

Table 2

*	0	1
0	0	0
1	1	0

Table 3

*	0	1
0	0	1
1	0	0

Table 4

*	0	1
0	1	0
1	0	0

Table 5

Three 0s total 4

*	0	1
0	0	0
1	1	1

Table 6

*	0	1
0	0	1
1	0	1

Table 7

*	0	1
0	0	1
1	1	0

Table 8

Two 0's total 6

*	0	1
0	1	0
1	0	1

Table 9

*	0	1
0	1	0
1	1	0

Table 10

*	0	1
0	1	1
1	0	0

Table 11

*	0	1
0	0	1
1	1	1

Table 12

*	0	1
0	1	0
1	1	1

Table 13

*	0	1
0	1	1
1	0	1

Table 14

*	0	1
0	1	1
1	1	0

Table 15

One 0 Total 4

*	0	1
0	1	1
1	1	1

Table 16

No 0 total 1

Total number of binary operations is 16.

The number of commutative operations is 8. They appear in table 1, 2, 5, 8, 9, 12, 15, 16.

Example 5.4 : Show that $(\mathbb{N}, *)$ is a semi-group where $x * y = \min\{x, y\}$ for any $x, y \in \mathbb{N}$.

Is $(\mathbb{N}, *)$ a monoid ? **(P.U. 2012)**

Solution : $\mathbb{N} = \{1, 2, 3, 4, \ldots\}$ and $x * y = \min\{x, y\}$ for any $x, y \in \mathbb{N}$.

Closure Property :

Let x and y be any two members of $\mathbb{N}$.

If $x < y$ then $x * y = x \in \mathbb{N}$

If $x > y$ then $x * y = y \in \mathbb{N}$

If $x = y$ then $x * y = x * x = x \in \mathbb{N}$.

Thus, $x * y \in \mathbb{N}$ for all $x, y \in \mathbb{N}$.

∴ Set $\mathbb{N}$ is closed under the operation *.

Associative Law :

Let $x, y, z \in \mathbb{N}$. We can assume that $x \leq y \leq z$.

Then $x * (y * z) = x * \min\{y, z\} = x * y = \min\{x, y\} = x$

and $(x * y) * z = \min\{x, y\} * z = x * z = \min\{x, z\} = x$

Thus, $x * (y * z) = (x * y) * z$ for any $x, y, z \in \mathbb{N}$.

Therefore operation * is associative.

∴ (ℕ, *) is a semi-group.

The greatest positive integer does not exist in ℕ which could act as an identity w.r.t. operation *. So there is no identity w.r.t. *. Therefore (ℕ, *) is not a monoid.

Example. 5.5 : Let < G * > be a commutative semi-group. Prove that if a * a = a and b * b = b for some a ∈ G, b ∈ G, then (a * b) * (a * b) = a * b.

Solution : <G, *> is a commutative semi-group. a, b ∈ G such that a * a = a and b * b = b consider (a * b) * (a * b).

$$
\begin{aligned}
(a * b) * (a * b) &= a * [b * (a * b)] &&\text{∵ by associative law}\\
&= a * [(b * a) * b] &&\text{∵ by associative law}\\
&= a * [(a * b) * b] &&\text{∵ by commutative law}\\
&= a * [a * (b * b)] &&\text{∵ by associative law}\\
&= (a * a) * (b * b) &&\text{∵ by associative law}\\
&= a * b &&\text{∵ given } a * a = a \text{ and } b * b = b \text{ (Proved)}
\end{aligned}
$$

Example 5.6 : Let G = {a, b, c, d} and * be the operation on G defined by Cayley table.

*	a	b	c	d
a	a	b	c	d
b	b	c	d	a
c	c	d	a	b
d	d	a	b	c

Is G abelian group ? **(P.U. 2010)**

Solution : Closure property : All 4 × 4 = 16 entries in the composition table are elements of set G itself; i.e. x * y ∈ G for all x, y ∈ G. Therefore set G is closed under *.

Associative law : The given binary operation is associative. We verify it

b * (c * d) = b * b = c. Also (b * c) * d = d * d = c.

Identity element : In the row of a and in the column of a the elements a, b, c, d of G appear in that order. This means x * a = x and a * x = x for all x ∈ G. Therefore a ∈ G is identity element.

Inverse of an element : From the table

$$
\begin{aligned}
a * a &= a = \text{identity}\\
b * d &= d * b = a = \text{identity}\\
c * c &= a = \text{identity}
\end{aligned}
$$

∴ $a^{-1} = a \in G$, $b^{-1} = d \in G$, $c^{-1} = c \in G$, $d^{-1} = b \in G$

∴ Every element of G possesses inverse in G.

Commutative law : From the given table x * y = y * x for all x, y ∈ G.

Thus, G satisfies all the axioms of abelian group.

∴ (G, *) is abelian group.

Example 5.7 : Let (A, *) be a monoid such that $x * x = e$ for every $x \in A$; where e is the identity element. Show that <A, *> is an abelian group.

Solution : <A, *> is a monoid; Given.

Therefore by definition, the set A is closed under *; the operation * is associative; and identity $e \in A$.

For <A, *> to be abelian group, we need to show that every element in A possesses inverse in A and the operation * is commutative.

Now $x * x = e$; for every $x \in A$

Therefore $\quad\quad\quad x^{-1} = x \in A$ for every $x \in A$. $\quad\quad\quad$ ... (1)

Let a, b be any two elements of A. Then $a * b \in A \quad\quad$ ∵ by closure property

∴ $\quad\quad\quad (a * b)^{-1} = a * b \quad\quad\quad\quad$ ... (2) $\quad$ ∵ by (1)

Also we have $\quad (a * b)^{-1} = b^{-1} * a^{-1} = b * a \quad\quad$ ... (3) $\quad$ ∵ by (1)

From equations (2) and (3), we get

$\quad\quad\quad a * b = b * a.$ This holds for every $a, b \in A$

∴ Operation * is commutative.

Hence <A, *> is abelian group.

Example 5.8 : Give example of infinite abelian group. Explain all properties of abelian group for example given.

Solution : The set $\mathbf{Z} = \{0, \pm 1, \pm 2, \pm 3, ...\}$ of all integers forms an infinite abelian group w.r.t. operation of usual addition.

Closure property : The sum of any two integers is again integer.

$\quad\quad x \in \mathbf{Z}, y \in \mathbf{Z} \Rightarrow x + y \in \mathbf{Z}.$

∴ **Z** is closed under addition.

Associative law : The usual addition is associative.

$\quad\quad x, y, z \in \mathbf{Z} \Rightarrow x + (y + z) = (x + y) + z.$

Identity element : The integer $0 \in \mathbf{Z}$ is additive identity.

$\quad\quad x + 0 = x, \ 0 + x = x$ for all $x \in \mathbf{Z}.$

Inverse of an element : If x is any integer then $-x$ is also integer and

$\quad\quad x + (-x) = 0, \ (-x) + x = 0$

∴ Every member of **Z** possesses additive inverse in **Z** itself.

Commutative law : The usual operation of addition obeys commutative law.

$\quad\quad x + y = y + x$ for all $x, y \in \mathbf{Z}.$

Therefore (**Z**, +) is infinite abelian group.

Example 5.9 : Prepare composition table for $\mathbf{Z}_5^* = \{\overline{1}, \overline{2}, \overline{3}, \overline{4}\}$ w.r.t. multiplication modulo 5, X_5 operation.

Is it abelian group ? If yes, solve the equation $\overline{2} \ X_5 \ \overline{x} \ X_5 \ \overline{4} = \overline{3}$.

Also compute $(\overline{3})^4 \ X_5 \ (\overline{2})^3$.

Solution :

X_5	$\bar{1}$	$\bar{2}$	$\bar{3}$	$\bar{4}$
$\bar{1}$	$\bar{1}$	$\bar{2}$	$\bar{3}$	$\bar{4}$
$\bar{2}$	$\bar{2}$	$\bar{4}$	$\bar{1}$	$\bar{3}$
$\bar{3}$	$\bar{3}$	$\bar{1}$	$\bar{4}$	$\bar{2}$
$\bar{4}$	$\bar{4}$	$\bar{3}$	$\bar{2}$	$\bar{1}$

$\bar{a} \, X_5 \, \bar{b}$ is the remainder when the product ab is divided by 5.

Closure property : In the composition table all entries are elements of Z_5^*.

$$\bar{x} \in Z_5^*, \, \bar{y} \in Z_5^* \Rightarrow \bar{x} \, X_5 \, \bar{y} \in Z_5^*.$$

∴ Z_5^* is closed under multiplication modulo 5.

Associative law : The operation of multiplication modulo 5 obeys associative law.

For example $\quad \bar{3} \, X_5 \, (\bar{4} \, X_5 \, \bar{2}) = \bar{3} \, X_5 \, \bar{3} = \bar{4}$

and $\quad (\bar{3} \, X_5 \, \bar{4}) \, X_5 \, \bar{2} = \bar{2} \, X_5 \, \bar{2} = \bar{4}$

∴ $\quad \bar{3} \, X_5 \, (\bar{4} \, X_5 \, \bar{2}) = (\bar{3} \, X_5 \, \bar{4}) \, X_5 \, \bar{2}$

Identity element : $\bar{1} \in Z_5^*$ and from the table $\bar{a} \, X_5 \, \bar{1} = \bar{1} \, X_5 \, \bar{a} = \bar{a}$ for every $\bar{a} \in Z_5^*$.

∴ $\bar{1} \in Z_5^*$ is identity element.

Inverse of an element : From the table, we have

$$\bar{1} \, X_5 \, \bar{1} = \bar{1}; \text{ identity}$$

$$\bar{2} \, X_5 \, \bar{3} = \bar{3} \, X_2 \, \bar{2} = \bar{1}; \text{ identity}$$

$$\bar{4} \, X_5 \, \bar{4} = \bar{1}; \text{ identity}$$

∴ $(\bar{1})^{-1} = \bar{1}, \, (\bar{2})^{-1} = \bar{3}, \, (\bar{3})^{-1} = \bar{2}, \, (\bar{4})^{-1} = \bar{4}$

(note operation is multiplicative).

Each element Z_5^* possesses inverse in Z_5^*.

Commutative law : From the table the entries which are symmetrically situated w.r.t. main diagonal are equal.

∴ $\bar{a} \, X_5 \, \bar{b} = \bar{b} \, X_5 \, \bar{a}$ for all $\bar{a}, \bar{b} \in Z_5^*$

Hence (Z_5^*, X_5) is an abelian group. Consider the equation

$$\bar{2} \, X_5 \, \bar{x} \, X_5 \, \bar{4} = \bar{3}$$

Premultiply by $(\bar{2})^{-1} = \bar{3}$ and post multiply by $(\bar{4})^{-1} = 4$ on both sides.

$$(\bar{2})^{-1} X_5 (\bar{2}) X_5 \bar{x} X_5 \bar{4} X_5 (\bar{4})^{-1} = (\bar{2})^{-1} X_5 \bar{3} X_5 (\bar{4})^{-1}$$

$$\bar{1} X_5 \bar{x} X_5 \bar{1} = \bar{3} X_5 \bar{3} X_5 \bar{4}$$

$\therefore \quad \bar{x} = \bar{4} X_5 \bar{4}$

$\therefore \quad \bar{x} = \bar{1}$

Finally, $\quad (\bar{3})^4 X_5 (\bar{2})^3 = \bar{1} X_5 \bar{3} \qquad (\bar{3})^4 = \bar{3} X_5 \bar{3} X_5 \bar{3} X_5 \bar{3} = \overline{81} = \bar{1}$

$\qquad\qquad\qquad\qquad = \bar{3} \qquad\qquad\qquad (\bar{2})^3 = \bar{2} X_5 \bar{2} X_5 \bar{2} = \bar{8} = \bar{3}$

Example 5.10 : Prove that every row or column in the composition table of a group <G, *> is a permutation of the elements of G.

Solution : We prepare a composition table for a finite group.

So we take <G, *> to be a finite group containing n elements $x_1, x_2, \ldots, x_n$. Some element being identity.

	x_1	x_2	x_i	x_n
x_1				
x_2				
x_i				
x_n				

To show that each row in the composition table is a permutation of elements of G, we show that in each row every element of G appears once and only once.

If possible, suppose row of x_i contains x_j twice i.e. in the kth column and l^{th} column.

Then $x_i x_k = x_j$ and $x_i x_l = x_j$

$\therefore \quad x_i x_k = x_i x_l$

Then by cancellation law $x_k = x_l$ which is a contradiction.

Therefore, any x_j cannot appear more than once in the row of x_i.

Next suppose x_j does not appear in the row of x_i. Then since the length of any row is n; some element x_m will appear more than once in the row of x_i which leads to the contradiction as above.

Finally, each row of the composition table contains each element of G exactly once.

Hence it is a permutation of elements of G.

Similarly, each column of the composition table is some permutation of elements of G.

Example 5.11 : Prepare a composition table for a group of order 3 and comment.

Solution : Let G = {e, a, b} be a group w.r.t. binary operation * where e denotes the identity.

Now consider the following table.

*	e	a	b
e	e	a	b
a	a		
b	b		

Since e is identity the row of e and column of e consists of e, a, b as shown above.

Now consider a * b. It has 3 choices a * b = e or a * b = a or a * b = b.

If a * b = a then a * b = a * e. This implies by cancellation law b = e which is not true.

Similarly, a * b ≠ b

Therefore, a * b must be e and on the same lines b * a = e

*	e	a	b
e	e	a	b
a	a		e
b	b	e	

Now consider a * a.

We know that in the composition table of a group each element of G appears exactly once in each row and also in each column.

Therefore,   a * a = b

Similarly,   b * b = a

	e	a	b
e	e	a	b
a	a	b	e
b	b	e	a

This gives the composition table for a group of order 3. We observe the following two results.

A group of order 3 is abelian. Any two groups of order 3 have the same algebraic structure.

Example 5.12 : Find whether {1, 2, 3, 4, 5, 9} is a group under multiplication modulo 11. **(P.U. 2010)**

Solution : A = {1, 2, 3, 4, 5, 9} 2 ∈ A, 3 ∈ A but 2 * 3 = 6 ∉ A.

The set A is not closed under multiplication modulo 11.

Therefore A does not form a group under multiplication modulo 11.

Example 5.13 : If $A = \{\bar{2}, \bar{4}, \bar{6}, \bar{8}\}$ then show that $<A, X_{10}>$ is abelian group.

Solution : We prepare a composition table.

X_{10}	$\bar{2}$	$\bar{4}$	$\bar{6}$	$\bar{8}$
$\bar{2}$	$\bar{4}$	$\bar{8}$	$\bar{2}$	$\bar{6}$
$\bar{4}$	$\bar{8}$	$\bar{6}$	$\bar{4}$	$\bar{2}$
$\bar{6}$	$\bar{2}$	$\bar{4}$	$\bar{6}$	$\bar{8}$
$\bar{8}$	$\bar{6}$	$\bar{2}$	$\bar{8}$	$\bar{4}$

Closure property : All the entries in the composition table are elements of A.

∴ $\bar{a} \in A, \bar{b} \in A \Rightarrow \bar{a} X_{10} \bar{b} \in A$

∴ Set A is closed under the operation multiplication modulo 10.

Associative law : The operation multiplication modulo 10 is associative.

$\bar{a}, \bar{b}, \bar{c} \in A \Rightarrow \bar{a} X_{10} (\bar{b} X_{10} \bar{c}) = (\bar{a} X_{10} \bar{b}) X_{10} \bar{c}$

For example, $\bar{2} X_{10} (\bar{4} X_{10} \bar{8}) = \bar{2} X_{10} \bar{2} = \bar{4}$

and $(\bar{2} X_{10} \bar{4}) X_{10} \bar{8} = \bar{8} X_{10} \bar{8} = \bar{4}$

Identity element : From the composition table, we see that

$$\bar{2} X_{10} \bar{6} = \bar{2}, \ \bar{6} X_{10} \bar{2} = \bar{2}$$

$$\bar{4} X_{10} \bar{6} = \bar{4}, \ \bar{6} X_{10} \bar{4} = \bar{4}$$

$$\bar{6} X_{10} \bar{6} = \bar{6}$$

$$\bar{8} X_{10} \bar{6} = \bar{8}, \ \bar{6} X_{10} \bar{8} = \bar{8}$$

Thus, $\bar{6} \in A$ is identity element.

Inverse of an element : From the composition table,

$$\bar{2} X_{10} \bar{8} = \bar{8} X_{10} \bar{2} = \bar{6}; \text{ identity}$$

$$\bar{4} X_{10} \bar{4} = \bar{6}, \text{ identity}$$

$$\bar{6} X_{10} \bar{6} = \bar{6}, \text{ identity}$$

Thus each element of A possesses inverse in A.

∴ $<A, X_{10}>$ is a group.

Further the operation of multiplication modulo 10 obeys commutative law i.e. $\bar{a} X_{10} \bar{b} = \bar{b} X_{10} \bar{a}$ for all $a, b \in A$.

Therefore group is abelian.

Example 5.14 : Show that a group G is abelian if and only if $(ab)^2 = a^2b^2$ for all $a, b \in G$.

(P.U. 2011)

Solution : Let G be a group.

First Part : Suppose G is abelian. Let a, b be any two elements of G.

Then
$$(ab)^2 = (ab)(ab)$$
$$= a[b(ab)] \qquad \because \text{Associative property in G}$$
$$= a[(ba)b] \qquad \because \text{Associative property in G}$$
$$= a[(ab)b] \qquad \because \text{G is abelian}$$
$$= a[a(bb)] \qquad \because \text{Associative property}$$
$$= (aa)(bb) \qquad \because \text{Associative property}$$
$$= a^2b^2$$

Second Part : Suppose $(ab)^2 = a^2b^2$ for all $a, b \in G$.

$$(ab)^2 = a^2b^2$$
$$\therefore (ab)(ab) = (aa)(bb)$$
$$\therefore a[b(ab)] = a[a(bb)] \qquad \because \text{Associative property}$$
$$\therefore b(ab) = a(bb) \qquad \because \text{Cancellation law}$$
$$\therefore (ba)b = (ab)b \qquad \because \text{Associative property}$$
$$\therefore ba = ab \qquad \because \text{Cancellation law}$$

$\therefore$ G is abelian group.

Example 5.15 : Show that the symmetric group S_3 is not abelian. Also find elements in S_3 such that $(a * b)^2 \neq a^2 * b^2$.

Solution : Consider the permutations

$$\alpha = \begin{pmatrix} 1 & 2 & 3 \\ 2 & 1 & 3 \end{pmatrix} \text{ and } \beta = \begin{pmatrix} 1 & 2 & 3 \\ 3 & 1 & 2 \end{pmatrix} \text{ in } S_3$$

$$\alpha\beta = \begin{pmatrix} 1 & 2 & 3 \\ 2 & 1 & 3 \end{pmatrix}\begin{pmatrix} 1 & 2 & 3 \\ 3 & 1 & 2 \end{pmatrix} = \begin{pmatrix} 1 & 2 & 3 \\ 1 & 3 & 2 \end{pmatrix}$$

$$\beta\alpha = \begin{pmatrix} 1 & 2 & 3 \\ 3 & 1 & 2 \end{pmatrix}\begin{pmatrix} 1 & 2 & 3 \\ 2 & 1 & 3 \end{pmatrix} = \begin{pmatrix} 1 & 2 & 3 \\ 3 & 2 & 1 \end{pmatrix}$$

$$\alpha\beta \neq \beta\alpha.$$

Therefore S_3 is not abelian. Also for above permutations α and β, we have

$$(\alpha\beta)^2 = \begin{pmatrix} 1 & 2 & 3 \\ 1 & 3 & 2 \end{pmatrix}\begin{pmatrix} 1 & 2 & 3 \\ 1 & 3 & 2 \end{pmatrix} = \begin{pmatrix} 1 & 2 & 3 \\ 1 & 2 & 3 \end{pmatrix}$$

$$\alpha^2 = \begin{pmatrix} 1 & 2 & 3 \\ 2 & 1 & 3 \end{pmatrix}\begin{pmatrix} 1 & 2 & 3 \\ 2 & 1 & 3 \end{pmatrix} = \begin{pmatrix} 1 & 2 & 3 \\ 1 & 2 & 3 \end{pmatrix}$$

$$\beta^2 = \begin{pmatrix} 1 & 2 & 3 \\ 3 & 1 & 2 \end{pmatrix}\begin{pmatrix} 1 & 2 & 3 \\ 3 & 1 & 2 \end{pmatrix} = \begin{pmatrix} 1 & 2 & 3 \\ 2 & 3 & 1 \end{pmatrix}$$

Then
$$\alpha^2\beta^2 = \begin{pmatrix} 1 & 2 & 3 \\ 1 & 2 & 3 \end{pmatrix}\begin{pmatrix} 1 & 2 & 3 \\ 2 & 3 & 1 \end{pmatrix} = \begin{pmatrix} 1 & 2 & 3 \\ 2 & 3 & 1 \end{pmatrix}$$

$\therefore \quad (\alpha\beta)^2 \neq \alpha^2\beta^2$

Example 5.16 : Consider the set Q of all rational numbers and let $*$ be the operation on Q defined by $a * b = a + b - ab$. Is $(Q, *)$ a group ? **(P.U. 2010)**

Solution : Given $a * b = a + b - ab$ in Q.

Closure property : Let a, b be any two rational numbers. Then $a + b - ab$ is a rational number $a \in Q$, $b \in Q \Rightarrow a * b \in Q$.

∴ Set Q is closed under the operation $*$.

Associative law : Let a, b, c be any three members of Q.

$$a * (b * c) = a * (b + c - bc) = a + (b + c - bc) - a(b + c - bc)$$
$$= a + b + c - bc - ab - ac + abc \qquad \ldots (1)$$

Also $(a * b) * c = (a + b - ab) * c = (a + b - ab) + c - (a + b - ab) c$
$$= a + b - ab + c - ac - bc + abc \qquad \ldots (2)$$

From equations (1) and (2), we have

$$a * (b * c) = (a * b) * c \text{ for all } a, b, c \in Q.$$

∴ Operation $*$ is associative.

Identity element : we have $0 \in Q$.

If a is any member of Q then

$$a * 0 = a + 0 - a \times 0 = a$$
$$0 * a = 0 + a - 0 \times a = a$$

Therefore $0 \in Q$ is identity element w.r.t. operation $*$.

Inverse of an element : We show that inverse of some element of Q does not exist w.r.t. operation $*$.

Let $a \in Q$; and b be inverse of a w.r.t. $*$.

Then, $\qquad a * b = $ identity

∴ $\qquad a * b = 0$

∴ $\qquad a + b - ab = 0$

∴ $\qquad b(1 - a) = -a$

∴ $\qquad b = -\dfrac{a}{1-a}$

This value of b does not exist for $a = 1 \in Q$.

∴ $1 \in Q$ does not possess inverse w.r.t. operation $*$.

Therefore $(Q, *)$ is not a group.

Example 5.17 : Show that $Z_6 = \{\bar{0}, \bar{1}, \bar{2}, \bar{3}, \bar{4}, \bar{5}\}$ forms an abelian group under the operation addition module 6; a * b = Remainder when a + b is divided by 6.

Solution : We prepare a composition table.

$+_6$	$\bar{0}$	$\bar{1}$	$\bar{2}$	$\bar{3}$	$\bar{4}$	$\bar{5}$
$\bar{0}$	$\bar{0}$	$\bar{1}$	$\bar{2}$	$\bar{3}$	$\bar{4}$	$\bar{5}$
$\bar{1}$	$\bar{1}$	$\bar{2}$	$\bar{3}$	$\bar{4}$	$\bar{5}$	$\bar{0}$
$\bar{2}$	$\bar{2}$	$\bar{3}$	$\bar{4}$	$\bar{5}$	$\bar{0}$	$\bar{1}$
$\bar{3}$	$\bar{3}$	$\bar{4}$	$\bar{5}$	$\bar{0}$	$\bar{1}$	$\bar{2}$
$\bar{4}$	$\bar{4}$	$\bar{5}$	$\bar{0}$	$\bar{1}$	$\bar{2}$	$\bar{3}$
$\bar{5}$	$\bar{5}$	$\bar{0}$	$\bar{1}$	$\bar{2}$	$\bar{3}$	$\bar{4}$

Closure property : All 6 × 6 = 36 entries in the composition table are elements Z_6.

x * y ∈ Z_{16} for all x, y ∈ Z_6.

∴ Z_6 is closed under addition modulo 6 operation.

Associative law : The operation $+_6$ is associative. For example $\bar{2} +_6 (\bar{3} +_6 \bar{5}) = \bar{2} +_6 \bar{2} = \bar{4}$ and $(\bar{2} +_6 \bar{3}) +_6 \bar{5} = \bar{5} +_6 \bar{5} = \bar{4}$

$\bar{x} +_6 (\bar{y} +_6 \bar{z}) = (\bar{x} +_6 \bar{y}) +_6 \bar{z}$ for every $\bar{x}, \bar{y}, \bar{z} \in Z_6$.

Identity element : $\bar{0} \in Z_6$ and $\bar{x} +_6 \bar{0} = \bar{0} +_6 \bar{x} = \bar{x}$ for all $\bar{x} \in Z_6$.

∴ $\bar{0}$ is identity element.

Inverse of an element : From the table, we have

$$\bar{0} +_6 \bar{0} = \bar{0}, \text{ identity}$$
$$\bar{1} +_6 \bar{5} = \bar{5} +_6 \bar{1} = \bar{0}, \text{ identity}$$
$$\bar{2} +_6 \bar{4} = \bar{4} +_6 \bar{2} = \bar{0}, \text{ identity}$$
$$\bar{3} +_6 \bar{3} = \bar{0}$$

The operation is additive, we denote the inverse by minus sign –.

Thus,
$$-\bar{0} = \bar{0} \in Z_6$$
$$-\bar{1} = \bar{5} \in Z_6$$
$$-\bar{2} = \bar{4} \in Z_6$$
$$-\bar{3} = \bar{3} \in Z_6$$

$$-\bar{4} = \bar{2} \in \mathbf{Z}_6$$
$$-\bar{5} = \bar{1} \in \mathbf{Z}_6$$

Thus, every element of $\mathbf{Z}_6$ has inverse in $\mathbf{Z}_6$.

Commutative law : The operation of addition modulo 6 is commutative. In the composition table the elements which are symmetrically situated w.r.t. main diagonal, are equal conclusion is that $(\mathbf{Z}_6, +_6)$ forms an abelian group.

Example 5.18 : Write the composition tables for $<\mathbf{Z}_7, +_7>$ and $<\mathbf{Z}_7^*, X_7>$ where $\mathbf{Z}_7^* = \mathbf{Z}_7 - \{[0]\}$.

Solution : $\mathbf{Z}_7 = \{\bar{0}, \bar{1}, \bar{2}, \bar{3}, \bar{4}, \bar{5}, \bar{6}\}$.

The composition table for $<\mathbf{Z}_7, +_7>$ under addition modulo 7 is as below.

$+_7$	$\bar{0}$	$\bar{1}$	$\bar{2}$	$\bar{3}$	$\bar{4}$	$\bar{5}$	$\bar{6}$
$\bar{0}$	$\bar{0}$	$\bar{1}$	$\bar{2}$	$\bar{3}$	$\bar{4}$	$\bar{5}$	$\bar{6}$
$\bar{1}$	$\bar{1}$	$\bar{2}$	$\bar{3}$	$\bar{4}$	$\bar{5}$	$\bar{6}$	$\bar{0}$
$\bar{2}$	$\bar{2}$	$\bar{3}$	$\bar{4}$	$\bar{5}$	$\bar{6}$	$\bar{0}$	$\bar{1}$
$\bar{3}$	$\bar{3}$	$\bar{4}$	$\bar{5}$	$\bar{6}$	$\bar{0}$	$\bar{1}$	$\bar{2}$
$\bar{4}$	$\bar{4}$	$\bar{5}$	$\bar{6}$	$\bar{0}$	$\bar{1}$	$\bar{2}$	$\bar{3}$
$\bar{5}$	$\bar{5}$	$\bar{6}$	$\bar{0}$	$\bar{1}$	$\bar{2}$	$\bar{3}$	$\bar{4}$
$\bar{6}$	$\bar{6}$	$\bar{0}$	$\bar{1}$	$\bar{2}$	$\bar{3}$	$\bar{4}$	$\bar{5}$

$\mathbf{Z}_7^* = \{\bar{1}, \bar{2}, \bar{3}, \bar{4}, \bar{5}, \bar{6}\}$. The composition table for $<\mathbf{Z}_7^*, X_7>$ is as below.

X_7	$\bar{1}$	$\bar{2}$	$\bar{3}$	$\bar{4}$	$\bar{5}$	$\bar{6}$
$\bar{1}$	$\bar{1}$	$\bar{2}$	$\bar{3}$	$\bar{4}$	$\bar{5}$	$\bar{6}$
$\bar{2}$	$\bar{2}$	$\bar{4}$	$\bar{6}$	$\bar{1}$	$\bar{3}$	$\bar{5}$
$\bar{3}$	$\bar{3}$	$\bar{6}$	$\bar{2}$	$\bar{5}$	$\bar{1}$	$\bar{4}$
$\bar{4}$	$\bar{4}$	$\bar{1}$	$\bar{5}$	$\bar{2}$	$\bar{6}$	$\bar{3}$
$\bar{5}$	$\bar{5}$	$\bar{3}$	$\bar{1}$	$\bar{6}$	$\bar{4}$	$\bar{2}$
$\bar{6}$	$\bar{6}$	$\bar{5}$	$\bar{4}$	$\bar{3}$	$\bar{2}$	$\bar{1}$

EXERCISE (5.1)

1. Determine whether or not the binary operation * defined on the given set is associative or not:
   - (i) $x * y = \min\{x, y\}$; $\mathbb{N}$
   - (ii) $x * y = x + y + 12$; $\mathbb{N}$
   - (iii) $x * y = x + 3y$; $\mathbb{N}$
   - (iv) $x * y = \min\{x, y + 3\}$; $\mathbb{N}$
   - (v) $x * y = x \cdot |y|$; $\mathbb{R}$
   - (vi) $x * y = xy + 2y$; $\mathbb{R}$
   - (viii) $x * y = \dfrac{x + y}{2}$; $\mathbb{Q}$

2. In exercise 1 above find which of the binary operations are commutative. Also find the identity element if it exists.

3. A binary operation □ on the set S = {a, b, c} is defined as

□	a	b	c
a	b	c	b
b	a	b	c
c	c	a	b

   - (i) Is the operation □ commutative ?
   - (ii) Is the operation □ associative ?
   - (iii) Compute a □ (b □ c) and (a □ b) □ c.

4. On the set $\mathbb{N}$ of positive integers show that the operation * defined by $a * b = \dfrac{a + 2b}{3}$ is idempotent but neither commutative nor associative.

5. Show that the set $\mathbb{Z}_4 = \{0, 1, 2, 3\}$ forms a semigroup w.r.t. the operation of multiplication modulo 4.

6. Let A = {1, 3, 5, 15, 30} and $a * b = $ G.C.D. {a, b}. Show that <A, *> is a semigroup. Is it a monoid ? If yes, what is the identity element ?

7. Show that the set of all even integers is a monoid w.r.t. $a * b = \dfrac{ab}{2}$. What is the identity element ? Is it commutative ?

8. Determine whether the set of positive integers is a semigroup, monoid under the given operation. In case of monoid state the identity element. Is the semigroup/monoid commutative ?
   - (i) $a * b = \max\{a, b\}$
   - (ii) $a * b = a$
   - (iii) $a * b = $ G.C.D. {a, b}

9. Let < {a, b}, * > be a semigroup in which a * a = b. Show that :
   (i) a * b = b * a   (ii) b * b = b.

10. Determine whether (Z^+, *) is a commutative group or not where Z^+ is the set of positive integers and * denotes the usual multiplication. **(P.U. 2011)**

11. In a group <G, *> if every element is its own inverse, show that G is abelian. Give example of such group.

12. Show that the set {..., 6^{-4}, 6^{-3}, 6^{-2}, 6^{-1}, 1, 6, 6^2, 6^3, 6^4, ...} is an abelian group of infinite order under usual multiplication.

13. Let < G, □ > be a group and a ∈ G such that a □ a = a. Then show that a = e.

14. Explain which of the group axioms fail to satisfy in the following :
    (i) A = {0, ±1, ±3, ±5, ...} w.r.t. addition.
    (ii) A = {0, ±1, ±2, ±3, ±4, ...} w.r.t. multiplication.

15. Show that the set of all real numbers except −1 forms an abelian group under the operation a * b = a + b + ab. In this group solve the equation 3 * x * 1 = 23.

16. Give example of :
    (i) Finite abelian group.
    (ii) Finite non-abelian group.
    (iii) Infinite abelian group.
    Justify your answer.

17. Solve the following equations in the group Z_5 = {$\bar{0}$, $\bar{1}$, $\bar{2}$, $\bar{3}$, $\bar{4}$} under addition modulo 5 operation.
    (i) $x^2 + \bar{2}x + \bar{3} = \bar{4}$
    (ii) $x^2 + \bar{4}x + \bar{1} = \bar{3}$

ANSWERS (5.1)

1. (i) Yes, (ii) Yes, (iii) No, (iv) No, (v) Yes, (vi) No, (vii) No
2. (i) Commutative, identity does not exist.
   (ii) Commutative; e = − 12
   (iii) Not commutative; identity does not exist.
   (iv) Not commutative; identity does not exist.
   (v) Not commutative; identity does not exist.
   (vi) Not commutative; identity does not eixst.
   (vii) Commutative; identity does not exist.
3. (i) No, (ii) No, (iii) b, b
6. Yes, e = 30
7. e = 2, Yes

8. (i) It is monoid, e = 1, commutative.
   (ii) Semigroup, not monoid, non-commutative.
   (iii) Commutative semigroup; not monoid.
10. No; inverse does not exist.
11. G = {1, 3, 5, 7} under multiplication modulo 8.
14. (i) A is not closed under addition.
    (ii) Inverse does not exist.
15. 2
17. (i) x = $\bar{3}$, (ii) x = $\bar{1}$

5.4 Cyclic Group

Let us consider following three group structues.

(i) G = {1, 2, 3, 4} w.r.t. multiplication modulo 5 is a group; with identity element 1. Now for 2 ∈ G, we have

$2^1 = 2$, $2^2 = 2 \times_5 2 = 4$,
$2^3 = 2^2 \times_5 2 = 4 \times_5 2 = 3$,
$2^4 = 2^3 \times_5 2 = 3 \times_5 2 = 1$ = identity.

We note that all the elements of this group can be written as integral powers of 2 ∈ G. This we describe by saying that 2 ∈ G generates all the elements of G i.e. 2 ∈ G generates G. Also 3 ∈ G, $3^1 = 3, 3^2 = 4, 3^3 = 2, 3^4 = 1$.

∴ 3 ∈ G also generates G and 4 ∈ G generates G.

In this group the binary operation is multiplicative.

(ii) Z_4 = {0, 1, 2, 3} w.r.t. addition modulo 4 is a group with identity element 0.

Now, $1 +_4 1 = 2$ i.e. 2.1 = 2
$1 +_4 1 +_4 1 = 2 +_4 1 = 3$ i.e. 3.1 = 3
$1 +_4 1 +_4 1 + 1 = 0$ i.e. 4.1 = 4.

The elements 1 and 3 of Z_4 generate all elements of Z_4.

However 2 ∈ Z_4 generates only two elements of Z_4.

$2^1 = 2$, $2 +_2 2 = 0$.

In this group the operation is additive. Hence we write n a for a * a * ... * a; instead of a^n.

(iii) A = {1, 5, 7, 11} forms a group w.r.t. multiplication modulo 12. 5 ∈ A generates only 2 elements

$5^1 = 5$, $5^2 = 5 * 5 = 1$ = identity
$7^1 = 7$, $7^2 = 7 * 7 = 1$ = identity
$11^1 = 11$, $11^2 = 11 * 11 = 1$ = identity

In this group no element of A generate the whole group A.

The groups G and Z_4 in (i) and (ii) above, are called cyclic groups and the group A in (iii) is non-cyclic.

Definition :

Let (G, *) be a group. If there exists an element a ∈ G such that every element x ∈ G can be written as some integral power of a i.e $x = a^n$; n is integer, then the group G is called cyclic group and element 'a' is called generator of G.

We write this as G = <a>. It is then clear that if a is a generator of G, then a^{-1} is also a generator of G.

Examples :

(A) (i) The additive group (Z, +) of all integers is cyclic. It has two generators 1 and −1.

(ii) The four fourth roots of unity 1, −1, i, −i where $i = \sqrt{-1}$ is a group under multiplication. It is a cyclic group. The generators are i and −i.

(iii) The set {1, 2, 3, 4, 5, 6} forms a group w.r.t. multiplication modulo 7 operation. This group is cyclic; the generators being 2, 3, 4, 5, 6.

(iv) Z_8 = {0, 1, 2, 3, 4, 5, 6, 7} is a cyclic group w.r.t. addition modulo 8 binary operation. Its generators are 1, 3, 5 and 7.

$2 \in Z_8$ is not a generator because 2 generates only four elements 2, 4, 6 and 0 of Z_8. Similarly, 4 and 6 are not generators of Z_8.

(B) (i) The set **Q** of all rational numbers. w.r.t. usual addition is a group. It is non-cyclic, since there is no rational number a ∈ **Q** such that after adding a (or − a) to itself we get all rational numbers.

(ii) The set of non-zero rational numbers forms a group w.r.t. multiplication. It is non-cyclic group.

We note that if (G, *) is a cyclic group having a as its one generator, then G is of the form G = {..., a^{-2}, a^{-1}, $a^0 = e$, a, a^2, a^3, ...}.

If G is a finite cyclic group, G = <a> then G = {$a^0 = e$, a, a^2, a^3, ..., a^{n-1}}.

Theorem : Every cyclic group is abelian.

Proof : Let G = <a> be a cyclic group whose one generator is 'a'.

Let x, y be any two elements of G. Then there exist integers r and s such that $x = a^r$ and $y = a^s$.

Now,
$$x * y = a^r * a^s = a^{r+s}$$
$$= a^{s+r} = a^s * a^r$$
$$= y * x$$

Hence G is abelian.

The converse of the above theorem is not true. Consider Klein − 4 group structure G = {e, a, b, c}. The composition table of Klein − 4 group (G, *) is as below.

*	e	a	b	c
e	e	a	b	c
a	a	e	c	b
b	b	c	e	a
c	c	b	a	e

e is identity element. Now $a^1 = a$, $a^2 = a * a = e$; identity. Thus $a \in G$ generates only two elements of G.

Similarly, $b \in G$ generates only two elements b and e.

Also $c \in G$ generates only two elements c and e.

The binary operation * is commutative.

Hence the group is abelian but not cyclic.

Number of generators : Consider the groups of order 1, 2, 3 and 4.

If $O(G) = 1$ then G consist singleton identity; $G = \{e\}$. It is a cyclic group having one generator i.e. e itself.

If $O(G) = 2$ then $G = \{e, a\}$ where e is identity. The composition table of G is

*	e	a
e	e	a
a	a	e

It is a cyclic group having only one generator i.e. a.

If $O(G) = 3$ then $G = \{e, a, b\}$ where e is identity and a and b are inverses of each other. There is only one group structure for this group.

*	e	a	b
e	e	a	b
a	a	b	e
b	b	e	a

It is a cyclic group having two generators viz. a and b.

If $O(G) = 4$ then $G = \{e, a, b, c\}$; where e is identity.

A group of order 4 has two group structures given by the composition table as below.

*	e	a	b	c
e	e	a	b	c
a	a	b	c	e
b	b	c	e	a
c	c	e	a	b

*	e	a	b	c
e	e	a	b	c
a	a	e	c	b
b	b	c	e	a
c	c	b	a	e

         Cyclic structure   Klein – 4 structure

Cyclic structure has 2 generators a and c.

A group of order 4 is the smallest non-cyclic group.

We now state without proof the result which helps us in finding the number of generators for a cyclic group or order n.

Let $(G, *)$ be a cyclic group of order n and whose one generator is a.

$G = \{a, a^2, a^3, ..., a^n = e\}$.

Then a^m is also a generator of G if and only if G.C.D. of m and n is 1.

Consider a cyclic group of order 24, generated by a.

$G = \{a, a^2, a^3, ..., a^{24} = e\}$.

The integers 1, 5, 7, 11, 13, 17, 19, 23 have G.C.D. 1 with the integer 24.

Therefore $a, a^5, a^7, a^{11}, a^{13}, a^{17}, a^{19}, a^{23}$ are generators of G. These are 8 in number.

Example 5.19 : Consider the group $G = \{1, 2, 3, 4, 5, 6\}$ under multiplication modulo 7.

(i) Prepare a multiplication table of G.

(ii) Is G cyclic ?

(iii) How many generators G has ?

Solution :

X_7	1	2	3	4	5	6
1	1	2	3	4	5	6
2	2	4	6	1	3	5
3	3	6	2	5	1	4
4	4	1	5	2	6	3
5	5	3	1	6	4	2
6	6	5	4	3	2	1

It is a cyclic group.

It has two generators 3 and 5.

Since $3^1 = 3, 3^2 = 2, 3^3 = 6, 3^4 = 4, 3^5 = 5, 3^6 = 1$.

Thus $G = <3>$

Also $G = <5>$

EXERCISE (5.2)

1. Show that the additive group of even integers $\{0, \pm 2, \pm 4, \pm 6, ...\}$ is cyclic. What are its generators ?

2. Show that $Z_6 = \{\bar{0}, \bar{1}, \bar{2}, \bar{3}, \bar{4}, \bar{5}\}$ w.r.t. addition modulo 6 is cyclic group. Find its generators.

3. How many generators does not group $\{a, a^2, a^3, ..., a^{20} = e\}$ have ?

4. Give example of :
   (i) Finite cyclic group.
   (ii) Infinite cyclic group.
   (iii) Finite non-cyclic group.
   (iv) Infinite non-cyclic group.
5. Find the number of generators of a cyclic group of order 40.

ANSWERS (5.2)

1. 2, –2
2. $\bar{1}, \bar{5}$
3. 8
5. 16

5.5 Sub Group

Let (A, *) be an algebraic system. A non-empty subset B of A, together with operation * is a subsystem of (A, *) if all the axioms of system (A, *) also hold in (B, *).

Definition : Let (A, *) be a semigroup. A non-empty subset B of A is called a sub-semigroup if (B, *) is itself a semigroup.

Definition : Let (A, *) be a monoid. A non-empty subset B of A is called a submonoid if (B, *) is itself a monoid having identity e of A.

Definition : Let (G, *) be a group. A non-empty subset H of G is a subgroup of G if (H, *) is itself a group.

Illustration 3 :

(i) The set $\mathbf{Z} = \{..., -3, -2, -1, 0, 1, 2, 3, ...\}$ is a group w.r.t. addition. Consider the set E of all even integers $E = \{..., -4, -2, 0, 2, 4, ...\}$.

Then (E, +) is also a group. All four group axioms hold in the system (E, +). Therefore, (E, +) is a subgroup of the group (Z, +).

(ii) $A = \{1, -1\}$ is a group w.r.t. usual multiplication; and $A \subset \mathbf{Z}$.

(A, ×) is not a subgroup of (Z, +). The reason is that the binary operation is not the same in (A, ×) and (Z, +).

(iii) (Z, ×) is a semigroup.

$E = \{..., -4, -2, 0, 2, 4, ...\}$ is a sub-semigroup; under multiplication. Again (Z, ×) is a monoid but (E, ×) is not a sub-monoid; since multiplicative identity $1 \notin E$.

(iv) Consider a Klein - 4 group $G = \{e, a, b, c\}$. Refer preceding article.

Then $A = \{e, a\}$, $B = \{e, b\}$, $C = \{e, c\}$ are subgroups of Klein - 4 group (G, *).

Let (G, *) be a group with identity e. Then the subsets {e} and G itself of G are always subgroups of G. Thee two subgroups of G are improper or trivial subgroups of G. Any other subgroup of G lying between these two trivial subgroups is called a non-trivial or proper subgroup of G.

Let now (G, *) be a group with identity e and let H be a non-empty subset of G. In order to show that H is a subgroup of G, we must show that H satisfies all 4 group axioms. However, this task can be reduced at least to some extent.

First, we note that associative law holds in G and $H \subset G$. Therefore associative law holds in H. So we need not check this group axiom.

The following two theorems further reduce the number of axioms to be checked in H.

Theorem 3 : Let (G, *) be a group. A non-empty subset H of G is a subgroup of G if and only if $a \in H, b \in H \Rightarrow a * b^{-1} \in H$.

Proof :

First Part : Assume that H is a subgroup of G.

Then (H, *) is itself a group. Let $a \in H$ and $b \in H$.

∴ $a \in H, b^{-1} \in H$ ∵ inverse exists in a group

∴ $a * b^{-1} \in H$ ∵ closure property in group H.

Thus the condition holds.

Second Part : Assume that H satisfies the condition $a \in H, b \in H \Rightarrow a * b^{-1} \in H$.

Now $H \neq \phi$ ∴ let $a \in H$

Then $a \in H, a \in H \Rightarrow a * a^{-1} \in H$ ∵ by given condition

                         $\Rightarrow e \in H$

Next $e \in H, a \in H \Rightarrow e * a^{-1} \in H$ ∵ by given condition

                         $\Rightarrow a^{-1} \in H$

Also, $a \in H, b^{-1} \in H \Rightarrow a * (b^{-1})^{-1} \in H$ ∵ by given condition

                         $\Rightarrow a * b \in H$

Also associative law holds in H since it holds in G.

Hence (H, *) is a group.

∴   H is a subgroup of G.

Theorem 4 : Let (G, *) be a group and H non-empty subset of G. If H is finite and H is closed under the binary operation * then H is a subgroup of G.

Proof : H is non-empty finite subset of group G such that H is closed under the binary operation *.

Let a be any element of H. By closure property of H, a, a^2, a^3, ... are all elements of H.

Since H is given to be finite the above list a, a^2, a^3, ... is not infinite list; and there is a repetition of elements in it so that we have for some i and j with i < j, that $a^i = a^j$.

This implies $a^i = a^i * a^{j-i}$.

This suggests that a^{j-i} is an identity element in (G, *) and it is included in H.

If $j - i > 1$ then $a^{j-i} = a * a^{j-i-1}$ implies that a^{j-i-1} is the inverse of a and it is included in H.

If $j - i = 1$ then we have $a^i = a^i * a$. This implies that a is identity element which is its own inverse.

Also H is closed under operation *; Given.

Thus (H, *) satisfies all 4 group axioms.

∴ (H, *) is a group.

∴ H is a subgroup of G.

Example 5.20 : Show that $H = <\{1, 4, 13, 16\}, X_{17}>$ is a subgroup of $<Z_{17}^*, X_{17}>$.

Solution : $Z_{17}^* = \{1, 2, 3, ..., 16\}$.

$H = \{1, 4, 13, 16\}$; binary operation is multiplication modulo 17.

H is a finite subset of Z_{17}^*. Hence to show that H is a subgroup of Z_{17}^*, we need only show that H is closed under the operation of multiplication modulo 17.

The composition table for H is as below.

X_{17}	1	4	13	16
1	1	4	13	16
4	4	16	1	13
13	13	1	16	4
16	16	13	4	1

All $4 \times 4 = 16$ entries in the composition table are elements of H.

$$x \in H, y \in H \Rightarrow x * y \in H$$

∴ H is closed under the operation multiplication modulo 17.

∴ H is a subgroup of Z_{17}^*.

Example 5.21 : Let G be the group of integers under the operation of addition and let $H = \{5k; k \text{ is integer}\}$ show that H is a subgroup of G.

Solution :
$$G = \{0, \pm 1, \pm 2, \pm 3, ...\}$$
$$H = \{0, \pm 5, \pm 10, \pm 15, ...\}$$

Let $a = 5k_1$ and $b = 5k_2$ be any two elements of H. Then k_1, k_2 are integers. The inverse of b under addition is $-b$ i.e. $-(5k_2)$.

Now $\quad a * b^{-1} = a + (-5k_2) = 5k_1 - 5k_2 = 5(k_1 - k_2)$

Let $\quad k_1 - k_2 = k_3$ which is integer

∴ $\quad a * b^{-1} = a - b = 5k_3 \in H$.

Hence H is a subgroup of G.

Example 5.22 : Let G be an abelian group with identity e, and let $H = \{x \in G; x^2 = e\}$. Show that H is a subgroup of G.

Solution : $H = \{x \in G;\ x^2 = e\}$; given. Let a, b be any two elements of H. We shall show $ab^{-1} \in H$

$a \in H \quad \therefore\ a^2 = e$

$b \in H \quad \therefore\ b^2 = e$

Now consider $(ab^{-1})^2$.

$$\begin{aligned}
(ab^{-1})^2 &= (ab^{-1})(ab^{-1}) = a\,[b^{-1}(ab^{-1})] \\
&= a\,[(b^{-1}a)\,b^{-1}] && \because \text{ by associative law} \\
&= a\,[(ab^{-1})\,b^{-1}] && \because \text{ G is abelian given} \\
&= a\,[a\,(b^{-1}b^{-1})] && \because \text{ by associative law} \\
&= (aa)\,(b^{-1}b^{-1}) && \because \text{ by associative law} \\
&= a^2\,(b^{-1})^2
\end{aligned}$$

$\therefore \qquad (ab^{-1})^2 = ee$

$\qquad\qquad\qquad\quad = e$

$\therefore\quad ab^{-1} \in H$

Thus $a \in H,\ b \in H \Rightarrow ab^{-1} \in H$.

$\therefore\quad$ H is a subgroup of G.

Cosets :

Let (G, *) be a group and H subgroup of G.

Let a be any element of G; a may or may not be in H.

Then the right coset of H in G generated by a is the set of all products of the type $h_i * a$ where h_i varies in H.

It is denoted by Ha.

Thus $\qquad Ha = \{h_i * a;\ h_i \in H\}$

Conveniently we drop (with clear understanding) the * and write

$\qquad Ha = \{h_i\,a;\ h_i \in H\}$

Similarly, the left coset of H in G generated by a is denoted by aH

and $\qquad aH = \{a * h_i;\ h_i \in H\}$

i.e. $\qquad aH = \{ah_i;\ h_i \in H\}$

It will be more clear by an example.

The set **Z** of all integers is a group w.r.t. addition.

$\qquad H = \{0, \pm 4, \pm 8, \pm 12, \ldots\}$ is a subgroup of (**Z**, +)

$0 \in$ **Z** is identity element.

The right coset of H generated by 0 is

$\qquad H + 0 = \{h + 0;\ h \in H\} = \{h;\ h \in H\} = H$

$\qquad H + 1 = \{h + 1;\ h \in H\} = \{\ldots, -7, -3, 1, 5, 9, 13, \ldots\}$

$$H + 2 = \{h + 2; h \in H\} = \{\ldots, -10, -6, -2, 2, 6, 10, \ldots\}$$
$$H + 3 = \{h + 3; h \in H\} = \{\ldots, -9, -5, -1, 3, 7, 11, \ldots\}$$

Any other right coset of H is exactly equal to one of the above four right cosets.

We see that the above four cosets are pairwise disjoint, their union gives the set **Z**.

Also the coset of H generated by identity 0 is H itself.

As an another example, consider the group S_3 of permutations on 3 symbols 1, 2, 3.

We have already prepared a composition table of permutation multiplication on 6 permutations. We reproduce it here for convenience.

$$i = \begin{pmatrix} 1 & 2 & 3 \\ 1 & 2 & 3 \end{pmatrix}, \alpha = \begin{pmatrix} 1 & 2 & 3 \\ 2 & 3 & 1 \end{pmatrix}, \beta = \begin{pmatrix} 1 & 2 & 3 \\ 3 & 1 & 2 \end{pmatrix}$$

$$\rho = \begin{pmatrix} 1 & 2 & 3 \\ 1 & 3 & 2 \end{pmatrix}; \mu = \begin{pmatrix} 1 & 2 & 3 \\ 3 & 2 & 1 \end{pmatrix}; \nu = \begin{pmatrix} 1 & 2 & 3 \\ 2 & 1 & 3 \end{pmatrix}$$

.	i	α	β	ρ	μ	ν
i	i	α	β	ρ	μ	ν
α	α	β	i	μ	ν	ρ
β	β	i	α	ν	ρ	μ
ρ	ρ	ν	μ	i	β	α
μ	μ	ρ	ν	α	i	β
ν	ν	μ	ρ	β	α	i

The three permutations i, α, β (they are called even permutations) form a subgroup of S_3 say H.

∴ $H = \{i, \alpha, \beta\}$

The right coset of H generated by μ is

$$H\mu = \{i\mu, \alpha\mu, \beta\mu\} = \{\mu, \nu, \rho\}$$

The left coset of H generated by ρ is

$$\rho H = \{\rho i, \rho\alpha, \rho\beta\} = \{\rho, \nu, \mu\}$$

Similarly, we can find the right cosets and left cosets of H generated by all the elements of S_3.

The following table gives the various cosets.

Generator	Right Coset	Left Coset
i	$H_i = H$	$iH = H$
α	$H\alpha = H$	$\alpha H = H$
β	$H\beta = H$	$\beta H = H$
ρ	$H\rho = \{\rho, \mu, \nu\}$	$\rho H = \{\rho, \nu, \mu\}$
μ	$H\mu = \{\mu, \nu, \rho\}$	$\mu H = \{\mu, \rho, \nu\}$
ν	$H\nu = \{\nu, \rho, \mu\}$	$\nu H = \{\nu, \mu, \rho\}$

There are only two pairwise disjoint right cosets whose union is S_3.

Also there are only two pairwise disjoint left cosets whose union is S_3.

Let G be abelian group and H subgroup of G. If a is any element of G then, we have

$$Ha = \{h * a; h \in H\} = \{a * h; h \in H\} \quad \because G \text{ is abelian}$$

$\therefore \quad Ha = aH$

This shows that if G is abelian group and H is a subgroup of G then the right coset of H generated by a is equal to left coset of H generated by a.

In S_3, we observe that the right coset of H generated by any permutation is equal to the left coset of H generated by that element. But S_3 is not abelian.

Let us now prove one result.

Theorem 5 : Let $(G, *)$ be a group and H be subgroup of G. If $a \in G$ then $Ha = H$ if and only if $a \in H$.

Proof : We prove the result in two parts.

First Part : Assume $Ha = H$. Since H is a subgroup of G, the identity e of G belongs to H.

Now $e \in H$, $a \in G$ $\quad \therefore ea \in Ha$

i.e. $ea \in H \quad \because Ha = H$

$\therefore \quad a \in H$ proved.

Second Part : Assume that $a \in H$. To prove that $Ha = H$, we need to prove that $Ha \subset H$ and $H \subset Ha$.

For any $xa \in Ha$, we have $x \in H$.

Then $\quad\quad x \in H, a \in H \Rightarrow xa \in H \quad\quad \because H$ is a subgroup

Thus $\quad\quad xa \in Ha \Rightarrow xa \in H$

$\therefore \quad\quad Ha \subset H$ ... (1)

Next $\quad\quad a \in H \Rightarrow a^{-1} \in H \quad\quad \because H$ is a subgroup

Then $\quad\quad z \in H, a^{-1} \in H \Rightarrow za^{-1} \in H$

$\quad\quad\quad\quad \Rightarrow (za^{-1}) a \in Ha$

$\quad\quad\quad\quad \Rightarrow z(a^{-1} a) \in Ha$

$\quad\quad\quad\quad \Rightarrow ze \in Ha$

$\quad\quad\quad\quad \Rightarrow z \in Ha$

Thus, $\quad\quad z \in H \Rightarrow z \in Ha$

$\therefore \quad\quad H \subset Ha$ ... (2)

From (1) and (2), we get $Ha = H$.

On the same lines as above, we can prove that $aH = H$, if and only if $a \in H$.

We accept various results about cosets without proof.

1. If G is abelian group and H is a subgroup of G then $Ha = aH$ for every $a \in G$.
2. Let G be a group and H subgroup of G. If a, b are any two elements of G then

$$Ha = Hb \Leftrightarrow ab^{-1} \in H$$

and $\quad\quad aH = bH \Leftrightarrow b^{-1}a \in H$

3. Any two right (left) cosets of H in G are either disjoint or identical.
4. If H is a subgroup of a group G then the number of distinct right cosets of H in G is equal to the number of distinct left coset of H in G.
5. If H is a subgroup of G and a ∈ G is arbitrary element of G then there is a one-one correspondence between the elements of H and Ha (H and aH).
6. **Lagrange's theorem :** If G is a finite group and H is a subgroup of G then O(H) divides O(G).

For example consider the group Z_{12} = {0, 1, 2, 3, ..., 11} under addition modulo 12.

$$H = \{0, 2, 4, 6, 8, 10\} \text{ is a subgroup of } Z_{12}$$
$$O(Z_{12}) = 12 \text{ and } O(H) = 6.$$

Clearly 6 is a divisor of 12. i.e. O(H) divides $O(Z_{12})$.

Again let G = {a, a^2, a^3, ..., a^{18} = e}.

It is a cyclic group of order 18. Let H be a subgroup of G; generated by a^4.

$$H = <a^4> = \{a^4, a^8, a^{12}, a^{16}, a^2, a^6, a^{10}, a^{14}, a^{18} = e\}$$

Thus, O(H) = 9.

Clearly 9 divides 18 i.e. O(H) | O(G).

A subgroup N of G is called a normal subgroup if Na = aN for every a ∈ G. In words the right coset of N generated by a is equal to the left coset of N generated by a holds for all a ∈ G.

In the above definition the condition Na = aN is equivalent to $Naa^{-1} = aNa^{-1}$

i.e. $Ne = aNa^{-1}$ i.e. $N = aNa^{-1}$; which means ana^{-1} ∈ N for every a ∈ G.

In order to determine whether or not a subgroup N of G is normal in G, we take arbitrary elements n ∈ N, g ∈ G and check whether or not gng^{-1} ∈ N.

Illustration 4 : (i) We know that if G is abelian group and H is a subgroup of G then Ha = aH for every a ∈ G. Therefore any subgroup H of abelian group is a normal subgroup.

(ii) Consider the permutation group S_3 = {i, α, β, ρ, μ, ν}. H = {i, α, β} is a subgroup of S_3. This H is a normal subgroup of S_3 β ∈ H, μ ∈ S_3 then $μβμ^{-1} = μβμ = μρ = α$ ∈ H.

Also ρ ∈ S_3, α ∈ H. We have $ρ α ρ^{-1} = ρ α ρ = ρμ = β$ ∈ H.

Note : We look carefully to the condition Na = aN for all a ∈ G. Na = aN does not mean that na = an for all a ∈ G and for all n ∈ N. It means that $n_1 a = a n_2$ for some n_1 and n_2 ∈ N and for all a ∈ G.

Isomorphism and Homomorphism :

Let (G, *) and (G', *') be two groups. A mapping f : G → G' is said to be isomorphic mapping or simply isomorphism if f satisfies the following three conditions.

(i) f is one-one (injective) i.e. $x_1 \neq x_2$ in G $\Rightarrow f(x_1) \neq f(x_2)$ in G'.

(ii) f is onto (surjective) i.e. corresponding to any y ∈ G' there exists preimage x ∈ G such that f(x) = y.

(iii) f preserves the compositions i.e. if x_1, x_2 are any two elements of G then
$$f(x_1 * x_2) = f(x_1) *' f(x_2)$$

When such a mapping exists, we say that group (G, *) is isomorphic to group (G', *') and denote it by $G \cong G'$.

Let us drop the first two conditions laid down for isomorphism.

A mapping f from a group (G, *) to a group (G', *') is called homomorphic mapping (or homomorphism) if f preserves the compositions between two groups i.e. if x_1, x_2 are any two elements of G then $f(x_1 * x_2) = f(x_1) *' f(x_2)$.

Let us consider two groups viz. $Z_4 = \{0, 1, 2, 3\}$ under addition modulo 4 and G $\{1, 2, 3, 4\}$ under multiplication modulo 5.

We define maping $f : Z_4 \to G$ by

$$0 \xrightarrow{f} 1$$
$$1 \xrightarrow{f} 2$$
$$2 \xrightarrow{f} 4$$
$$3 \xrightarrow{f} 3$$

Clearly this mapping f is one-one and onto.

Also f preserves the compositions

$$f(1 +_4 2) = f(3) = 3$$
and $\quad f(1) \times_5 f(2) = 2 \times_5 4 = 3$
Thus $\quad f(1 +_4 2) = f(1) \times_5 f(2)$
Again $\quad f(3 +_4 2) = f(1) = 2$
and $\quad f(3) \times_5 f(2) = 3 \times_5 4 = 2$
$\therefore \quad f(3 +_4 2) = f(3) \times_5 f(2)$

In this way the compositions are preserved.

Therefore $\quad (Z_4, +_4) \cong (G, \times_5)$

If (G, *) and (G', *') are two groups and there exists a mapping $f : G \xrightarrow{\text{isomorphism}} G'$ then G and G' have the same algebraic structure except for the labels of their elements and binary operations.

This means under isomorphic mapping $f : G \to G'$

(i) The identities of G and G' correspond i.e. $f(e) = e'$.
(ii) Inverses of elements correspond i.e. when $a \in G$ and $f(a) \in G'$, we have $f(a^{-1}) = (f(a))^{-1}$
(iii) The corresponding elements have the same order. i.e. if for $a \in G$ order of a is r then for f(a) in G' order of f(a) is also r.

All above results can be proved easily. We omit the proofs.

In order to show that the two groups (G, *) and (G', *') are isomorphic, we proceed as below :

(i) First define a mapping f : G → G'.
(ii) To show that f is one-one mapping i.e. $x_1 \neq x_2$ in G ⇒ $f(x_1) \neq f(x_2)$ in G'.
We make use of contrapositive, we assume that $f(x_1) = f(x_2)$ and show that $x_1 = x_2$.
(iii) To show that f is onto we take any y ∈ G' and find x ∈ G whose image under the mapping is y.
(iv) To show that f preserves the compositions, we take any two elements x_1, x_2 ∈ G; find their images $f(x_1)$ and $f(x_2)$; and show that $f(x_1 * x_2) = f(x_1) *' f(x_2)$.

To show that f : G → G' is a homomorphism, we have only to show that $f(x_1 * x_2) = f(x_1) *' f(x_2)$ for all x_1, x_2 ∈ G.

Let f : G → G' be a group homomorphism. It can be easily seen that f(e) = e' where e and e' are identities of G and G' respectively. In addition to e there may be some other elements of G which map onto identity e' of G'. The set of those elements of G which map onto identity e' of G' is called Kernel of homomorphism f.

It is denoted by ker. f. Thus, ker. f = {x ∈ G; f(x) = e'}

SOLVED EXAMPLES

Example 5.23 : Consider the group G = {0, 1, 2, 3, 4, 5, 6} under addition modulo 7.
(i) Prepare the addition table of G.
(ii) Obtain the left and right cosets of G. **(P.U. 2010)**

Solution : (i)

$+_7$	0	1	2	3	4	5	6
0	0	1	2	3	4	5	6
1	1	2	3	4	5	6	0
2	2	3	4	5	6	0	1
3	3	4	5	6	0	1	2
4	4	5	6	0	1	2	3
5	5	6	0	1	2	3	4
6	6	0	1	2	3	4	5

(ii) The operation addition modulo 7 is commutative. Therefore group G is abelian. Hence every left cost is also a right coset.

0 ∈ G	∴	G $+_7$ 0 = 0 $+_7$ G = G
1 ∈ G	∴	G $+_7$ 1 = 1 $+_7$ G = G
2 ∈ G	∴	G $+_7$ 2 = 2 $+_7$ G = G
3 ∈ G	∴	G $+_7$ 3 = 3 $+_7$ G = G
4 ∈ G	∴	G $+_7$ 4 = 4 $+_7$ G = G
5 ∈ G	∴	G $+_7$ 5 = 5 $+_7$ G = G
6 ∈ G	∴	G $+_7$ 6 = 6 $+_7$ G = G

Example 5.24 : Let $< I, + >$ be the group and H_3 the set of all multiples of 3. Show that H_3 is a subgroup of I. Determine all left cosets of H_3 in I where I is the set of all integers.

Solution :
$$I = \{0, \pm 1, \pm 2, \pm 3, \ldots\}$$
$$H_3 = \{0, \pm 3, \pm 6, \pm 9, \pm 12, \ldots\}.$$

Let $a = 3k_1$ and $b = 3k_2$ by any two elements of H_3. Then k_1, k_2 are integers.

Now $\quad a - b = 3k_1 - 3k_2 = 3(k_1 - k_2) = 3k_3 \in H_3$

Since $\quad k_3 = k_1 - k_2$ is integer.

Thus, $\quad a \in H_3, b \in H_3 \Rightarrow a - b \in H_3$

Therefore, H_3 is a subgroup of I.

$0 \in H_3 \quad \therefore \quad$ left coset $0 + H_3 = H_3$

$1 \in I \quad \therefore \quad$ left coset $1 + H_3 = \{1 + h; h \in H_3\}$

$\therefore \quad 1 + H_3 = \{1, 4, 7, 10, \ldots, -2, -5, -8, \ldots\}$

$2 \in I \quad \therefore \quad 2 + H_3 = \{2 + h; h \in H_3\}$

$\therefore \quad 2 + H_3 = \{2, 5, 8, 11, \ldots, -1, -4, -7, \ldots\}$

After these cosets there is a repetition.

There are 3 distinct left cosets of H_3 in I. They are $H, 1 + H_3, 2 + H_3$.

Example 5.25 : Find the left cosets of $H = \{[0], [3]\}$ in the group $<Z_6, +_6>$.

Solution :
$$Z_6 = \{[0], [1], [2], [3], [4], [5]\}$$
$$H = \{[0], [3]\} \text{ is a subgroup of } Z_6.$$

$[0] \in H \quad \therefore \quad$ left coset $[0] +_6 H = H$

$[3] \in H \quad \therefore \quad$ left coset $[3] +_6 H = H$

Now $\quad [1] +_6 H = \{[1] +_6 [h]; [h] \in H\}$
$$= \{[1] +_6 [0], [1] +_6 [3]\} = \{[1], [4]\}$$

$[2] +_6 H = \{[2] +_6 [h]; [h] \in H\}$
$$= \{[2] +_6 [0], [2] +_6 [3]\} = \{[2], [5]\}$$

$[4] +_6 H = \{[4] +_6 [h]; [h] \in H\}$
$$= \{[4] +_6 [0], [4] +_6 [3]\} = \{[4], [1]\}$$

$[5] +_6 H = \{[5] +_6 [h]; [h] \in H\}$
$$= \{[5] +_6 [0], [5] +_6 [3]\} = \{[5], [2]\}$$

Example 5.26 : Let f and g be homomorphisms from a group $(A, *)$ to a group $(B, \square)$ and $C = \{x \in A; f(x) = g(x)\}$.

Show that $(C, *)$ is a subgroup of $(A, *)$.

Solution : Given that $f : A \to B$ and $g : A \to B$ are homomorphisms.

$C = \{x \in A; f(x) = g(x)\}$.

First, we show that C contains at least one element.

Let e and e' be identity elements in A and B respectively.

Then $f(e) = e', \; g(e) = e'$

∴ $f(e) = g(e)$

∴ $e \in C$. Therefore C is non-empty subset of A.

Now we show that the condition for a subgroup holds in C.

Let $x \in C$ and $y \in C$ be any two elements of C.

Out claim is $x * y^{-1} \in C$.

$x \in C$ ∴ $f(x) = g(x)$
$y \in C$ ∴ $f(y) = g(y)$

Now consider $x * y^{-1}$.

$$\begin{aligned} f(x * y^{-1}) &= f(x) \,\square\, f(y^{-1}) & &\because \text{f is homomorphism} \\ &= f(x) \,\square\, (f(y))^{-1} & &\because \text{f is homomorphism} \\ &= g(x) \,\square\, (g(y))^{-1} & &\because f(x) = g(x) \text{ and } f(y) = g(y) \\ &= g(x * y^{-1}) & &\because \text{g is homomorphism} \end{aligned}$$

Thus, $f(x * y^{-1}) = g(x * y^{-1})$

∴ $x * y^{-1} \in C$ $\because$ definition of set C

Hence $(C, *)$ is a subgroup of $(A, *)$.

Example 5.27 : Let $<G, *>$ and $<H, \Delta>$ be groups and $g : G \to H$ be a homomorphism. Prove that the Kernel of g is a normal subgroup of G.

Solution : $g : G \xrightarrow{\text{homomorphism}} H$: Given.

The Kernel of g is Ker. $g = \{x \in G; \; g(x) = e'\}$ where e' is identity in H.

First, we show Ker. g is a subgroup of G.

Let $x \in$ Ker. g and $y \in$ Ker. g be any two elements of Ker. g.

Now consider $x * y^{-1}$.

$$\begin{aligned} g(x * y^{-1}) &= g(x) \,\Delta\, g(y^{-1}) & &\because \text{g is a homomorphism} \\ &= g(x) \,\Delta\, [g(y)]^{-1} & &\because g(y^{-1}) = (g(y))^{-1} \text{ under homomorphism} \\ &= e' \,\Delta\, (e')^{-1} \\ &= e' \,\Delta\, e' \\ &= e' \end{aligned}$$

∴ $x * y^{-1} \in$ Ker. g

Thus, $x \in$ Ker. g, $y \in$ Ker. g $\Rightarrow x * y^{-1}$ Ker. g

∴ Ker. g is a subgroup of G.

Next we show that Ker. g is normal in G.

Let a be any element of G and x be any element of Ker. g.

Consider the element $a * x * a^{-1}$

$$\begin{aligned} g(a * x * a^{-1}) &= g(a) \,\Delta\, g(x) \,\Delta\, g(a^{-1}) & &\because \text{g is a homomorphism} \\ &= g(a) \,\Delta\, e' \,\Delta\, g(a^{-1}) & &\because x \in \text{Ker. g} \end{aligned}$$

$$\begin{aligned}
&= g(a) \,\Delta\, g(a^{-1}) && \because e' \text{ is identity in H} \\
&= g(a * a^{-1}) && \because g \text{ is homomorphism} \\
&= g(e) && \because a * a^{-1} = e \\
&= e' && \because g(e) = e' \text{ under homomorphism}
\end{aligned}$$

$\therefore \quad a * x * a^{-1} \in \text{Ker. } g$.

Thus, $a \in G$, $x \in \text{Ker. } g \Rightarrow a * x * a^{-1} \in \text{Ker. } g$

Therefore, Ker. g is normal in G.

Example 5.28 : Let <G, *> be a group and $a \in G$.

Let $f : G \to G$ be given by $f(x) = ax\, a^{-1}$ for every $x \in G$. Prove that f is an isomorphism of G onto G.

Solution : A mapping $f : G \to G$ itself is defined by $f(x) = ax\, a^{-1}$; $x \in G$, $a \in G$.

f is one-one : For this $\quad f(x) = f(y)$

$\Rightarrow \quad\quad\quad\quad\quad ax\, a^{-1} = ay\, a^{-1}$

$\Rightarrow \quad\quad\quad\quad\quad x = y \quad\quad \because$ by left and right cancellation laws in G.

Therefore, f is one-one.

f is onto : Let z be any elements of G.

Then $a^{-1} z\, a \in G$. $\quad \because$ G is a group.

Now, $\quad\quad\quad f(a^{-1} za) = a(a^{-1} za)\, a^{-1}$

$$\begin{aligned}
&= (aa^{-1})\, z\, (aa^{-1}) && \because \text{ by associative law} \\
&= eze && \because aa^{-1} = e \\
&= z && \because e \text{ is identity}
\end{aligned}$$

Thus $z \in G$ has preimage $a^{-1} z\, a \in G$.

Therefore, f is onto mapping.

f preserves compositions : Let x and y be any two elements of G.

Then, $\quad\quad\quad f(xy) = a(xy)\, a^{-1} \quad\quad\quad \because$ by definition of f

$$\begin{aligned}
&= (ax)(ya^{-1}) && \because \text{ by associative law} \\
&= (ax)(a^{-1} a)(ya^{-1}) && \because a^{-1} a = e \\
&= (ax\, a^{-1})(ay\, a^{-1}) && \because \text{ by associative law} \\
&= f(x) f(y) && \because \text{ definition of f}
\end{aligned}$$

Thus f is preserves the compositions.

Conclusion is that f is an isomorphism of G onto G.

Example 5.29 : Let T be the set of all even integers. Show that the semigroups (Z, +) and (T, +) are isomorphic. **(P.U. 2010)**

Solution : $\quad\quad\quad\quad Z = \{0, \pm 1, \pm 2, \pm 3, \ldots\}$

$\quad\quad\quad\quad\quad\quad\quad\quad\quad T = \{0, \pm 2, \pm 4, \pm 6, \ldots\}$

We define a mapping $f : Z \to T$ by $f(x) = 2x$ for every $x \in Z$.

f is one-one : For x, y ∈ **Z**, we have f(x) = f(y) ⇒ 2x = 2y ⇒ x = y

Therefore, f is one-one.

f is onto : Let 2k be any element of T. Then k is integer; k ∈ **Z**. Then f(k) = 2k. Thus every element of T has preimage in **Z**. Therefore f is onto.

f preserves the compositions : For any x, y ∈ **Z**, we have

$$f(x + y) = 2(x + y) = 2x + 2y$$
$$= f(x) + f(y)$$

Thus, f preserves the compositions.

Hence f is an isomorphism.

EXERCISE (5.3)

1. Let <G, *> be the group of integers under addition. Determine whether the set of all even integers is a subgroup of G or not. **(P.U. 2011)**

2. Let G be the set of non-zero integers under multiplication and H = {3^n; n ∈ **Z**}. Is H a subgroup of G ? Justify your answer.

3. G is abelian group and H = {x ∈ G, x^2 = e}. Show that H is a subgroup of G.

4. Show that the set m**Z** of all integral multiples of integer m is a subgroup of the additive group of integers. Is it a normal subgroup ?

5. Prove that the intersection of two subgroups of a group G is a subgroup of G. Give example to show that union of two subgroups need not be a subgroup.

6. Determine whether or not (**Z**, +) is a subgroup of (**Q**, +).

7. {G, *} is a group and A = {a ∈ G, ax = xa for all x ∈ G}. Show that A is a subgroup of G.

8. In the group $\mathbf{Z}_8$ under addition modulo 8 show that H = {[0], [2], [4], [6]} is a subgroup of $\mathbf{Z}_8$. Determine its all left cosets.

9. Show that H = {1, 9} is a subgroup of the group G = {1, 3, 7, 9} under multiplication modulo 10. Find all right cosets of H in G.

10. Let G = {1, −1, i, −i} be a multiplicative group of 4 fourth roots of unity; i = $\sqrt{-1}$ show that H = {1, −1} is a subgroup of G. Find all right cosets of H in G.

11. Show that all integral multiples of integer m forms a subgroup of the additive group of integers. What are right cosets ? Comment if m = 2.

12. Show that if (H, *) is a subgroup of group (G, *), then a * H = H if and only if a ∈ H.

13. Let (H, *) be a subgroup of group (G, *). Show that the collection of all left cosets of H in G forms a partition of G.

14. In a group <G, *>, show that H = {x ∈ G; xa = ax} is a normal subgroup of G.

15. Show that the intersection of two normal subgroups of group G is a normal subgroup of G.

16. Let $(\mathbf{Z}, +)$ and $(E, +)$ be groups where $\mathbf{Z}$ is the set of integers and E is the set of even integers. Is the mapping $f : \mathbf{Z} \to E$ defined by $f(x) = 4x$ a homomorphism ?

    (P.U. 2011)

17. Let $(\mathbf{Z}_6, +)$ be a group and $S = \{[0], [3]\}$ be a subgroup. Is S normal in $\mathbf{Z}_6$?

18. Prove that the Kernel of a homomorphism ϕ from a group $<G, *>$ to a group $<H, \Delta>$ is a subgroup of $<G, *>$. **(P.U. 2009, 2012)**

19. Let $G = \{e, a, a^2, a^3, a^4, a^5\}$ be a group under the operation $a^i * a^j = a^r$ where $i + j = r \pmod{6}$. Show that $f : (G, *) \to (\mathbf{Z}_6, +_6)$ defines an isomorphism.

20. Show that $f : \mathbf{Z} \to \mathbf{Z}$ defined by $f(x) = -x$ is isomorphic mapping.

21. Two groups G_1 and G_2 have the composition tables :

*	a	b	c
a	a	b	c
b	b	c	a
c	c	a	b

□	x	y	z
x	z	x	y
y	x	y	z
z	y	z	x

    Show that $G_1 \cong G_2$.

ANSWERS (5.3)

1. Yes
2. No; G is not a group.
4. Yes, $m\mathbf{Z}$ is normal in $\mathbf{Z}$.
6. Yes
8. H and $[1] + H = \{[1], [3], [5], [7]\}$
9. H and $H * 3 = \{3, 7\}$
10. H and $H * i = \{i, -i\}$
11. $H = \{0, \pm m, \pm 2m, \pm 3m, \ldots\}$

    $H + 1, H + 2, H + 3, \ldots, H + (m - 1)$ are m distinct right cosets. If m = 2 there are 2 distinct right cosets viz. {All even integers} and {all odd integers}.

16. Yes
17. Yes

5.6 Group Codes

One of the most important applications of Algebra and Discrete Mathematics lies in the theory of error correcting codes.

First, we explain the problem before us briefly. Suppose we are given four bits (binary digits) of the information say 1001 which can be some data of experiment or some part of a computer program. The string 1001 is called a word.

We have to transmit this word from one point to the other point through some transmission channel. In the process of transmission it is likely that some disturbances called noises may occur, due to electricity problems, equipment problems etc. As a result the receiving station may not receive the word 1001 correctly. It is likely that some 0s are received as 1s and vice versa.

By using algebra and discrete mathematics it is possible for us to gain some protection against such transmission errors.

In order to overcome the difficulties mentioned above the data to be sent is not sent in its original form. It is first encoded and encoded form is sent through the transmission channel. At the receiving centre the received data is decoded by the decoder.

The following picture makes the process clear.

| Data | → | Incode | → | Tranmission Channel | → | Received Data | → | Decode |

In the discussion that follows, we shall accept almost all the required result about groups, normal subgroups, homomorphism etc. without proof.

We need the following results in the beginning.

1. In the set $B = \{0, 1\}$ of binary digits the operations addition module 2 and multiplication modulo 2 have the composition tables.

$+_2$	0	1
0	0	1
1	1	0

$\times_2$	0	1
0	0	0
1	0	1

2. If m is a positive integer, then $\underbrace{B \times B \times \ldots \times B}_{m \text{ factors}}$ consists of all m-tuples $(x_1, x_2, \ldots, x_m)$ each $x_i = 0$ or 1.

$$B^m = \{(x_1, x_2, \ldots, x_m); x_i = 0 \text{ or } 1\}$$

Contains 2^m m-tuples and it forms an abelian group w.r.t. the operation $\oplus$ defined by $(x_1, x_2, \ldots, x_m) \oplus (y_1, y_2, \ldots, y_m) = (x_1 +_2 y_1, x_2 +_2 y_2, x_3 +_2 y_3, \ldots, x_m +_2 y_m)$.

In this group identity is $(0, 0, 0, \ldots, 0)$ and each element is its own inverse. We write $(x_1, x_2, \ldots, x_m)$ as $x_1 x_2 \ldots x_m$.

3. Let m and n be positive integers with $m < n$ and $r = n - m$.

Let H be $n \times r$ Boolean matrix. The function $f_H : B^n \to B^r$ defined by

$$f_H(x) = x * H$$
$$= [x_1, x_2, \ldots, x_n] * H$$

Satisfies $\quad f_H(x \oplus y) = f_H(x) \oplus f_H(y)$

[* denotes Boolean multiplication of matrices]

This means f_H is a homomorphism from B^n to B^r.

Further $N = \{x \in B^n;\ x * H = \bar{0}\}$ is a normal subgroup of B^n.

Now the first part of our problem is that of encoding.

Let $b \in B^m$ is a word that is to be sent to the destination.

For encoding, we choose integer $n > m$ and define a one-one mapping denoted by $e : B^m \to B^n$. It is called (m, n) encoding function. The mapping e being one-one the different b^s in B^m have different images in B^n.

Let us write $x = e(b)$.

This word x is then sent to B^n via the transmission channel, and received as $x_t \in B^n$; as shown below.

| $b \in B^m$ to be sent | $\xrightarrow{e}$ | Encoded word $x = e(b) \in B^n$ | $\xrightarrow{\text{Transmission Channel}}$ | Received word $x_t \in B^n$ |

If any error does not occur, then $x_t = x$. But this is not the case always and $x_t \neq x$ generally.

If x and x_t differ in k or fewer positions out of n positions then we say that the encoding function e detects k or fewer errors.

If $x_t \neq x$ then x_t is not a code word; and if $x_t = x$ then x_t is a codeword.

For $x \in B^n$ then number of places at which 1 appears is called weight of x and it is denoted by $|x|$.

For example, $x = (1, 1, 0, 1, 0, 0, 1) \in B^7$ and $|x| = 4$. Also $y = (0, 0, 1, 1, 1) \in B^5$; $|y| = 3$

Parity Check Code :

Let m be a positive integer. Consider encoding function $e : B^m \longrightarrow B^{m+1}$ defined as below.

For $\quad\quad\quad\quad\quad\quad b = b_1 b_2 b_3 \ldots b_m$

$$e(b) = b_1 b_2 \ldots b_m b_{m+1}$$

where $\quad\quad\quad\quad b_{m+1} = \begin{cases} 0; & \text{if } |b| \text{ is even} \\ 1; & \text{if } |b| \text{ is odd} \end{cases}$

For example suppose m = 2 then $B^2 = \{00, 01, 10, 11\}$

Weight of 00 is 0; even

Weight of 01 is 1; odd

Weight of 10 is 1; odd

Weight of 11 is 2; even

According to the above definition of $e : B^2 \to B^3$, we get

$$\left.\begin{array}{l} e(00) = 000 \\ e(01) = 011 \\ e(1, 0) = 101 \\ e(1, 1) = 110 \end{array}\right\} \text{Code words}$$

The weight of all code words is even. Now if the word say 10 is mapped onto 111 under the mapping e then clearly an error is detected because weight of 111 is 3 which is odd.

In this example, the encoding function e detects at least one error. It can detect 3 errors also. But it cannot detect even number of errors.

The encoding function $e : B^2 \to B^3$ defined above is called parity (m, m + 1) check code.

Here it is parity (2, 3) check code.

Hamming Distance :

Let $x = x_1 x_2 \ldots x_m$ and $y = y_1 y_2 \ldots y_m$ be two elements in B^m. Then

$$x \oplus y = (x_1 +_2 y_1, x_2 +_2 y_2, \ldots, x_m +_2 y_m)$$

The Hamming distance between x and y is defined as $|x \oplus y|$. It is denoted by $\delta(x, y)$.

It is then clear that $\delta(x, y)$ is exactly equal to the number of places at which x and y differ.

Suppose, $\quad x = 1001110$

and $\quad y = 1100011$ be two elements of B^7.

Then x and y differ at 4 places viz. 2nd, 4th, 5th and 7th place.

$\therefore \quad \delta(x, y) = 4$

We have $\quad x \oplus y = (0, 1, 0, 1, 1, 0, 1)$

$\quad |x \oplus y| = 4$

$\therefore \quad \delta(x, y) = 4$

The Hamming distance defined as above satisfies four properties of a distance function.

Theorem 6 : Let x, y, z be any element of B^m. Then the Hamming distance satisfies the following properties :

(i) Non-negativity : $\delta(x, y) \geq 0$ for all $x, y \in B^m$.

(ii) Symmetry : $\delta(x, y) = \delta(y, x)$ for all $x, y \in B^m$.

(iii) $\delta(x, y) = 0$ iff $x = y$.

(iv) Triangle inequality : $\delta(x, y) \leq \delta(x, z) + \delta(z, y)$ for all $x, y, z \in B^m$.

Proof : Let $\quad x = x_1 x_2 \ldots x_m, y = y_1 y_2 \ldots y_m,$

$z = z_1 z_2 \ldots z_m$ be any elements of B^m.

$\delta(x, y) = $ number of places at which x and y differ

(i) **Non-negativity :** From the definition of $\delta(x, y)$ the minimum number of places at which x and y differ is 0. Therefore $\delta(x, y) \geq 0$.

(ii) **Symmetry :** The number of places at which x and y differ is equal to the number of places at which y and x differ.

$\therefore \quad \delta(x, y) = \delta(y, x)$

(iii) Suppose $\delta(x, y) = 0$

Then the number of places at which x and y differ is 0.

∴ at each of m places x and y have the same entry.

∴ x = y.

The above steps are reversible.

∴ $x = y \Rightarrow \delta(x, y) = 0$

(iv) Triangle inequality : Since at any place where x and y differ, one of them must be 1. This implies that

$$|x \oplus y| \leq |x| + |y| \quad \ldots (1)$$

Now,
$$\begin{aligned}
\delta(x, y) &= |x \oplus y| = |x \oplus 0 \oplus y| \\
&= |x \oplus (z \oplus z) \oplus y| \quad \because z \oplus z = 0 \\
&= |(x \oplus z) \oplus (z \oplus y)| \\
&\leq |x \oplus z| + |z \oplus y| \quad \because \text{by equation (1)} \\
&= \delta(x, z) + \delta(z, y) \quad \text{Proved.}
\end{aligned}$$

Definition : Let $e : B^m \to B^n$ be (m, n) encoding function. The minimum distance of e is the minimum of the distances between all distinct pairs of code words;

i.e. min $\{\delta(e(x), e(y)); x, y \in B^m, x \neq y\}$.

Consider (2, 6) encoding function $e : B^2 \to B^6$ defined below.

$$e(00) = 000000$$
$$e(01) = 011110$$
$$e(10) = 111011$$
$$e(11) = 110010$$

By taking into consideration the symmetry property of the distance function, we find only 6 distances as shown in the table below.

δ	000000	011110	111011	110010
000000	–	4	5	3
011110		–	3	3
111011			–	2
110010				–

The minimum distance of encoding function e is 2.

Theorem 7 : An (m, n) encoding function $e : B^m \to B^n$ can detect k or fewer errors if and only if its minimum distance is at least k + 1.

Proof : $e : B^m \to B^n$

Suppose minimum distance of e is at least k + 1. Then the minimum distance between any two code words is at least k + 1.

Let $b \in B$ and $x = e(b) \in B^n$ be the code word.

Now x is transmitted as x_t. If x_t is a code word and $x_t \neq x$ then $\delta(x, x_t) \geq k + 1$ and x is transmitted with k + 1 or more errors.

Thus, if x is transmitted with k or fewer errors, then x_t cannot be a code word. Therefore e can detect k or fewer errors.

Conversely, suppose that the minimum distance between the code words is $r \leq k$ and x, y be code words with $\delta(x, y) = r$.

if now $x_t = y$ i.e. x is transmitted and received as y, then $r \leq k$ errors are committed and have not been detected.

This means e can detect k or fewer errors is a false statement.

Example 5.30 : Consider the (2, 6) encoding function
e(00) = 000000, e(01) = 011110, e(10) = 101010, e(11) = 111000
(i) Find the minimum distance of e.
(ii) How many errors can e detect ?

Solution : (i) To find the minimum distance of e, we prepare following table.

δ	000000	011110	101010	111000
000000	–	4	3	3
011110	–	–	3	3
101010	–	–	–	2
111000	–	–	–	–

The minimum distance of e is 2.

(ii) e can detect k or fewer errors if and only if minimum distance is $\geq k + 1$

$\therefore$ $\quad 2 \geq k + 1$

$\therefore$ $\quad 1 \geq k$

$\therefore$ $\quad k \leq 1$

$\therefore$ e can detect 1 or less errors.

Now e detects less than 1 errors mean e detects 0 number of errors i.e. e does not detect any error.

Finally, therefore e detects only one error.

Group Code : We know that $(B^n, \oplus)$ is a group.

Let now $e : B^m \to B^n$ be an (m, n) encoding function.

If the range of e i.e. $\quad e(B^m)$ = {the images of all elements of B^m}
$\quad\quad\quad\quad\quad\quad\quad\quad\quad\quad$ = {e(x); x $\in B^m$}

is a subgroup of the group B^n then e is called a group code.

In the preceding example, $e : B^2 \to B^6$ the range of e is
$\quad\quad\quad e(B^2)$ = {000000, 011110, 101010, 111000}

The four code words do not form a subgroup of B^6 because this set of code words is not closed under the operation $\oplus$. For example, consider two code words 101010 and 111000.

We have, $101010 \oplus 111000 = 010010$ which is not a code word.

On the other hand consider $(2, 5)$ encoding function $e : B^2 \to B^5$ defined as
$$e(0, 0) = 00000, \; e(01) = 01110, \; e(10) = 10101, \; e(11) = 11011$$

The composition table for the range of e w.r.t. $\oplus$ operation is as below.

$\oplus$	00000	01110	10101	11011
00000	00000	01110	10101	11011
01110	01110	00000	11011	10101
10101	10101	11011	00000	01110
11011	11011	10101	01110	00000

The set $e(B^2)$ is closed under the operation $\oplus$. Therefore $e(B^2)$ is a subgroup of B^5. Hence e is a group code.

The group code e has the property that the minimum distance of e is the minimum weight of the non-zero code word in it.

In the above example, $|01110| = 3$, $|10101| = 3$, $|11011| = 4$

The minimum weight of a non-zero code word is 3.

Therefore the minimum distance of e is 3.

Let now $m < n$ so that $n - m = r$. Then a Boolean matrix.

$$H_{n \times r} = \begin{bmatrix} h_{11} & h_{12} & \cdots & h_{1r} \\ h_{21} & h_{22} & \cdots & h_{2r} \\ \vdots & \vdots & & \vdots \\ h_{m1} & h_{m2} & \cdots & h_{mr} \\ 1 & 0 & \cdots & 0 \\ 0 & 1 & \cdots & 0 \\ \vdots & \vdots & & \vdots \\ 0 & 0 & \cdots & 1 \end{bmatrix} \begin{matrix} \} m \times r \\ \\ \\ \} r \times r \end{matrix}$$

where the bottom $r \times r$ submatrix is identity matrix; H is called a parity check matrix.

The first m bits are information bits and the last r bits are parity bits.

To find (m, n) encoding function $e : B^m \to B^n$ so that the code words form a group code the following procedure is to be adopted.

Step 1 : $\qquad b = b_1 b_2 \ldots b_m \in B^m$

and $\qquad x = e(b) = b_1 b_2 \ldots b_m x_1 x_2 \ldots x_r \in B^n$.

Step 2 : Write the equation $x * H = 0$, where * denotes the Boolean multiplication of matrices.

$$[b_1 b_2 \ldots b_m x_1 x_2 \ldots x_r] \begin{bmatrix} h_{11} & h_{12} & \cdots & h_{1r} \\ h_{21} & h_{22} & \cdots & h_{2r} \\ \vdots & \vdots & & \vdots \\ h_{m1} & h_{m2} & \cdots & h_{mr} \\ 1 & 0 & \cdots & 0 \\ 0 & 1 & \cdots & 0 \\ \vdots & \vdots & & \vdots \\ 0 & 0 & \cdots & 1 \end{bmatrix} = 0$$

This matrix equation gives

$$\left.\begin{array}{l} b_1h_{11} + b_2h_{21} + \ldots + b_mh_{m1} + x_1 = 0 \\ b_1h_{12} + b_2h_{22} + \ldots + b_mh_{m2} + x_2 = 0 \\ \text{------------------------------} \\ \text{------------------------------} \\ b_1h_{1r} + b_2h_{2r} + \ldots + b_mh_{mr} + x_r = 0 \end{array}\right\}$$

Then

$$\left.\begin{array}{l} x_1 = b_1h_{11} + b_2h_{21} + \ldots + b_mh_{m1} \\ x_2 = b_1h_{12} + b_2h_{22} + \ldots + b_mh_{m2} \\ \text{------------------------------} \\ \text{------------------------------} \\ x_r = b_1h_{1r} + b_2h_{2r} + \ldots + b_mh_{mr} \end{array}\right\}$$ Note that $a + a = 0$

Hence $x = e(b) = b_1b_2 \ldots b_m x_1x_2 \ldots x_r$

Step 3 : By using the values of $x_1, x_2, \ldots, x_r$ found in sep 2, we can write $e(B^m)$ which forms a group code. We illustrate by an example.

Illustration 5 : Let $m = 2$, $n = 5$ so that $r = n - m = 5 - 2 = 3$.

Let parity check matrix be $H = \begin{bmatrix} 1 & 0 & 1 \\ 1 & 1 & 0 \\ 1 & 0 & 0 \\ 0 & 1 & 0 \\ 0 & 0 & 1 \end{bmatrix}$

We have to find a group code $e : B^2 \to B^5$.

If $b = b_1b_2 \in B^2$ then $x = e(b) = b_1b_2x_1x_2x_3$.

Now, $\quad x * H = 0 \quad$ gives

$$[b_1 \ b_2 \ x_1 \ x_2 \ x_3] \begin{bmatrix} 1 & 0 & 1 \\ 1 & 1 & 0 \\ 1 & 0 & 0 \\ 0 & 1 & 0 \\ 0 & 0 & 1 \end{bmatrix} = [0 \ 0 \ 0]$$

$\therefore \quad \left.\begin{array}{l} b_1 +_2 b_2 +_2 x_1 = 0 \\ b_2 +_2 x_2 \quad\quad\quad = 0 \\ b_1 +_2 x_3 \quad\quad\quad = 0 \end{array}\right\}$

$\therefore \quad \left.\begin{array}{l} x_1 = b_1 +_2 b_2 \\ x_2 = b_2 \\ x_3 = b_1 \end{array}\right\} \quad\quad\quad \because a + a = 0$

Now we have to find the images of 00, 01, 10, 11 under the mapping $e : B^2 \to B^5$.

For 00 we have $b_1 = 0$, $b_2 = 0$

$\therefore \quad x_1 = 0, \ x_2 = 0, \ x_3 = 0$

$\therefore \quad e(00) = 00 \ x_1x_2x_3 = 00000$

For 01, we have $b_1 = 0$, $b_2 = 1$

$$\therefore \quad x_1 = 0 + 1 = 1$$
$$x_2 = 1$$
$$x_3 = 0$$
$$\therefore \quad e(01) = 01\, x_1 x_2 x_3 = 01110$$

For 10, we have $b_1 = 1,\ b_2 = 0$

$$\therefore \quad x_1 = b_1 + b_2 = 1 + 0 = 1$$
$$x_2 = b_2 = 0$$
$$x_3 = b_1 = 1$$
$$\therefore \quad e(10) = 10\, x_1 x_2 x_3 = 10101$$

Finally for 11, we have $b_1 = 1,\ b_2 = 1$

$$\therefore \quad x_1 = b_1 + b_2 = 1 + 1 = 0$$
$$x_2 = b_2 = 1$$
$$x_3 = b_1 = 1$$
$$\therefore \quad e(11) = 11\, x_1 x_2 x_3 = 11011$$
$$\therefore \quad e(B^2) = \{00000,\ 01110,\ 10101,\ 11011\}$$

It is easy to verify that this set is a subgroup of B^5 since it is closed under the operation $\oplus$. Hence it is a group code.

The above process can be simplified with the help of table as shown below.

b_1, b_2 are information bits and x_1, x_2, x_3 are parity bits. There are 4 combinations of the values of b_1 and b_2 i.e. 00, 01, 10, 11.

We prepare a table as below.

b_1	b_2	$x_1 = b_1 +_2 b_2$	$x_2 = b_2$	$x_3 = b_1$
0	0	0	0	0
0	1	1	1	0
1	0	1	0	1
1	1	0	1	1

$$\therefore \quad e(00) = 00000$$
$$e(01) = 01110$$
$$e(10) = 10101$$
$$e(11) = 11011 \text{ which is as before.}$$

Decoding :

Now we consider the converse problem i.e. of decoding of the word which is being received. This task is performed by the decoder at the receiving centre.

Suppose $e : B^m \to B^n$ is encoding function where the code words in $e(B^m)$ may or may not form a group. If the word $x \in B^m$ is received as $x_t \in B^n$ then we have to find the decoding function d associated with e such that $d(x_t) = x$.

For this purpose, we use the technique called 'maximum likelihood technique'. The technique is as below.

There are 2^m code words in B^n. We list these 2^m code words in a fixed order say
$$x^{(1)}, x^{(2)}, x^{(3)}, \ldots, x^{(2^m)}.$$
Suppose now x_t is a word which is received.

We compute the distance of x_t from each $x^{(i)}$; i.e. $\delta(x^{(i)}, x_t)$ for $1 \leq i \leq 2^m$.

Let s be the first integer such that $\delta(x^{(s)}, x_t)$ is the minimum of all 2^m distances computed above i.e.
$$\delta(x^{(s)}, x_t) = \min_{1 \leq i \leq 2^m} \delta(x^{(i)}, x_t)$$
In words, $x^{(s)}$ is the first code word in the list that is closest to the received word x_t.

Now if $x^{(s)} = e(b)$ then we write $d(x_t) = b \in B^m$.

It may be noted here that if the original list of code words is changed then we get different value of $x^{(s)}$.

Illustration 6 : Let the encoding function $e : B^2 \to B^4$ be given by
$e(00) = 0000$, $e(01) = 0111$, $e(10) = 1001$, $e(11) = 1111$ and 1101 is the received word.
The list of code words is $x^{(1)} = 0000$, $x^{(2)} = 0111$, $x^{(3)} = 1001$, $x^{(4)} = 1111$.
We now find the distances of $x_t = 1101$ from each code word.

$x^{(1)} \oplus x_t = 0000 \oplus 1101 = 1101 \qquad \therefore \delta(x^{(1)}, x_t) = |x^{(1)} \oplus x_t| = 3$

$x^{(2)} \oplus x_t = 0111 \oplus 1101 = 1010 \qquad \therefore \delta(x^{(2)}, x_t) = |x^{(2)} \oplus x_t| = 2$

$x^{(3)} \oplus x_t = 1001 \oplus 1101 = 0100 \qquad \therefore \delta(x^{(3)}, x_t) = |x^{(3)} \oplus x_t| = 1$

$x^{(4)} \oplus x_t = 1111 \oplus 1101 = 0010 \qquad \therefore \delta(x^{(4)}, x_t) = |x^{(4)} \oplus x_t| = 1$

The minimum of these four distances is 1. According to the above listing of $x^{(1)}, x^{(2)}, x^{(3)}, x^{(4)}$ the first minimum distance is $|x^{(3)} \oplus x_t| = 1$.

$\therefore \quad x^{(3)}$ is the code word which is closest to $x_t = 1101$.

Now $\qquad\qquad\qquad x^{(3)} = 1001 = e(10)$

$\therefore \qquad\qquad\qquad d(1101) = 10$

Thus, the received word 1101 is decoded as 10.

If $e : B^m \to B^n$ is a group code then there is a simple and effective technique i.e. 'minimum distance decoding criterian' for the purpose of decoding.

Let $(G, \oplus)$ be a group code and $x_1, x_2, \ldots, x_N$ denote the code words in G. Further let y be the received word. We compute the distances $\delta(y, x_i)$ for $i = 1, 2, \ldots, N$ and conclude that x_k is the transmitted word if $\delta(y, x_k)$ is the minimum distance among all the distances computed. This is the 'minimum distance decoding criterian'.

Now for a received word y, we have $\delta(y, x_i) = |y \oplus x_i|$ which is weight of $y \oplus x_i$.

As x_i varies in G, the coset of G generated by y is
$$y \oplus G = \{y \oplus x_1, y \oplus x_2, \ldots, y \oplus x_N\}.$$
Suppose now $\varepsilon = y \oplus x_j$ denotes the word of minimum weight in the above coset $y \oplus G$, for some j.

Then according to the minimum distance decoding criterian
$$y \oplus \varepsilon = y \oplus (y \oplus x_j) = (y \oplus y) \oplus x_j = 0 \oplus x_j = x_j \text{ is the transmitted word.}$$
The above argument is valid for all y in the coset $y \oplus G$.

We adopt the following procedure while using the minimum distance decoding criterion.

1. Find all cosets of G and write them row-wise; the first row being the elements of G itself.
2. For each coset, pick the word of the smallest weight. This word of smallest weight is the coset leader for that coset.
3. If y is a received word then $y + \epsilon$ is the transmitted word where ϵ is the coset leader. It appears at the top of the column in which y lies.

The following illustration will make the idea clear.

Illustration 7 : Consider the group code G = {0000, 0011, 1101, 1110}.

The set G is closed under the operation $\oplus$. Hence it is a subgroup of B^4 and $(G, \oplus)$ is a group.

In B^4 there are $2^4 = 16$ elements and each coset contains equal number of elements because there is a one-one correspondence between the elements of any two cosets.

Thus, there are $\frac{16}{4} = 4$ distinct cosets and G itself is one of them. Thus the first row of the decoding table is

     0000   0011   1101   1110   (First row)

These 4 words have weights 0, 2, 3, 3.

In B^4 there are 4 words of next smallest weight 1. They are 0001, 0010, 0100 and 1000.

Consider any one of them say 0001.

It will be a coset leader for the next coset; which is obtained by adding 0001 to each element of the first row.

     $0001 \oplus 0000 = 0001$, $0001 \oplus 0011 = 0010$,
     $0001 \oplus 1101 = 1100$ $0001 \oplus 1110 = 1111$

Therefore, second row of the decoding table is

     0001   0010   1100   1111   (second row)

Upto now 2 elements of weight 1 in B^4 have been utilised; viz. 0001 and 0010.

There are two elements of minimum weight 1 available to us. They are 0100 and 1000.

We choose any one of them say 0100 as the next coset leader.

Therefore, the 3rd row of the decoding table has following elements.

     $0100 \oplus 0000 = 0100$, $0100 \oplus 0011 = 0111$,
     $0100 \oplus 1101 = 1001$, $0100 \oplus 1110 = 1010$

Thus,   0100   0111   1001   1010   (third row)

We have still one element of weight 1 available i.e. 1000. It is a leader for the next coset. The elements of the fourth row of decoding table has elements.

     $1000 \oplus 0000 = 1000$, $1000 \oplus 0011 = 1011$,
     $1000 \oplus 1101 = 0101$, $1000 \oplus 1110 = 0110$

Thus,   1000   1011   0101   0110   (fourth row)

Finally the decoding table looks as below.

Decoding Table - 1 :

0000	0011	1101	1110
0001	0010	1100	1111
0100	0111	1001	1010
1000	1011	0101	0110

Suppose now the word received is 0111 which is in the third row and second column of the table.

In the second column the element at the top is 0011. Hence the word which was sent is 0011.

Again consider the received word 0110 which is in the fourth row and fourth column of the decoding table.

We have 1110 at the top of the fourth column. Therefore the word which was sent is 1110.

Note : In the above illustration, let us prepare a decoding table as below.

    0000   0011   1101   1110 (first row)

Now consider 1000 as the coset leader which does not appear in the first row.

Then $1000 \oplus 0000 = 1000$, $1000 \oplus 0011 = 1011$

           $1000 \oplus 1101 = 0101$, $1000 \oplus 1110 = 0110$

$\therefore$ 1000   1011   0101   0110 (second row)

Then 0100 does not appear in first and second row.

So we take 0100 as coset leader

           $0100 \oplus 0000 = 0100$, $0100 \oplus 0011 = 0111$

           $0100 \oplus 1101 = 1001$, $0100 \oplus 1110 = 1010$

$\therefore$ 1000   1011   0101   0110 (second row)

Then 0100 does not appear in first and second row.

So we take 0100 as coset leader

           $0100 \oplus 0000 = 0100$, $0100 \oplus 0011 = 0111$

           $0100 \oplus 1101 = 1001$, $0100 \oplus 1110 = 1010$

$\therefore$ 0100   0111,   1001,   1010 (third row)

Next coset leader is 0010 of weight 1 and does not appear in the above three rows.

           $0010 \oplus 0000 = 0010$, $0010 \oplus 0011 = 0001$,

           $0010 \oplus 1101 = 1111$, $0010 \oplus 1110 = 1100$

$\therefore$ Fourth row of table is

           0010   0001   1111   1100 (fourth row)

Decoding Table - 2

0000	0011	1101	1110
1000	1011	0101	0110
0100	0111	1001	1010
0010	0001	1111	1100

Now suppose the word that is received is 1100.

According to decoding table - 1 the transmitted word is 1101 but according to decoding table - 2 the transmitted word is 1110.

Similarly, if the received word is 1111 then the transmitted word is 1110 according to table - 1 but 1101 according to table - 2.

If a parity check matrix is given, the process of decoding technique is further simplied. Here we are not required to prepare a decoding table.

We explain the method with the help of example.

Consider the parity check matrix

$$H = \begin{bmatrix} 1 & 1 \\ 1 & 0 \\ 1 & 0 \\ 0 & 1 \end{bmatrix}$$

The last two rows of H form 2×2 identity matrix.

In the first step, we find encoding function $e : B^2 \to B^4$.

For $b_1 b_2 \in B^2$, we have $e(b_1 b_2) = b_1 b_2 x_1 x_2$.

Now, $[b_1 b_2 \; x_1 x_2] \begin{bmatrix} 1 & 1 \\ 1 & 0 \\ 1 & 0 \\ 0 & 1 \end{bmatrix} = 0$ gives

$$\left. \begin{array}{c} b_1 +_2 b_2 +_2 x_1 = 0 \\ b_1 +_2 x_2 = 0 \end{array} \right\}$$

$\therefore$
$$\left. \begin{array}{c} x_1 = b_1 +_2 b_2 \\ x_2 = b_1 \end{array} \right\}$$

Consider now the table of values of b_1, b_2, x_1, x_2 which is as below.

b_1	b_2	x_1	x_2
0	0	0	0
0	1	1	0
1	0	1	1
1	1	0	1

Then the encoding function e is

$$e(00) = 0000$$
$$e(01) = 0110$$
$$e(10) = 1011$$
$$e(11) = 1101$$

It forms a group code and $N = \{0000, 0110, 1011, 1101\}$ is a normal subgroup of B^4.

In the second step, we find all $\dfrac{2^4}{2^2} = \dfrac{16}{4} = 4$ cosets of N, in increasing order of the weights of coset leaders.

We recall the following properties of cosets.

If N is a subgroup of a group G, then:

(i) $a + N = N$ iff $a \in N$

(ii) any two cosets of N are either disjoint or identical.

Now N is itself a coset in B^4; the leader being identity element 0000 whose weight is 0.

$\quad$ N : 0000 $\quad$ 0110 $\quad$ 1011 $\quad$ 1101

Now 0001 of weight 1 is not in N.

$\quad$ 0001 $\oplus$ N : 0001 $\quad$ 0111 $\quad$ 1010 $\quad$ 1100

Then 0010 of weight 1 is not in above two cosets.

$\quad$ 0010 $\oplus$ N : 0010 $\quad$ 0100 $\quad$ 1001 $\quad$ 1111

Here note that 0100 of weight 1 is included in this coset.

So consider 1000 of weight 1 which is not included in above three cosets.

$\quad$ 1000 $\oplus$ N : 1000 $\quad$ 1110 $\quad$ 0011 $\quad$ 0101

In the third step, we find the syndrome of each coset leader. The syndrome of $x \in B^4$ is $x * H$.

The syndrome of 0000 is $[0000] * H = [0000] * \begin{bmatrix} 1 & 1 \\ 1 & 0 \\ 1 & 0 \\ 0 & 1 \end{bmatrix} = 00$

Syndrome of 0001 is $[0001] * H = [0001] * \begin{bmatrix} 1 & 1 \\ 1 & 0 \\ 1 & 0 \\ 0 & 1 \end{bmatrix} = 01$

Syndrome of 0010 is $[0010] * \begin{bmatrix} 1 & 1 \\ 1 & 0 \\ 1 & 0 \\ 0 & 1 \end{bmatrix} = 10$

Syndrome of 1000 is $[1000] * \begin{bmatrix} 1 & 1 \\ 1 & 0 \\ 1 & 0 \\ 0 & 1 \end{bmatrix} = 11$

We prepare now a table showing the coset leader and its syndrome.

Coset Leader	Syndrome
0000	00
0001	01
0010	10
1000	11

Now we are in the last phase of the solution to the problem. Suppose we are asked to decode the received word $x_t = 0011$.

We find syndrome of $x_t = 0011$.

It is $$[0011] * \begin{bmatrix} 1 & 1 \\ 1 & 0 \\ 1 & 0 \\ 0 & 1 \end{bmatrix} = 11$$

Now refer the table of coset leaders and their syndromes. The coset leader corresponding to the syndrome 11 is 1000. This means $x_t = 0011$ lies in the coset.

Whose leader is 1000.

Now compute
$$x = x_t +_2 1000$$
$$= 0011 +_2 1000$$
$$= 1011.$$

Finally, we know that $e(10) = 1011$

Thus, the received word 0011 is decoded as transmitted word 10.

SOLVED EXAMPLES

Example 5.31 : Find the number of code words generated by the following parity check matrix H. Also find the codewords generated.

$$H = \begin{bmatrix} 0 & 1 & 0 \\ 1 & 0 & 1 \\ 1 & 0 & 0 \\ 0 & 1 & 0 \\ 0 & 0 & 1 \end{bmatrix}$$ (P.U. 2011)

Solution : In the given matrix H the last three rows form 3×3 identity matrix. So we have to find encoding function $e : B^2 \to B^5$ which is a group code.

Now, $B^2 = \{00, 01, 10, 11\}$

$\therefore$ $e(B^2)$ contains 4 code words. For any $b_1 b_2 \in B^2$, we have $e(b_1 b_2) = b_1 b_2\, x_1\, x_2\, x_3$ where b_1, b_2 are information bits and x_1, x_2, x_3 are parity bits.

Consider the equation $x * H = 0$

$$[b_1 b_2\, x_1\, x_2\, x_3] * \begin{bmatrix} 0 & 1 & 0 \\ 1 & 0 & 1 \\ 1 & 0 & 0 \\ 0 & 1 & 0 \\ 0 & 0 & 1 \end{bmatrix} = 0$$

∴
$$\left. \begin{array}{r} b_2 +_2 x_1 = 0 \\ b_1 +_2 x_2 = 0 \\ b_2 +_2 x_3 = 0 \end{array} \right\}$$

∴ $x_1 = b_2$, $x_2 = b_1$, $x_3 = b_2$ [$a +_2 a = 0$]

There are 2 information bits.

So we prepare a table of values containing $2^2 = 4$ rows.

b_1	b_2	$x_1 = b_2$	$x_2 = b_1$	$x_3 = b_2$
0	0	0	0	0
0	1	1	0	1
1	0	0	1	0
1	1	1	1	1

The group code consists of 4 code words :

$$e(00) = 00000$$
$$e(01) = 01101$$
$$e(10) = 10010$$
$$e(11) = 11111$$

Example 5.32 : Write the code words generated by parity check matrix.

$$H = \begin{bmatrix} 1 & 0 & 1 & 1 & 0 & 0 \\ 1 & 1 & 0 & 0 & 1 & 0 \\ 1 & 1 & 1 & 0 & 0 & 1 \end{bmatrix}$$

What is the minimum weight of non-zero code word ? How many errors can be detected by this group code ? **(P.U. 2009)**

Solution : In the given matrix H the last three columns form 3×3 identity matrix; and H is of order 3×6. We have to find $e : B^3 \to B^6$ which is a group code.

Now,
$$H^t = \begin{bmatrix} 1 & 1 & 1 \\ 0 & 1 & 1 \\ 1 & 0 & 1 \\ 1 & 0 & 0 \\ 0 & 1 & 0 \\ 0 & 0 & 1 \end{bmatrix}$$

If $b = b_1 b_2 b_3 \in B^3$ then $x = e(b) = b_1 b_2 b_3 x_1 x_2 x_3$.

Now, $x * H^t = 0$ gives

$$[b_1\ b_2\ b_3\ x_1\ x_2\ x_3] \begin{bmatrix} 1 & 1 & 1 \\ 0 & 1 & 1 \\ 1 & 0 & 1 \\ 1 & 0 & 0 \\ 0 & 1 & 0 \\ 0 & 0 & 1 \end{bmatrix} = 0$$

$$\therefore \quad \left.\begin{array}{r} b_1 +_2 b_3 +_2 x_1 = 0 \\ b_1 +_2 b_2 +_2 x_2 = 0 \\ b_1 +_2 b_2 +_2 b_3 + x_3 = 0 \end{array}\right\}$$

$$\therefore \quad \left.\begin{array}{r} x_1 = b_1 +_2 b_3 \\ x_2 = b_1 +_2 b_2 \\ x_3 = b_1 +_2 b_2 +_2 b_3 \end{array}\right\}$$

Now we prepare a table for values of b_1, b_2, b_3 and x_1, x_2, x_3 containing $2^3 = 8$ rows.

b_1	b_2	b_3	$x_1 = b_1 +_2 b_3$	$x_2 = b_1 +_2 b_2$	$x_3 = b_1 +_2 b_2 +_2 b_3$
0	0	0	0	0	0
0	0	1	1	0	1
0	1	0	0	1	1
0	1	1	1	1	0
1	0	0	1	1	1
1	0	1	0	1	0
1	1	0	1	0	0
1	1	1	0	0	1

$\therefore \quad e(B^3) = \{000000, 001101, 010011, 011110, 100111, 101010, 110100, 111001\}$

It is a group code.

The minimum weigh of non-zero code word is 3.

$\therefore$ The minimum distance of group code is 3.

We know that a group code can detect k or fewer errors if and only if the minimum distance is $\geq k + 1$.

$\therefore \quad 3 \geq k + 1$
$\therefore \quad 2 \geq k$
$\therefore \quad k \leq 2$

Thus, 2 or less than 2 errors can be detected.

Example 5.33 : Determine the code words generated by the parity check matrix.

$$H = \begin{bmatrix} 1 & 0 & 1 & 1 & 1 & 0 & 0 \\ 1 & 1 & 0 & 0 & 0 & 1 & 0 \\ 1 & 0 & 0 & 1 & 0 & 0 & 1 \end{bmatrix}$$

How many errors are detected by this group code ? **(P.U. 2011)**

Solution : From a given matrix, we get

$$H^t = \begin{bmatrix} 1 & 1 & 1 \\ 0 & 1 & 0 \\ 1 & 0 & 0 \\ 1 & 0 & 1 \\ 1 & 0 & 0 \\ 0 & 1 & 0 \\ 0 & 0 & 1 \end{bmatrix}$$

We have to find (4, 7) encoding function $e : B^4 \to B^7$.

i.e. to find $x = e(b_1 b_2 b_3 b_4) = b_1 b_2 b_3 b_4 \, x_1 x_2 x_3$.

The matrix equation $x * H^t = 0$ gives

$$[b_1 b_2 b_3 b_4 \, x_1 x_2 x_3] \begin{bmatrix} 1 & 1 & 1 \\ 0 & 1 & 0 \\ 1 & 0 & 0 \\ 1 & 0 & 1 \\ 1 & 0 & 0 \\ 0 & 1 & 0 \\ 0 & 0 & 1 \end{bmatrix} = 0$$

$\therefore \quad b_1 +_2 b_3 +_2 b_4 +_2 x_1 = 0$
$\quad\quad\quad b_1 +_2 b_2 +_2 x_2 = 0$
$\quad\quad\quad b_1 +_2 b_4 +_2 x_3 = 0$

$\therefore \quad x_1 = b_1 +_2 b_3 +_2 b_4$
$\quad\quad\quad x_2 = b_1 +_2 b_2$
$\quad\quad\quad x_3 = b_1 +_2 b_4$

Now, we prepare a table of $2^4 = 16$ rows since information bits b^s are 4 in number.

b_1	b_2	b_3	b_4	$x_1 = b_1 +_2 b_3 +_2 b_4$	$x_2 = b_1 +_2 b_2$	$x_3 = b_1 +_2 b_4$
0	0	0	0	0	0	0
0	0	0	1	1	0	1
0	0	1	0	1	0	0
0	0	1	1	0	0	1
0	1	0	0	0	1	0
0	1	0	1	1	1	1
0	1	1	0	1	1	0
0	1	1	1	0	1	1
1	0	0	0	1	1	1
1	0	0	1	0	1	0
1	0	1	0	0	1	1
1	0	1	1	1	1	0
1	1	0	0	1	0	1
1	1	0	1	0	0	0
1	1	1	0	0	0	1
1	1	1	1	1	0	0

The group code $e(B^4)$ consists of 16 code words.

0000000, 0001101, 0010100, 0011001,
0100010, 0101111, 0110110, 0111011,
1000111, 1001010, 1010011, 1011110,
1100101, 1101000, 1110001, 1111100.

The minimum weight of the non-zero code word is 2.

∴ The minimum distance of the group code is 2.

We know that e can detect k or fewer errors if minimum distance is $\geq k + 1$.

∴ $\qquad 2 \geq k + 1$

∴ $\qquad 1 \geq k$

∴ $\qquad k \leq 1$

∴ e can detect 1 or less errors. Hence e can detect only one error.

Example 5.34 : Show that (2, 4) encoding function given by e(00) = 0000, e(01) = 0111, e(10) = 1001, e(11) = 1110 is a group code.

How many errors will be detected by e ?

Decode the words 0011, 1100 and 1101.

Solution : Let us prepare a composition table for e w.r.t. $\oplus$ operation.

$\oplus$	0000	0111	1001	1110
0000	0000	0111	1001	1110
0111	0111	0000	1110	1001
1001	1001	1110	0000	0111
1110	1110	1001	0111	0000

From the composition table, we see that $\oplus$ of any two elements of the given set is again element of the set.

Therefore it is a subgroup of B^4.

∴ Given set is a group.

The minimum distance of e = minimum weight of non-zero code word
$\qquad = 2$

If minimum distance is at least k + 1 then k or fewer errors can be detected.

Now k + 1 = 2 ∴ k = 1.

∴ e can detect only one error.

Now we prepare a decoding table. There are $\dfrac{2^4}{2^2} = \dfrac{16}{4} = 4$ cosets.

$\qquad$ 0000 $\quad$ 0111 $\quad$ 1001 $\quad$ 1110 $\quad$ (first row)

For the next coset the coset leader is taken as 0001 that does not appear in the first row.

$\qquad$ 0001 $\oplus$ 0000 = 0001, $\quad$ 0001 $\oplus$ 0111 = 0110

$\qquad$ 0001 $\oplus$ 1001 = 1000, $\quad$ 0001 $\oplus$ 1110 = 1111

$\qquad$ 0001 $\quad$ 0110 $\quad$ 1000 $\quad$ 1111 $\quad$ (second row)

For the next coset choose the coset leader 0010 which does not appear in above two rows.

$\qquad$ 0010 $\oplus$ 0000 = 0010, $\quad$ 0010 $\oplus$ 0111 = 0101

$\qquad$ 0010 $\oplus$ 1001 = 1011, $\quad$ 0010 $\oplus$ 1110 = 1100

∴ $\qquad$ 0010 $\quad$ 0101 $\quad$ 1011 $\quad$ 1100 $\quad$ (third row)

For the next coset choose the coset leader 0100 which does not appear in above three rows.

$$0100 \oplus 0000 = 0100, \quad 0100 \oplus 0111 = 0011$$
$$0100 \oplus 1001 = 1101, \quad 0100 \oplus 1110 = 1010$$

∴ 0100   0011   1101   1010 (fourth row)

Decoding Table

0000	0111	1001	1110
0001	0110	1000	1111
0010	0101	1011	<u>1100</u>
0100	<u>0011</u>	<u>1101</u>	1010

Received Word	Transmitted Word
0011	0111
1100	1110
1101	1001

SOLVED EXAMPLES

Example 5.35 : Show that (2, 5) encoding function e(00) = 00000, e(10) = 10101, e(01) = 01110, e(11) = 11011 is a group code.

Decode the following received words by applying minimum distance decoding criterian.

(i) 11110   (ii) 10011   (iii) 10100.

Solution : The composition table for $\oplus$ in B^5 for given four elements is as below.

$\oplus$	00000	10101	01110	11011
00000	00000	10101	01110	11011
10101	10101	00000	11011	01110
01110	01110	11011	00000	10101
11011	11011	01110	10101	00000

From this table, we see that the $\oplus$ of any two elements of given four elements is again element of that set. Therefore the set {00000, 10101, 01110, 11011} is closed under the operation $\oplus$. Therefore it is a subgroup of B^5.

∴ Given set is a group code.

We now prepare a decoding table. Given group code has 4 elements and B^5 has $2^5 = 32$ elements. hence there are $\frac{32}{4} = 8$ distinct coset of G in B^5; and G is one of them. First row of the table is

00000   10101   01110   11011   (first row)

Consider 00001 of minimum weight 1 which does not appear in the above row; and it is a coset leader for next coset.

$$00001 \oplus 00000 = 00001, \quad 00001 \oplus 10101 = 10100,$$
$$00001 \oplus 01110 = 01111, \quad 00001 \oplus 11011 = 11010$$

∴ 00001   10100   01111   11010   (second row)

Next consider 00010 as the next leader which does not appear in above two rows and has weight 1 i.e. minimum.

$$00010 \oplus 00000 = 00010, \quad 00010 \oplus 10101 = 10111,$$
$$00010 \oplus 01110 = 01100, \quad 00010 \oplus 11011 = 11001$$

∴ 00010   10111   01100   11001   (third row)

Next leader of minimum weight 1 and not appearing in above three rows is 00100.

$$00100 \oplus 00000 = 00100, \quad 00100 \oplus 10101 = 10001,$$
$$00100 \oplus 01110 = 01010, \quad 00100 \oplus 11011 = 11111$$

∴ 00100   10001   01010   11111   (fourth row)

Next available leader is 01000, which does not appear in above four rows.

$$01000 \oplus 00000 = 01000, \quad 01000 \oplus 10101 = 11101,$$
$$01000 \oplus 01110 = 00110, \quad 01000 \oplus 11011 = 10011$$

∴ 01000   11101   00110   10011   (fifth row)

Next available element for leadership is 10000 and it is not in above five rows.

$$10000 \oplus 00000 = 10000, \quad 10000 \oplus 10101 = 00101,$$
$$10000 \oplus 01110 = 11110, \quad 10000 \oplus 11011 = 01011$$

∴ 10000   00101   11110   01011   (sixth row)

Now next minimum weight is 2. Consider 00011 as coset leader which does not appear in above six rows.

$$00011 \oplus 00000 = 00011, \quad 00011 \oplus 10101 = 10110,$$
$$00011 \oplus 01110 = 01101, \quad 00011 \oplus 11011 = 11000$$

∴ 00011   00010   01101   11000   (seventh row)

Next minimum weight is 2 and 01001 does not appear in above seven rows, it acts as a coset leader.

$$01001 \oplus 00000 = 01001, \quad 01001 \oplus 10101 = 11100,$$
$$01001 \oplus 01110 = 00111, \quad 01001 \oplus 11011 = 10010$$

∴ 01001   11100   00111   10010   (eighth row)

Decoding Table

00000	10101	01110	11011
00001	<u>10100</u>	01111	11010
00010	10111	01100	11001
00100	10001	01010	11111
01000	11101	00110	<u>10011</u>
10000	00101	<u>11110</u>	01011
00011	10110	01101	11000
01001	11100	00111	10010

Received Word	Word Sent
11110	01110
10011	11011
10100	10101

Example 5.36 : A parity check matrix is $H = \begin{bmatrix} 0 & 1 & 1 \\ 1 & 0 & 1 \\ 1 & 0 & 0 \\ 0 & 1 & 0 \\ 0 & 0 & 1 \end{bmatrix}$.

Decode the words (i) 01110 (ii) 11100

Solution : In the given matrix the last 3 rows form 3×3 identity matrix. So we have to find the encoding function $e : B^2 \to B^5$.

For $b_1 b_2 \in B^2$, we have $e(b_1 b_2) = b_1 b_2 \, x_1 x_2 x_3$

$$[b_1 b_2 \, x_1 x_2 x_3] * \begin{bmatrix} 0 & 1 & 1 \\ 1 & 0 & 1 \\ 1 & 0 & 0 \\ 0 & 1 & 0 \\ 0 & 0 & 1 \end{bmatrix} = 0 \text{ gives}$$

$$\left. \begin{array}{r} b_2 +_2 x_1 = 0 \\ b_1 +_2 x_2 = 0 \\ b_1 +_2 b_2 +_2 x_3 = 0 \end{array} \right\}$$

$\therefore$ $\left. \begin{array}{r} x_1 = b_2 \\ x_2 = b_1 \\ x_3 = b_1 +_2 b_2 \end{array} \right\}$

Consider the following table

b_1	b_2	x_1	x_2	x_3
0	0	0	0	0
0	1	1	0	1
1	0	0	1	1
1	1	1	1	0

$\therefore$
$$e(00) = 00000$$
$$e(01) = 01101$$
$$e(10) = 10011$$
$$e(11) = 11110$$

This forms a group code and N = {00000, 01101, 10011, 11110} is a normal subgroup of B^5.

Now we find $\dfrac{2^5}{2^2} = \dfrac{32}{4} = 8$ cosets such that the coset leaders are in increasing order of their weights.

The cosets are as follows :

```
00000   01101   10011   11110
00001   01100   10010   11111
00010   01111   10001   11100
00100   01001   10111   11010
01000   00101   11011   10110
10000   11101   00011   01110
11000   10101   01011   00110
10100   11001   00111   01010
```

The coset leaders are listed in the first column above.

Now we find syndromes of coset leaders

Clearly syndrome of 00000 is 000

Syndrome of 00001 is $[00001] * \begin{bmatrix} 0 & 1 & 1 \\ 1 & 0 & 1 \\ 1 & 0 & 0 \\ 0 & 1 & 0 \\ 0 & 0 & 1 \end{bmatrix} = 001$

Syndrome of 00010 is $[00010] * \begin{bmatrix} 0 & 1 & 1 \\ 1 & 0 & 1 \\ 1 & 0 & 0 \\ 0 & 1 & 0 \\ 0 & 0 & 1 \end{bmatrix} = 010$

Syndrome of 00100 is $[00100] * \begin{bmatrix} 0 & 1 & 1 \\ 1 & 0 & 1 \\ 1 & 0 & 0 \\ 0 & 1 & 0 \\ 0 & 0 & 1 \end{bmatrix} = 100$

Syndrome of 01000 is $[01000] * \begin{bmatrix} 0 & 1 & 1 \\ 1 & 0 & 1 \\ 1 & 0 & 0 \\ 0 & 1 & 0 \\ 0 & 0 & 1 \end{bmatrix} = 101$

Syndrome of 10000 is $[10000] * \begin{bmatrix} 0 & 1 & 1 \\ 1 & 0 & 1 \\ 1 & 0 & 0 \\ 0 & 1 & 0 \\ 0 & 0 & 1 \end{bmatrix} = 011$

Syndrome of 11000 is $[11000] * \begin{bmatrix} 0 & 1 & 1 \\ 1 & 0 & 1 \\ 1 & 0 & 0 \\ 0 & 1 & 0 \\ 0 & 0 & 1 \end{bmatrix} = 110$

Syndrome of 10100 is $[10100] * \begin{bmatrix} 0 & 1 & 1 \\ 1 & 0 & 1 \\ 1 & 0 & 0 \\ 0 & 1 & 0 \\ 0 & 0 & 1 \end{bmatrix} = 111$

Coset Leader	Syndrome
00000	000
00001	001
00010	010
00100	100
01000	101
10000	011
11000	110
10100	111

(i) Received word is $x_t = 01110$. Syndrome of $x_t = 01110$ is

$$[01110] * \begin{bmatrix} 0 & 1 & 1 \\ 1 & 0 & 1 \\ 1 & 0 & 0 \\ 0 & 1 & 0 \\ 0 & 0 & 1 \end{bmatrix} = 011$$

From the table of coset leaders and syndromes the coset leader corresponding to 011 is 10000.

This means $x_t = 01110$ lies in the coset whose leader is 10000.

∴ $x = x_t +_2 10000 = 01110 +_2 10000 = 11110$

Finally, we know $e(11) = 11110$.

∴ 01110 is decoded as 11.

(ii) Received word is $x_t = 11100$. syndrome of $x_t = 11100$ is

$$[11100] * \begin{bmatrix} 0 & 1 & 1 \\ 1 & 0 & 1 \\ 1 & 0 & 0 \\ 0 & 1 & 0 \\ 0 & 0 & 1 \end{bmatrix} = 010$$

From the table of coset leader and syndromes the coset leader corresponding to 010 is 00010.

This means $x_t = 11100$ lies in the coset whose leader is 00010.

∴ $x = x_t +_2 00010 = 11100 +_2 00010 = 11110$.

Finally we know $e(11) = 11110$.

Hence 11100 is decoded as 11.

EXERCISE (5.4)

1. Find $|x|, |y|$ and the distance between x and y in the following :
   (i) x = 11010010, y = 10101001
   (ii) x = 00100111, y = 00111000

2. Find the minimum distance of (2, 4) encoding function e given by
   $e(00) = 0000$, $e(01) = 0100$,
   $e(10) = 1001$, $e(11) = 1110$

   It is a group code ? Explain.

3. Consider (2, 6) encoding function e
   $e(00) = 000000$, $e(01) = 011010$,
   $e(10) = 101000$, $e(11) = 111110$

   (i) Find the minimum distance of e.
   (ii) How many errors can be detected by e ?
   (iii) Explain why e is not a group code.

4. Show that (2, 5) encoding function defined as
   $e(00) = 00000$, $e(01) = 01110$,
   $e(10) = 10101$, $e(11) = 11011$

   is a group code.

   What is the minimum distance of e ?

5. Determine the group code $e : B^2 \to B^5$ when the parity check matrix H is

(i) $H = \begin{bmatrix} 1 & 1 & 0 \\ 0 & 1 & 1 \\ 1 & 0 & 0 \\ 0 & 1 & 0 \\ 0 & 0 & 1 \end{bmatrix}$ (P.U. 2010)   (ii) $H = \begin{bmatrix} 0 & 1 & 1 \\ 0 & 1 & 1 \\ 1 & 0 & 0 \\ 0 & 1 & 0 \\ 0 & 0 & 1 \end{bmatrix}$

6. A parity check matrix H is given below. In each case find the code words generated by H. Also find the minimum weight of a non-zero code word and state how many errors can be detected by the group code.

(i) $H = \begin{bmatrix} 1 & 0 & 1 & 1 & 0 & 0 \\ 1 & 1 & 0 & 0 & 1 & 0 \\ 1 & 0 & 1 & 0 & 0 & 1 \end{bmatrix}$ (P.U. 2012)   (ii) $H = \begin{bmatrix} 1 & 1 & 0 & 1 & 0 & 0 \\ 0 & 1 & 1 & 0 & 1 & 0 \\ 1 & 0 & 1 & 0 & 0 & 1 \end{bmatrix}$

(iii) $H = \begin{bmatrix} 1 & 1 & 0 & 1 & 0 & 0 \\ 1 & 0 & 1 & 0 & 1 & 0 \\ 0 & 1 & 1 & 0 & 0 & 1 \end{bmatrix}$ (P.U. 2010)   (iv) $H = \begin{bmatrix} 1 & 0 & 1 & 1 & 1 & 0 & 0 \\ 1 & 1 & 1 & 0 & 0 & 1 & 0 \\ 0 & 1 & 1 & 1 & 0 & 0 & 1 \end{bmatrix}$

7. Write the code words generated by the parity check matrix $H = \begin{bmatrix} 1 & 1 & 1 \\ 1 & 1 & 0 \\ 1 & 0 & 1 \\ 0 & 1 & 1 \\ 1 & 0 & 0 \\ 0 & 1 & 0 \\ 0 & 0 & 1 \end{bmatrix}$.

What is the minimum weight of non-zero code word ? How many errors can be detected by the group code ?

8. Show that (3, 5) encoding function e defined by

e(000) = 00000,   e(001) = 11110,
e(010) = 01101,   e(011) = 10011,
e(100) = 01010,   e(101) = 10100,
e(110) = 00111,   e(111) = 11001

is a group code. How many errors will be detected by e ?

9. Let (2, 4) encoding function e be defined by

e(00) = 0000,   e(01) = 0111,
e(10) = 1001,   e(11) = 1111

Decode (i) 1101, (ii) 0110 by using maximum likelihood function.

10. Consider (2, 4) encoding function $e : B^2 \to B^4$ defined by

e(00) = 0000, e(01) = 1011, e(10) = 0110, e(11) = 1101.

Show that e is a group code. Decode the words (i) 1111, (ii) 0111, (iii) 1001 by minimum distance decoding criterian.

11. A parity check matrix is $H = \begin{bmatrix} 1 & 1 & 0 \\ 1 & 0 & 1 \\ 1 & 0 & 0 \\ 0 & 1 & 0 \\ 0 & 0 & 1 \end{bmatrix}$. Determine (2, 5) group code function $e : B^2 \to B^5$.

12. Determine whether or not the (3, 7) encoding function is a group code. What is the minimum distanc of e ?

    e(000) = 0000000, e(001) = 0010110, e(010) = 0101000,

    e(011) = 0111110, e(100) = 1000101, e(101) = 1010011,

    e(110) = 1101101, e(111) = 1111011.

13. Consider (2, 4) encoding function

    e(00) = 0000, e(01) = 0111, e(10) = 1001, e(11) = 1100

    Decode 1101 according to maximum likelihood decoding function.

14. The encoding function $e : B^2 \to B^5$ is given by parity check matrix.

    $H = \begin{bmatrix} 1 & 1 & 0 \\ 0 & 1 & 1 \\ 1 & 0 & 0 \\ 0 & 1 & 0 \\ 0 & 0 & 1 \end{bmatrix}$. Decode the word 11100.

15. Show that the encoding function $e : B^2 \to B^4$ defined by

    e(00) = 0000, e(01) = 1101, e(10) = 0011, e(11) = 1110 is a group code. Use the minimum distance decoding criterian and decode the words. (i) 1001, (ii) 0111.

ANSWERS (5.4)

1. (i) $|x| = 4$, $|y| = 4$, distance = 6
   (ii) $|x| = 4$, $|y| = 3$, distance = 5
2. Minimum distance is 1. $e(B^2)$ is not subgroup of B^4.
3. (i) 2   (ii) 1   (iii) $e(B^2)$ is not a subgroup of B^6.
4. 3
5. (i) $e(B^2)$ = {00000, 01011, 10110, 11101}
   (ii) $e(B^2)$ = {00000, 01011, 10011, 11000}
6. (i) {000000, 001101, 010010, 011111, 100111, 101010, 110101, 111000}
   minimum weight = 2. 1 error can be detected.
   (ii) {000000, 001011, 010110, 011101, 100101, 101110, 110011, 111000}
   minimum weight = 3. 2 or less errors can be detected.

(iii) {000000, 001011, 010101, 011110, 100110, 101101, 110011, 111000}

minimum weight = 3. 2 or less errors can be detected.

(iv) {0000000, 0001101, 0010111, 0011010, 0100011, 0101110, 0110100, 0111001, 1000110, 1001011, 1010001, 1011100, 1100101, 1101000, 1110010, 1111111}

minimum weight = 3. 2 or less errors can be detected.

7. {0000000, 0001011, 0010101, 0011110, 0100110, 0101101, 0110011, 0111000, 1000111, 1001100, 1010010, 1011001, 1100001, 1101010, 1110100, 1111111}

minimum weight = 3. 2 or less errors can be detected.

8. 1 error
9. (i) 10   (ii) 01
10. (i) 1101   (ii) 0110   (iii) 1011
11. e(00) = 00000, e(01) = 01101, e(10) = 10110, e(11) = 11011
12. Yes, 2
13. 10
14. 11
15. (i) 1101   (ii) 0011

www.ingramcontent.com/pod-product-compliance
Lightning Source LLC
Chambersburg PA
CBHW080428230426
43662CB00015B/2215